Mastering Criminal Procedure
Volume 2

Carolina Academic Press Mastering Series

Russell Weaver, Series Editor

Mastering Administrative Law
William R. Andersen

Mastering Alternative Dispute Resolution
Kelly M. Feeley, James A. Sheehan

Mastering American Indian Law
Angelique Townsend EagleWoman, Stacy L. Leeds

Mastering Appellate Advocacy and Process
Donna C. Looper, George W. Kuney

Mastering Art Law
Herbert Lazerow

Mastering Bankruptcy
George W. Kuney

Mastering Civil Procedure 2d e
David Charles Hricik

Mastering Constitutional Law 2d e
John C. Knechtle, Christopher J. Roederer

Mastering Contract Law
Irma S. Russell, Barbara K. Bucholtz

Mastering Corporate Tax
Reginald Mombrun, Gail Levin Richmond, Felicia Branch

Mastering Corporations and Other Business Entities
Lee Harris

Mastering Criminal Law
Ellen S. Podgor, Peter J. Henning, Neil P. Cohen

Mastering Criminal Procedure, Volume 1: The Investigative Stage 2d e
Peter J. Henning, Andrew Taslitz, Margaret L. Paris,
Cynthia E. Jones, Ellen S. Podgor

Mastering Criminal Procedure, Volume 2: The Adjudicatory Stage 2d e
Peter J. Henning, Andrew Taslitz, Margaret L. Paris,
Cynthia E. Jones, Ellen S. Podgor

Mastering Elder Law 2d e
Ralph C. Brashier

Mastering Employment Discrimination Law
Paul M. Secunda, Jeffrey M. Hirsch

Mastering Criminal Procedure
Volume 2: The Adjudicatory Stage

Second Edition

Peter J. Henning
PROFESSOR OF LAW
WAYNE STATE UNIVERSITY LAW SCHOOL

Andrew Taslitz
PROFESSOR OF LAW
LATE OF AMERICAN UNIVERSITY, WASHINGTON COLLEGE OF LAW

Margaret L. Paris
PROFESSOR OF LAW
UNIVERSITY OF OREGON SCHOOL OF LAW

Cynthia E. Jones
PROFESSOR OF LAW
AMERICAN UNIVERSITY, WASHINGTON COLLEGE OF LAW

Ellen S. Podgor
GARY R. TROMBLEY FAMILY WHITE-COLLAR CRIME RESEARCH PROFESSOR
PROFESSOR OF LAW
STETSON UNIVERSITY COLLEGE OF LAW

CAROLINA ACADEMIC PRESS
Durham, North Carolina

Library of Congress Cataloging-in-Publication Data

Mastering criminal procedure / Peter J. Henning, Andrew Taslitz, Margaret L. Paris, Cynthia E. Jones, and Ellen S. Podgor.
    2 volumes cm. -- (Carolina academic press mastering series)
    Includes bibliographical references and index.
    Contents: volume 1. The investigative stage -- volume 2. The adjudicatory stage.
    ISBN 978-1-61163-550-8 (volume 1) -- ISBN 978-1-61163-551-5 (volume 2)
    1. Criminal procedure--United States. I. Henning, Peter J., author.

KF9619.85.M378 2014
345.73'05--dc23

2014037524

Carolina Academic Press
700 Kent Street
Durham, NC 27701
Telephone (919) 489-7486
Fax (919) 493-5668
www.cap-press.com

Printed in the United States of America

To the Hennings
(Eugene, Mildred, William, Phyllis, and Philip)
Peter J. Henning

To my wife, Patty, who makes life worthwhile;
my sister, Ellen, who taught me to read and write in the first place;
and my students, who give me more than I can ever say.
Andrew Taslitz

To Shel, who makes everything possible.
Margaret L. Paris

To the memory of my wonderful mother, Ernestine C. Jones (1932–2004),
who continues to motivate and inspire me.
Cynthia E. Jones

To all my students.
Ellen S. Podgor

Contents

Table of Cases

Series Editor's Foreword

The Carolina Academic Press Mastering Series is designed to provide you with a tool that will enable you to easily and efficiently "master" the substance and content of law school courses. Throughout the series, the focus is on quality writing that makes legal concepts understandable. As a result, the series is designed to be easy to read and is not unduly cluttered with footnotes or cites to secondary sources.

In order to facilitate student mastery of topics, the Mastering Series includes a number of pedagogical features designed to improve learning and retention. At the beginning of each chapter, you will find a "Roadmap" that tells you about the chapter and provides you with a sense of the material that you will cover. A "Checkpoint" at the end of each chapter encourages you to stop and review the key concepts, reiterating what you have learned. Throughout the book, key terms are explained and emphasized. Finally, a "Master Checklist" at the end of each book reinforces what you have learned and helps you identify any areas that need review or further study.

We hope that you will enjoy studying with, and learning from, the Mastering Series.

Russell L. Weaver
Professor of Law & Distinguished University Scholar
University of Louisville, Louis D. Brandeis School of Law

Preface

It is difficult to synthesize all of criminal procedure in two volumes. One finds state and federal differences in procedure, and systems that constantly change as a result of new statutes, rules, and court interpretations. The authors hope that this overview of criminal procedure will offer students an accessible study guide in understanding this important subject. The book, however, is not intended to serve as a guide for resolving a specific problem or case.

This Volume covers the major issues in criminal procedure that relate to the Fourth, Fifth, and Sixth Amendment rights provided in the U.S. Constitution and also covers entrapment. Volume Two examines procedure issues from the bail through the jail process and also considers post-conviction matters. Because the law is not stagnant, it is important to note in using the Mastering Criminal Procedure volumes that one needs to look to recent cases and legislative developments that may modify the existing law.

As we were preparing the second edition, we lost our friend and colleague, Andy Taslitz. His prodigious knowledge of criminal procedure continues to suffuse this book, and he remains as a co-author.

There are many to thank:

- Professor Peter J. Henning thanks his assistant, Olive Hyman, who makes it all work, the research assistance of Allison Bars (Wayne State University Law School Class of 2014) and Pamela Wall (Wayne State Univsity Law School Class of 2015), and co-authors who made this a pleasure.
- Professor Andrew Taslitz (from the first edition) thanks his wife, Patricia V. Sun, Esq., and his dogs, Odo and B'lanna, for their support, patience, love, and feedback on early drafts of several chapters (trust me — the dogs can give you a look that says, "Oh, come on! You can do better than that!"); his research assistants, Melissa Bancroft, Jasmine Modoor, Jeanne Laurenceau, Natasha Williams, and Cassandra Thomas, for their excellent work; his secretary, Gay Kirsch, for her outstanding production skills; and his co-authors, criminal procedure geeks all, albeit with warm hearts and an instinctive way of knowing just how to make me smile.

- Professor Margaret L. Paris thanks her co-authors, who always inspire.
- Professor Cynthia E. Jones thanks her wonderful deans fellows, Caitlin Marchand and Paul Turkevich for their research assistance, and her Criminal Procedure students — past, present and future — at the American University Washington College of Law.
- Professor Ellen S. Podgor thanks Gordon J. Kirsch, Shannon Mullins, Scott Tolliver, Giovanni P. Giarratana, Stetson University College of Law, and her incredible co-authors.

Peter J. Henning
Margaret L. Paris
Cynthia E. Jones
Ellen S. Podgor
July 2014

Mastering Criminal Procedure
Volume 2

Chapter 1

Preliminary Proceedings

Roadmap

- Timely hearing requirement for warrantless arrests
- Bail procedures
- Standards for pretrial detention
- Preliminary examination

Once a person is arrested or charged with a crime, the workings of the criminal justice system begin to move forward. There are a number of preliminary judicial proceedings in which the court may make initial determinations about the defendant's status, the nature of the charges, the continued detention of the defendant, and the conditions to be imposed before releasing the person to ensure an appearance at future proceedings. Moreover, different constitutional rights and statutory procedures come into play at this early phase. This Chapter describes the important steps in the beginning stage of the judicial process, some of which may be combined into a single proceeding. Different jurisdictions may have a variety of labels for these proceedings; this Chapter provides a general overview without going into detail about how a particular state might move the case through the system. As with many other constitutional and statutory rights, a defendant can waive some or all the protections afforded and proceed through the adjudicatory process.

I. Preliminary Proceedings

A. *Gerstein* Hearing

A person may be arrested without a warrant if the arresting officer has probable cause to believe the individual committed a crime. In *Gerstein v. Pugh*, 420 U.S. 103 (1975), the Supreme Court held that when a person is arrested without a warrant "the Fourth Amendment requires a judicial determination of probable cause as a prerequisite to extended restraint of liberty following arrest." Depending upon the state at issue, a person could be held for a month or more before a court makes a preliminary determination of the validity of the arrest, with no right to challenge the detention before that time.

The Court concluded that any delay in bringing the person before a judicial officer is permissible only to "take the administrative steps incident to arrest." The basis for requiring the hearing is the protection of an arrestee's liberty interest under the Due Process Clause. The Court also requires a hearing if release is "accompanied by burdensome conditions that effects a significant restraint on liberty."

1. Right to Counsel

The *Gerstein* hearing may be conducted in a less formal manner than other types of preliminary proceedings, and it is often non-adversarial. Importantly, the Supreme Court found in *Gerstein* that an arrestee does not have the right to counsel under the Sixth Amendment because the hearing is not a "critical stage." The proceeding does not significantly affect any defense on the merits at a subsequent trial, so the presence of counsel is not required. The sole focus of the proceeding is to determine whether there was probable cause for the arrest and whether to continue pretrial custody, not the basis of any possible criminal charge. Along these lines, an arrestee does not have the right to be present at the *Gerstein* hearing, or to offer evidence or cross-examine witnesses. The decision by the judicial officer regarding the propriety of an arrest can be based on hearsay or evidence otherwise subject to the exclusionary rule.

2. Timing

The probable cause standard for continued detention is the same as that of an arrest—that there are sufficient facts "to warrant a prudent man in believing the suspect had committed or was committing an offense." The hearing must be held *promptly* to determine whether there was probable cause for the arrest and the continued restraint of the person. The hearing is not adversarial and may be based on the allegations in a criminal complaint, so witnesses are not called to establish the defendant committed an offense. The standard is the same as that for obtaining an arrest warrant: Whether the judicial officer has sufficient facts to determine whether there was probable cause to arrest the person. The probable cause question can be revisited later in the case if a defendant files a challenge to how evidence was obtained as a result of the arrest, for example seeking suppression of items seized during a search incident to the arrest.

In *County of Riverside v. McLaughlin*, 500 U.S. 44 (1991), the Supreme Court "articulate[d] more clearly the boundaries of what is permissible under the Fourth Amendment," holding that a period of less than 48 hours between the arrest and the *Gerstein* hearing did not violate due process *so long as* the delay was reasonable. For example, it would be unreasonable to delay the hearing to permit the police to gather additional evidence to help establish probable cause for the arrest. But a gap in time between an arrest and the hearing due to transferring a prisoner or finding an available magistrate would not be unreasonable.

The Court further held that when there is a delay beyond the 48-hour period, the government has the burden to "demonstrate the existence of a bona fide emergency or other extraordinary circumstance" justifying the interval between arrest and the probable cause determination. But, if a person is arrested pursuant to a warrant, or is held after being charged in a grand jury indictment, then a *Gerstein* hearing is not required because there has already been a determination of probable cause.

3. Effect of a Violation

The *Gerstein* hearing imposes a procedural requirement on the government to give an arrestee the opportunity to appear in court within a reasonably limited period of time, but a violation of this obligation may have few practical consequences on any subsequent prosecution. While the decisions in *Gerstein* and *McLaughlin* secured a right for detainees, violation of that right will not preclude conviction. A conviction subsequent to the improper detainment or an unreasonable delay in the *Gerstein* hearing will not be invalidated solely on the basis of the impermissible treatment. Though it is possible that a statement taken from a defendant during such an unlawful detention could be precluded from the government's case-in-chief, or the results of a search undertaken in connection with the detention may be subject to the exclusionary rule, that remedy is rarely applied. In *Powell v. Nevada*, 511 U.S. 79 (1994), the Supreme Court declined the opportunity to decide the appropriate remedy for the failure to hold a prompt hearing. *Gerstein* and *McLaughlin* were private class actions alleging a constitutional violation brought under 42 U.S.C. § 1983, and damages may be available for a violation even if there is no direct relief provided in a subsequent criminal prosecution.

B. Initial Appearance

Most jurisdictions require by statute or rule that those accused of a crime be brought before the court within a short period of time for an initial appearance to apprise them of their rights. Different terminology is used to describe the proceeding, such as "preliminary appearance," "initial presentment," or "first appearance." It is often fairly brief, and may be adjourned while the defendant obtains counsel or appointed counsel is provided. The proceeding occurs whether the accused was arrested, issued a summons, or made a voluntary appearance after being notified of the charge. A person may be arraigned on a charge at this appearance and be asked to enter a plea, although those proceedings can be postponed to a later date or a not guilty plea entered by the court as a matter of course without the defendant having to decide whether or not to enter a specific plea.

Federal Rule of Criminal Procedure 5(a)(1) requires that a person arrested be brought before a magistrate or other appropriate judicial officer "without unnecessary delay." Rule 5(d)(1) requires the court to inform the defendant of the following at the initial appearance:

(A)   the complaint against the defendant, and any affidavit filed with it;
(B)   the defendant's right to retain counsel or to request that counsel be appointed if the defendant cannot obtain counsel;
(C)   the circumstances, if any, under which the defendant may secure pretrial release;
(D)   any right to a preliminary hearing; and
(E)   the defendant's right not to make a statement, and that any statement made may be used against the defendant.

The judge must also allow the defendant an opportunity to consult with counsel during the proceeding, and decide whether to detain or release the person.

1. Right to Counsel

A court may combine the *Gerstein* hearing on the arrest and possible continued detention with the initial appearance into a single proceeding. Unlike the determination of probable cause to arrest, however, a defendant will have the right to counsel at the initial appearance because the exercise of certain rights makes it a "critical stage" of the prosecution. For example, if a defendant enters a plea to a charge, then counsel must be present, although the failure to provide counsel when the court enters a "not guilty" plea is usually viewed as harmless error because there is no prejudice to the defendant. The initial proceeding is not adversarial, and under Rule 5(f) the defendant may appear by videoconference rather than being physically present in the courtroom.

2. Effect of a Violation

Delay between an arrest and an initial appearance can be considered when a court undertakes an analysis of the voluntariness of any statement obtained during that period. In *McNabb v. United States*, 318 U.S. 332 (1943), and *Mallory v. United States*, 354 U.S. 449 (1957), the Supreme Court used its supervisory power over the federal courts to render inadmissible statements taken from defendants obtained during an unnecessary delay that violated Federal Rule of Criminal Procedure 5(a)(1)(A), which requires a defendant be presented to the court "without unnecessary delay" after an arrest. That analysis does not create a constitutional protection for those held beyond the "without unnecessary delay" required by the federal rule if the person makes an otherwise voluntary statement.

II. Bail

A. The Bail System

Bail is the money or other item of value that defendants offer to the court as a means of securing their release before trial. If the person appears at subsequent hearings and for trial as required, the bail is returned. The amount of bail required to obtain release from custody should be sufficient to ensure the defendant's appearance at later proceedings, but not so high that the defendant has no chance of being released. In *Stack v. Boyle*, 342 U.S. 1 (1951), the Supreme Court explained that "[b]ail set at a figure higher than an amount reasonably calculated to fulfill this purpose is 'excessive' under the Eighth Amendment." A court looks at a number of factors in deciding whether to grant bail, and how much property or money must be furnished to ensure future appearances. If the defendant does not appear at a subsequent hearing or otherwise violates a condition of release, then the defendant forfeits the bail to the court. It is also a crime for a defendant not to appear when ordered by the court, which could subject the person to additional criminal charges.

The likelihood of flight is usually a key determinant in setting the amount of bail. The bail required—whether posted by the defendant, family, friends, or a professional who agrees to post bond in exchange for a payment—should be sufficient to give the defendant a strong incentive to appear without making it impossible for the person to secure release from custody. Another factor in setting bail is the nature of the crime charged and the potential punishment anticipated. The more serious the offense, and the greater the possible prison term if convicted, the more likely a defendant may abscond to avoid punishment.

The court also looks to the personal circumstances of the accused when setting bail. For example, strong personal or family ties to the jurisdiction weigh in favor of a finding that the person is likely to appear for trial. Similarly, a defendant's financial condition can affect the analysis, along with prior convictions and — if applicable — a history of compliance with the terms of release in other cases.

B. Bail Bonds

For defendants who cannot afford to put up the amount required for bail, many jurisdictions allow a bail bondsman to post security for the accused. Typically, the bonding company requires the defendant to pay a percentage of the total amount of bail, usually 10%, which is not refunded. The bonding company posts the defendant's bail or agrees to be liable for the full amount of bail should the defendant not appear. Under this approach, the bonding company, or "bondsman," rather than the government, oversees defendants released on bail; the bondsman has a financial incentive to ensure that defendants comply with the conditions of release and appear at future hearings.

The bonding system has been subject to abuse, and some states have taken steps to eliminate bonding companies by making it easier for individual defendants and their families to post a percentage of the cash bail or to pledge property to secure the person's release. The costs of bail are especially steep for the poor, who may be unable to put up the cash required for bail and may not be able to afford the fees charged by bonding companies.

In federal prosecutions, Rule 45(e) requires that a "surety" who posts a bond, other than a corporation, must establish that he or she is "qualified" to cover the costs if the defendant violates the terms of the bond. Courts require the surety to file an affidavit providing the following information:

(1) the property that the surety proposes to use as security;
(2) any encumbrance on that property;
(3) the number and amount of any other undischarged bonds and bail undertakings the surety has issued; and
(4) any other liability of the surety.

A defendant's violation of a bond condition can result in forfeiture of the amount posted, although a court can rescind the forfeiture if the defendant is surrendered into custody or "it appears that justice does not require bail forfeiture." Fed. R. Crim. P. 45(f).

C. Release on Defendant's Own Recognizance

Not all offenses require a person to post cash or property to secure release from custody. For those charged with less serious crimes, or defendants with particularly deep roots in the community who do not pose any threat of violence or flight risk, the court may order release on his or her "own recognizance" based only on the promise to appear at future proceedings. Some courts permit a relative or friend to agree to monitor the defendant's compliance with any conditions of release and ensure the person's appearance. It is common to require defendants to remain at a specified location, usually a residence, and to wear an electronic monitoring device that permits the government to track their movements and ensure they do not flee the jurisdiction or go to a prohibited location. If the defendant fails to appear or violates any release conditions, both the defendant and the person who agrees to act as a monitor may be required to pay a specified amount as a bail forfeiture.

D. Constitutional Protection

The Eighth Amendment provides that "excessive bail shall not be required." The Supreme Court has never specifically held that this protection applies to the states, although the constitutions of every state address bail, so there has not been a compelling reason to extend this provision. In *Schilb v. Kuebel*, 404 U.S. 357 (1971), the Supreme Court noted that bail is "basic to our system of law" and that "the Eighth Amendment's proscription of excessive bail has been assumed to have application to the States through the Fourteenth Amendment."

1. No Right to Bail

The Eighth Amendment does not grant a *right* to bail in every case, but instead only guarantees that when bail is granted it cannot be "excessive." In *United States v. Salerno*, 481 U.S. 739 (1987), the Supreme Court stated that "[t]he only arguable substantive limitation of the Bail Clause is that the Government's proposed conditions of release or detention not be 'excessive' in light of the perceived evil." Bail is frequently prohibited in capital cases in which a defendant faces a term of life imprisonment or the death penalty.

The Eighth Amendment prohibition on "cruel and unusual punishments" does not apply to bail because that provision only relates to those convicted of crimes and not to defendants awaiting trial. The Due Process and Equal Protection Clauses provide some measure of protection beyond the Excessive Bail Clause by requiring uniform procedures and equal access to bail.

2. Reasonable Bail

In *Stack v. Boyle*, 342 U.S. 1 (1951), the Supreme Court considered a challenge to the trial court's decision to require a uniform bail for twelve defendants based solely on the charge without taking into account the circumstances of each individual. It held, "Since the function of bail is limited, the fixing of bail for any individual defendant must be based upon standards relevant to the purpose of assuring the presence of that defendant." If a defendant has a statutory right to bail, then the amount imposed cannot be greater than that required to ensure appearance at future proceedings and compliance with the conditions of release.

While a court can consider a defendant's financial situation, the Eighth Amendment does not guarantee bail, thus it is *not* a constitutional violation to set the amount at a level beyond what the defendant can pay so long as the amount is not "excessive." Lower courts have also rejected an equal protection argument that a person who cannot make bail has suffered any impermissible discrimination.

Stack v. Boyle should not be read to mean that assuring the defendant's appearance is the only basis for determining the amount of bail. In *Salerno*, the Court held that the government can seek to vindicate other objectives in the bail determination, such as protecting the safety of the community, which can lead to a outright denial of bail or setting it at a prohibitively high rate.

III. Release and Pretrial Detention

A. Authority

Because a defendant does not have a right to bail under the Eighth Amendment, pretrial detention may be permissible if that person poses a danger to the community or is a flight risk. In the Bail Reform Act of 1984, Congress authorized pretrial detention of federal defendants if the prosecution establishes by clear and convincing evidence that no condition or set of conditions for release on bail can reasonably assure the safety of the community. The federal statute does not address the standard for showing a risk of flight, and lower courts have generally required proof of that risk by a preponderance of the evidence.

In *United States v. Salerno*, 481 U.S. 739 (1987), the Supreme Court held that pretrial detention based on the danger that would be posed to the community if the defendant were released did not violate Due Process or the prohibition of "excessive bail." A pretrial detention order must be based on a "sufficiently compelling governmental interest" and not constitute a punishment of the defendant, which may only be imposed *after* a criminal conviction. The Court in *Salerno* rejected a facial challenge to the Bail Reform Act's pretrial detention provisions seeking to have them declared unconstitutional. Individual cases could rise to the level of a violation of a defendant's due process right, even though the statute itself is constitutional. For example, if the duration of the detention is sufficiently long to constitute punishment—not protection of the community—then a due process violation has occurred.

Pretrial detention standards under state law are diverse because some state constitutions grant a right to bail, unlike *Salerno*'s interpretation of the Eighth Amendment. For example, a number of state constitutions provide, "All prisoners shall, before conviction, be bailable by sufficient sureties, except for capital offenses, where the proof is evident, or the presumption great." Many state statutes permit pretrial detention in limited circumstances.

B. Release

The availability of bail is among the most important issues defense counsel needs to address at the early stages of a case. The court decides the appropriate bail and conditions of release, and if the parties differ regarding the conditions or the amount of bail, or whether a person should remain in custody, then a hearing will be held. The federal Bail Reform Act of 1984 provides a judicial officer can order one of the following for the defendant:

- release on personal recognizance or upon execution of an unsecured appearance bond;
- release on a condition or combination of conditions, including posting a bond;
- temporary detention to consider revocation of conditional release, deportation, or exclusion; or
- detention pending trial.

18 U.S.C. § 3142(a). The key issues are ensuring the defendant will appear for future proceedings and protecting the community from potential danger.

1. Personal Recognizance or Unsecured Appearance Bond

If the court orders the defendant's release on personal recognizance or an unsecured appearance bond, then bail is not posted and the person can be released upon signing the appropriate forms. The Bail Reform Act requires that the conditions of release must include a statement "that the person not commit a Federal, State, or local crime during the period of release," and agrees to the collection of a DNA sample if authorized by the DNA Analysis Backlog Elimination Act of 2000 (42 U.S.C. 14135a). 18 U.S.C. § 3142(b).

2. Release on Conditions

The Bail Reform Act authorizes a number of additional conditions, in addition to the two required for release on personal recognizance or pursuant to an unsecured appearance bond, to ensure the defendant's appearance at future proceedings and the safety of the community. The defendant must:

- remain in the custody of a designated person, who agrees to assume supervision and to report any violation of a release condition to the court;
- maintain employment or actively seek employment;
- maintain or begin an educational program;
- abide by restrictions on associating with certain persons, where to live, and travel;
- avoid all contact with alleged victims and witnesses;
- report regularly to a designated agency or law enforcement office;
- comply with a curfew;
- not possess a weapon;
- refrain from excessive use of alcohol or use of any narcotic without a prescription;
- undergo medical or psychiatric treatment, or participate in a drug or alcohol dependency program;
- execute a bail bond or agree to forfeit specified property for any failure to promptly appear; and
- "satisfy any other condition that is reasonably necessary to assure the appearance of the person as required and to assure the safety of any other person and the community."

18 U.S.C. § 3142(c).

In determining whether there are conditions that can be imposed on the defendant to reasonably assure his appearance and protect the safety of the community, the court must consider the following factors:

- The nature and circumstances of the offense charged, including whether it is a crime of violence, a Federal crime of terrorism, or involves a minor victim or a controlled substance, firearm, explosive, or destructive device;
- The weight of the evidence against the defendant;
- The history and characteristics of the defendant, including physical and mental condition, family and community ties, financial resources and

employment history, prior drug or alcohol abuse, criminal history, and record of court appearances, including whether he was on probation or parole for another offense at the time of the charged crime; and

- The nature and seriousness of any danger posed to another person or the community if released from custody.

18 U.S.C. § 3142(g).

C. Pretrial Detention

The Bail Reform Act provides detailed procedures for considering whether to order the pretrial detention of a defendant. A detention hearing can be held on the government's motion, or the judicial officer's own motion, if there is a serious risk of flight, obstruction of justice, or threat to a witness or juror. A hearing must be held for defendants charged with crimes of violence, offenses with a sentence of death or life imprisonment, drug offenses punishable by ten or more years of imprisonment, or if the defendant has been convicted of two or more specified offenses.

The statute also provides a rebuttable presumption that no set of conditions will reasonably assure the safety of individuals or the community if the defendant was convicted previously of certain crimes, such as crimes of violence or drug offenses, or if there is probable cause to believe the defendant committed specified offenses involving drugs, guns, or a minor victim. The detention hearing must be held at the defendant's initial appearance on the charge, although the court may grant a continuance for a limited period of time.

The rules of evidence do not apply at the hearing, yet a defendant is entitled to have counsel appointed, to testify, and to call or cross-examine witnesses. In addition, a defendant can offer evidence by "proffer" through the attorney rather than providing actual documents or testimony; although the statute does not specifically allow this practice, judges generally allow it to happen rather than require the presentation of evidence through live witnesses. The court must issue a written report if it orders a defendant detained before trial, and a defendant has the right to appeal the detention order.

IV. Preliminary Examination

Most states and the federal government provide a preliminary examination—also called a "preliminary hearing" or "bindover hearing" in some jurisdictions—to ascertain whether there is *probable cause* for any criminal charge against a defendant. If a grand jury returns an indictment, that often precludes the need for the preliminary examination, although some states require a proceeding to examine the basis for the charges even after the grand jury acts. Unlike a criminal information (a formal charge made by the prosecutor that does not require an indictment—see Chapter 3), a grand jury indictment usually encompasses a finding that there is probable cause that the defendant committed the offense, and in the federal system there is no need to hold a preliminary hearing once the grand jury hands up the indictment.

A preliminary examination is not a mini-trial in which each side is permitted to call witnesses to have their credibility assessed. The standard for upholding a charge is whether there is sufficient evidence—evidence which need not meet the standard for admission at trial—to show there is probable cause that the defendant committed the offense(s) alleged in the charging document. In many states, the defendant does not have the right to call witnesses, although there is usually a limited opportunity to cross-examine those presented by the prosecution. A preliminary examination is not mandated in every case. Federal Rule of Criminal Procedure 5.1(a)(4) is similar to provisions in almost every state in providing a misdemeanor charge does not require a preliminary examination of the basis for the charge, and instead the case proceeds to a trial or other resolution.

Some states permit direct filing of charges by the prosecutor, and do not mandate an adversarial proceeding to review its evidentiary support. In these jurisdictions, a defendant can file a motion to dismiss the charge, which triggers a court hearing on whether to permit the case to proceed. A few states require an *ex parte* hearing before the court authorizes the prosecutor to file a criminal information or other charging document detailing the offense.

A. Screening Function

The preliminary examination has been viewed as a means to filter out weak cases before the defendant must expend significant time and resources defending against a charge. The proceeding must be held within a relatively short period of time after the filing of charges and the initial proceedings described above. For example, Federal Rule of Criminal Procedure 5.1(c) requires the court hold a preliminary examination no more than ten days after a defendant's initial appearance if the person is in custody, or within twenty days if not in custody. Under Rule 5.1(d), with the defendant's consent and after a showing of good cause, the preliminary hearing can be postponed. If a defendant does not consent to a delay, then the prosecution must show "extraordinary circumstances exist and justice requires the delay." A defendant can also waive the preliminary examination completely and elect to proceed to trial.

B. Procedure

The prosecution usually calls witnesses and submits documentary evidence for the court to consider in deciding whether there is probable cause for the defendant to be made to answer the charge in a criminal trial. The government bears the burden of proof at the preliminary examination, and it is an adversarial proceeding at which the defendant can cross-examine witnesses and offer evidence, including testimony. As a "critical stage" of the prosecution, an indigent defendant has the right to appointed counsel. *Coleman v. Alabama*, 399 U.S. 1 (1970). The purpose of the proceeding is more limited than a trial, however, so the court may curtail the defendant's ability to present evidence if there is proof sufficient to establish probable cause. Unlike the *Gerstein* hearing, which is limited to determining whether there was probable cause at the time of the arrest, the preliminary examination involves weighing the evidence and, in some states, the credibility of the witnesses in deciding whether the government has shown there is a sufficient basis to believe that both a crime occurred and that the defendant committed the offense.

C. Not a Constitutional Requirement

In *Lem Woon v. Oregon*, 229 U.S. 586 (1913), the Supreme Court rejected a due process challenge to a state provision allowing a prosecution to move forward upon a criminal information filed by the district attorney without requiring a preliminary examination into whether probable cause supported the charges. The Court determined that because the grand jury indictment requirement of the Fifth Amendment does not apply to the states (see Chapter 2), due process cannot compel a state to conduct a preliminary examination. This position does not conflict with the requirement of a hearing on the defendant's arrest imposed in *Gerstein* because that right is triggered by the defendant's continued detention, thereby implicating the liberty interest protected by due process. *Gerstein* stated that "we adhere to the Court's prior holding that a judicial hearing is not prerequisite to prosecution by information."

Due process also does not protect a defendant from a prosecution for which there was no supporting evidence. In *Albright v. Oliver*, 510 U.S. 266 (1994), the plaintiff filed a § 1983 civil rights lawsuit claiming that he had been improperly prosecuted based solely on information from an unreliable informant. A plurality of the Court found that only the Fourth Amendment applied to a claim that a charge was not based on probable cause, noting that *Lem Woon* and *Gerstein* made it clear that "the accused is not entitled to oversight or review of the decision to prosecute."

A preliminary examination does not protect a defendant's liberty interest because it only concerns whether the defendant will have to stand trial, regardless of whether the person is in custody. While not constitutionally required, the vast majority of the states and the federal government provide for some form of review of criminal charges, although when a grand jury issues an indictment, in many states and at the federal level that obviates the need for a preliminary hearing because the charges must be based on an assessment of probable cause (see Chapter 2).

D. Benefits

In addition to possibly eliminating weak cases, both the defendant and the prosecutor can benefit from a preliminary examination. For the prosecution, the proceeding allows it to test how well witnesses testify in court and hold up on cross-examination. Moreover, the hearing allows the government to preserve evidence for trial. For example, if a witness testifies at the preliminary examination and is later unavailable, a transcript of the person's testimony may be admissible evidence at a subsequent trial if the defendant had an opportunity to cross-examine the witness, thus fulfilling the requirements of the Confrontation Clause (see Chapter 13).

The defendant can realize significant benefits from the proceeding by getting a preview of the government's case and obtaining discovery of at least some of the most important evidence that the prosecution intends to use at trial. In jurisdictions that do not permit pre-trial depositions of witnesses, the opportunity to hear direct testimony and then cross-examine a witness may provide invaluable information not otherwise available. The government may also introduce physical evidence or documents, such as police reports or recorded witness statements, which become immediately available to the defendant at the hearing rather than having to wait until a later point to review them.

The testimony may also reveal impeachment material for use at trial if a witness makes inconsistent statements. For example, a witness who is tentative at the preliminary examination in identifying a defendant or recalling the details of a crime, but who is much firmer in that recollection at trial, may be impeached regarding how the person's memory suddenly improved and whether the government has suggested information to help its case. In addition, the presentation of strong evidence by the prosecution at the preliminary hearing may lead a defendant to consider a plea offer.

E. Waiver

Even if the defendant has the right to a preliminary examination, there may be good reasons to forego it by waiving the right to the hearing and allowing the case to move forward to trial. As with other proceedings, most preliminary examinations are open to the public, so any publicity generated by the hearing can have an adverse effect on the jury pool, because, in large part, only the government's evidence will be introduced.

To the extent the defendant is afforded the opportunity to cross-examine a witness, that person's testimony at the preliminary examination may be admissible at trial if the person is unavailable at that time, thereby preserving potentially adverse testimony. For these and other reasons, counsel may conclude that it is better to forego the preliminary examination, especially in a jurisdiction that has liberal discovery rules. Some states do not allow a waiver of the preliminary examination without the prosecutor's consent, which may be withheld if the prosecutor is concerned about preserving the testimony of a witness who may become unavailable by the time of trial.

F. Right to Counsel

Although the Constitution does not require a preliminary examination to determine whether there is probable cause for a charge, if such a proceeding is provided, then it is a "critical stage" and counsel must be furnished to the defendant (see Chapter 7). In *Coleman v. Alabama*, 399 U.S. 1 (1970), the Supreme Court held that "the guiding hand of counsel at the preliminary hearing is essential to protect the indigent accused against an erroneous or improper prosecution." The Court noted that counsel's cross-examination could expose "fatal weaknesses in the State's case that may lead the magistrate to refuse to bind the accused over." In addition, the Court noted that the lawyer's interrogation of a witness could create impeachment material useful at trial, and counsel could engage in discovery and perhaps even argue in favor of an early psychiatric exam of the defendant.

G. Burden of Proof

In most states and in federal cases, the prosecutor bears the burden of showing that there is probable cause to conclude that a crime was committed and that the defendant committed the offense, either as the perpetrator or by any other theory of criminal liability. Similar to the standard for issuance of a warrant, the probable cause threshold is lower than the typical preponderance of the evidence requirement in civil litigation. A minority of states require that the government establish a *prima facie* case that the defendant committed the crime, which is higher than the probable cause determination for a warrant but does not reach the preponderance of the evidence level. Under the *prima facie* standard, the court must determine whether a reasonable jury would convict based on the evidence presented, not just that it is probable that the person committed the crime.

The exclusionary rule does not apply to preliminary examinations, so the court could rely on evidence that would be unavailable in the prosecution's case-in-chief at trial. For example, Federal Rule of Criminal Procedure 5.1(e) provides that the defendant "may not object to evidence on the ground that it was unlawfully acquired." In many jurisdictions, the preliminary examination is held prior to a decision on a Motion to Suppress Evidence, so courts are reluctant to revisit the propriety of the charges if it turns out that certain evidence cannot be used at trial. Some states prohibit the use of evidence illegally obtained by the government.

H. Credibility

During preliminary examinations, the court assesses the credibility of any witnesses presented, although the standard is usually whether a reasonable juror could credit the testimony and not whether the judge actually believes it. Defendants are generally permitted to cross-examine witnesses, but the Confrontation Clause does not apply at a preliminary examination. The cross-examination of a witness may be limited by the court because the proceeding is only to determine whether there is sufficient evidence to go to trial, not a determination of guilt, so once the evidence is found to be sufficient, further inquiry may be unnecessary. If the government is concerned that a witness may be unavailable to testify at trial or could change the testimony, however, then under the Confrontation Clause the defendant must be afforded full and fair opportunity to cross-examine the witness or the testimony would not be admissible at trial.

I. Rules of Evidence

In the majority of the states, and in federal prosecutions, the rules of evidence do not apply at a preliminary examination. Federal Rule of Evidence 1101(d) specifically exempts "preliminary examinations in criminal cases" from the requirements for admission of evidence. Constitutional and evidentiary testimonial privileges are available to a witness in a preliminary hearing even if the other evidence rules are not applicable. For example, a defendant can assert Fifth Amendment privilege against self-incrimination and refuse to testify; similarly, a person cannot be compelled to provide information protected by attorney-client privilege or marital privilege, unless an exception is available. On the other hand, statements constituting hearsay would *not* be excluded from the hearing in almost every jurisdiction, so that they can help to establish the basis for determining whether there is sufficient evidence to proceed to trial. For example, a common scenario in which hearsay is used is when a police officer recounts what an eyewitness reported about the crime: such statements may indicate that there are sufficient grounds for the case to proceed to trial, yet this testimony would not be admitted at trial, unless it met the requirements of the evidence rules and did not violate the Confrontation Clause (see Chapter 14).

Some states require the prosecution's evidence at the preliminary hearing be admissible under the evidence rules, but provide an exception for certain types of hearsay statements and evidence subject to an exclusionary rule, such as evidence obtained in violation of a federal or state statute. A few states apply the evidence rules fully to a preliminary examination, but it is not clear whether the erroneous admission of evidence at this stage would authorize a court to overturn a subsequent conviction.

J. Probable Cause

If the court determines there is sufficient evidence of probable cause that the defendant committed the offense, then the case moves forward to trial on the charges approved by the court. In some jurisdictions, the case proceeds to a grand jury for an independent determination that there is probable cause for the charges to be included in an indictment. In these states, the preliminary examination is only an initial step that allows a defendant to be held in custody on the charges. In either scenario, a defendant can still seek dismissal of the charges by the trial judge, but the credibility determinations made at the preliminary examination will be accorded weight, and the decision to allow the prosecution to proceed can be overturned only if there was an abuse of discretion. Most states, and the federal system, do not allow an interlocutory appeal of a finding of probable cause, which means a defendant must go to trial to challenge the strength of the government's case.

Some states permit a defendant to offer an affirmative defense to the charge at the preliminary examination, although such permission may be limited so as to prevent the proceeding from becoming a full-scale trial. Other states do not allow evidence relating to an affirmative defense because the only issue in the proceeding is whether the prosecution can produce sufficient evidence establishing probable cause or a *prima facie* case that the defendant committed the crime, and defenses are for a jury to decide after the government proves all the elements of the offense. The affirmative defenses most likely to be raised at this stage of the case are insanity, entrapment, and justification.

K. Dismissal

If the court determines there is insufficient evidence at the end of the preliminary examination to allow the case to proceed further, then it may dismiss the charges. In some jurisdictions, the court can also find that the evidence only supports a lesser-included offense, and allow the prosecutor to amend the charge to the lower crime before permitting the case to move forward. Even if the charge is dismissed, however, that is not necessarily the end of the case.

In almost every jurisdiction, the prosecutor has discretion to refile the charges and begin the process again. For example, Federal Rule of Criminal Procedure 5.1(f) provides that dismissal "does not preclude the government from later prosecuting the defendant for the same offense." Double jeopardy does not apply to a pre-trial dismissal of charges because jeopardy does not attach until the trial begins; there is no constitutional prohibition on pursuing the same charges in a subsequent proceeding.

Some jurisdictions allow the prosecutor to appeal a dismissal of charges, rather than refiling the charges and perhaps suffering a second dismissal. In states that do not authorize an appeal, the prosecutor may seek an extraordinary writ from a higher court to allow the prosecution to proceed, although the standard for issuance is usually quite high and makes review of the decision difficult to obtain.

L. Refiling Charges

Most states and the federal system do not require the prosecutor to obtain additional evidence before charging the defendant again after charges were dismissed, although, as a strategic matter, it may be preferable to do so. As a general proposition, prosecutors do not want to put on the entire case during the preliminary examination; some evidence may have been withheld in the first hearing that can be introduced in a second proceeding. A minority of states require the government to obtain additional evidence before refiling charges, although what constitutes such evidence is not always clear. If a jurisdiction provides for indictment by a grand jury, then the prosecutor can pursue charges by that avenue, because an indictment requires a determination of probable cause and, thus, there is no need for another preliminary examination.

M. Harmless Error

Even if the preliminary examination should have resulted in the dismissal of charges, if a fact-finder validly found the defendant guilty beyond a reasonable doubt, then the initial error is considered harmless in most cases. A few states allow for reversal of a conviction based on an erroneous finding of probable cause for the charge, but the procedure, then, is to hold another preliminary examination and permit the case to move forward to trial if the court finds probable cause. The second preliminary examination may be before the same judge or magistrate, or a new one, depending on the local court's procedures.

Constitutional errors at the preliminary examination are subject to harmless error review. For example, while the Supreme Court found that the denial of counsel in *Coleman v. Alabama* was a constitutional violation, it remanded the case to determine whether or not the error tainted the subsequent convictions.

Checkpoints

- The *Gerstein* hearing on whether there was probable cause to arrest without a warrant must be held within a reasonable period, no more than forty-eight hours after the arrest, save for certain extraordinary circumstances.

- The *Gerstein* hearing determines whether there was probable cause for a warrantless arrest.

- Bail should be set at an amount that will assure the presence of the defendant at future proceedings, but nothing greater can be required.

- Key factors in determining whether to grant bail, and the amount required, are the likelihood of flight; the nature of the crime charged and potential punishment involved; and potential threat to the community and witnesses if the defendant is released.

- A *Gerstein* hearing, bail determination, and arraignment can be combined into a single proceeding.

- The Eighth Amendment prohibits excessive bail, but does not grant a right to bail in any particular case.

- Pretrial detention statutes are permissible under due process so long as they fulfill a strong government interest.

- Detention in an individual case may violate the defendant's liberty interest if it is punitive.

- A preliminary determination of probable cause for the filing of criminal charges is not required by the Constitution.

- If a preliminary examination is authorized, then counsel must be provided to the defendant.

- In most jurisdictions, the rules of evidence do not apply at a preliminary examination, or do so with significant exceptions.

- A defendant may have only a limited right to cross-examine witnesses and introduce evidence at a preliminary examination.

- The preliminary examination can provide a defendant with certain collateral benefits, such as discovery of the government's case.

- Dismissal of charges after the preliminary examination does not prevent the government from filing identical charges again or seeking a grand jury indictment, because double jeopardy does not attach at the pre-trial stage.

Chapter 2

Grand Jury

Roadmap

- Authority of the grand jury
- Standard for an indictment
- Selection and function
- Constitutional limitations
- Investigative and accusatory roles
- Fifth Amendment rights of witnesses
- Challenges to the grand jury process

I. Historical Development

The Fifth Amendment provides: "No person shall be held to answer for a capital, or otherwise infamous crime, unless on a presentment or indictment of a grand jury." In colonial times, the grand jury was viewed as a significant bulwark against prosecutorial abuses, because it placed a body of ordinary citizens between a potential defendant and the government. In a famous pre-Revolutionary War case, three grand juries in New York refused to charge John Peter Zenger for his newspaper articles criticizing monarchical abuses. As the Supreme Court noted in *Wood v. Georgia*, 370 U.S. 375 (1962), "this body has been regarded as a primary security to the innocent against hasty, malicious and oppressive persecution."

The grand jury traces its roots to fourteenth-century England, when a group of twenty-four knights, called *le grand inquest*, were given the authority to initiate a prosecution. The grand jury members would provide the information necessary to determine whether there was probable cause that an individual committed an offense, and then a petit jury would determine the defendant's guilt. Great Britain has abolished the grand jury, but it remains an integral component in criminal cases in approximately twenty states and most federal prosecutions.

Over time, the grand jury developed its authority to investigate possible crimes by compelling witnesses to produce evidence and to testify in aid of the determination whether an offense had occurred. This leads to the dual function of the grand jury today: as an *investigative* body, it gathers evidence of potential wrongdoing; and as an *accusatory* body, it judges whether there is probable cause to charge an individual with a crime. These two functions, sometimes referred to as a "sword and shield," may actually conflict when prosecutors largely control the investigative function.

II. Grand Jury Procedures

A. Method of Charging

The Fifth Amendment requires a grand jury indictment or presentment for all capital offenses and "infamous crimes," which today means all felonies. An indictment is a charging document drafted by the prosecutor and approved by the grand jury, while a presentment is a charge crafted by the grand jurors on their own initiative, usually based on their personal knowledge or information provided directly to them by an individual. While early grand juries often charged crimes by presentment, that is no longer the case today, and in the federal courts the prosecutor must sign the charging document for it to be effective. Under federal law, a special grand jury convened to investigate organized crime can furnish the court with a report "(1) concerning noncriminal misconduct, malfeasance, or misfeasance in office involving organized criminal activity by an appointed public officer or employee as the basis for a recommendation of removal or disciplinary action; or (2) regarding organized crime conditions in the district." 18 U.S.C.A. § 3333(a).

Federal Rule of Criminal Procedure 7(c)(1) provides that the indictment "must be a plain, concise, and definite written statement of the essential facts constituting the offense charged and must be signed by an attorney for the government." A count of the indictment can incorporate by reference information related to another charge, and it can include multiple means for committing the offense or state that the manner of committing the crime is unknown to the grand jury.

B. Standard of Proof

The primary standard used by the grand jury to determine whether to return an indictment is *probable cause*, although in some states the evidence must establish a *prima facie* case that, if unrebutted, would lead a petit jury to convict a person for an offense. The requirement of proof beyond a reasonable doubt is not applied to the decision whether to return an indictment, and defendants rarely have a right to present evidence to rebut the prosecutor's case.

Grand juries in most states and the federal system are not subject to close judicial supervision, unlike a petit jury that receives case-specific instructions. The decision to return an indictment usually is not subject to review for possible legal or factual error. At the federal level, and for those states that still employ the grand jury, the grand jury approves the charges by voting in favor of an indictment—known as returning a "true bill"—or rejects them—returning what is called a "no bill."

C. Constitutional Right

The right to a grand jury is one of the few criminal protections in the Constitution that has not been applied to the states under the incorporation analysis used by the Supreme Court in the 1960s. Beginning in the mid-nineteenth century, a number of states began authorizing local prosecutors to file criminal charges without requiring initiation of the more laborious grand jury process. The charges were contained in a *complaint* or *criminal information* that sets forth the elements of the offense in much the same way an indictment, except that there is no independent, advance determination of probable cause. In *Hurtado v. California*, 110 U.S. 516 (1884), the Supreme Court held that due process did not require that grand jury to initiate a felony prosecution, upholding the practice of prosecutorial filing of charges without outside review.

Since *Hurtado*, a majority of the states allow prosecutors to use a complaint or criminal information in felony cases. These states do not prohibit an indictment, but in many of them the grand jury has fallen into disuse. In some states, a grand jury is used in special situations, particularly when that body's investigative powers are needed to complete the inquiry, such as police shootings and public corruption cases. After the prosecutor files a complaint or criminal information, in most instances, the states provide a preliminary hearing to determine probable cause for the charges (see Chapter 1). A few states only require a grand jury indictment for specified crimes, usually those involving the death penalty or life in prison without the possibility of parole.

D. Selection

Grand juries range in size from sixteen to twenty-three members in federal districts to as few as six members in some states. As representatives of the community, the grand jurors are selected largely in the same way as members of the petit juries that decide a defendant's guilt. In some jurisdictions, the court calls in a group of potential jurors, called the "venire," and grand and petit juries can be selected from the same pool, depending on the particular need that day. A grand jury, however, sits for a designated period of time rather than deciding a particular case, and usually hears evidence from a number of investigations that may result in returning indictments in hundreds of prosecutions. Under Federal Rule of Criminal Procedure 6(g), a grand jury is impaneled for eighteen months, although its term can be extended six months; in certain exceptional situations, a statute may authorize a grand jury to sit for three years.

Unlike a trial (or petit) jury, there are no peremptory challenges to remove a grand juror, and indeed there is no involvement of prosecutors or defense counsel in their selection. Grand jurors are selected from the same pool as a petit jury, but the decision regarding who will be named to a grand jury is made by the clerk of the court rather than an attorney for a party. Federal Rule of Criminal Procedure 6(b)(1) authorizes challenges to the composition of a grand jury by either the prosecution or defense "on the ground that it was not lawfully drawn, summoned, or selected, and may challenge an individual juror on the ground that the juror is not legally qualified."

Because a grand jury usually sits for a longer period than a trial jury, courts often excuse individuals from service after they were impaneled. The membership of a grand jury can shift over time, so that as jurors are excused, or perhaps removed for lack of diligence, alternate grand jurors can be added without affecting its operation. The same individual jurors need not hear all the evidence in a case before voting to indict, and not all must be present for the proper return of an indictment.

E. Constitutional Protections in Selecting Grand Jurors

1. Equal Protection

The Equal Protection Clause of the Fourteenth Amendment prohibits discrimination on the basis of race or gender in the selection of grand jurors. In *Campbell v. Louisiana*, 523 U.S. 392 (1998), the Supreme Court applied the rule of *Powers v. Ohio*, 499 U.S. 400 (1990),which permits a defendant to raise an equal protection claim regarding intentional exclusion of members of one race from service as the grand jury foreman even if the defendant is of a different race. The Court held that "[r]egardless of his or her skin color, the accused suffers a significant injury in fact when the composition of the grand jury is tainted by racial discrimination."

2. Due Process

In addition to an equal protection claim, in *Peters v. Kiff*, 407 U.S. 493 (1972), the Supreme Court held that "a State cannot, consistent with due process, subject a defendant to indictment or trial by a jury that has been selected in an arbitrary and discriminatory manner, in violation of the Constitution and laws of the United States." It found that the exclusion of "a substantial and identifiable class of citizens" from grand jury service would have a subtle effect on the decision to indict, and, therefore, a defendant of *any race* could challenge the exclusion of a class of persons from being eligible to serve as grand jurors.

In *Rose v. Mitchell*, 443 U.S. 545 (1979), the Court stated that a finding of unlawful discrimination affecting the composition of a grand jury would result in the reversal of a conviction and quashing the indictment "without inquiry into whether the defendant was prejudiced in fact by the discrimination at the grand jury stage." The alleged discrimination in *Rose* involved the appointment of the grand jury foreman, who was added to the grand jury by the local court and had the authority to block an indictment. The Court reaffirmed this rule of automatic reversal of a conviction in *Vasquez v. Hillary*, 474 U.S. 254 (1986), when it held that "discrimination in the grand jury undermines the structural integrity of the criminal tribunal itself, and is not amenable to harmless-error review."

In *Hobby v. United States*, 468 U.S. 339 (1984), the Court reaffirmed the *Peters* holding that discrimination in the selection of a grand jury could be challenged as a violation of due process; the Court concluded, however, that alleged discrimination in the selection of the foreman of a federal grand jury did not constitute a violation of due process because the foreman was selected from among the grand jurors and that person's role was largely ministerial, with no authority to affect the grand jury's decisions beyond voting on an indictment. Therefore, reversal of the conviction was not required when there was no impact from the discrimination on the decision to indict.

3. Fair Cross-Section

Peters, *Rose*, and *Hobby* involved claims of racial discrimination, which can now be the basis for both due process and equal protection claims. In addition, under the Sixth Amendment, there is a "fair cross-section" requirement for the venire from which petit juries are drawn. In *Taylor v. Louisiana*, 419 U.S. 522 (1975), the Supreme Court held that "the selection of a petit jury from a representative cross section of the community is an essential component of the Sixth Amendment right to a jury trial." It is a constitutional violation to exclude from jury service "large, distinctive groups" (see Chapter 10). *Taylor* based its analysis on the Sixth Amendment jury trial right, which does not apply to grand juries.

In *Campbell v. Louisiana*, 523 U.S. 392 (1998), the Court declined to consider a "fair cross-section" claim regarding the selection of grand jury foremen because the defendant had not met the burden of establishing the exclusion of an identifiable group. It is not clear whether such a claim regarding other groups, for example based on religion or age, can succeed as part of a due process argument challenging the grand jury, or whether a claim is limited to discrimination based on race or sex.

III. Investigative Role

In its earliest form, the grand jury relied on the observations and information provided by its members to determine whether a crime occurred. The modern grand jury obtains evidence and compels witnesses to appear through the use of *subpoenas*, which require the recipient to appear and provide evidence. The grand jury's authority is supported by the *contempt power* of the court, which can send a person to jail—perhaps for the remainder of the grand jury's term— to coerce compliance with the subpoena. This is not a criminal punishment; rather, under civil contempt, the person "holds the keys" to the jail cell and can be released upon compliance with the subpoena, or if the court determines there is no possibility the person will succumb to coercive authority by complying.

A. Authority

The grand jury can require a person to appear to testify, through a subpoena *ad testificandum*, and to provide documents and other physical evidence, through a subpoena *duces tecum*. In the modern grand jury, the decision regarding which witnesses to subpoena is made by the prosecutor and not, in most cases, by the individual grand jurors. The prosecutor serves as the legal advisor to the grand jury, and investigative agencies often conduct a preliminary review of a case before the prosecutor decides whether to present it to the grand jury. In federal investigations, and in many states, a grand jury subpoena need not be approved by the body itself, and frequently prosecutors issue them on behalf of the grand jury before it even begins to review evidence and hear testimony.

The grand jury is entitled to compel the production of "every man's evidence" as part of its investigation: "Because its task is to inquire into the existence of possible criminal conduct and to return only well-founded indictments, its investigative powers are necessarily broad." *Branzburg v. Hayes*, 408 U.S.

665 (1972). The grand jury can initiate an investigation "merely on suspicion that the law is being violated, or even just because it wants assurance that it is not." *United States v. Morton Salt Co.*, 338 U.S. 632 (1950). The grand jury "may act on tips, rumors, evidence offered by the prosecutor, or their own personal knowledge." *United States v. Dionisio*, 410 U.S. 1 (1973).

B. Limitations

A grand jury's investigative power, though expansive, is not unlimited. Evidentiary privileges — such as the protection for attorney-client or marital communications, and the Fifth Amendment privilege against self-incrimination — apply in the grand jury and may be a valid basis to resist providing evidence and testimony. If a witness asserts the Fifth Amendment in the grand jury and then testifies at trial, the prosecution may not bring out that fact to impeach the defendant. *Grunewald v. United States*, 353 U.S. 391 (1957). Moreover, in *United States v. R. Enterprises*, 498 U.S. 292 (1991), the Supreme Court noted that a grand jury is not "licensed to engage in arbitrary fishing expeditions, nor may they select targets of investigation out of malice or an intent to harass." The propriety of a subpoena for records is assessed by the relevance of the categories of documents it seeks from the recipient to the subject matter of the investigation, but a court would not determine relevancy "with respect to particular documents within those categories or particular portions of documents." *In re Grand Jury Proceedings*, 616 F.3d 1186, 1205 (10th Cir. 2010).

C. Advantages and Disadvantages

Using a grand jury to investigate a case in place of, or in conjunction with, the police and other law enforcement agencies may provide significant advantages to prosecutors. Unlike a search warrant, a grand jury subpoena can be issued without prior judicial approval, and need not meet any standard such as probable cause for its issuance. Regarding federal grand jury subpoenas, the Supreme Court in *R. Enterprises* held that the subpoena cannot be quashed "unless the district court determines that there is no reasonable possibility that the category of materials the Government seeks will produce information relevant to the general subject of the grand jury's investigation." Witnesses testifying before a grand jury are usually placed under oath, so they may be subject to a perjury prosecution if they lie. The presence of a group of citizens observing and participating in the proceeding may exert pressure on the witness to testify truthfully.

On the other hand, grand jury investigations can be more cumbersome than a traditional law enforcement investigation: due to the time exhausted awaiting compliance with a subpoena, evidence remains for some time in the control of the recipient, who may delay responding, destroy it, or otherwise place it beyond the reach of the authorities. The element of surprise, which almost necessarily comes along with police officer interviews or execution of search warrants, is lost due to the period of time to comply offered by grand jury subpoenas.

D. Individual Rights

While police investigations are constrained by the Fourth and Fifth Amendments, those protections are largely inapplicable to grand jury investigations. In *Dionisio*, the Supreme Court rejected the argument that a grand jury subpoena for voice exemplars was subject to review under the Fourth Amendment. The Court held, "Since neither the summons to appear before the grand jury nor its directive to make a voice recording infringed upon any interest protected by the Fourth Amendment, there was no justification for requiring the grand jury to satisfy even the minimal requirement of 'reasonableness' ...." If a subpoena is the *functional equivalent* of a search because of its breadth, however, lower courts may order it quashed and require that a narrower one be issued, because, otherwise, the subpoena would be a violation of the Fourth Amendment prohibition on unreasonable searches.

A witness appearing before a grand jury does not have the right to be warned that he or she is a target of the investigation. *United States v. Washington*, 431 U.S. 181 (1977). Moreover, because testifying in a grand jury is not considered a custodial interrogation, *Miranda* warnings need not be given to the witness. *United States v. Mandujano*, 425 U.S. 564 (1976). As a matter of good practice, prosecutors should (and usually do) provide some warnings to a witness regarding the requirement to testify truthfully and the potential uses for the testimony.

In federal grand juries and those of some states, a witness has no right to be accompanied by counsel, unlike a police interrogation. The witness may be permitted to consult with counsel outside the grand jury room, but because neither *Miranda* nor the Sixth Amendment right to counsel attach to an appearance before the grand jury, there is no constitutional requirement to furnish counsel, nor that the lawyer be present during the testimony. In those states that permit counsel to be present, the lawyer serves as a monitor of the proceedings but generally does not participate, neither by examining witnesses nor commenting on the evidence, except in some instances to provide clarifications for the record.

In addition to barring counsel from the grand jury room in many jurisdictions, a putative defendant may be denied the opportunity to testify before the grand jury. New York is the only state primarily using indictments that grant a prospective defendant the *right to testify*. Many prosecutors are willing to allow a target of the investigation to testify before the grand jury in light of the advantages provided to the government — including the absence of counsel from the grand jury room in many jurisdictions and the right to cross-examine a witness largely unfettered by the rules of evidence. It is uncommon for an investigative target to testify before a grand jury because of the risks involved.

E. Grand Jury Subpoenas

A federal grand jury can require a person to appear to testify, by means of what is called a subpoena *ad testificandum*, and to provide documents and other physical evidence, pursuant to what is called a subpoena *duces tecum*. In addition, the subpoena recipient can be required to furnish certain items or information, such as a handwriting or voice exemplar. There is no Fourth Amendment limitation on their use because the Supreme Court has held that the witness does not have a reasonable expectation of privacy regarding certain external characteristics. *See United States v. Mara*, 410 U.S. 19 (1973) (handwriting); *United States v. Dionisio*, 410 U.S. 1 (1973) (voice).

Federal Rule of Criminal Procedure 17(c)(1) authorizes the issuance of a subpoena in both grand jury investigations and for trial that compels a

> witness to produce any books, papers, documents, data, or other objects the subpoena designates. The court may direct the witness to produce the designated items in court before trial or before they are to be offered in evidence. When the items arrive, the court may permit the parties and their attorneys to inspect all or part of them.

Rule 17(c)(2) authorizes the court to quash a subpoena in response to a timely motion "if compliance would be unreasonable or oppressive." A trial subpoena directed to a victim may only be issued by order of the court, and Rule 17(c)(3) provides that before issuance "the court must require giving notice to the victim so that the victim can move to quash or modify the subpoena or otherwise object."

A subpoena may be directed at a natural person or a legal entity. Where documents from a business or other organization are sought, the subpoena may be directed to a "custodian of records" for the entity.

The description of the subpoenaed records will often include phrases like "any and all documents reflecting, referring, or relating to," or "any and all documents in the possession, custody, or control of" an identified person or organization. The broad terminology is designed to make it more difficult for the recipient to find a loophole in the subpoena to avoid producing potentially incriminating records.

Federal prosecutors often are willing to make arrangements for service of the subpoena and delivery of documents and other materials so that the recipient does not have to appear before the grand jury. It is common for the subpoena recipient's counsel to request an extension of time for delivery of the materials, and also to seek clarification of the scope of the subpoena. Counsel and prosecutors may negotiate terms such as the time limit allowed for production of the records sought, or whether production may be performed in stages as the documents are retrieved and reviewed.

F. Enforcing Subpoenas

Grand jury subpoenas are supported by the court's authority to hold in contempt any person who willfully refuses, without legal justification, to comply with a subpoena's directive. The court's authority includes both civil and criminal contempt. In *Shillitani v. United States*, 384 U.S. 364 (1966), the Supreme Court directed lower courts to consider civil contempt first to enforce a subpoena, and pursue criminal contempt only when they conclude that the civil contempt has been ineffective.

For civil contempt, the recalcitrant subpoena recipient is sent to a local jail or given a fine (which may increase daily), but the person may purge the contempt by complying with the subpoena. "It has been said," the Second Circuit stated in *Armstrong v. Guccione*, 470 F.3d 89 (2d Cir. 2006), "that a civil contemnor who is incarcerated to compel compliance with a court order holds the key to his prison cell: Where defiance leads to the contemnor's incarceration, compliance is his salvation."

A witness refusing to purge the contempt can be incarcerated until the grand jury completes its term and is discharged. Under the Recalcitrant Witness Act, 28 U.S.C. § 1826(a), the period of incarceration for civil contempt for refusing to testify before a federal grand jury is limited to eighteen months. If prosecutors still need the information or documents held by the person, a new grand jury subpoena can be issued and, if the person again refuses to comply, then another civil contempt charge can be imposed. Once civil contempt shifts from being coercive to punitive, however, the witness must be released. While some contemnors have spent the entire term of the grand jury in jail, a person may be released at an earlier point if the court can be convinced that further incarceration will not produce a response.

The most common ground for refusing to comply with a grand jury subpoena is the assertion of a common law, statutory, or constitutional privilege. The full range of privileges that apply in federal courts also apply to grand jury proceedings, such as the Fifth Amendment privilege against self-incrimination and attorney-client privilege. These types of refusals to comply do not contest the validity of the subpoena, but only seek to interpose the privilege claim to prevent having to respond to certain questions, or avoid producing particular records. Where the challenge goes to the underlying validity of the subpoena, it is presented through a motion to quash under Federal Rule 17(c) on the ground that enforcement would be "unreasonable or oppressive."

1. "Unreasonable or Oppressive"

The Supreme Court gave a broad reading to the validity of grand jury subpoenas in *United States v. R. Enterprises*, 498 U.S. 292 (1991), in which the Court considered a challenge to subpoenas on the ground that the items sought were irrelevant to the investigation because they were outside the grand jury's jurisdiction. The Court stated that "a grand jury subpoena issued through normal channels is presumed to be reasonable, and the burden of showing unreasonableness must be on the recipient who seeks to avoid compliance." When assessing the validity of a grand jury subpoena, *R. Enterprises* held that "the motion to quash must be denied unless the district court determines that there is no reasonable possibility that the category of materials the government seeks will produce information relevant to the general subject of the grand jury's investigation." Given the broad reach of the federal criminal law and the grand jury's expansive authority to investigate possible violations, *R. Enterprises* makes it very difficult to successfully challenge a subpoena on the ground that the information sought is irrelevant to the investigation or not within the power of the grand jury to review.

Subpoena recipients occasionally have been successful in challenging document requests based on the overbreadth doctrine. Invoking the limitations of the Fourth Amendment on unreasonable searches, a subpoena recipient may claim that the volume of records sought by the subpoena essentially converts it to a general search. In determining whether a subpoena is overbroad, in *In re Corrado Brothers, Inc.*, 367 F.Supp. 1126 (D. Del. 1973), the federal district court summarized the key factors to be considered in deciding whether to grant a motion to quash: "(1) that the subpoena command only the production of materials relevant to the investigation; (2) that the subpoena specify the materials to be produced with reasonable particularity; and (3) that the subpoena command production of materials covering only a reasonable period of time."

If a court denies a motion to quash and orders the recipient to comply with the subpoena, the only way to appeal that decision is to suffer a civil contempt, with the risk that the person will be incarcerated while the appellate court decides the case. The Supreme Court, in *United States v. Ryan*, 402 U.S. 530

(1971), rejected the argument that a person challenging a subpoena should be
allowed to appeal without being found in contempt, stating

> we have consistently held that the necessity for expedition in the ad-
> ministration of the criminal law justifies putting one who seeks to re-
> sist the production of desired information to a choice between
> compliance with a trial court's order to produce prior to any review of
> that order, and resistance to that order with the concomitant possibil-
> ity of an adjudication of contempt if his claims are rejected on appeal.

There are strategic considerations in deciding whether to challenge a grand
jury subpoena. Even if a subpoena is successfully challenged, the prosecutor can
issue a narrower one that may survive a challenge and require the production
of certain records. Where the government has asked for a large number of documents, the recipient may respond by turning over everything that could possibly fall within the subpoena and then rely on the prosecutor's lack of resources
to sort out potentially damaging material. Even if the motion to quash is unlikely to succeed, the process of reviewing the motion may force the government to disclose information not otherwise available to the subpoenaed party,
which may be helpful in later tactical decisions.

2. Act of Production Privilege

The Fifth Amendment privilege against self-incrimination can be the basis for
refusing to testify before the grand jury. At one time, the Fifth Amendment was
also viewed as extending to the production of documents, based on the Supreme
Court's decision in *Boyd v. United States*, 116 U.S. 616 (1883). The Court stated
that "any forcible and compulsory extortion of a man's ... private papers to be used
as evidence to convict him of a crime or to forfeit his goods" violated the witness's right to privacy under the Fourth and Fifth Amendments. It limited *Boyd*
in *Hale v. Henkel*, 201 U.S. 43 (1906), in holding a custodian subpoenaed for a
corporation's records could not assert the privilege against self-incrimination because the Fifth Amendment did not apply to business organizations.

The most significant limitation on the scope of *Boyd* came in *Fisher v. United
States*, 425 U.S. 391 (1976), when the Court held that the contents of voluntarily created records were not protected by the Fifth Amendment because
there was no compulsion in their creation, and thus they did not qualify for
the protection afforded by the privilege against self-incrimination. The Court
did not dispense completely with the protection for documents, however, because it recognized that the *act of production* in response to a subpoena com-
municated information about the existence, possession, and authenticity of

the records sought. Thus, while an individual could not assert the Fifth Amendment because a document might be incriminating, the act-of-production privilege could be asserted if turning over the documents, a *communicative act*, would be incriminating by providing the government with information.

The Fifth Amendment is not available to resist every subpoena for personal records. In *Fisher*, the Court held that the communicative aspect of the act of production may not be protected if the information conveyed was not incriminating because it was "a foregone conclusion and the [witness] adds little or nothing to the sum total of the Government's information by conceding that he in fact has the papers." In other words, if the government can show that it already knows about the existence, possession, and authenticity of the records sought, then there is no incriminating communication by producing them and the witness can be compelled to comply with the subpoena. The foregone conclusion analysis requires the government to show that it possessed this information regarding the existence, possession, and authenticity of the records *at the time* it issued the subpoena. *In re Grand Jury Subpoena Dated April 18, 2003*, 383 F.3d 905 (9th Cir. 2004).

If prosecutors are unable to establish the foregone conclusion regarding the records, then they can compel production of the records if the witness is granted use/fruits immunity under 18 U.S.C. §6001 et seq., which prohibits the government from making any direct or derivative use of the communicative aspect of the act of production (see Chapter 12). In *United States v. Hubbell*, 530 U.S. 27 (2000), the Supreme Court rejected the argument that such immunity only prohibits the government from referring to the defendant's act of production but allows complete use of the contents of the records at trial. Instead, the Court held that "[i]t is abundantly clear that the testimonial aspect of respondent's act of producing subpoenaed documents was the first step in a chain of evidence that led to this prosecution," and therefore any use of the documents would violate the immunity provided to the defendant.

In *United States v. Doe*, 465 U.S. 605 (1984), the Court extended *Fisher's* act of production analysis to a sole proprietorship, finding that the business is effectively an extension of its individual owner. For corporations and larger business organizations, however, there is no Fifth Amendment right to resist producing the organization's documents. In *Braswell v. United States*, 487 U.S. 99 (1988), the Court reaffirmed its position in *Hale v. Henkel* regarding the unavailability of the privilege against self-incrimination for corporations, upholding the *collective entity doctrine*, which denies the Fifth Amendment privilege against self-incrimination to business organizations. *Braswell* held that a custodian of records "may not resist a subpoena for corporate records on Fifth Amendment grounds," regardless of the size or complexity of the organization. The entity was a small corporation, with only a single shareholder, but by choosing the corporate form there was no right to resist a subpoena *duces tecum* directed to it.

Although the collective entity doctrine bars an organization from asserting the Fifth Amendment in response to a subpoena for its records, the act of producing those records cannot be used against the custodian in a subsequent prosecution of that person. *Braswell* explained in a footnote that limiting the evidentiary use of the corporation's document production was a "necessary concomitant of the notion that a corporate custodian acts as an agent and not an individual when he produces corporate records in response to a subpoena addressed to him in his representative capacity." If the person holding the records is no longer an employee of the organization, then those may now be personal documents for which the act-of-production privilege could be asserted to resist supplying them to the grand jury in response to a subpoena. *In re Three Grand Jury Subpoenas*, 191 F.3d 173 (2d Cir. 1999).

Required records are not subject to a Fifth Amendment privilege claim even when held by an individual. To come within this exception, there are three requirements: (1) the purpose of the government's inquiry must be regulatory and not criminal; (2) the documents are of a type that the regulated party customarily keeps; and (3) the records have public aspects which make them analogous to public documents. *Shapiro v. United States*, 335 U.S. 1 (1948). The required records analysis has been applied in recent years to compel the production of documents from owners of overseas bank accounts who must maintain them for tax purposes. *In re Grand Jury Subpoena*, 696 F.3d 428 (5th Cir. 2012); *In re Special February 2011-1 Grand Jury Subpoena Dated September 12, 2011*, 691 F.3d 903 (7th Cir. 2012).

If prosecutors are concerned that a person will assert the privilege against self-incrimination to resist producing records, they can seek a warrant to seize the documents because the Fifth Amendment cannot be used to resist a search. This alternative may not be available, however, if the government cannot establish probable cause regarding the location of the records or their relationship to criminal activity, which is not required to issue a grand jury subpoena.

IV. Accusatory Role

A. Screening Function

The grand jury has long been viewed as a shield to protect citizens from overzealous prosecutors who may seek to initiate prosecutions for vindictive reasons. The grand jury can serve as an independent body that screens cases to determine whether there is sufficient evidence that the person committed the crime and whether it is appropriate to pursue a prosecution. Much like a petit jury, a grand jury has the power to effectively nullify the law by refusing to indict, *even if* there is sufficient evidence of a crime. Unlike a jury at trial, however, a "no bill" returned by a grand jury does not have any preclusive effect under double jeopardy to bar the prosecutor from presenting the case to another grand jury, which could vote to return a "true bill." Some states require judicial approval before submitting a case to another grand jury.

Some question whether the modern grand jury has any real screening function because of the control over the process exercised by prosecutors. Statistics on the number of indictments returned by federal grand juries show that in over 99% of cases the grand jury votes to return an indictment. The grand jury system, however, may effectively weed out weaker cases because prosecutors can drop an investigation before seeking an indictment if it appears the grand jurors are skeptical about pursuing charges. A grand jury can also serve an important function by allowing prosecutors to evaluate a case in private in deciding whether to proceed, rather than filing charges and having them aired at a preliminary hearing or trial.

B. Rules of Evidence

In federal grand jury investigations and in a majority of the states, the rules of evidence do not apply to the material presented to establish probable cause, except that witnesses may assert valid privileges. Even evidence obtained in violation of a person's constitutional rights, which would otherwise be subject to the exclusionary rule, may be considered by the grand jury. In *Gelbard v. United States*, 408 U.S. 41 (1972), the Supreme Court described what it called the "general rule" that "a defendant is not entitled to have his indictment dismissed before trial simply because the Government acquired incriminating evidence in violation of the law." Similarly, in *Lawn v. United States*, 355 U.S. 339 (1958), the Court held that a defendant could not have his conviction reversed on the ground that the indictment had been procured by evidence obtained in violation of his Fifth Amendment right.

Prosecutors may rely primarily on hearsay in presenting a case to a grand jury by having an agent or police officer testify about what was learned in the investigation and recount the statements of witnesses. While this is hearsay, and would not be permitted at trial, in those jurisdictions that do not apply the rules of evidence in the grand jury, this more streamlined approach can be used. Some jurisdictions require the victim to testify before the grand jury, rather than having the person's statements summarized, to ensure that the grand jurors hear evidence from a central witness in the proceeding.

In some instances, the prosecutor will call a number of witnesses to testify before the grand jury for strategic purposes, even if the evidence could be presented through a summary witness, like a case agent. One reason to do so is to observe how well a witness will testify in a formal setting, and respond to questions in a controlled setting. In some cases, the prosecutor may view grand jury testimony as a means of pressuring a reluctant witness to provide more complete information because the person is under oath and may be questioned by the grand jurors in addition to the government attorney. One downside to presenting a number of witnesses to the grand jury, however, is that the testimony may have to be made available to the defense if the case proceeds to trial, providing fodder for cross-examination on any inconsistencies between the trial testimony and earlier statements.

C. Challenging the Sufficiency of the Evidence

In addition to allowing grand jurors to hear evidence that might not be admissible at trial, the Supreme Court has ruled out challenges to the *sufficiency* of the evidence for federal charges except by going to trial. In *Costello v. United States*, 350 U.S. 359 (1956), the Court rejected a defendant's request to overturn a conviction on the ground that the grand jury did not have sufficient admissible evidence to charge him with a crime. The grand jury indicted the defendant for tax evasion based on the testimony of three government agents who summarized the evidence, while at trial 144 witnesses testified and 368 exhibits were introduced. The Court stated,

> [N]either the Fifth Amendment nor any other constitutional provision prescribes the kind of evidence upon which grand juries must act ... An indictment returned by a legally constituted and unbiased grand jury, like an information drawn by the prosecutor, if valid on its face, is enough to call for trial of the charge on the merits.

The Court's concern was to avoid having "mini trials" on indictments by limiting a defendant's ability to challenge the evidentiary basis for the charges before a full trial.

Costello effectively rules out direct challenges to the substance of an indictment, and requires a defendant to go to trial to test the strength of the government's case. While *Costello* only governs federal indictments, a majority of the states follow its approach to preclude a defendant from disputing the evidence used to obtain an indictment. In those states that reject *Costello*, a judge can review the evidentiary support for the charges, similar to the review of a criminal information conducted at a preliminary hearing. In order to mount such a challenge, the defendant needs access to the grand jury transcripts, which is usually provided in states that do not follow *Costello*. Even then, the grand jury's probable cause determination is accorded deference, and charges will not be dismissed just because it is a close case that could result in an acquittal.

D. Secrecy

As an investigatory body, there is a need to keep the grand jury's proceedings secret: the system has an interest in allowing witnesses to provide information without being subjected to public scrutiny, and in protecting the interests of potential defendants who may suffer if word leaked about an investigation. There are strict rules that prohibit disclosure of grand jury information. For example, Federal Rule of Criminal Procedure 6(e)(2) states that participants "must not disclose a matter occurring before the grand jury." The one person who is usually not covered by the secrecy requirement is a witness, who is free to disclose what he or she said to the grand jury, although prosecutors often ask witnesses not to disclose such information for fear of prejudicing the case.

One effect of the grand jury secrecy rule is to keep information obtained in the investigation away from discovery by civil litigants and often the defendant who was the subject of the investigation. While the criminal discovery rules may give access to grand jury transcripts, the secrecy rules prohibit general discovery of what occurred before the grand jury.

Federal Rule 6(e)(3)(E) allows the court to order disclosure of grand jury transcripts to a defendant "who shows that a ground may exist to dismiss the indictment because of a matter that occurred before the grand jury." A number of states have a similar provision, which can be used to establish a claim of prosecutorial misconduct before the grand jury. Courts tend to impose a significant evidentiary requirement on the defendant before granting such discovery because of the concern about maintaining grand jury secrecy. It is often the case that a court will deny a motion for discovery of grand jury transcripts because the defense's evidence is "speculative" or does not show "a substantial likelihood" of misconduct.

While Federal Rule 6 imposes a strict secrecy requirement, testimony before a grand jury may have to be disclosed by the prosecution to a defendant as part of the required discovery in the criminal case. The rule in *Brady v. Maryland* requiring disclosure of exculpatory evidence, and the requirement in Federal Rule 26.2 that prior statements of witnesses must be disclosed after their testimony, are the most common grounds for requiring disclosure of grand jury testimony to the defense (see Chapter 8).

E. The Decision to Indict

At the conclusion of the investigation, the prosecutor usually makes the initial determination whether to seek an indictment, and will draft one for the grand jury's consideration. As the legal adviser to the body, the prosecutor in most cases makes a presentation on the applicable laws and outlines the evidence that supports the indictment. The prosecutor may, but is not constitutionally required to, provide exculpatory evidence supplied by a putative defendant for the grand jurors to consider. *United States v. Williams*, 504 U.S. 36 (1992). A prosecutor's ethical duty is to present the evidence and legal analysis in an unbiased manner so the grand jury can make a fair judgment, but there is little opportunity to police prosecutorial conduct in the grand jury due to the strict secrecy rule.

After the prosecutor's presentation, the grand jurors alone consider whether to vote in favor of an indictment, with no one else present. Federal Rule 6(f) provides that "[a] grand jury may indict only if at least 12 jurors concur" out of twenty-three on the panel. This is called returning a "true bill," and the indictment must be presented in open court after the grand jury's vote, or if 12 jurors do not concur in approving the indictment then that must be reported.

Those voting in favor of the indictment need not have been present for all the evidence, and one or more could have been impaneled at any time during the grand jury's term if another member was excused or removed. States with smaller grand juries usually require a supermajority vote in favor of an indictment, such as two-thirds or three-fourths of the members.

V. Prosecutorial Misconduct Challenges

After *Costello*, a defendant cannot, in most jurisdictions, mount a direct challenge to the sufficiency of the evidence supporting an indictment. Given that limitation, some cases involve claims that the *process* of obtaining the indictment was tainted by prosecutorial misconduct, and therefore the charges should be dismissed due to violations of a defendant's rights or the need to deter future impropriety. At one time, a number of lower federal courts dismissed indictments based on the supervisory authority of judges over conduct in the courtroom, and by extension to investigations that resulted in the filing of criminal charges. Unlike the evidentiary challenge prohibited in *Costello*, the exercise of *supervisory power* to dismiss charges did not involve directly a review of the sufficiency of the evidence, only the propriety of the government's conduct in obtaining the indictment. The Supreme Court responded by cutting back substantially on the supervisory authority of judges over conduct in the grand jury.

A. Supervisory Power

In exercising supervisory power over federal prosecutors, some lower courts adopted rules for the conduct of grand jury investigations. In *United States v. Williams*, 504 U.S. 36 (1992), the Supreme Court substantially limited the supervisory authority of federal judges to dismiss indictments based on action a judge determined was misconduct. In *Williams*, the Tenth Circuit dismissed an indictment because prosecutors failed to provide the grand jury with exculpatory evidence provided by the defendant that may have negated the government's proof of probable cause. The Supreme Court noted that

> the supervisory power can be used to dismiss an indictment because of misconduct before the grand jury, at least where that misconduct amounts to a violation of one of those few, clear rules which were carefully drafted and approved by this Court and by Congress to ensure the integrity of the grand jury's functions....

Despite that inherent judicial power, the Court held that the supervisory power did *not* authorize a court to adopt a requirement that prosecutors present exculpatory evidence to a grand jury because "any power federal courts may have to fashion, on their own initiative, rules of grand jury procedure is a very limited one, not remotely comparable to the power they maintain over their own proceedings." According to the Court, the Tenth Circuit's holding "requiring the prosecutor to present exculpatory as well as inculpatory evidence would alter the grand jury's historical role, transforming it from an accusatory to an adjudicatory body." Four Justices dissented in *Williams*, arguing that "[w]e do not protect the integrity and independence of the grand jury by closing our eyes to the countless forms of prosecutorial misconduct that may occur inside the secrecy of the grand jury room."

Williams called into question rules adopted by lower federal courts allowing dismissal of indictments based on prosecutorial misconduct in presenting evidence to the grand jury or the issuance of subpoenas. Many of those rulings did not tie the misconduct standards to a specific statutory prohibition, court rule, or constitutional requirement, instead relying only on the court's supervisory authority to prescribe general standards of fairness. While some of those misconduct standards can be preserved by reference to statutory protections, such as the prohibition on direct use of immunized testimony, dismissals of indictments for prosecutorial misconduct diminished significantly after *Williams*.

One area in which courts have on occasion used their supervisory power is when the government refuses to grant immunity to a defense witness to allow the person to testify without fear of being prosecuted for what will be said. If a court finds that the prosecutor's refusal to authorize immunity is for the purpose of keeping important evidence away from the defense, then it can use its supervisory power to issue an immunity order to permit the witness to testify.

B. State Courts

While *Williams* is the rule for federal courts, and many states take the same approach, some state courts interpret their constitutions to prohibit certain types of prosecutorial misconduct, or apply their supervisory authority to impose a rule similar to the one rejected by the Court in *Williams*. For example, the New Jersey Supreme Court used its supervisory power over lower state courts to require prosecutors to present exculpatory evidence to a grand jury in *State v. Hogan*, 676 A.2d 533 (N.J. 1996). It later extended the rule to recognize a prosecutor's obligation to instruct the grand jury on possible defenses as a corollary to the responsibility to present exculpatory evidence. California by statute requires prosecutors to disclose exculpatory evidence to the grand jury. CAL. PENAL CODE § 939.71. Some states also permit claims of prosecutorial misconduct in the grand jury to be considered on a motion to dismiss even if there was not a violation of a particular rule or constitutional protection. *State v. Johnson*, 441 N.W.2d 460 (Minn. 1989).

C. Fifth Amendment

The Supreme Court noted in *Williams* that there was no claim that the alleged prosecutorial misconduct of failing to provide exculpatory evidence amounted to a constitutional violation. The Court has said very little about what prosecutorial action before a grand jury would constitute a violation of the Fifth Amendment right to a grand jury indictment that would justify dismissing an indictment. Lower court rulings have dealt more extensively with the question of what types of prosecutorial misconduct reach the level of a constitutional violation. For example, the prosecutor's intentional introduction of perjured testimony on a critical issue has been characterized by several courts as a constitutional violation authorizing dismissal of an indictment. In addition, a court may use its supervisory power if the prosecutor's misconduct threatens the impartiality or independence of the grand jury process, which is derived from the Grand Jury Clause of the Fifth Amendment.

D. Timing of the Challenge

1. Post-Trial Dismissal

In *United States v. Mechanik*, 475 U.S. 66 (1986), the defense moved for dismissal of an indictment during trial on the ground that prosecutors violated Federal Rule 6(d)(1), which specifies those persons who may be present at grand jury proceedings. The jury returned a guilty verdict, but the Court of Appeals reversed, holding that the violation required automatic reversal. The Supreme Court rejected that position, however, holding that the impact of any violation of a defendant's rights should be evaluated in light of the supervening jury verdict. The effect of this position is that

> the petit jury's subsequent guilty verdict not only means that there was probable cause to believe that the defendants were guilty as charged, but that they are in fact guilty as charged beyond a reasonable doubt. Measured by the petit jury's verdict, then, any error in the grand jury proceeding connected with the charging decision was harmless beyond a reasonable doubt.

After *Mechanik*, few (if any) errors during the grand jury phase of a case can be remedied by dismissal of the charges if there was a conviction. Some circuit courts, however, interpret *Mechanik* in a more limited way, finding that it did not extend to misconduct which denied fundamental fairness involving a constitutional claim, even though it extended to the broad range of nonconstitutional improprieties that can occur at the charging process.

2. Pre-Trial Dismissal

If a trial court grants a *pre-trial* motion to dismiss due to prosecutorial misconduct based on supervisory power, the Supreme Court in *Bank of Nova Scotia v. United States*, 487 U.S. 250 (1988), spelled out the governing standard for the dismissal of an indictment prior to conviction. The Court held that "a federal court may not invoke supervisory power to circumvent the harmless error inquiry prescribed by Federal Rule of Criminal Procedure 52(a)." The trial judge must find that the prosecutorial errors prejudiced the defendant, which requires a showing that "the violation substantially influenced the grand jury's decision to indict, or if there is 'grave doubt' that the decision to indict was free from the substantial influence of such violations." Only constitutional errors subject to automatic reversal because they involve structural error—such as discrimination on the basis of race or sex in selecting grand jurors—would not require a harmless error analysis.

3. Interlocutory Appeal

In *Midland Asphalt Corp. v. United States*, 489 U.S. 794 (1989), the Supreme Court held that a trial court's refusal to dismiss a federal indictment before trial because of the improper disclosure of grand jury material was not appealable under the *collateral order doctrine*. Under that doctrine, an order of a trial court cannot be appealed until the case is concluded, unless it falls into a narrow category of rulings that are "claims of right separable from, and collateral to, rights asserted in the action" which are "too important to be denied review and too independent of the cause itself to require that appellate consideration be deferred until the whole case is adjudicated." *Cohen v. Beneficial Industrial Loan Corp.*, 337 U.S. 541 (1949) (see Chapter 16). If the judge denies a motion to dismiss an indictment because of prosecutorial misconduct in the grand jury and the defendant is subsequently convicted, there may be no effective review of the alleged violation under the analysis adopted in *Mechanik*. A district court could simply defer ruling on a motion to dismiss until after trial, avoiding the need for a ruling on the merits since an acquittal would render the motion moot and a conviction would render the error *per se* harmless.

E. Prosecutorial Misuse of the Grand Jury

1. Continuing Investigation

In addition to prosecutorial misconduct related to the indictment of a defendant, prosecutors may improperly use the grand jury's investigative authority to assist in the preparation of a case for trial, or to assist a related civil proceeding. The grand jury's investigation generally ends when an indictment is returned, but its investigatory authority continues and it may gather evidence about additional crimes by a defendant already charged. Once a grand jury returns an indictment, the government is prohibited from using its authority to conduct discovery or otherwise prepare its case for trial. But where the primary purpose of a continuing investigation is to determine whether others were involved in the same criminal activity, or whether an indicted person committed additional crimes, prosecutors may go forward with the grand jury investigation even though one result may be uncovering evidence that could then be used at the trial of a pending indictment.

In analyzing whether a continuing investigation is a violation, abuse of the grand jury process occurs when the government's "sole or dominant purpose" in convening a grand jury is to gather evidence for pending litigation; if there is another valid purpose, then the investigation may proceed and evidence obtained could be used to prosecute a pending indictment. If there is misuse of the grand jury, then the remedy is to exclude the evidence from the government's case-in-chief at trial.

2. Use in Civil Case

Another type of misuse involves employing the grand jury's investigatory power to assist in gathering evidence for a civil case. In *United States v. Procter & Gamble*, 356 U.S. 677 (1958), a district court permitted disclosure of grand jury testimony to defendants in a civil antitrust action brought by the government because the judge found that prosecutors used the grand jury investigation at which the testimony was given "to elicit evidence" for its subsequent civil action. The Supreme Court rejected the district court's disclosure order because it was not supported by a showing of particularized need, and also acknowledged that the alleged government use of the grand jury process to prepare a civil case would have been improper. If the grand jury had been employed in that fashion, the Court noted, the government clearly would have been guilty of "flouting the policy of the law," both in using the grand jury for a purpose other than criminal investigation *and* in circumventing limits that would be placed upon a plaintiff in civil discovery. The Court added, however, that if the grand jury investigation was aimed at developing evidence for the possible issuance of an indictment, then there was no need to deny the government the incidental benefit of civil use of properly acquired evidence.

Checkpoints

- The Fifth Amendment requires a grand jury indictment for all capital offenses and "infamous crimes."

- The grand jury requirement has not been imposed on the states.

- The grand jury determines whether there is probable cause that the defendant committed the offense.

- A grand jury will consider a number of cases for an extended period of time.

- The Equal Protection and Due Process Clauses prohibit discrimination in the selection of grand jurors.

- The grand jury has the right to compel evidence from any person, but it may not engage in "arbitrary fishing expeditions."

- If a subpoena is so broad as to constitute a search, it may be challenged as a violation of the Fourth Amendment.

- Witnesses testifying before a grand jury do not have a right to receive *Miranda* warnings or to be told about their status in the investigation.

- Evidentiary privileges, most importantly the Fifth Amendment self-incrimination privilege, may be asserted to refuse to testify before a grand jury.

- A grand jury screens cases to determine whether charges should be filed, although in the vast majority of cases an indictment is returned.

- A grand jury is not limited to considering only admissible evidence, although some states require compliance with evidence rules.

- Grand jury secrecy prohibits the prosecutor and members of the grand jury from disclosing any information about what has occurred.

- Federal grand jury subpoenas are considered proper upon issuance, and can be challenged if they are "unreasonable or oppressive."

- A subpoena recipient can assert the range of testimonial privileges available under the evidence rules, including the Fifth Amendment privilege against self-incrimination and the attorney-client privilege.

- A court can enforce a subpoena by holding the witness in civil contempt, and the person can be jailed for the term of the grand jury, up to 18 months.

- In order to challenge a trial court's order enforcing a subpoena, the recipient must suffer a civil or criminal contempt because there is no right to a direct appeal of the decision under the collateral order doctrine.

- The Fifth Amendment does not protect the content of voluntarily created records, but an individual or sole proprietor of a business can resist producing records under the act of production doctrine.

- The government can overcome a Fifth Amendment act of production claim if it can show that it is a foregone conclusion about the existence, possession, and authenticity of the records held by the subpoena recipient.

- A business organization has no Fifth Amendment right to resist producing its business records.

- The custodian of the corporate records must comply with a subpoena to produce the organizations records, but that act of production cannot be used against that person in a subsequent prosecution.

- In the federal system, challenges to an indictment based on alleged prosecutorial misconduct in the grand jury will not result in the dismissal of charges except in very limited circumstances.

- In the federal system, a defendant cannot appeal a decision not to dismiss an indictment before trial until after a conviction.

Chapter 3

Filing Charges

Roadmap

- The scope of prosecutorial discretion
- Limitations on adding and increasing charges
- Selective prosecution claims
- Requirements for a valid indictment
- Amendments to the charges
- Variances between the charge and proof
- Duplicity and multiplicity

I. Prosecutorial Discretion

A. The Decision Not to Charge

In the American criminal justice system, the police and prosecutors have enormous discretion to decide whether to file charges, and what charges to prosecute. The decision not to pursue charges exemplifies this discretion at its height; the choice not to charge is virtually unreviewable by the judiciary or legislature. For example, a police officer who observes minor misconduct can decide not to address the matter with a formal arrest or citation, perhaps giving the person a warning instead. Similarly, a prosecutor can review the evidence in a case and decide that it is insufficient to establish liability for an offense, that the violation is one better left to a civil or administrative system, or that there are insufficient resources to pursue the matter further. Courts are reluctant to second-guess a prosecutor's decision *not* to pursue charges because of the variety of factors that can come into play in the decision.

A key limitation on reviewing prosecutorial decision-making is the lack of judicial expertise in the field. As then-Circuit Judge Warren Burger stated in *Newman v. United States*, 382 F.2d 479 (D.C. Cir. 1967), "Few subjects are less adapted to judicial review than the exercise by the Executive of his dis-

cretion in deciding when and whether to institute criminal proceedings, or
what precise charge shall be made, or whether to dismiss a proceeding once
brought."

B. The Decision to Charge

While less broad than the discretion *not* to charge a crime, the prosecutor
still has considerable authority in deciding to file charges, what particular vi-
olation(s) to allege, when to initiate the prosecution (subject to the applicable
statute of limitations), and, in certain instances, the jurisdiction where it will
be pursued. The prosecutor's discretionary authority is increased by the ex-
pansiveness of state and federal criminal codes, which often allow charges
under multiple provisions based on a single course of conduct.

The tension between allowing unfettered exercise of the prosecutor's powers
and authorizing judicial review of charging decisions reveals the conflict underlying the role of the prosecutor, who must act as both a zealous advocate
and as an official charged with a broad duty to ensure justice. Courts cannot simply abdicate all authority to oversee the fairness of such an important process,
yet the impetus to engage in judicial review conflicts with an important pre-
cept of the criminal justice system: the executive branch decides the proper
means of enforcing the criminal law, largely to the exclusion of the judiciary.

There are constraints on the prosecutor's decision to charge an offense due
to the availability of outside review of the charges and the evidence to support
them. For example, a criminal information is subject to a preliminary examination in most states, and for cases utilizing a grand jury, that body must
make the first determination whether to initiate a prosecution (see Chapter 2).
While the standard for filing charges is fairly low — probable cause — there remains a judicial forum for at least some independent review of the prosecutor's
decision.

Allowing prosecutors such broad discretion, especially at the charging stage,
raises the issue of monitoring the fairness of their decisions. Outside of a preliminary hearing, the Supreme Court recognizes judicial authority to review
prosecutorial charging decisions in two situations: when the decision to multiply the number or severity charges was *vindictive*, and when the government
engaged in an improper *selective prosecution* based on an impermissible classification in violation of the Equal Protection Clause.

II. Vindictive Prosecutions

A. The *Pearce* Rule

The proscription against vindictive prosecutorial charging decisions originated, not in the setting of the prosecutor's decision to pursue a case, but in the context of judicial sentencing. A prosecutor's reasons for pursuing a case are generally private. A judge, on the other hand, announces a sentencing decision in open court after conviction, often describing on the record the reasons for imposing a particular sentence. In *North Carolina v. Pearce*, 395 U.S. 711 (1969), the Supreme Court reviewed two defendants' harsher sentences imposed on remand by the prosecution after they had successfully challenged their convictions on appeal. The Court stated that "vindictiveness against a defendant for having successfully attacked his first conviction must play no part in the sentence he receives after a new trial," and that due process "requires that a defendant be freed of apprehension of such a retaliatory motivation on the part of the sentencing judge." The Court limited a judge's authority to impose a higher sentence after appeal because "the imposition of a penalty upon the defendant for having successfully pursued a statutory right of appeal or collateral remedy would be no less a violation of due process of law."

B. Actual Vindictiveness

1. Post-Trial

The Supreme Court expanded the *Pearce* rule in *Blackledge v. Perry*, 417 U.S. 21 (1974), to cover a claim of prosecutorial vindictiveness when the prosecutor increased charges against the defendant after he appealed to a higher court for a trial *de novo*. The Court held that, although there was no evidence of actual prosecutorial bad faith, "the opportunities for vindictiveness in this situation are such as to impel the conclusion that due process of law requires a rule analogous to that of the *Pearce* case." What constitutes impermissible vindictiveness was not considered solely from the point of view of the defendant, however, because the possibility of increased punishment only violates the Due Process Clause if the circumstances "pose a realistic likelihood of 'vindictiveness.'" That means a court makes an objective assessment of the potential for vindictiveness in the prosecutor's actions without asking whether the defendant actually perceived the prosecutor acted vindictively.

After applying the *Pearce* presumption to prosecutors, the Supreme Court resisted any inquiry into actual prosecutorial motives by noting that genuine good faith would not justify the increased charges because the "potential for vindictiveness" in response to the defendant's assertion of his right to appeal triggered the due process violation. *Blackledge v. Perry*'s prophylactic rule substituted a judicial determination of the likelihood of an improper motivation for any factual inquiry into the prosecutor's actual state of mind. A presumption of vindictiveness may arise when the government re-indicts the defendant on an increased charge or for additional crimes carrying a more severe punishment after the assertion of a constitutional or statutory right in the post-trial phase of a case.

2. Pre-Trial

The Supreme Court took a more restrictive approach to finding prosecutorial vindictiveness when the charge was increased *before trial* rather than after a verdict. In *United States v. Goodwin*, 457 U.S. 368 (1982), the government charged the defendant with misdemeanor assault, and, after plea negotiations were unsuccessful, the defendant asserted his right to a jury trial. The original prosecutor did not have the authority to conduct jury trials, so another attorney reviewed the matter and decided to seek an indictment charging four felonies with significantly heightened potential sentences compared to the original misdemeanor charge. The defendant challenged the more severe charges on the ground of prosecutorial vindictiveness, arguing that the government retaliated against him for exercising his right to a jury trial.

To determine whether the more serious charges violated the *Blackledge v. Perry* presumption of vindictiveness, the Court looked at the type of right invoked and the timing of the government's response. First, the Court found the assumption that the prosecutor would retaliate against invocation of the right to a jury trial "unrealistic": these "procedural" rights are such an integral part of the system that defendants assert them routinely.

Second, the Court stated that the presumption of vindictiveness did not apply when the government acted before trial, as opposed to after a successful challenge to a conviction, as in *Blackledge v. Perry*. The Court expressly rejected any attempt to ascertain the prosecutor's motives for bringing charges:

> The imposition of punishment is the very purpose of virtually all criminal proceedings. The presence of a punitive motivation, therefore, does not provide an adequate basis for distinguishing governmental action that is fully justified as a legitimate response to perceived criminal conduct from governmental action that is impermissible response to noncriminal, protected activity. Motives are complex and difficult to prove.

The Court in *Goodwin* made it clear that the judiciary would not abdicate all authority to police the conduct of prosecutors, despite its assertion that prosecutorial motives are irrelevant. At the end of the opinion, the Court noted that "we of course do not foreclose the possibility that a defendant in an appropriate case might prove objectively that the prosecutor's charging decision was motivated by a desire to punish him for doing something that the law plainly allowed him to do." The Court, however, did not describe what "objective" evidence might establish a case of actual vindictiveness.

C. Plea Bargaining

The limits of the Supreme Court's prophylactic approach to prosecutorial vindictiveness also arose in *Bordenkircher v. Hayes*, 434 U.S. 357 (1978), a case in which the prosecutor threatened the defendant with more serious charges unless he agreed to plead guilty to the pending indictment. The prosecutor's stated reason for seeking the plea bargain was to "save the court the inconvenience and necessity of a trial." The defendant refused the offer, and after being charged with additional offenses carrying significantly higher penalties as a recidivist, was convicted and sentenced to life imprisonment. It was clear that the prosecutor sought to dissuade the defendant from exercising his Sixth Amendment jury trial right, and that the superseding charge came in retaliation for forcing the government to prove its case at trial.

The prosecution's conduct clearly violated the defendant's due process right if one reads *Blackledge v. Perry* as prohibiting *any* appearance of vindictiveness in response to the exercise of a constitutional or statutory right. The Court stated in that case, "A person convicted of an offense is entitled to pursue his statutory right to a trial de novo, without apprehension that the State will retaliate by substituting a more serious charge for the original one, thus subjecting him to a significantly increased potential period of incarceration." Yet, the Court rejected the due process claim, holding that "in the 'give-and-take' of plea bargaining, there is no such element of punishment or retaliation so long as the accused is free to accept or reject the prosecution's offer." The prosecutor's acknowledged retaliatory reason for increasing the charges did not violate due process, so certainly the defendant's mere apprehension of vindictiveness during plea bargaining could not suffice for a constitutional violation.

The Court sought to temper the effect of its analysis by emphasizing the forthrightness of the prosecutor, that his intent to increase the charges "was clearly expressed at the outset of the plea negotiations. Hayes was thus fully informed of the true terms of the offer when he made his decision to plead not guilty." While superficially reassuring, *Bordenkircher*'s reference to the forthrightness of the prosecutor was irrelevant to the Court's holding. Similarly, if the prosecutor did not inform the defendant of the possible increase in charges, *Bordenkircher* suggested that it would not violate due process because the Court essentially defined the prophylactic rule in such a way that it did not apply to vindictive prosecutorial acts during plea bargaining. The government's failure to inform the defendant of a potentially higher charge that it may file would not make the additional charge any more retaliatory than if the defendant knew in advance the effect of rejecting the plea offer.

Outside of the post-trial setting of *Blackledge v. Perry*, the prophylactic rule against prosecutorial vindictiveness does not appear to prohibit the prosecutor from increasing charges, regardless of how questionable the timing of the government's decision might seem or clear the intent of the prosecutor to seek an increased sentence due to the exercise of a constitutional or statutory right.

D. Selective Prosecution

1. Equal Protection (Yick Wo v. Hopkins)

The Supreme Court has noted on more than one occasion that a prosecutor's discretion is "subject to constitutional constraints," and a prosecution based on "an unjustifiable standard such as race, religion or other arbitrary classification" is impermissible. The Equal Protection Clause is the basis for the prohibition on selective prosecutions, grounded in the Court's seminal analysis in *Yick Wo v. Hopkins*, 118 U.S. 356 (1886). The decision overturned the denial of a writ of habeas corpus for a defendant who suffered from the sheriff's enforcement of a municipal ordinance only against laundries owned by Chinese Americans and not others. *Yick Wo*'s language has become the standard for measuring an unequal application of a law:

> Though the law itself be fair on its face, and impartial in appearance, yet, if it is applied and administered by public authority with an evil eye and an unequal hand, so as practically to make unjust and illegal discriminations between persons in similar circumstances, material to their rights, the denial of equal justice is still within the prohibition of the constitution.

2. Vietnam War Era Cases

For a brief period during the Vietnam War, a few lower federal courts found instances of improper selective prosecution and dismissed charges. *See United States v. Falk*, 479 F.2d 616 (7th Cir. 1973); *United States v. Steele*, 461 F.2d 1148 (9th Cir. 1972); *United States v. Robinson*, 311 F.Supp. 1063 (W.D. Mo.

1969). The cases are interesting mainly for their historical character, revealing that judges were caught up in the political tenor of the times. The cases involved acts of civil disobedience and, in one instance, reflected the growing perception that law enforcement agents used overwrought investigatory tactics against fringe groups. After that brief flowering of successful selective prosecution challenges, courts have been unwilling for the most part to find a prosecutor's exercise of discretion was improperly motivated. Since then, the Supreme Court has made the standard for obtaining discovery to establish the equal protection violation almost insurmountable, and so selective prosecution claims are almost doomed at the outset.

3. *Raising the Burden* (Wayte v. United States)

The virtual impossibility of proving a selective prosecution claim can be traced to the sentiment expressed in *Oyler v. Boles*, 368 U.S. 448 (1962), in which the Supreme Court recognized that "the conscious exercise of some selectivity in enforcement is not in itself a federal constitutional violation." Picking up on that theme in *Wayte v. United States*, 470 U.S. 598 (1985), the Court showed a decided lack of sympathy toward equal protection claims involving the exercise of prosecutorial discretion, adopting an approach that significantly diminished a defendant's chance of success in raising a claim that the prosecutor singled him out for criminal charges based on an impermissible criterion.

The Court in *Wayte*, revealing how attitudes had changed since the end of the Vietnam War, reinstated the indictment of a defendant who refused to register for the draft despite evidence that the government selected him for prosecution under a policy that made vocal proponents of non-registration more likely to be charged. The defendant was among a rather exclusive group of young men numbering less than twenty, out of a total of approximately 674,000 nonregistrants, picked for prosecution. The Court held that to demonstrate selective prosecution, a defendant must show that the government's decision "had a discriminatory effect and that it was motivated by a discriminatory purpose."

Proof of discriminatory purpose required a defendant to demonstrate "that the government prosecuted him because of his protected activities," not just that his involvement in protected speech was *one reason* for the decision to prosecute. The Court emphasized the problem with judicial scrutiny of the government's reasons for choosing to pursue a particular defendant. The Court stated that "[e]xamining the basis of a prosecution delays the criminal proceeding, threatens to chill law enforcement by subjecting the prosecutor's motives and decision making to outside inquiry, and may undermine prosecutorial effectiveness by revealing the Government's enforcement policy."

4. *Restricting Discovery* (United States v. Armstrong)

The burden established by *Wayte* for a selective prosecution claim was heavy, but certainly not insurmountable if defendants could ascertain the prosecutor's motives for selecting the person to be charged. The Supreme Court, however, made discovery of a prosecutor's reasons nearly impossible in *United States v. Armstrong*, 517 U.S. 456 (1996).

In *Armstrong*, the district court dismissed an indictment for selling crack cocaine after the United States Attorney's Office refused to comply with an order requiring it to provide information regarding prosecutions for similar offenses and "to explain its criteria for deciding to prosecute the … defendants for federal cocaine offenses." According to the defendants, the federal government prosecuted only African Americans for crack offenses. Information from the federal defender's office for the district in which the prosecution took place indicated that all of the twenty-four crack cocaine cases defended by that office in 1991 involved a black defendant.

Without considering the merits of the selective prosecution claim, the Court focused on whether the defendants had made the requisite showing to obtain discovery of the prosecution's reasons. It began by noting the "background presumption" for a selective prosecution claim "that the showing necessary to obtain discovery should itself be a significant barrier to the litigation of insubstantial claims." The standard adopted, indeed, created a hurdle that is virtually insurmountable. "In order to dispel the presumption that a prosecutor has not violated equal protection, a criminal defendant must present 'clear evidence to the contrary.'" *Armstrong* effectively required proof of an equal protection violation before a court could allow the defendant to engage in discovery of the prosecution's motive. Such discovery would then be used to establish the equal protection violation.

The circularity of the *Armstrong* standard is difficult to deny, although the Court asserted that the high threshold for establishing invidious discrimination "does not make a selective-prosecution claim impossible to prove." Perhaps not impossible, but *Armstrong* makes the standard of proof necessary just to obtain discovery so rigorous that it is difficult to see how raising such a claim can be anything but an exercise in futility.

5. *Applying* Armstrong

Does *Armstrong* mean that a successful selective prosecution case will never be brought? Only a few cases even get to the point where the court allows discovery of the prosecution's motives, and those have primarily centered on whether to seek the death penalty rather than on the decision to charge. The Supreme Court has been unwilling to permit the use of broad statistical evidence showing a discriminatory *impact* in prosecutions as the basis for discovery when there is no direct proof of a discriminatory motive in the actual charging decision at issue. In *United States v. Bass*, 536 U.S. 862 (2002), the Court summarily overturned the dismissal of a death penalty notice because the government refused to provide discovery on the charging decision. It stated, "Even assuming that the *Armstrong* requirement can be satisfied by a nationwide showing (as opposed to a showing regarding the record of the decisionmakers in respondent's case), raw statistics regarding overall charges say nothing about charges brought against similarly situated defendants."

As the Court noted in *Reno v. American-Arab Anti-Discrimination Comm.*, 525 U.S. 471 (1999), "Even in the criminal-law field, a selective prosecution claim is a *rara avis* [rare bird] ... [T]he standard for proving [it] is particularly demanding, requiring a criminal defendant to introduce 'clear evidence' displacing the presumption that a prosecutor has acted lawfully." Similar to vindictive prosecution claims, a successful selective prosecution case may well require a defendant to produce an admission by the prosecutor that an impermissible criterion played a significant role in the decision to prosecute. That type of evidence would provide the "but for" reason referenced in *Wayte* that can result in a dismissal for violating the Equal Protection Clause. Absent such proof, the Court has made discovery of the reason for the selection of the defendant virtually impossible to obtain.

III. The Charging Instrument

The Fifth Amendment's Grand Jury Clause requires that federal criminal prosecutions for all capital or "otherwise infamous" crimes be brought by grand jury indictment. The Supreme Court has defined an "infamous crime" as one punishable by imprisonment in a penitentiary or for a term of years at hard labor. The constitutional protection applies to the decision to pursue a prosecution, not the actual punishment imposed after a conviction. Any crime with a potential penalty of at least one year is "infamous" because the defendant can be confined in a penitentiary. Unlike almost all other criminal protections afforded in the Bill of Rights, the Supreme Court has not applied this provision to the states.

In *Hurtado v. California*, 110 U.S. 516 (1884), the Court held that due process does not require a state to proceed in a capital case by grand jury indictment, upholding the use of a criminal information, subject to a preliminary hearing, to determine probable cause for the charge. *Hurtado* was one of the first cases in which the Court determined whether a provision in the Bill of Rights, which applies in all federal prosecutions, should also be applied to the states. Although most protections afforded criminal defendants were later made applicable to state defendants through the Due Process Clause of the Fourteenth Amendment, the Court has never revisited its decision in *Hurtado*, which came long before it developed the incorporation doctrine.

If a grand jury indictment is not required, the prosecutor may initiate a case by filing a criminal information. Regardless of the method of charging the defendant, the charging document must meet certain constitutional requirements that provide a defendant with notice of the charges. In addition, the description of the offenses must have sufficient information to allow for a determination whether the defendant's double jeopardy rights have been implicated. Once the case goes to trial, the government is generally bound by the terms of the charging instrument, and a variance between the charges and the proof may result in a conviction being overturned.

A. Sufficiency of the Indictment

At one time, the common law had highly technical pleading rules that in many ways were a trap for the unwary. The Federal Rules of Criminal Procedure put an end to technical and formalized pleading, and for the most part the complex requirements of common-law criminal pleading are now obsolete. The precision and detail formerly demanded are no longer required in most states, and certain imperfections that are not prejudicial can be disregarded. Federal Rule of Criminal Procedure 7(c)(1) is typical of provisions throughout the states on the requirements for a valid charge: "[t]he indictment or information must be a plain, concise, and definite written statement of the essential facts constituting the offense charged and must be signed by an attorney for the government. It need not contain a formal introduction or conclusion."

1. Charging the Offense

With the advent of less technical pleading, prosecutors can now bring allegations in one count that may then be incorporated by reference into other counts. Much like a complaint in a civil case, the prosecutor need not recite information in other counts but only states that prior paragraphs are incorporated into the charge. Nevertheless, each count of an indictment or information is considered as if it were a separate charging document, so it must be sufficient in itself in identifying the offense without reference to other counts unless they are expressly incorporated by reference. Federal Rule 7(c)(1) also provides that a "count may allege that the means by which the defendant committed the offense are unknown or that the defendant committed it by one or more specified means." This eliminates the use of multiple counts each alleging the commission of the offense by a different means or in a different way.

An indictment or criminal information must provide a defendant with sufficient notice of the charge in order to be able to prepare a defense and, if necessary, invoke the Double Jeopardy Clause to bar a second prosecution. In *Hamling v. United States*, 418 U.S. 87 (1974), the Supreme Court explained that "an indictment is sufficient if it, first, contains the elements of the offense charged and fairly informs a defendant of the charge against which he must defend, and, second, enables him to plead an acquittal or conviction in bar of future prosecutions for the same offense." Reciting the words of the statute allegedly violated can be sufficient in most cases to provide the defendant with adequate notice of the charge so long as it is "accompanied with such a statement of the facts and circumstances as will inform the accused of the specific offence, coming under the general description, with which he is charged." *United States v. Hess*, 124 U.S. 483 (1888).

The issue of whether the indictment enables a defendant "to plead an acquittal or conviction" relates to the double jeopardy protection of a defendant from re-prosecution for the same offense (see Chapter 15). At one time, courts determined whether a charge in a second prosecution was for the same offense prosecuted in an earlier case by comparing the charging documents. The need to protect a defendant's double jeopardy right by requiring a sufficient description of the facts underlying a charge is now much less important because courts can review the transcript or recording of an earlier proceeding to determine whether a later charge is for the same offense, information that was no available in the past. While courts frequently recite the double jeopardy concern as a rationale for requiring some measure of specificity in an indictment or information, it is no longer a valid basis on its own for dismissing a charge due to a lack of sufficient information in the charging document.

2. Factual Specificity

An indictment or criminal information must provide the defendant with certain factual information about the charged offense(s). Simply alleging that a defendant "committed a burglary" without including the location of the crime, date and time of its occurrence, and the intended offense upon entry would not provide a basis to discern what the government intends to prove. At the same time, the prosecution is not required to include its theory of guilt, nor must it provide detailed information or a description of the evidence or witnesses it intends to call to prove the case.

For certain types of offenses, such as those involving a single act or result, providing a general statement of the date—and perhaps the time—of the crime, which need not be exact, and the location and identity of the defendant and victim(s) is often sufficient. For example, it is common for a criminal charge to state that the offense took place "on or about July 1" so that any error in the exact date cannot be the basis for dismissing a charge or overturning a conviction.

For the purpose of establishing venue, the charge need only state that the offense took place in the district, state, or county in which the prosecution is occurring. For more complex crimes, such as conspiracy or a fraudulent scheme, greater detail is required in the charging document, such as the manner and means of the criminal agreement or illegal object of the scheme. The government bears the burden of proving that venue is proper, but the indictment need not plead all the facts necessary to establish that the location of the prosecution is proper.

3. Sufficiency of the Charging Language

Even with more forgiving pleading standards than under the common law, prosecutors must draft the charging instrument with some care, or risk reversal of a conviction. In *Russell v. United States*, 369 U.S. 749 (1962), the Supreme Court overturned the convictions because the indictment simply tracked the statute but did not identify a key aspect of the crime. The defendants were charged with contempt of Congress for refusing to testify before a Congressional subcommittee, but there was no identification of the subject matter of the hearing. The statute at issue made it a crime to refuse to answer questions "pertinent to the question under inquiry" by the subcommittee, so the failure to allege the subject matter of the proceeding was a fatal error in the indictment. According to the Court:

> A cryptic form of indictment in cases of this kind requires the defendant to go to trial with the chief issue undefined. It enables his conviction to rest on one point and the affirmance of the conviction to rest on another. It gives the prosecution free hand on appeal to fill in the gaps of proof by surmise or conjecture.

The failure to provide the specifics of the congressional inquiry in the indictment, which instead only quoted the statutory language on pertinence, meant that the convictions had to be overturned. In refusing to give a more flexible reading to the indictment, the Court noted that "[t]o allow the prosecutor, or the court, to make a subsequent guess as to what was in the minds of the grand jury at the time they returned the indictment would deprive the defendant of a basic protection which the guaranty of the intervention of a grand jury was designed to secure."

The sufficiency of the recitation of the elements of the offense depends on the meaning of the statutory terms and to what they refer. Unlike *Russell*, in *United States v. Resendiz-Ponce*, 549 U.S. 102 (2007), the Court overturned a lower court decision finding that an indictment's failure to identify "any specific overt act that is a substantial step" toward an attempt to illegally reenter the country after a prior deportation required dismissal of the charge. The Court found that the term "attempt" sufficiently identified the requisite intent and conduct for a violation of the statute when accompanied by additional factual information so that it satisfied the two constitutional requirements of fairly informing the defendant of the charge and enabling a determination of any double jeopardy claim after an acquittal or conviction.

Courts have not been as restrictive in their reading of indictments since *Russell*, although a prosecutor risks dismissal of charges or reversal of a conviction if the indictment is sloppy or the factual description cursory.

4. Sentencing Facts

The traditional rule was that an indictment need not set forth allegations relevant only to sentencing and not guilt. In a series of cases beginning with *Apprendi v. New Jersey*, 530 U.S. 466 (2000), the Supreme Court has held that any fact — other than a prior conviction increasing a sentence — that increased the penalty for an offense beyond the statutory maximum should be submitted to a jury and proved beyond a reasonable doubt. In *Alleyne v. United States*, 133 S. Ct. 2151 (2013), the Court reversed its position in *Apprendi* and held that any fact increasing a mandatory minimum sentence for crime is an "element" of the offense that must be submitted to the jury.

These decisions mean that prosecutors must add certain facts in the charging document to establish the defendant's liability for a sentencing enhancement. For example, if an assault is punishable by five years imprisonment, but if the motivating factor for the attack is racial animus for which a ten-year sentence is authorized, then that factor must be alleged in the indictment and proven to the jury beyond a reasonable doubt.

This requirement is especially important where aggravating circumstances in a case expose a defendant to a possible death sentence. In *Ring v. Arizona*, 536 U.S. 584 (2002), the Court held that aggravating factors in capital cases are statutory maximum enhancing facts, so at least one such aggravating factor must be alleged in the indictment for submission to the jury. In a federal death penalty case, however, the government need not allege non-statutory aggravating factors.

5. Remedy

An issue the Supreme Court did not decide in *Resendiz-Ponce* was whether an invalid indictment required that a conviction be automatically reversed, or whether it was subject to the harmless error analysis (see Chapter 16). The traditional view of an invalid indictment was that the failure to properly identify the offense meant that the court had no authority to proceed in the case, depriving it of jurisdiction. In *Russell*, the Supreme Court reversed the conviction without discussing the reason for granting that remedy.

In *United States v. Cotton*, 535 U.S. 625 (2002), the Court applied the plain error analysis, which requires finding that the error affected the defendant's "substantial rights," (see Chapter 16), rather than automatically reversing the conviction when a defendant had not objected in the trial court to the failure of the indictment to allege facts affecting the sentence, as required by *Apprendi v. New Jersey* (see also Chapter 14). The Court in *Cotton* explained that application of the plain error standard was appropriate because the view that omissions in an indictment deprived a court of jurisdiction to hear the case was no longer correct. That may mean that, even in those instances in which the indictment does not provide sufficient detail, as in *Russell*, the court must find that the error prejudiced the defendant before granting a remedy rather than automatically overturning the conviction.

B. Bill of Particulars

Defendants frequently seek greater detail from the prosecutor about the charges in discovery of the government's evidence and, if necessary, through a *bill of particulars*. Many states and the federal government explicitly authorize a court to order the prosecutor to provide information by this means. Even those jurisdictions that do not specifically provide for such a procedure generally allow a court to require the government to provide additional information to overcome shortcomings in an indictment or information.

A bill of particulars is a formal written statement by the prosecutor providing additional information about the charge(s), sometimes based on areas identified by the defendant as needing further clarification or explication. Federal Rule 7(f) provides, "The court may direct the government to file a bill of particulars. The defendant may move for a bill of particulars before or within 14 days after arraignment or at a later time if the court permits."

A bill of particulars serves two functions: first, to give the defendant notice of the essential facts supporting the crimes alleged in the indictment or criminal information; second, to avoid prejudicial surprise to the defense at trial. A court will deny a request for a bill of particulars if the information sought would merely be helpful to the defense rather than being necessary for a fair trial. At the same time, it is a commonly repeated mantra that if the indictment or information is insufficient it must be dismissed, and cannot be saved by a bill of particulars. Therefore, while the bill of particulars can assist the defendant in receiving a fair trial, it does not protect the government from a fatally flawed indictment or information.

A defendant is not entitled to a bill of particulars as a matter of right, so the decision whether to order the prosecution to produce one, and the information required in it, is usually left to the discretion of the trial court. Importantly, a bill of particulars is *not primarily a means of discovery*, which is covered by more specific rules in the jurisdiction (see Chapter 8). The focus of the bill of particulars is to provide additional facts and not to disclose evidence or the government's theory of the case. Courts usually refuse to order a bill of particulars if the information is available to the defendant through some other means. For example, if sufficient information is already contained in the indictment or information but the defendant simply wants more details, the motion will usually be denied. Similarly, a bill of particulars is not required if the government has provided the desired information through pretrial discovery or in some other acceptable manner, such as a letter from the prosecutor explaining a charge.

C. Essential Elements Requirement

In many jurisdictions, the indictment or information simply recites the relevant statutory language and includes certain minimal identifying information for the particular defendant and the offense, such as the date(s) of the crime and its location. A technical error in the charging document, such as citing the wrong statute, usually is not fatal to a charge or conviction.

The danger with simply quoting the statute is that the indictment must contain all the relevant elements of the offense to provide fair notice to the defendant, and it may be that the statutory language does not include a crucial element. Some statutes do not contain an express *mens rea* element, which have been supplied by courts in construing the provision. For example, a homicide statute may provide, "Manslaughter is the unlawful killing of a human being without malice." Courts can interpret that to require proof that the defendant acted recklessly or with criminal negligence, even though those terms are not in the provision. Quoting the statute in the charging document without *also* including the intent required for the offense means that the indictment or information may be inadequate, and could result in dismissal of a charge or reversal of a conviction.

In federal prosecutions, a defendant must raise a challenge to the institution of a prosecution before trial, but Federal Rule of Criminal Procedure 12(b)(3)(B) provides that "at any time while the case is pending, the court may hear a claim that the indictment or information fails to invoke the court's jurisdiction or to state an offense." A failure to allege an essential element of the crime means that the indictment does not "state an offense" and the charge can be dismissed at any point when the case is pending, including during an appeal.

The Supreme Court ruled in *Ex Parte Bain*, 121 U.S. 1 (1887), that failure to properly state the elements of an offense in the charging document was a *jurisdictional* defect, and, therefore, the court did not have the power to hear the case if the indictment was defective. Under this analysis, there was no consideration of prejudice to the defendant from a defect in the indictment because a jurisdictional error meant that the court could not even entertain the prosecution. The effect of *Bain* was to encourage defendants to avoid raising the possibility of an error in the indictment before trial, if it were recognized. If the prosecution resulted in a guilty verdict, then the defect in the indictment could be raised later to have the conviction overturned, thereby giving the defendant the benefit of hearing the government's evidence at the first proceeding.

The Court overruled the jurisdictional analysis of *Bain* in *United States v. Cotton*, 535 U.S. 625 (2002), a case involving defendants convicted of conspiracy to distribute cocaine. The statute provided a maximum penalty of 20 years imprisonment for a detectable quantity of narcotics but a maximum sentence of life imprisonment where the offense involved 50 grams or more. On appeal, defendants for the first time raised the claim that their sentences in excess of 20 years were invalid because the issue of drug quantity, a fact that became an element of the offense after *Apprendi v. New Jersey*, was not alleged in the indictment (see Chapter 14).

The Court held that the defect in the indictment was not jurisdictional because it did not deprive the court of its power to hear the case, but only whether the sentence was proper. It then analyzed whether the error required the court to correct a serious injustice under the plain error rule (see Chapter 16): the Court found such remedial action unnecessary because "evidence that the conspiracy involved at least 50 grams of cocaine base was 'overwhelming' and 'essentially uncontroverted.'" By allowing courts to consider harm from the defective charge, *Cotton* now requires defendants to establish prejudice arising from the error in the charging document, at least if it was not raised in the trial court but only later on appeal.

IV. Amendments and Variances

The move away from technical pleading requirements substantially reduced successful attacks on prosecutorial filings due to inadequacies in the charging language. When a case goes to trial and a problem emerges at that point with the indictment or information, the court will allow an amendment to the document so long as the change does not prejudice the defendant or effectively charge a different offense. Most states allow such changes to be made both to indictments, which are returned by a grand jury, and to criminal informations, which are filed by the prosecutor.

At the federal level, Rule 7(e) permits amendment of an information before a verdict: "Unless an additional or different offense is charged or a substantial right of the defendant is prejudiced, the court may permit an information to be amended at any time before the verdict or finding."

An indictment, however, is treated differently because it was returned by a grand jury that determined the charge based on the evidence presented. Applying *Ex parte Bain*, the federal courts do not allow changes to an indictment because it reflects the decision of the grand jury regarding what should be charged. In *Russell v. United States*, 369 U.S. 749 (1962), the Supreme Court recognized that minor changes to an indictment could be made, stating that "an indictment may not be amended except by resubmission to the grand jury, unless the change is merely a matter of form." Permissible changes to an indictment include a correction in the spelling of a defendant's name or the location of an offense, but anything more extensive requires re-indictment by the grand jury. A few states follow the federal rule that greatly restricts amendments to indictments and prohibits a substantial variance between the crime charged and the proof of the offense.

Even if the indictment is not actually altered, the government's proof at trial may not match exactly what it alleged in the charging document. If the change amounts to a *constructive amendment* of the indictment, then it is improper and the conviction must be overturned. If the difference in proof is only minor, then it is termed a *permissible variance* and the defendant must establish prejudice in order to receive any relief. There is a fine line between an impermissible amendment and a mere variance, a difference more of degree between the evidence and the indictment, and not a categorical distinction.

A. Amendments

1. Form and Substance

It is frequently said that an amendment to the charging document that only goes to *form* is permissible, but one altering the *substance* of the offense should not be allowed, particularly once trial has begun. For example, a change in the date of the crime may only be to form when there is no dispute about when the crime actually took place. On the other hand, changing the date so that the charge does not fall outside of the limitations period in which to commence a prosecution would clearly be a substantive change. An amendment involving only form includes a court striking surplusage, *i.e.* unnecessary language, or correcting a miscited statute. Federal Rule 7(c)(1) requires the indictment to cite the statute or rule claimed to have been violated, but Federal Rule 7(c)(2) provides that "[u]nless the defendant was misled and thereby prejudiced, neither an error in a citation nor a citation's omission is a ground to dismiss the indictment or information or to reverse a conviction." Unfortunately, the form/substance distinction is often conclusory, with courts relying on it to justify a decision either permitting a change or finding that it was impermissible without a clear explanation about why it reached that result.

2. Prejudice

A better way to analyze changes in the charging document that avoids the unhelpful form/substance terminology is determining whether an amendment prejudiced a defendant. If the change was prejudicial, then it was impermissible regardless of how extensive or trivial the alteration appears. For example, changing the date of the offense may substantially affect the defense case in a murder prosecution if the defendant were offering an alibi defense, but not if the person claimed self-defense or insanity.

A frequent prejudice argument regarding amendments is *surprise*—that the alteration in the charge left defense counsel ill-prepared to respond to the government's evidence or prevented the defendant from mounting a defense. In many cases, the trial court can deal with the surprise claim by granting a continuance to allow counsel an opportunity to respond to the amendment, but there may be situations when the time allowed by the court is insufficient. The claim of unfair surprise is often coupled with an argument that the government did not comply with its discovery obligations by failing to turn over evidence in a timely manner (see Chapter 8).

3. Charging a Different Offense

A more difficult question arises when a defendant claims that the amendment to the charge made for a different offense than that set forth in the indictment or information. At one time, federal courts were not allowed to make any changes to indictments because the alteration invaded the province of the grand jury. In *Ex parte Bain*, the Supreme Court held that striking out the name of one of two victims of the defendant's deceptive practices from the indictment was impermissible because it denigrated the grand jury's decision to charge the crime in a particular manner. The Court stated:

> If it lies within the province of a court to change the charging part of an indictment to suit its own notions of what it ought to have been, or what the grand jury would probably have made it if their attention had been called to suggested changes, the great importance which the common law attaches to an indictment by a grand jury, as a prerequisite to a prisoner's trial for a crime, and without which the Constitution says 'no person shall be held to answer,' may be frittered away until its value is almost destroyed.

The language at issue in *Bain* could now be removed from an indictment under Federal Rule 7(d) if the defendant so requested: "Upon the defendant's motion, the court may strike surplusage from the indictment or information." Note that the rule does *not* authorize the *prosecutor* to move for deleting surplus language from the charging document. Nevertheless, a court may accede to a prosecutor's request, or even act on its own initiative, to remove surplusage absent an objection by the defendant. A few states continue to adhere strictly to the *Bain* rule, prohibiting any alteration of an indictment without returning to the grand jury for its approval of an alteration in the language through the issuance of a superseding indictment.

In the federal courts, the historical rule against amendments is still applied fairly rigorously, except for the correction of minor flaws with the defendant's acquiescence. The prohibition against changing the language of an indictment has even been applied when the offense charged was a misdemeanor, so that the government could have proceeded by information rather than by indictment in the first instance. If a grand jury is used as the vehicle for charging the case, then only minor flaws in an indictment can be changed without the grand jury handing up a superseding indictment.

4. Narrowing the Charge

The Supreme Court distinguished amendments to an indictment from steps by the prosecution to withdraw part of a charge. In *United States v. Miller*, 471 U.S. 130 (1985), the Court clarified how the charges in an indictment can be *narrowed* permissibly by the government's proof of the offense without violating the Grand Jury Clause. The indictment charged the defendant with fraud, alleging he arranged a burglary of his business and then lied to the insurance company about the value of the stolen items. At trial, prosecutors dropped the burglary aspect of the fraud charge and instead sought to prove only that the defendant overstated the loss from the theft.

A lower court overturned the conviction, relying on *Bain* to find that the government's proof amended the indictment by proving a crime different from what the grand jury charged. The Supreme Court distinguished *Bain* and upheld the conviction, holding that

> an indictment may charge numerous offenses or the commission of any one offense in several ways. As long as the crime and the elements of the offense that sustain the conviction are fully and clearly set out in the indictment, the right to a grand jury is not normally violated by the fact that the indictment alleges more crimes or other means of committing the same crime.

Miller conflicted with the broad proposition announced in *Bain* that any change to an indictment was an impermissible violation of the grand jury's authority to determine the charge. The Court noted that, after *Bain,* it had limited the scope of its prior decision to allow modest changes to an indictment. Federal Rule 7(e) now provides that "[u]nless an additional or different offense is charged or a substantial right of the defendant is prejudiced, the court may permit an information to be amended at any time before the verdict or finding." This provision, which was approved by the Court long before *Miller,* would conflict with a broad reading of *Bain.*

Rather than distinguish *Bain* again, the Court in *Miller* chose to overrule it, insofar as a *narrowing* of an indictment could be considered an impermissible change to the charging document. It stated, "To the extent *Bain* stands for the proposition that it constitutes an unconstitutional amendment to drop from an indictment those allegations that are unnecessary to an offense that is clearly contained within it, that case has simply not survived. To avoid further confusion, we now explicitly reject that proposition."

B. Variances

A variance occurs when the prosecution's proof of the offense at trial differs modestly from the crime alleged in the indictment or information. A defendant could object at trial to the introduction of irrelevant evidence, because testimony and documents that do not prove the offense charged usually would not be admissible. Where the court admits evidence at trial that diverges significantly from the crime described in the charging document, and subsequently the jury convicts the defendant, a claim can be made that the variance was a constructive amendment that violated the defendant's right to be tried on the charged offense.

1. Permissible Variance (Berger v. United States)

In every trial, there will not be a perfect match between the prosecution's allegations in the indictment or information and the offence established by the evidence. Many variances are comparatively minor — such as an incorrect date or location — while others may be significant — such as proof of a different means of committing the crime. As with the requirements for a valid indictment or information, the issue is frequently fair notice to the defendant. Defense counsel will prepare the defense for one charge, but if the proof is sufficiently different then a defendant may be surprised by the government's case and unable to adequately defend against the charge.

In *Berger v. United States*, 295 U.S. 78 (1935), the defendant challenged his conviction for conspiracy when the government charged a single agreement to utter counterfeit notes, but the proof at trial established two different conspiracies, of which the defendant was a member of only one. Thus, while there was sufficient proof that the defendant joined a conspiracy, it was not exactly the conspiracy charged in the indictment. In analyzing whether the variance was fatal to the conviction, the Supreme Court stated:

> The general rule that allegations and proof must correspond is based upon the obvious requirements (1) that the accused shall be definitely informed as to the charges against him, so that he may be enabled to present his defense and not be taken by surprise by the evidence offered at the trial; and (2) that he may be protected against another prosecution for the same offense.

In upholding the conviction, the Court concluded that the defendant was not prejudiced by the difference between the conspiracy charged and the proof at trial because there was sufficient evidence of the scope of the conspiracy and the defendant had notice of the crime the government intended to prove at trial.

2. *Constructive Amendment* (**Stirone v. United States**)

In determining whether a defendant was prejudiced by a variance, a court looks to whether the defendant was misled in some way by the difference between the indictment or information and the government's proof at trial. If a defendant did not object to the variance at trial, received the evidence of the offense in pretrial discovery, or offered a defense at trial unaffected by the different proof, then there would not be a basis to find sufficient prejudice to show the variance violated the defendant's rights. For example, a defendant who offers an alibi defense would not be prejudiced if the government proved that the victim was attacked with a knife rather than a baseball bat, as stated in an assault charge. On the other hand, if the government's proof varied the time when the attack occurred, that would likely have a substantial prejudicial impact on the defendant's alibi defense, which depends on establishing his or her whereabouts at a specific time.

The Supreme Court held that if the variance between the charge and the proof at trial was significant, then it constituted a *constructive amendment* to the indictment, which was impermissible under the Fifth Amendment's Grand Jury Clause. In *Stirone v. United States*, 361 U.S. 212 (1960), the Court overturned a defendant's conviction for violating the Hobbs Act because the government charged one means of affecting interstate commerce while the proof at trial involved a different means. The charge required proof of some interference with interstate commerce, and the indictment accused the defendant — a union official — with extorting the victim by preventing the importation of sand from another state that would be used for the concrete to build a steel mill. At trial, the judge admitted into evidence and charged the jury that it could find the requisite interference with interstate commerce from the victim's inability to build the mill and then ship steel in interstate commerce.

While the proof of affecting interstate commerce, a key element in a Hobbs Act prosecution, was established beyond a reasonable doubt, the government's evidence was completely different from the means charged in the indictment. The Court concluded that the variance constituted a constructive amendment of the indictment, in violation of *Ex parte Bain*. The Court stated:

> The right to have the grand jury make the charge on its own judgment is a substantial right which cannot be taken away with or without court amendment. Here, as in the *Bain* case, we cannot know whether the grand jury would have included in its indictment a charge that commerce in steel from a nonexistent steel mill had been interfered with. Yet because of the court's admission of evidence and under its charge this might have been the basis upon which the trial jury

convicted petitioner. If so, he was convicted on a charge the grand jury never made against him. This was fatal error.

Stirone prevented the government from proving a different offense, or a different element of an offense, from that charged in the indictment. In *United States v. Miller*, 471 U.S. 130 (1985), the Court explained the import of its decision: "In *Stirone* the offense proved at trial was not fully contained in the indictment, for trial evidence had 'amended' the indictment by broadening the possible bases for conviction from that which appeared in the indictment." A variance is not fatal if it proves a *narrower* crime from the one charged in the indictment, as in *Miller*, or a more conscripted scope of a criminal agreement, as in *Berger*. If the proof established a *different* crime, or an element substantially changed from that described in the indictment or information, then there is a *constructive amendment* that is fatal to the conviction.

3. Remedy

The Supreme Court in *Stirone* did not consider whether the defendant was prejudiced by the variance in proof, similar to the approach taken in *Bain* in which it found an amendment to an indictment to be an automatic violation of the Fifth Amendment grand jury right. It is not clear whether a constructive amendment like that in *Stirone* is still subject to automatic reversal, or whether a defendant must also show prejudice from the difference in proof under the harmless error rule.

In *United States v. Cotton*, 535 U.S. 625 (2002), the Court rejected *Bain*'s holding that a change to an indictment deprived the court of jurisdiction over the matter, which would require automatic reversal of the conviction because there was no power to hear the case. Instead, the Court applied the plain error rule to the failure to include in the indictment the applicable drug quantity that triggered an enhanced sentence. It is not clear after *Cotton* whether a harmless error analysis, or plain error if there was no contemporaneous objection in the trial court, would also apply to a variance that rises to the level of a constructive amendment. *Stirone* was decided before the Court applied the harmless error analysis to constitutional errors, so it may be that a constructive amendment would be analyzed differently today.

The federal circuits are split regarding the burden on a defendant to demonstrate some prejudice, either under the plain error or harmless error rule, or whether automatic reversal, such as the result in *Stirone*, still applies. The trend is toward considering whether the error was harmful, consistent with the Supreme Court's more recent jurisprudence allowing most errors to be analyzed to determine prejudice to the defendant. (See Chapter 16).

V. Specifying the Offense

A. Duplicity

An indictment or information that charges two (or more) different offenses in a single count is *duplicitous*. A charging document that alleges different means to commit an offense is not duplicitous. For example, a single charge of distribution of a controlled substance that alleges the defendant sold different types of drugs would not be duplicitous.

If a charge is duplicitous, then it presents a number of problems for a successful prosecution. First, duplicity violates a defendant's constitutional right to notice of the charges against him or her because it is not clear what violation will be proven at trial. Second, on the other hand, duplicity makes it more difficult for a defendant to raise a double jeopardy claim in a subsequent prosecution by identifying what was decided in the first prosecution.

Third, duplicity may allow a jury to find a defendant guilty without it being clear whether the jurors were unanimous regarding which offense the defendant committed, thus violating the right to a unanimous verdict. Fourth, a duplicitous indictment could allow the court to admit evidence on one charge that would not be admissible for a second charge, thus raising the possibility of prejudicial spillover from the improperly admitted evidence.

Duplicity in an indictment or information is not, however, necessarily fatal to the case if it comes to the court's attention before the jury begins its deliberations. Courts usually allow the prosecution to correct the error by selecting a single crime on which it will proceed if the defendant raises the issue before trial. If the duplicity only becomes apparent during trial, a corrective instruction to the jury may also cure the violation, or the court can dismiss a duplicitous charge if it finds prejudice to the defendant. Another method of curing the defect is to require the jury to complete a special verdict form, which identifies the specific crime on which it unanimously agrees.

A trial court's refusal to dismiss a duplicitous charge is analyzed under the harmless error rule, and a conviction can be upheld when there is no doubt that the jury verdict was unanimous or where the record shows that the prosecution proved one offense and the double jeopardy protection from a subsequent prosecution for that offense is not compromised. A defendant who does not object to a duplicitous indictment before or during trial can only have a conviction overturned under the plain error rule (see Chapter 16).

B. Multiplicity

An indictment or information that charges the same offense in different counts is *multiplicitous*. Multiplicity is improper because the defendant may receive more than one sentence for a *single* offense, in clear violation of the Double Jeopardy Clause. Separate charges related to a single course of conduct are not necessarily considered multiplicitous if each charge requires proof of facts that the other count does not.

For example, under the federal mail fraud statute, each separate mailing can be charged as a separate offense even though there is only one scheme to defraud. Similarly, a defendant who makes multiple efforts to steal one person's identity could be charged with the same crime in multiple counts. Even if a statute appears to require proof of different facts, however, courts usually consider whether the legislature intended to provide for multiple punishments under the Double Jeopardy Clause. If not, then charging the offense more than once would be multiplicitous.

As with duplicity, multiplicity in an indictment or information is not necessarily fatal. When it is apparent before or during trial that charges are multiplicitous, the court may require the government to choose which count it will prosecute and dismiss any other count(s) charging the same offense. A court usually will not dismiss a multiplicitous indictment or information *after trial,* so long as the convictions did not result in an increased sentence, which would violate the double jeopardy protection against multiple punishments (see Chapter 15). If the defendant does not object to multiplicitous charges that were apparent before trial, then a reviewing court applies the plain error analysis (see Chapter 16). Courts generally find that the error was plain and vacate the conviction on the multiplicitous count(s) when it resulted in a longer sentence than the defendant would have received.

Checkpoints

- Prosecutors have largely unreviewable discretion to file charges.

- The prosecutor cannot multiply the number or severity of charges after a successful appeal except in limited circumstances.

- Before trial, a prosecutor can increase the charge if a defendant rejects a plea bargain and chooses to proceed to trial.

- The government cannot charge a defendant with a crime by selecting him on the basis of race, sex, or other arbitrary classification.

- To establish a selective prosecution claim, the defendant must show that the prosecutor acted based on a discriminatory intent.

- To obtain discovery of the charging decision, a defendant must present clear evidence of a discriminatory intent before a court can order disclosure.

- An indictment need not meet technical pleading requirements, but it must provide a defendant with sufficient notice of the charge to allow for preparation of the defense.

- The indictment or information need not include all of the facts or the government's theory of the case, but the key elements of the crime must be included.

- A bill of particulars can supplement an indictment by providing additional information about the charge, but it does not cure an invalid indictment.

- While older cases reverse a conviction when the indictment does not have the requisite specificity or there is a variance between the charge and the proof, courts are tending more toward requiring the defendant to show prejudice from a violation before granting a remedy.

- Minor flaws in an indictment can be cured by an amendment, but a substantive change in the charge violates the grand jury right.

- A court cannot significantly change the alleged crime, although proof of a narrower violation than the one charged in the indictment or information is permissible.

- A significant variance between the charge and the government's proof at trial may result in overturning a conviction due to insufficient evidence of the offense charged.

- A duplicitous indictment alleges more than one offense in a single charge.

- A multiplicitous indictment charges the same offense more than once in different charges.

- Problems arising from duplicity or multiplicity may be cured by amending the charge to specify the particular offense or by removing the improper charge.

Chapter 4

Joinder and Severance

Roadmap

- Basis for joining charges and defendants for a single trial
- Requirements for proper joinder of charges and defendants
- Prejudice requirement for severance if joinder is proper

I. Joinder of Crimes and Defendants

The prosecution of multiple offenses against a defendant in a single proceeding and the joining of two or more defendants for a single trial are common methods utilized to ensure the efficient use of judicial resources. In addition, trying two or more defendants together reduces the possibility of inconsistent verdicts, while bringing an array of charges for different crimes against a single defendant in one proceeding reduces the delay inherent in the criminal justice system. There are risks to bringing multiple charges or defendants into a single proceeding, however, such as jury confusion and the possibility of prejudicial "spillover" of the evidence from one charge—or defendant—to another.

In the federal system, more than half of all defendants are charged with multiple counts, approximately one-third are joined with other defendants, and one-quarter face a single proceeding with multiple charges plus one or more co-defendants. Prosecutors make the initial decision whether to file multiple charges against a defendant, and whether to join two or more defendants in one criminal information or indictment. Joinder is permissive in most jurisdictions, and the states have rules that provide limitations on the right to join charges or defendants in a single proceeding. Some states have mandatory joinder rules, requiring the prosecutor to bring charges arising out of the "same transaction" to avoid violating a defendant's double jeopardy rights (see Chapter 15). There is no constitutional limitation on joinder unless a court concludes it violated a defendant's due process rights, or if venue was improper in the jurisdiction in which a defendant was charged.

Federal Rule of Criminal Procedure 8 is representative of the provisions in most states by providing general instructions to courts regarding the propriety of multiple charges or defendants in a case, and allows defendants to seek a severance of the charges or separate trial for one or more of them. Federal Rule 8 allows for joinder of offenses and defendants if the crimes charged are closely related. Federal Rule of Criminal Procedure 14 provides a means to challenge joinder of offenses or defendants that is otherwise proper under Federal Rule 8 if the defendant or prosecutor can show that a single proceeding will be prejudicial. The Federal Rules will be the focus of this chapter because they are representative of the provisions found in most states.

II. Rationale for Joinder

The primary rationale behind the joinder rules is efficiency. Conducting multiple trials of a defendant on similar charges, such as a string of purse-snatchings, would entail a significant drain on scarce judicial resources, as well as impose a burden on witnesses who may be called upon to repeat their testimony multiple times. Joinder of defendants may also avoid what the Supreme Court described in *Richardson v. Marsh*, 481 U.S. 200 (1987), as the "scandal and inequity of inconsistent verdicts" in which juries in different proceedings reach conflicting results on virtually the same evidence. The Court noted there that "[j]oint trials generally serve the interests of justice by avoiding inconsistent verdicts and enabling more accurate assessment of relative culpability—advantages which sometimes operate to the defendant's benefit."

There is a preference for joint trials, which "play a vital role in the criminal justice system." *Zafiro v. United States*, 506 U.S. 534 (1993). Thus, courts have tended to broadly construe the joinder provisions of Federal Rule 8, relying on the prejudice ground provided in provisions like Federal Rule 14 to sever cases where the joinder would be harmful, effectively creating a presumption that a single indictment will result in a single trial. It is certainly questionable whether judicial efficiency should be the primary goal of the joinder rules when a defendant's freedom is at stake.

III. Misjoinder and Motion for Severance

Either party is entitled to ask the court for severance, but in most cases the defendant will seek a severance because he or she will suffer the harm from the joinder. Because the prosecutor controls the decision whether to charge multiple crimes and defendants in a single proceeding, the initial determination whether the requirements of Federal Rule 8 are satisfied will be made by that office.

There may be cases in which the prosecutor requests a severance due to circumstances that develop after the filing of the charges. For example, if there are multiple defendants and one becomes incapacitated, the prosecutor may request the severance of that defendant so the case can proceed against the others. A defendant, however, does not have a right to be tried with another defendant or to have distinct charges joined together.

Federal Rule of Criminal Procedure 13 provides that a court may order a single trial for separate cases "if all offenses and all defendants could have been joined in a single indictment or information." Because of the emphasis on efficiency, courts tend to grant motions to consolidate cases under Federal Rule 13.

If the joinder of charges or defendants are is sufficiently related to meet the requirements of Federal Rule 8, then there is a *misjoinder* and the court usually orders the prosecution to redraft the charging document to properly allege the offenses or name the defendants. If the requirements of Federal Rule 8 for joinder are met, then a challenge can be brought under Federal Rule 14 seeking severance of the charges or defendants due to prejudice from the joinder. In deciding whether to grant the severance motion, which must be made before trial, the court considers whether the efficiency of a single proceeding overcomes the potential prejudice from trying the charges in a single proceeding.

IV. Joinder of Offenses

Federal Rule 8(a) describes when it is permissible to join more than one count in a single indictment or information. The Rule provides that an indictment or information can contain two or more in separate counts, whether felonies or misdemeanors, when they "are of the same or similar character, or are based on the same act or transaction, or are connected with or constitute parts of a common scheme or plan." Because the Rule is permissive and not mandatory, a defendant could be subjected to multiple trials, perhaps even in different jurisdictions, for crimes that are similar or arise out of the same basic chain of events.

The policy of the Department of Justice regarding joinder is that "several offenses arising out of a single transaction should be alleged and tried together and should not be made the basis of multiple prosecutions, a policy dictated by considerations both of fairness to defendants and of efficient and orderly law enforcement." *Petite v. United States*, 361 U.S. 529 (1960). This so-called *Petite* policy is only a guideline for federal prosecutors, and a defendant cannot claim any violation of rights if the federal government files charges that violate its terms.

A. Same Act or Transaction

Joinder is permitted when the various charged offenses arise from the "same act or transaction," and the latter term has been construed by the lower courts to require that there be some logical connection between the charges. For example, in *United States v. Cardwell*, 433 F.3d 378 (4th Cir. 2005), the Fourth Circuit stated that "[s]uch a relationship exists when consideration of discrete counts against the defendant paints an incomplete picture of the defendant's criminal enterprise."

One factor courts consider in determining whether charges arise out of the same transaction is whether the evidence supporting the different offenses overlaps sufficiently such that the same evidence would be admissible if there were separate trials. For example, courts have upheld fraud and tax evasion charges when the same financial information would be used to establish both offenses, even though the victims and elements of the offenses are quite different. On the other hand, joinder of theft and assault on a police officer charges was improper when the assault occurred at the time of the arrest on the theft charge, but there was no other connection between them. The fact that two crimes are contemporaneous may not be sufficient to permit joinder, while a significant gap in time between the offenses does not preclude charging them as arising from the same transaction.

B. Common Scheme or Plan

Rule 8(a) allows joinder of offenses against a single defendant if the different charges are "connected with or constitute parts of a common scheme or plan." Similar to the "same act or transaction" basis for joinder, courts look for a logical connection between the offenses to find that they are part of a continuous course of conduct. Indeed, courts analyzing whether charges are proper under Rule 8(a) often fail to distinguish between these first two grounds for joinder. For example, courts frequently assert that the evidence is "inextricably intertwined" or "factually interrelated" as the basis to find the joinder was acceptable under the rule without going into further detail.

There are some common types of criminal charges that courts routinely allow to be joined absent strong evidence from the defendant that the charges are clearly unrelated. For example, many narcotics prosecutions include charges of illegal possession or use of a firearm, money laundering, and conspiracy. Similarly, federal mail and wire fraud offenses often include tax evasion, money laundering, false statements, and conspiracy charges. For certain crimes involving administrative agencies, false filing, perjury, and obstruction of justice charges will often be included in the indictment or information.

C. Same or Similar Character

While the first two grounds for joinder discussed are fairly uncontroversial, the third basis, that the crimes are "of the same or similar character," is more difficult to assess. The benefits of joinder are less obvious in this circumstance, and the risk of an unfair trial more prevalent, because the connection between the offenses is not based on any particular relationship among them other than their "character" — a broad term.

Allowing charges under this prong of Federal Rule 8(a) may make it more difficult for a defendant to testify about one charge but not another, or permitting a jury to hear evidence about other crimes that would have been inadmissible if there had been separate trials on the charges. As one English judge stated in the nineteenth century, it would be

> a scandal that an accused person should be put to answer such an array of counts containing as these do, several distinct charges. Though not illegal, it is hardly fair to put a man upon his trial on such an indictment, for it is almost impossible that he should not be grievously prejudiced as regards each one of the charges by the evidence which is being given up on the others.

Regina v. King, 1 Q.B. 214 (1897).

Courts take different — and sometimes inconsistent — approaches to determining whether offenses are of a similar character. Some decisions are based on a categorical approach, looking at the elements of the crimes charged, not whether there is any temporal or evidentiary overlap between the actual offenses alleged by the government. Other courts look to both the objective aspects of the crimes along with the particular allegations in the charging document, such as the timing and location of the crimes and whether there is overlapping evidence that justifies the use of a single proceeding to converse judicial resources. In *United States v. Scott*, 732 F.3d 910 (8th Cir. 2013), the court found that a seventeen-month gap between the first and third robberies was "a sufficiently short time" to permit joinder of all three in a single indictment under Federal Rule 8(a). Courts usually focus only on the allegations contained in the indictment or information to determine whether joinder is proper, although any consideration of the admissibility of evidence in separate proceedings will require some consideration of the underlying facts of the case.

Even if the evidence of one crime would not be admissible if there were separate trials on the charges, courts may allow joinder by relying on jury instructions requiring segregation of the evidence so that the jurors do not view it cumulatively to find the defendant guilty on all charges. Whether an instruction is sufficient to overcome the possibility that the jurors will view the defendant as a bad character deserving of punishment regardless of the sufficiency of the evidence on a particular charge is an open question. Allowing a trial on similar but otherwise unconnected charges does entail a small efficiency gain because only one jury is needed and the consolidation of the charges will allow for a better use of all participants' time. It is arguable whether that modest benefit overcomes the potential harm to a defendant facing a single trial on multiple charges that are only connected by their similar character.

D. Prejudicial Joinder of Offenses

Federal Rule of Criminal Procedure 14(a) allows a court to sever counts of an indictment for separate trial if joinder prejudices the defendant or the prosecution. The Rule provides: "If the joinder of offenses or defendants in an indictment, an information, or a consolidation for trial appears to prejudice a defendant or the government, the court may order separate trials of counts, sever the defendants' trials, or provide any other relief that justice requires."

Studies of joinder in the federal courts have found that a defendant faces a significantly increased risk of conviction on the most serious charge when there are multiple counts in the indictment or information as compared to when there is only a single charge. Federal Rule 14 authorizes the severance of charges so that they can be tried separately, but courts are generally reluctant to do so if the joinder was proper under Federal Rule 8. One reason for such reluctance is the difficulty a defendant faces in demonstrating prejudice. Courts require proof of more than a possibility of prejudice, often stating that the risk of harm from the joinder must be shown to be "compelling, specific, and actual prejudice." *United States v. Saadey*, 393 F.3d 669 (6th Cir. 2005). In *United States v. Blair*, 661 F.3d 755 (4th Cir. 2011), the court stated, "Under Rule 14, a properly joined claim may be severed only if there is a serious risk that a joint trial would prevent the jury from making a reliable judgment about guilt or innocence." Prejudice will not be established if the only assertion is that the defendant would have a better chance of acquittal if the counts were tried separately; because the severance motion is filed before trial, there is always an element of speculation about the asserted harm, and courts tend to reject vague claims that a defendant will suffer unfairness or prejudice from a single proceeding.

E. Sources of Prejudice

Courts have identified three related, but distinct, forms of prejudice that can flow from the joinder of offenses:

- *Bad Character*: The jury may conclude that a defendant charged with an array of crimes has a bad or criminal character, so that it cumulates the evidence to return guilty verdicts rather than viewing the evidence separately to determine whether there is proof beyond a reasonable doubt for each charge. Thus, it may be that the more counts in the indictment or information, the quicker the jury may assume that the accused must be guilty of something, and therefore return a verdict of guilty on at least some counts.
- *Spillover*: Evidence of guilt on one count may have a spillover effect on other counts. This is more likely to occur when the joinder is based on the charges being of a "same or similar character," so that a jury might be so persuaded by the evidence on some counts that it fails to notice that there was insufficient evidence on a similar count. This is especially problematic if the evidence on one charge would be inadmissible on the other charge if there were separate trials.
- *Inconsistent Defenses*: If a defendant has a plausible defense to some charges but not others, he will face a difficult strategic choice if there is a joinder of the charges. If the defendant wants to testify about one count because he has a valid alibi or justification defense, he opens himself to cross-examination on a second count for a crime he actually did commit. The defendant may have to admit to the second crime, which he would not otherwise have to do if there were separate trials in which he could choose not to testify in one proceeding but could in the other. If the defendant declines to testify in the multi-count trial to protect himself on the second count, he may forfeit the opportunity to offer probative evidence that will enhance the likelihood of an acquittal on the first count. The joinder of offenses would make it more difficult to offer a defense to some charges.

F. Protection Provided by Evidence Rules

While courts often acknowledge that the risk of trying multiple charges in a single proceeding may lead the jury to infer that the defendant has a criminal disposition and cumulate the evidence, they rarely find that risk sufficient to require severance. It is not enough to argue that the evidence on one count is significantly stronger than on another count.

Similarly, the limitation on admitting "crimes, wrongs, or other acts" evidence is usually found sufficient to protect against possible spillover. Federal Rule of Evidence 404(b). If the evidence of each crime would be independently admissible in a separate trial, courts routinely find no prejudice from trying the charges together.

The problem of spillover evidence arises frequently when a defendant is charged with being a felon in possession of a firearm in addition to other offenses. A prior offense is an element of the possession charge, so the evidence used to prove that prior offense will be available to the jury when determining guilt on the additional joined offenses. While judges may be more receptive to severance motions in this context, no court has found that severing the charges is presumptively required.

G. Limiting Instruction

Even if the evidence rules preclude introducing the evidence of a different offense at a separate trial, courts often deny severance motions when the evidence of the different crime is "simple and distinct," so that a proper jury instruction can be given, requiring the jury to compartmentalize the evidence and apply it separately to each charge. In *Drew v. United States*, 331 F.2d 85 (D.C. Cir. 1964), the court stated:

> In summary, then, even where the evidence would not have been admissible in separate trials, if, from the nature of the crimes charged, it appears that the prosecutor might be able to present the evidence in such a manner that the accused is not confounded in his defense and the jury will be able to treat the evidence relevant to each charge separately and distinctly, the trial judge need not order severance or election at the commencement of the trial.

The District of Columbia Circuit explained the type of prejudice that can arise when a defendant wants to testify about one charge but not another, which is a result of the rule that once the defendant chooses to testify, the Fifth Amendment cannot be selectively invoked as to certain questions. In *Cross v. United States*, 335 F.2d 987 (D.C. Cir. 1964), the court stated:

> If [the defendant] testifies on one count, he runs the risk that any adverse effects will influence the jury's consideration of the other count.

Thus he bears the risk on both counts, although he may benefit on only one. Moreover, a defendant's silence on one count would be damaging in the face of his express denial of the other. Thus he may be coerced into testifying on the count upon which he wished to remain silent. It is not necessary to decide whether this invades his constitutional right to remain silent, since we think it constitutes prejudice within the meaning of Rule 14.

While the risk from joinder may be clear, courts are skeptical of such claims when raised in a pretrial severance motion because defendants infrequently testify at their own trials, especially when the person has a prior criminal record that could be used in cross-examination. A defendant must make a convincing case about the need to testify regarding one count and the impact that will have on another count.

V. Joinder of Defendants

Federal Rule of Criminal Procedure 8(b) provides for the joinder of defendants in a single prosecution. The basis for joinder involves language similar to Federal Rule 8(a), permitting multiple defendants "if they are alleged to have participated in the same act or transaction, or in the same series of acts or transactions, constituting an offense or offenses." One important difference between the two subsections is that Federal Rule 8(a) allows offenses to be joined if they are of "the same or similar character" while Federal Rule 8(b) does not. Courts permit felony and misdemeanor charges to be joined against multiple defendants, even though only Federal Rule 8(a) so provides, not Federal Rule 8(b).

A. Relationship Among Charges

The Rule provides that "[a]ll defendants need not be charged in each count," so defendants with different levels of culpability can be joined together in a single prosecution. But courts do not permit joinder of charges of a similar character for one defendant under Federal Rule 8(a) and then in the same proceeding join additional defendants who have no connection with the added charges. In other words, what is permissible under Federal Rule 8(a) may not be under Federal Rule 8(b) when additional defendants are joined in the indictment.

For example, A committed armed robberies of three banks in the same area. In the first two robberies, B assisted by acting as a lookout, but not for the third (which A committed with a different person's help). If both subsections of Rule 8 were permitted to operate together, then A and B could be charged together for the first two robberies, and A could also be charged in the same indictment with the third robbery that did not involve B, solely because that robbery was of a similar character to the other two. While joinder of the third robbery in the indictment is arguably more efficient in prosecuting all of A's crimes in a single proceeding, the potential prejudice to B is significant because he had no connection to the third robbery, so joinder would be improper under Federal Rule 8(b). In *Cupo v. United States*, 359 F.2d 990 (D.C. Cir. 1966), the court noted:

> When similar but unrelated offenses are jointly charged to a single defendant, some prejudice almost necessarily results, and the same is true when several defendants are jointly charged with a single offense or related offenses. Rule 8(a) permits the first sort of prejudice and Rule 8(b) the second. But the Rules do not permit cumulation of prejudice by charging several defendants with similar but unrelated offenses.

Taking the analysis a step further, when two defendants are jointly charged with committing one offense, and there is an unrelated charge alleging that on some other occasion they committed a similar offense that is unrelated to the first crime, joinder of the second charge should not be permitted if the government wishes to have the defendants tried together. On the other hand, defendants do not have a right to a joint trial, and Federal Rule 13 provides that a court "may order that separate cases be tried together as though brought in a single indictment or information if all offenses and all defendants could have been joined in a single indictment or information."

B. Series of Acts

Federal Rule 8(b) does not define what is meant by "the same series of acts or transactions," and different approaches can be taken to determining the scope of the provision. For example, any set of acts may be viewed as part of a "series" so long as some plausible connection can be identified between them, but that seems to be too low a threshold for joining defendants together.

The better approach is to require a more concrete relationship among the acts to constitute a series, such as evidence of a common scheme or plan. Because the primary rationale for the joinder rules is efficiency, courts tend to allow a charge naming multiple defendants when there is substantially overlapping evidence that allows for the same proof at trial. Courts do not require that all of the evidence be admissible against each defendant, but there must be at least some core of evidence that can be used against all of them, even if some items might be excludable if there were separate trials.

Recall that each defendant need not be named in every charge in the indictment or information, so there is no requirement that the culpability of each person charged be the same. Although all defendants must have participated in some manner in the series of acts from which the charges arose, Federal Rule 8(b) does not require that each defendant have participated to the same degree in each act. For example, joinder has been allowed in cases with over fifty defendants involved in the importation and distribution of narcotics, with different levels of involvement in the crimes.

Prosecutors frequently charge a single conspiracy among the different defendants to aid in establishing joinder, but such a charge is not required. Even if a conspiracy charge were dismissed, joinder can still be permitted if the indictment or information sufficiently alleges a related series of crimes to support bringing the defendants into a single proceeding.

C. Conspiracy and Criminal Enterprise

Courts often find that a conspiracy charge is sufficient to establish that the defendants engaged in the same series of acts or transactions to allow for their joinder. The same approach is taken when there is a charge involving a criminal enterprise, such as under the RICO statute (18 U.S.C. § 1961 et seq.) or the Violent Crimes in Aid of Racketeering (18 U.S.C. § 1959) provision, which require proof of a continuing course of conduct by the members that are related to the criminal purpose of the organization.

The conspiracy or enterprise charge means that any substantive offenses that were the object of the conspiracy or perpetrated by the organization may properly be joined in the same case. Only some of the defendants may be charged with particular substantive offenses, such as when one member joins a conspiracy after it has commenced. Joinder of the co-conspirators does not require that each defendant join the agreement at the same time so long as all of the substantive counts arise out of the same conspiracy. It is even possible that a series of conspiracies may be joined in one prosecution if they are part of a related series of acts.

The problem of *retroactive misjoinder* most often arises in a multi-defendant conspiracy prosecution when that charge is dismissed. In *United States v. Vebeliunas*, 76 F.3d 1283 (2d Cir. 1996), the court stated that "[r]etroactive misjoinder arises where joinder of multiple counts was proper initially, but later developments — such as a district court's dismissal of some counts for lack of evidence or an appellate court's reversal of less than all convictions — renders the initial joinder improper."

For example, three defendants are joined together for trial based on a conspiracy count, and the indictment contains additional substantive charges against one or more of them arising out of the alleged conspiracy. If the jury acquits on the conspiracy count but convicts on the substantive offenses, courts hold that the convictions are permissible and the acquittal on the conspiracy does *not* operate retroactively to establish that joinder was improper. Similarly, if the jury convicts on all counts, but then an appellate court reverses the conspiracy conviction but not the substantive counts, perhaps because there was not a single conspiracy, then the conviction on the substantive counts will stand and the joinder was not improper.

A more difficult situation arises if the conspiracy count is dismissed due to insufficient evidence or other pleading failure prior to submission of the case to the jury. In *Schaffer v. United States*, 362 U.S. 511 (1960), the government charged three groups of defendants with interstate transportation of stolen property in separate counts, and the fourth count alleged a single conspiracy among the three groups of defendants—a classic "hub-and-spoke" conspiracy in which each group had no connection with the others except for the common source for transporting the stolen goods. At the close of the government's case-in-chief, the court dismissed the conspiracy charge because there was insufficient proof of a single conspiracy, which was the sole basis for joining the various defendants at trial. The Supreme Court held that when the requirements for joinder under Federal Rule 8(b) were satisfied because the defendants were alleged to have participated in the same conspiracy, then there was no violation absent a showing of prejudice under Federal Rule 14. "The terms of Rule 8(b) having been met and no prejudice under Rule 14 having been shown, there was no misjoinder."

The Court in *Schaffer* noted that "the trial judge has a continuing duty at all stages of the trial to grant a severance if prejudice does appear. And where, as here, the charge which originally justified joinder turns out to lack the support of sufficient evidence, a trial judge should be particularly sensitive to the possibility of such prejudice." Therefore, the convictions on the substantive counts were upheld because of the absence of any showing of prejudice. In light of *Schaffer*, lower courts look to whether the government brought the conspiracy count in good faith, and if so, dismissal of that charge does not require severance unless the defendants can meet the requirement of Federal Rule 14 by showing prejudice from the joinder.

D. Prejudicial Joinder of Defendants

A single trial with more than one defendant creates several risks for the accused, particularly for one whose culpability is significantly lower than a codefendant's. A defendant in that situation will naturally be concerned that the jury will vote to convict based on "guilt by association," especially if other defendants are charged with more serious offenses. If there are a number of defendants, then one accused of playing only a minor role in a large-scale criminal enterprise can reasonably fear that the jury will not look carefully at the evidence to determine individual guilt, but will lump all the defendants together. Similarly, defendants may have antagonistic defenses, and trying them together could reduce the impact of a claim of innocence or reduced culpability if the jury fails to distinguish among them in assessing guilt. Federal Rule 14(a) authorizes severance if the defendant or government will suffer prejudice, but there is no definition of what constitutes prejudice in a particular case.

1. Antagonistic Defenses

In *Zafiro v. United States*, 506 U.S. 534 (1993), the Supreme Court considered a claim that the district court should have granted the defendants' severance motions when they sought to blame others for the wrongdoing. Four defendants were charged with a variety of narcotics-related offenses: each sought to blame a co-defendant for the presence of the large volume of drugs found by the police. The Court noted that joining defendants with antagonistic defenses in a single trial could mean "a jury will conclude (1) that both defendants are lying and convict them both on that basis, or (2) that at least one of the two must be guilty without regard to whether the Government has proved its case beyond a reasonable doubt."

The Court found that "when defendants properly have been joined under Rule 8(b), a district court should grant a severance under Rule 14 only if there is a serious risk that a joint trial would compromise a specific trial right of one of the defendants, or prevent the jury from making a reliable judgment about guilt or innocence." The Court rejected the defendants' argument that a *per se* rule requiring severance was necessary to mitigate any potential prejudice when defendants assert that their defenses will be antagonistic.

Zafiro held that "Rule 14 does not require severance even if prejudice is shown; rather, it leaves the tailoring of the relief to be granted, if any, to the district court's sound discretion." In explaining when a severance motion should be granted under Federal Rule 14, the Court stated that the risk of prejudice

> might occur when evidence that the jury should not consider against a defendant and that would not be admissible if a defendant were tried alone is admitted against a codefendant. For example, evidence of a codefendant's wrongdoing in some circumstances erroneously could lead a jury to conclude that a defendant was guilty.

When many defendants are tried together in a complex case and they have markedly different degrees of culpability, the risk of prejudice is heightened. The Court explained that evidence

> probative of a defendant's guilt but technically admissible only against a codefendant also might present a risk of prejudice. Conversely, a defendant might suffer prejudice if essential exculpatory evidence that would be available to a defendant tried alone were unavailable in a joint trial. The risk of prejudice will vary with the facts in each case, and district courts may find prejudice in situations not discussed here.

2. Standard for Granting Motion

Whether to grant a motion to sever or provide some other type of relief comes within the discretion of the trial court, which balances the inconvenience and expense to the government of separate trials against the prejudice to the defendants from a joint trial. The burden is on the defendant to show that joinder, which otherwise meets the requirements of Federal Rule 8(b), will result in significant prejudice in order to obtain a severance under Federal Rule 14.

Even if some harm from joinder could be shown, *Zafiro* pointed out that a trial court has available "less drastic measures, such as limiting instructions, [which] often will suffice to cure any risk of prejudice." Unless defendants can show that joinder will prejudice a specific trial right, or that the risk of jury confusion is so great as to make a guilty verdict unreliable, then they are unlikely to prevail on a motion to sever based on conflicting defenses.

3. Other Grounds

Zafiro's analysis of Federal Rule 14 applies beyond claims of antagonistic defenses as the basis for severance. The Supreme Court's endorsement of joint trials has led lower courts to routinely reject severance motions based on claims a defendant might have a better chance for acquittal if tried separately, or might not be able to undertake the expense or strain of a lengthy trial precipitated by numerous codefendants. In addition, courts generally reject severance motions based on claimed differences in the culpability of the defendants, that codefendants have a criminal record that can be introduced against them, that there is hostility or other conflicts among the defendants, or that a co-defendant is absent from the trial.

Although courts consider whether evidence may be admissible against one defendant but not others in deciding the severance motion, the fact that there is a core of evidence admissible against all defendants is frequently the basis for justifying a joint trial. The ultimate question is whether the jury can make a reliable determination of guilt by compartmentalizing the evidence so that it only considers that which is relevant to each defendant. Courts generally rely on cautionary jury instructions to mitigate any prejudice that might otherwise arise from the joinder of defendants.

E. Codefendant Statements

The Sixth Amendment provides that "[i]n all criminal prosecutions, the accused shall enjoy the right … to be confronted with the witnesses against him." The Supreme Court has interpreted the confrontation right to require that a defendant be allowed a physical, face-to-face meeting with witnesses, although this right is not absolute (see Chapter 12). One area of special constitutional concern in joint trials is when the government seeks to use the statement of one co-defendant that implicates another co-defendant at a joint trial. While the statement is admissible against the co-defendant who made it, it is *not* admissible against the co-defendant named in the statement unless the person who made the statement testifies at trial.

For example, after being arrested for a bank robbery, A tells the police, "B and I robbed the bank." If A and B are tried together, the statement is admissible against A under the evidence rules as a statement of a party-opponent, but it is hearsay with regard to B. Even if the statement might be admissible under an exception to the hearsay rules, it would violate B's rights under the Confrontation Clause of the Sixth Amendment. If a defendant's statement that also implicates a co-defendant were introduced at trial, then there is no guarantee that the co-defendant will be able to cross-examine the person who made the statement, because that defendant could exercise the Fifth Amendment privilege and refuse to testify.

1. Bruton v. United States

While courts often deal with the problem of evidence inadmissible against a co-defendant in a joint trial by giving an appropriate jury instruction, the Supreme Court rejected this approach in the seminal decision in *Bruton v. United States*, 391 U.S. 123 (1968). Bruton was tried jointly with codefendant Evans, who had confessed that both he and Bruton committed an armed robbery. At trial, Evans did not testify, and the government called an investigator to testify about what Evans said in his confession. Bruton did not have an opportunity to cross-examine Evans, and the trial court gave a limiting instruction to the jury that it should not use Evans' confession in any way against Bruton.

The Court found that Bruton's Confrontation Clause right was violated, despite the limiting instruction. It determined that while a jury is usually presumed to follow instructions, sometimes that presumption is unavailing, so that "there are some contexts in which the risk that the jury will not, or cannot, follow instructions is so great, and the consequences of failure so vital to the defendant, that the practical and human limitations of the jury system cannot be ignored." The Court found that "[s]uch a context is presented here, where the powerfully incriminating extrajudicial statements of a codefendant, who stands accused side-by-side with the defendant, are deliberately spread before the jury in a joint trial.... It was against such threats to a fair trial that the Confrontation Clause was directed."

The Court in *Bruton* held that it violated the Sixth Amendment for an out-of-court statement by one defendant that implicated another defendant to be introduced in a joint trial where the speaker did not take the stand and was not available for cross-examination. This does not mean that there can never be a joint trial if one codefendant's otherwise admissible statement implicates a co-defendant. For example, if the statement comes within some other exception to the hearsay rule so that it would be admissible in a separate trial of the implicated codefendant, then there is no confrontation issue (see Chapter 12).

Because *Bruton* rests on the lack of opportunity to cross-examine the co-defendant who made the statement, the introduction of the statement at a joint trial is permissible if that codefendant takes the stand and is subject to cross-examination. Of course, the government cannot guarantee that a defendant will testify, so there is a substantial risk in conducting a joint trial in which a statement that otherwise violates *Bruton* is admitted on the hope (or belief) that the codefendant will testify and be available for cross-examination by any other defendant implicated by the statement.

2. Limitations on Bruton

Bruton does not apply to a bench trial. The rule is based on the inability of juries to follow a limiting instruction to use a statement only against the co-defendant who made and disregard when assessing the evidence against a different codefendant who was implicated in the statement. Thus, the rule has no application if the trial is to the court because the judge is equipped to assess the evidence properly.

Bruton does not automatically require severance even when a statement comes within its parameters. The Supreme Court noted that there are "alternative ways of achieving that benefit [the use of the defendant's statement at a joint trial] without at the same time infringing the non-confessor's right of confrontation." Federal Rule 14(b) provides that "[b]efore ruling on a defendant's motion to sever, the court may order an attorney for the government to deliver to the court for in camera inspection any defendant's statement that the government intends to use as evidence." This allows a trial court to consider various alternatives to avoid the *Bruton* rule while still conducting a joint trial.

For example, the prosecution may agree not to introduce the co-defendant's statement at trial, which avoids the problem altogether if the government prefers the advantage of a joint trial to the evidentiary benefits of the statement. A court could also have multiple juries, so that there is a single proceeding while excusing the jurors for one defendant when inadmissible evidence — such as a *Bruton*-type statement — is introduced against a codefendant.

The more common means to overcome a *Bruton* problem in a joint trial is to redact that portion of the statement that implicates the codefendant. For the statement "B and I robbed the bank," the "B and" could be removed so that all the jury heard was A's statement that "I robbed the bank." *United States v. Logan*, 210 F.3d 820 (8th Cir. 2000). Unfortunately, people rarely make inculpatory statements in such an easily edited fashion, so removing references to the other defendants could make the statement incoherent. In addition, the prosecution may object to removing all references to another defendant because it could render the statement misleading, as if the defendant asserted he acted alone in committing the crime — "I robbed the bank" makes it sound like a one-person crime.

One way a court may deal with a *Bruton* problem is to replace the name of the other defendant with a letter or symbol — *e.g.,* "* and I robbed the bank" — to indicate that another person was involved in the commission of the crime, but not *specifically* implicating the co-defendant by name. However, even this approach may not solve the *Bruton* problem if the context of the statement revealed that the co-defendant is the additional person in spite of the redaction of his name.

The Supreme Court has upheld the use of redactions to dissipate any Confrontation Clause problems. *Richardson v. Marsh*, 481 U.S. 200 (1987). But in *Gray v. Maryland*, 523 U.S. 185 (1998), the Court found a confrontation violation from the admission at a joint trial of a non-testifying codefendant's statements in which the implicated codefendant's name was replaced by "deleted" or "deletion" when a detective read the statement. Although the statement did not refer specifically to the defendant, the Court concluded that it "powerfully implicated" him:

> Redactions that simply replace a name with an obvious blank space or a word such as "deleted" or a symbol or other similarly obvious indi-

cations of alteration, however, leave statements that, considered as a class, so closely resemble *Bruton*'s unredacted statements that, in our view, the law must require the same result.

Although incriminating statements of a co-defendant continue to be used at joint trials, prosecutors and judges need to exercise great care editing statements to ensure there is no reference to a codefendant. *Quisenberry v. Commonwealth*, 336 S.W.3d 19 (Ky. 2011). A defendant concerned about a potential *Bruton* problem should raise the issue in a pretrial motion for severance, or at least during the trial, because failure to raise the issue until after a conviction runs the risk of having the appellate court find waiver of the Confrontation Clause issue. Federal Rule 14(b) provides that "[b]efore ruling on a defendant's motion to sever, the court may order an attorney for the government to deliver to the court for in camera inspection any defendant's statement that the government intends to use as evidence." In *United States v. Min*, 704 F.3d 314 (4th Cir. 2013), the court upheld the admission of a redacted statement by a codefendant because " [w]ritten in the third person and in grammatically correct phrases, the redacted confession referred generally and without facial incrimination to some number of individuals who could, or could not, be the other defendants. The statement did not implicate any one defendant in particular, nor did it leave the jury to fill in any obvious blanks."

Checkpoints

- Courts encourage joinder to preserve scarce judicial resources.
- Different offenses can be joined if they arise from the same act or transaction, are part of a common plan or scheme, or have the same or similar character.
- Offenses joined in a single indictment or information can be severed if the defendant is prejudiced by the joinder.
- Common grounds for finding prejudice are a spillover of evidence from separate charges, showing defendant has a bad character, and inconsistent defenses.
- Courts often rely on limiting instructions given to the jurors to mitigate prejudice from the joinder of charges.
- Joinder of defendants is permitted if the charges arise from the same act or transaction or are part of a common plan or scheme, but not if they only have the same or similar character.
- Defendants need not be named in every count of the indictment or information for joinder.
- A conspiracy charge is frequently charged to establish the basis for joinder of the defendants.
- If one defendant makes a statement incriminating of a second defendant in the trial, and the statement is not otherwise admissible against the second defendant, then under *Bruton* the court may have to sever the defendants to avoid violating the second defendant's Confrontation Clause right.

Chapter 5

Venue

Roadmap

- Subject-matter and personal jurisdiction over the defendant
- Venue and vicinage are based on the location of the criminal offense
- Where the crime occurs is based on the interpretation of the statute
- The standard of proof for venue is lower than for other elements

---

I. Jurisdiction

Jurisdiction can be understood as granting a court the *power* to adjudicate a case. A state has *subject-matter jurisdiction* over any offense that occurs within its borders. At least some part of the crime must occur in the state for it to be able to punish the conduct. A state may obtain *personal jurisdiction* over the perpetrator of the crime if that person is within the boundaries of the state, or if it can have another sovereign—*i.e.*, a state or a foreign country—take the person into custody and deliver him or her into the state. As a general rule, a state or the federal government seeking to prosecute a crime must have *both* subject matter and personal jurisdiction over the defendant, although there are limited instances in which a defendant can be tried *in absentia*—i.e., when they are absent.

The states have a general police power to identify and punish conduct as criminal. Most states have codified the offenses subject to criminal prosecution, although a few retain common law crimes—offenses recognized by courts rather than adopted by the legislature. The federal government has jurisdiction only over those crimes that are identified by statute, and there are no federal common law offenses. In certain regions, there is exclusive federal jurisdiction over crimes, such as those that occur on the high seas, on federal land, or in the District of Columbia. In addition, offenses involving specified subject matters, such as currency counterfeiting or copyrights, can only be prosecuted in federal court. As a practical matter, most conduct punishable by the states can also be prosecuted by the federal government.

Jurisdiction over an offense must be distinguished from *venue*, which denotes the location of the prosecution. While the two terms are sometimes (erroneously) used interchangeably, they apply to different aspects of a criminal prosecution. Venue rules in the states allocate judicial authority within its borders, so that it may provide which county or local government has the authority to prosecute a crime. The federal venue rules allocate the authority to pursue prosecutions among the different federal districts. Unlike subject-matter or personal jurisdiction, venue does not involve the power of the court to adjudicate a case but is a right granted to the defendant to have the case heard in a particular location. Thus, while a court cannot hear a case in which it does not have *jurisdiction*, a trial can be held even if *venue* is not proper because a defendant can waive any objection to the location of a trial.

II. Constitutional Venue and Vicinage Provisions

Venue in federal criminal cases involves the intersection of constitutional provisions, statutes, and rules. During the colonial period, the right to a trial by jury composed of residents of the location where the offense had been committed was considered vital. In 1769, Parliament — over strong objections — proposed taking Americans to England or to another colony for trial in treason cases. The colonial legislatures objected vehemently to this proposal, and the Declaration of Independence included a denouncement of the King "for transporting us beyond Seas to be tried for pretended offences."

The Constitution contains an explicit *venue* requirement as part of the right to trial, mandating that the proceeding take place where the crime occurred. Article III, Section 2 provides that the trial of all federal crimes "shall be held in the State where the said Crimes shall have been committed." While that provision also provides for a right to a jury trial, it does not address the location from which the jurors will be drawn, called the *vicinage*.

The Sixth Amendment requires that the jury be "of the State and district" where the crime was committed, a vicinage right. The term "district" does not have any clearly defined constitutional meaning, and it is up to Congress to determine the federal judicial districts from which a jury will be called. By statute, Congress has divided many states into different districts, and in single-district states, along with some larger districts, it has designated different divisions that further limit the source of the pool of potential jurors.

The vicinage requirement of the Sixth Amendment has not been imposed on the states, although most have their own constitutional or statutory provisions dictating where a crime can be prosecuted. Many states require that a crime be prosecuted in the county in which it was committed, although they allow more than one jurisdiction to pursue a case if different aspects of the crime occurred across county lines. In addition, the joinder rules in most states allow — or in some instances require — crimes that arise out of the same acts or transactions be prosecuted in a single county, even if some of the offenses did not occur within its boundaries. Some states also have "buffer" statutes that permit a prosecution in a neighboring county if the crime occurred within a specified distance from its borders, such as within a mile of the county line.

The technical distinction between venue and vicinage is of no real importance at the federal level. In practical terms, so long as the jurors come from a district in which the crime occurred, then for constitutional purposes, the trial will take place in the proper location.

III. Rationale for Venue

Crimes are most commonly committed in the place where the defendant resides. Yet, the drafters of the Constitution could not have anticipated the increased mobility of today's population, the expansion of commercial enterprises that operate on a global scale, and the breadth of potential vicarious liability for participation in a crime, such as corporate criminal liability based solely on the acts of individual employees who may be located throughout the world.

Although most crimes are prosecuted where a defendant lives, sometimes the prosecutorial location meets the constitutional venue requirement, yet is in a courtroom far from the defendant's home — even if the case could have been filed in a more convenient jurisdiction. For example, former WorldCom CEO Bernard J. Ebbers was prosecuted in New York City for securities fraud related to the collapse of the Mississippi-headquartered company, rather than closer to his home in Jackson, Mississippi. Venue was based on the fact that the company's shares were traded on the New York Stock Exchange, even though it would have been permissible to file the case closer to his residence. Similarly, a number of insider trading prosecutions are brought there because the trades are executed through Wall Street firms, even though the defendants may live anywhere in the country.

The government may choose a particular venue for the trial when the crime was committed in multiple locations to avoid what it may perceive as a potential bias in favor of a local defendant. Defendants have objected to the government's choice of venue on the ground that it is burdensome or inconvenient, and a court may transfer the case as provided by Federal Rule of Criminal Procedure 21(b). The trial court has broad discretion under that provision, and defendants have no right to a pre-trial hearing on whether venue is proper in a federal prosecution where a valid indictment shows sufficient facts to support a prosecution of the charges in the chosen district. Thus, if a court denies a motion for a change of venue on grounds of inconvenience, the only means to challenge the location of the trial is to seek an acquittal at trial based on insufficient evidence to establish venue. *United States v. Snipes*, 611 F.3d 855 (11th Cir. 2010).

The Supreme Court has not consistently viewed the scope of the constitutional protection afforded by the venue and vicinage provisions when a trial is located a significant distance from a defendant's home. Its four leading decisions on the issue revealed a deep split in the how the constitutional requirement should be applied, and the issue has not arisen again in the Court in nearly 50 years.

A. *United States v. Johnson*

In *United States v. Johnson*, 323 U.S. 273 (1944), the Supreme Court noted that the constitutional provisions on venue and vicinage protected defendants from "the unfairness and hardship to which trial in an environment alien to the accused exposes him." It concluded that allowing a trial in a distant jurisdiction could create "needless hardship to an accused by prosecution remote from home and from appropriate facilities for defense." To avoid the constitutional issue, *Johnson* held that a federal statute which proscribed the delivery of dentures ordered by an unlicensed facility could only be prosecuted where the item was sent and not where it was delivered, preventing the defendant from being hauled across the country to face charges. Four dissenting Justices asserted that the Constitution's venue and vicinage provisions had nothing to do with locating a trial close to a defendant's home, but instead was designed "to assure a trial in the place where the crime is committed and not to be concerned with the domicile of the criminal nor with his familiarity with the environment of the place of trial."

B. *Johnston v. United States*

In *Johnston v. United States*, 351 U.S. 215 (1956), the Supreme Court took a different approach in reviewing the prosecution of two conscientious objectors who reported to the draft board in the Western District of Pennsylvania but then later refused to report to their hospital assignments in the Eastern District of Pennsylvania. The Court held that the defendants could only be prosecuted in the district where the hospitals were located, rather than in the district where they lived. The majority stated, "This requirement of venue states the public policy that fixes the *situs* of the trial in the vicinage of the crime rather than the residence of the accused."

C. *United States v. Cores*

Only two years after *Johnston*, the Supreme Court again referenced the policy in favor of limiting venue to the district where the defendant resides. In *United States v. Cores*, 356 U.S. 405 (1958), the Court considered the proper venue for a foreign seaman charged with willfully remaining in the United States after his conditional landing permit had expired, at which time he was supposed to leave the country. In holding that the crime involved a continuing violation that authorized venue where the defendant was found, the Court stated, "[W]e think it not amiss to point out that this result is entirely in keeping with the policy of relieving the accused, where possible, of the inconvenience incident to prosecution in a district far removed from his residence."

D. *Travis v. United States*

Apparently changing its view of the scope of the venue protection again only three years later, in *Travis v. United States*, 364 U.S. 631 (1961), the Supreme Court reversed the conviction of a defendant union official who had been tried in his home jurisdiction of Colorado for mailing an allegedly false affidavit stating that he had no affiliation with the Communist Party. The Court held that venue would only lie in the District of Columbia, where the affidavit was required to be filed with the National Labor Relations Board.

The majority noted that a trial in Colorado "might offer conveniences and advantages to him which a trial in the District of Columbia might lack," but held that "[v]enue should not be made to depend on the chance use of the mails, when Congress has so carefully indicated the locus of the crime." As with many cases involving prosecution based on the defendant's supposed membership in the Communist Party, the Court's decision in *Travis* may reflect its unease with these cases, and therefore it used the venue provision as a means to overturn a conviction that it viewed as noxious.

E. Scope of the Venue Right

The starting point for any venue analysis is the underlying criminal statute that authorizes the prosecution. If it prescribes a particular location for the trial, then that language controls. Absent an explicit venue provision in the statute, a defendant can argue in favor of holding a trial near his home, so long as the offense involves conduct at that location. While the defendant's residence may be a factor in the venue analysis, in *Platt v. Minnesota Mining & Manufacturing Co.*, 376 U.S. 240 (1964), a criminal antitrust case, the Supreme Court rejected "the erroneous holding of the Court of Appeals that criminal defendants have a constitutionally based right to a trial in their home districts."

The analysis of the proper venue for an offense may entail some reference to constitutional provisions, but there is no constitutional right that trumps the venue designation in a statute, at least as long as one part of the offense took place in the district. For example, a Florida resident charged with assault on a federal officer while traveling in California cannot argue successfully that the case should be tried in Florida because that is where he resides and it would be more convenient for him to face the charges close to home. Federal Rule of Criminal Procedure 21(b) does allow for the transfer of a trial "[f]or the convenience of parties and witnesses," but that Rule is not based on the constitutional venue provisions but, rather, the equitable power of the court.

IV. Federal Venue Statutes

The constitutional requirement of prosecution where the crime was committed is easily understood in cases involving most common law offenses, such as murder or robbery, which usually occur in a single location. Even economic crimes, such as fraud and public corruption, frequently involve conduct in a particular locale, so venue in those cases is often easy to determine. For more complex schemes and extensive drug operations involving conduct over an extended period of time with a number of different participants, determining where the crime was committed is not always an easy task.

There is no requirement that a crime be prosecuted in only one location if the venue provision authorizes prosecution in different ones, in which case it is a matter of prosecutorial discretion about where to pursue the case. Federal Rule 21(b) permits a district court to transfer a case to another jurisdiction "for the convenience of the parties and witnesses and in the interest of justice." This Rule only authorizes a defendant to seek a transfer, not the prosecutor, who must live with the venue choice absent a request by the defendant to move the trial to a different district. If a court grants a defendant's motion, it can then transfer the case to any other district, regardless of whether venue would have been proper there in the first place. *United States v. Roberts*, 618 F.2d 530, 537 (9th Cir. 1980). While the court will, in most cases, transfer the prosecution to a more convenient location, the defendant does not have a right to object to the district selected because the Federal Rule 21(b) motion operates as a waiver of the constitutional venue protection.

A. Continuing Offenses

If a federal statute prescribes the appropriate venue for its prosecution, then that provision controls where the case can be filed. Most federal crimes, however, do not have a specific venue provision, so the general federal venue statute, 18 U.S.C. § 3237(a), controls the location of the prosecution. The statute is particularly important for "continuing" offenses that occur in multiple locations by permitting prosecution in different districts. The statute provides that an offense "begun in one district and completed in another, or committed in more than one district, may be inquired of and prosecuted in any district in which such offense was begun, continued, or completed."

A court must ascertain whether the venue chosen by the government was proper by analyzing the *conduct* that constitutes the offense. The initial question in a prosecution involving a statute which does not contain a specific venue provision is whether the crime can be committed in only a single location, which is then the sole proper venue for the case, or whether it can be committed in multiple locations because it is then a continuing offense. If it is a continuing offense, it comes within § 3237(a), which allows charges to be filed in any district where the crime "was begun, continued, or completed."

B. The Rise and (Apparent) Fall of the Verb Test

At one time, a number of courts analyzed statutes by looking at the verb(s) used to describe the offense. The so-called "verb test" focused on the essential act described in the statute that made it a crime, which would then guide the determination of the appropriate venue for the prosecution. If the key verb in the statute entailed continuing conduct, then under § 3237(a), the offense could be charged in any district where the relevant act occurred.

For example, a federal court held that a statute making it a crime to "knowingly deposit" obscene materials in the mail limited venue to the place where the item entered into the mails and not the location of its receipt. *United States v. Ross*, 205 F.2d 619 (10th Cir. 1953). In response, Congress amended the statute to proscribe the mailing *or delivery* of obscene matter, thus expanding the potential site of a criminal prosecution to where the item entered the mails or reached the intended recipient. 18 U.S.C. § 1461.

The Supreme Court rejected the nearly exclusive focus on just the key verb in a statute for a broader consideration of the *nature of the crime* charged in the indictment, including particular facts related to its commission, to ascertain a proper venue for prosecution. In *United States v. Cabrales*, 524 U.S. 1 (1998), the Court held that a money laundering prosecution could not be maintained in Missouri when the financial transactions occurred entirely in Florida, even though the money came from drug sales in Missouri. The Court held that "the *locus delicti* [of the charged offense] must be determined from the nature of the crime alleged and the location of the act or acts constituting it."

Cabrales noted that a charge of money laundering might be a continuing offense if it involved transporting money from one locale to another, but, in this case, the offense involved transactions only in Florida, so any prior criminal activity in Missouri was of "no moment." The Court explained that the defendant "dispatched no missive from one State into another. The counts before us portray her and the money she deposited and withdrew as moving inside Florida only." In response to *Cabrales*, Congress amended the money laundering statute three years later to expand venue for money laundering to include any location where the underlying specified unlawful activity generating the money, such as drug dealing or bribery, as a proper location for trial so long as the defendant participated in the transfer of the proceeds from that district. 18 U.S.C. § 1956(i)(B), as amended by USA Patriot Act, Pub. L. No. 107-56 (2001).

A year after *Cabrales*, in *United States v. Rodriguez-Moreno*, 526 U.S. 275 (1999), the Court limited—although did not reject completely—the verb test as a means of determining the appropriate venue:

> We have never before held, and decline to do so here, that verbs are the sole consideration in identifying the conduct that constitutes an offense. While the "verb test" certainly has value as an interpretative tool, it cannot be applied rigidly, to the exclusion of other relevant statutory language. The test unduly limits the inquiry into the nature of the offense and thereby creates a danger that certain conduct prohibited by statute will be missed.

The defendant was charged with kidnapping and using a weapon during the commission of a crime of violence after forcibly moving the victim from Texas to New Jersey and then to Maryland as part of a drug deal. The government charged the defendant in New Jersey, even though the only place the defendant had possession of the gun was in Maryland, and the Court held that venue was proper in any district in which the underlying crime of violence occurred. Thus, while the weapon was only used in one location, the crime of violence involved multiple acts that allowed for venue in a number of districts.

Rodriguez-Moreno's broader focus requires a more nuanced review of the crime covered by a statute to determine where proper venue lies. The Court adopted an expansive, although imprecise, description of the statutory analysis required: "[A] court must initially identify the conduct constituting the offense (the nature of the crime) and then discern the location of the commission of the criminal acts." Thus, in interpreting the scope of venue for a particular statute, a court should look at the *conduct* the legislature sought to prohibit, not just the particular wording used to describe the act that violated the provision. Of necessity, the operative words of the statute, *i.e.* the verbs, remain an important consideration in ascertaining venue.

Even before *Rodriguez-Moreno* rejected a strict application of the verb test as the sole means of determining venue, the lower courts rejected the position that the Constitution commands a single, exclusive venue for the prosecution. Some lower courts adopted a "substantial contacts" analysis for determining the proper venue, which could result in multiple jurisdictions qualifying as a proper venue for trying the case. The Second Circuit, in *United States v. Reed*, 773 F.2d 477 (2d Cir. 1985), explained that "the test is best described as a substantial contacts rule that takes into account a number of factors — the site of the defendant's acts, the elements and nature of the crime, the locus of the effect of the criminal conduct, and the suitability of each district for accurate factfinding...." Courts usually apply the substantial contacts test to determine whether venue is proper in a district when the defendant's own conduct did not occur there, but the effects of the criminal conduct impacted the district in which the charges were filed.

Cabrales and *Rodriguez-Moreno* take a flexible, highly fact-specific approach in federal prosecutions to determine venue based on the nature of the crime set forth in the statute and the type of conduct alleged in the indictment. The starting point in each case is the statutory language, including the verbs used to describe the offense, to determine whether the provision incorporates a description of the appropriate venue and whether it is a continuing offense. Once the statutory analysis is complete, then a court must determine whether the case has been filed in a proper location for adjudicating the charge(s). Note that it is possible for a district to be a proper venue for some charges against a defendant but not for others, which would require prosecutors to pursue cases in different districts. The requirements for proper joinder of charges and defendants in Federal Rule of Criminal Procedure 8 (see Chapter 4) do not trump the constitutional requirement that venue be proper for each charge.

C. No District Where Crime Committed

Article III, section 2 of the Constitution states that if an offense is "not committed within any State, the Trial shall be at such Place or Places as the Congress may by Law have directed." The First Congress implemented this constitutional provision by a statute, 18 U.S.C. § 3238, that — with only slight modifications — has been in effect ever since. It provides that any offense "begun or committed upon the high seas, or elsewhere out of the jurisdiction of any particular State or district" shall be prosecuted in the district where the defendant was arrested or first appeared in the United States. This provision is particularly important for cases involving international and transnational crimes in which charges are filed for conduct that occurred outside the borders yet affects the United States or a victim of the crime is an American citizen. Section 3238 allows the government to choose the jurisdiction it wants to try the case when a person is first found overseas by picking the district to which it will return the defendant. The statute further provides that if there are two or more joint offenders, trial may be held in the district in which any one of them is arrested or first brought.

The statute also provides that if a defendant is not arrested or brought into any district, an indictment or information may be filed in the district of the last known residence of the offender, or, if no such residence is known, in the District of Columbia. If a defendant is indicted before he is brought into the United States, he may be tried in the district in which he was indicted regardless of whether it was the district in which he was first arrested or brought into the United States.

D. Waiver and Proof

1. Waiver

Although the Supreme Court has never reached this issue, a number of lower courts have held that the Constitution's venue provisions are a privilege for the benefit of the accused but not a limitation on the jurisdiction of the court. Therefore, while the defendant can waive the constitutional venue and vicinage protections, a lack of jurisdiction would mean that a court would not have the authority to hear the case, which cannot be waived by the parties.

The usual requirement for defendant's waiver of a constitutional right is that it be knowing, intelligent, and voluntary. Unlike other trial protections, such as the right to a jury or the assistance of counsel, the courts have found a waiver of the venue right from the defendant's *inaction*, and do not require an explicit waiver. For example, the absence of an objection to venue by a motion specifically raising the defect in the charge can constitute a waiver of the issue.

Courts generally hold that if a venue appears improper on the face of the indictment or information, then a defendant waives any objection to venue by failing to raise the issue prior to trial, or by entering a guilty plea. If the charging document alleges venue for the offense, but proof at trial fails to establish venue was proper in the district, then the defendant can raise the objection at the close of trial. If an appellate court concludes the defendant waived an objection to venue, then it will not consider whether there was plain error in the selection of the location for the prosecution.

2. Standard of Proof

The prosecution need not specifically allege venue in the indictment or information, although as a practical matter it is best to do so in the charging document. Even if it is not referenced expressly, venue is a fact that the government must prove at trial unless the defendant has waived the protection. What distinguishes venue from other facts that the government must prove is that it requires a lower standard of proof in most states and in federal prosecutions. Unlike the elements of an offense that must be proven beyond a reasonable doubt, venue can be established by just a preponderance of the evidence.

Courts rationalize the different treatment of venue from other elements of the offense by asserting that it is *not an essential aspect of the crime*, so a lower standard of proof suffices. The Supreme Court has never explicitly held that venue can be proven by a preponderance of the evidence, but the lower federal courts are unanimous on the reduced standard of proof.

Like any other fact, venue may be proven by circumstantial evidence, and it is often inferred from the circumstances of the offense. Some judges have even taken judicial notice of venue for the offense, obviating any need for the prosecutor to offer additional proof of the location of the crime. Nevertheless, venue must be proper for every count in the indictment or information, so that if the location of the prosecution was proper for one count but not for another, the count on which the venue was improper must be dismissed.

Courts generally require defendants to contest venue at trial before instructing the jury to determine whether the prosecution was properly pursued in the district. Thus, if a defendant fails to raise the issue, or presents no material evidence raising a factual question about venue, then a court does not commit reversible error by failing to instruct the jury to determine the proper venue for the offense or refusing a defendant's proposed instruction on the issue.

Checkpoints

- A court must have subject-matter and personal jurisdiction over a defendant in order to proceed with the criminal prosecution.

- The Constitution provides for (1) the venue for a prosecution, which is where the crime was committed, and (2) the vicinage for the trial, which is the area from which the jury pool will be drawn from.

- There is no constitutional right to have a trial in a location close to the defendant's home.

- There may be multiple locations in which the crime was committed, and venue is proper in each location.

- Statutory interpretation is the key to ascertaining the proper venue for a prosecution, if the statute does not otherwise explicitly provide for the location of a prosecution.

- If the crime is a continuing offense, then, under federal law, venue is proper in any district in which it occurred.

- Congress can designate the location of a prosecution if the crime was not committed within any state.

- While venue is an element of every federal offense, the prosecution can prove that venue is proper by a preponderance of the evidence rather than beyond a reasonable doubt.

Chapter 6

Speedy Trial

Roadmap

- Defendants must receive a speedy trial
- A four-part test determines whether post-charge delay violated the speedy trial right
- The federal Speedy Trial Act supplements the constitutional protection
- Due process limits delay in filing charges

The Sixth Amendment provides that "[i]n all criminal prosecutions, the accused shall enjoy the right to a speedy ... trial." The right to a speedy trial is traceable to the Magna Carta, and all of the states provide in their own constitutions or statutes for a speedy disposition of charges. Delay in pursuing the resolution of criminal charges can affect a defendant in a number of ways. As the Supreme Court noted in *Smith v. Hooey*, 393 U.S. 374 (1969):

> [T]his constitutional guarantee has universally been thought essential to protect at least three basic demands of criminal justice in the Anglo-American legal system: (1) to prevent undue and oppressive incarceration prior to trial, (2) to minimize anxiety and concern accompanying public accusation and (3) to limit the possibilities that long delay will impair the ability of an accused to defend himself.

While delay may harm the prosecution's case, the harm most often falls on the defendant. This may be particularly true when the government does not file charges in a timely manner, which invokes the protections of the Sixth Amendment. One means of protecting individuals from delay in the filing of charges is the statute of limitations. In *United States v. Ewell*, 383 U.S. 116 (1966), the Court noted that the limitations period "is usually considered the primary guarantee against bringing overly stale criminal charges." The Due Process Clause also protects against improper delay in the institution of a criminal prosecution.

I. Speedy Trial Right

A. *Barker v. Wingo* Four-Part Test

The seminal decision on the Sixth Amendment speedy trial right is *Barker v. Wingo*, 407 U.S. 514 (1972). In that case, the Supreme Court considered a defendant's claim of a constitutional violation as a result of a four-year delay between being charged with murder until the trial finally began, due to numerous continuances granted at the government's request. A defendant usually suffers the harm from delay, but the Court pointed out that the Sixth Amendment also protects an important societal interest in the prompt disposition of criminal charges "which exists apart from, and at times in opposition to, the interest of the accused." For example, a backlog of cases

> enables defendants to negotiate more effectively for pleas of guilty to lesser offenses and otherwise manipulate the system. In addition, persons released on bond for lengthy periods awaiting trial have an opportunity to commit other crimes ... Moreover, the longer an accused is free awaiting trial, the more tempting becomes his opportunity to jump bail and escape.

Barker v. Wingo rejected a bright-line rule based on the amount of time elapsed after the filing of charges for assessing a speedy trial violation. Instead, the Court adopted a four-part balancing test that takes into consideration the possibility that a defendant is seeking to take advantage of a delay by suddenly moving for dismissal of the charges after having acquiesced in postponements of the prosecution. The test involves the following factors: (1) the length of delay; (2) any reason provided by the government for delay; (3) whether (and when) the defendant asserted the right to a speedy trial; and, (4) prejudice to the defendant from the delay.

The Court described the speedy trial right as "slippery," and one reason it adopted a balancing test rather than a bright-line rule was to avoid any hasty grant of the remedy available for a violation. The Court noted that "the only remedy" is dismissal of the charge and a prohibition on future proceedings for the crime, which "is indeed a serious consequence because it means that a defendant who may be guilty of a serious crime will go free, without having been tried." In *Strunk v. United States*, 412 U.S. 434 (1973), the Court affirmed that the sole remedy for a violation of the right to a speedy trial was dismissal of the charge rather than, for example, reducing a sentence for time served while awaiting trial.

Unlike other constitutional violations, which may result in the exclusion of evidence or the imposition of other trial-related restrictions on the government, a speedy trial violation means the case is over before it even begins—a result most courts are loath to order. Thus, the balancing test gives courts greater flexibility to assess the reasons for the delay and the harm before ordering the ultimate remedy of dismissal and a prohibition on any future prosecution for the offense.

B. Length of the Delay

The Supreme Court described the length of the delay as "to some extent a triggering mechanism." Any criminal case requires a period of time during which the parties prepare their case and a court schedules the proceeding, so *Barker v. Wingo* recognized that "[u]ntil there is some delay which is presumptively prejudicial, there is no necessity for inquiry into the other factors that go into the balance." The Court hesitated to draw a bright line even within this factor, noting that "the delay that can be tolerated for an ordinary street crime is considerably less than for a serious, complex conspiracy charge." Thus, the "peculiar circumstances" of the case would dictate whether the initial threshold to undertake a speedy trial analysis has been crossed.

1. Presumptive Prejudice

The Supreme Court refused to set a minimum amount of delay as the threshold for triggering the other *Barker v. Wingo* factors, but did acknowledge in *Doggett v. United States*, 505 U.S. 647 (1992), that "[d]epending on the nature of the charges, the lower courts have generally found postaccusation delay 'presumptively prejudicial' at least as it approaches one year." Thus, to raise a colorable speedy trial claim, the delay between the filing of charges or a defendant's arrest must be at least one year.

That does not mean, however, that such a delay automatically constitutes a violation. For example, courts have rejected Sixth Amendment claims in which the delay exceeded periods from three to five years. In *Barker v. Wingo*, the Supreme Court found after analyzing the various causes of the four-year delay in the defendant's trial that his right to a speedy trial had not been violated and upheld the conviction.

2. Measuring Delay

The starting point for the Sixth Amendment speedy trial right "clock" is important to the analysis. The usual trigger for the right is the defendant's arrest or the filing of criminal charges, the point at which the other protections of the

Sixth Amendment—most importantly the right to counsel—also attach. In *United States v. Marion*, 404 U.S. 307 (1971), the Supreme Court stated that "the protection of the Amendment is activated only when a criminal prosecution has begun and extends only to those persons who have been 'accused' in the course of that prosecution." The filing of a sealed indictment will trigger the calculation of what qualified as a "speedy" trial, even though the defendant is unaware of the charges. *United States v. Casas*, 356 F.3d 104 (1st Cir.2004); *United States v. Bergfeld*, 280 F.3d 486 (5th Cir.2002); *United States v. Hayes,* 40 F.3d 362, 365 (11th Cir.1994).

Delay may result from the government's decision to dismiss charges while it investigates further, or if a lower court dismisses the case due to a defect in the investigation or prosecution. In *United States v. MacDonald*, 456 U.S. 1 (1982), the Court held that there was no speedy trial right violation for the delay arising from the period between the dismissal of military court martial charges and the return of an indictment. The Court stated, "Once charges are dismissed, the speedy trial guarantee is no longer applicable. At that point, the formerly accused is, at most, in the same position as any other subject of a criminal investigation." Similarly, the delay caused by the government's appeal of a trial court's dismissal of an indictment did not count under the Speedy Trial Clause because "[d]uring much of the litigation, respondents were neither under indictment nor subject to bail." *United States v. Loud Hawk*, 474 U.S. 302 (1986).

C. Reason for the Delay

In *Barker v. Wingo*, the Supreme Court stated that "different weights should be assigned to different reasons" for the delay in beginning the trial. It outlined three different types of reasons and their effects on the analysis:

- "[A] deliberate attempt to delay the trial in order to hamper the defense should be weighted heavily against the government."
- "A more neutral reason such as negligence or overcrowded courts should be weighted less heavily but nevertheless should be considered since the ultimate responsibility for such circumstances must rest with the government rather than with the defendant."
- "Finally, a valid reason, such as a missing witness, should serve to justify appropriate delay."

The burden is on the government to explain the delay once it crosses the threshold of presumptive prejudice. Among the reasons that usually do not weigh heavily against the prosecution are the complexity of the case, the need to extradite a co-defendant or obtain the testimony of a witness outside the

United States, and meritorious interlocutory appeals by the government, such as a challenge to the suppression of evidence that did not lead to dismissal of the charges. In addition, delay caused by the defendant, such as the briefing and argument of pre-trial motions, hearings on competency, or the period during which the defendant was a fugitive, are not weighed against the government in the balancing process.

On the other hand, a delay in unsealing the indictment so that a co-defendant can be apprehended may count against the prosecution if law enforcement agents did not act diligently in pursuing the case or seeking to apprehend the defendant. While it is the rare case where there would be proof of a "deliberate attempt to delay the trial," courts have found that continuing negligence by the government should be weighed in favor of finding a violation.

In *Doggett v. United States*, which involved a delay of over eight years from indictment to trial, the Court noted that the greater the delay due to negligence, the more it would count against the government in determining whether there was a speedy trial violation. It stated:

> The Government's investigators made no serious effort to test their progressively more questionable assumption that Doggett was living abroad, and, had they done so, they could have found him within minutes. While the Government's lethargy may have reflected no more than Doggett's relative unimportance in the world of drug trafficking, it was still findable negligence.

Speedy trial right dismissals are rare, and usually occur because of the government's negligence in pursuing the case after indictment rather than intentional misconduct. For example, in *United States v. Mendoza*, 530 F.3d 758 (9th Cir. 2008), the Ninth Circuit reversed a defendant's conviction because of a ten-year delay between the return of an indictment and the defendant's arrest. The court found the only thing the government did once the defendant was charged was to file information about the charges in a criminal information database, and made no further effort to locate or contact him. In *United States v. Ferreira*, 665 F.3d 701 (6th Cir. 2011), the Sixth Circuit dismissed charges after a 35-month delay solely attributable to the government's "gross negligence" when it sent a writ to turn over the defendant to the wrong county jail, even though it had just been informed of where he was being held.

D. Defendant's Assertion of the Right

Most constitutional protections afforded to a criminal defendant can be waived, and the usual standard for judging whether the defendant gave up a right is whether the decision was knowing, intelligent, and voluntary. For the speedy trial right, however, the defendant's request for a speedy trial is one factor weighed in determining whether there was a violation. While the government must protect a defendant's rights and the accused need not demand their enforcement, in this context, the Supreme Court has acknowledged that delay could be in a defendant's interest, so it looks to whether the right has been asserted.

When and how often a defendant raises the speedy trial issue can work against the claimed constitutional violation. In *Barker v. Wingo*, the Court stated that the "failure to assert the right will make it difficult for a defendant to prove that he was denied a speedy trial." By looking at whether the defendant sought a prompt trial, and how frequently that issue was raised, the Court sought to avoid the potential for sandbagging, *i.e.* a defendant waiting silently while time passes and then, right before trial, seeking dismissal of the charges because the prosecution did not act quickly enough to resolve the charges.

Although a defendant cannot compel a judge to begin a trial, inaction on seeking to begin the trial will usually be viewed as a type of waiver of the claim, at least until the Sixth Amendment issue has been raised explicitly with the court. Similarly, defense requests for continuances and the filing of motions is weighted against a defendant who later asserts a speedy trial violation.

Filing a written motion seeking a prompt disposition of the case is not required, although it will be good evidence that the defendant asserted the right and put the court (and prosecutor) on notice that further delay may develop into a violation of the Sixth Amendment. Moreover, a single assertion of the right is unlikely to be sufficient and, in most cases, the defendant has, on multiple occasions, protested continued delay and demanded that trial commence as soon as possible as a pre-requisite for a court to find a violation of the right to a speedy trial.

E. Demonstrating Prejudice

As with other constitutional violations, the Supreme Court requires that a defendant suffer some actual prejudice from the delay before granting relief. As the Court noted in *Reed v. Farley*, 512 U.S. 339 (1994), "A showing of prejudice is required to establish a violation of the Sixth Amendment Speedy Trial Clause." In *Barker v. Wingo*, the Court identified three types of harm the right protects against: "(i) to prevent oppressive pretrial incarceration; (ii) to minimize anxiety and concern of the accused; and (iii) to limit the possibility that the defense will be impaired." In actuality, the first two types are rarely sufficient to support a finding of prejudice, and the Court asserted that "the most serious is the last, because the inability of a defendant adequately to prepare his case skews the fairness of the entire system."

For example, in *Hakeem v. Beyer*, 990 F.2d 750 (3rd Cir. 1993), the court of appeals found that the defendant's fourteen-month pre-trial incarceration was not *per se* prejudicial, and absent a showing of some harm to the defense, the delay was insufficient to constitute a speedy trial violation. The Third Circuit stated:

> Credit for time served cannot cure every unexcused delay but where the defendant has not pointed to any evidence of additional, specific prejudice flowing from the delay, we are unwilling to infer prejudice based on incarceration that the defendant would ultimately have had to serve solely because fourteen and one-half months had elapsed between arrest and trial.

Although actual prejudice is required to establish a speedy trial violation, the Supreme Court recognizes that demonstrating specific instances of harm traceable to the delay may be difficult. In *Doggett,* the Court found a violation based on *presumptive prejudice* arising solely from a delay of over eight years. The Court found that "consideration of prejudice is not limited to the specifically demonstrable, and, as [the prosecution] concedes, affirmative proof of particularized prejudice is not essential to every speedy trial claim." The delay was due to the government's negligence, as shown by the fact that Doggett was found after agents conducted a simple credit check and only then learned that he had returned to the United States years earlier.

In analyzing the prejudice from the delay, the Court viewed it in light of the reason for the delay, which it noted involved rather extreme negligence by law enforcement personnel. It held, "[S]uch is the nature of the prejudice presumed that the weight we assign to official negligence compounds over time as the presumption of evidentiary prejudice grows. Thus, our toleration of such negligence varies inversely with its protractedness, and its consequent threat to the fairness of the accused's trial." After *Doggett*, a defendant need not always demonstrate actual prejudice if there was a delay sufficiently long to be weighed heavily against the government.

Doggett illustrates that the four-factor *Barker v. Wingo* test is truly a balancing exercise, so the stronger one factor is, the less the others must be in order to reach a conclusion on a violation. For example, if a significant delay were due to an effort to extradite the defendant, or because of pre-trial defense motions that required resolution before trial could begin, then the lack of any weight against the government on the reason for the delay would require a stronger showing of prejudice by the defendant to establish a speedy trial violation. In that sense, the reason for the delay and any prejudice from it will be viewed together in analyzing a claimed violation of the Speedy Trial Clause.

II. Speedy Trial Act

In 1974, Congress adopted the Speedy Trial Act, 18 U.S.C. §§ 3161 *et seq.*, to create a system for the prompt disposition of criminal prosecutions in the federal courts. The Act does not supplant a defendant's speedy trial right, but, for those charged with federal crimes, it is another means to ensure that a trial takes place within a reasonable amount of time after charges were filed. Unlike the more amorphous balancing test adopted by the Supreme Court in *Barker v. Wingo*, the Speedy Trial Act provides a specific set of rules for calculating when a trial should take place and the range of permissible delays based on certain triggering events, such as a competency hearing or disposition of pretrial motions.

A. Timing Requirements

The Speedy Trial Act requires at least *thirty days* from when the defendant first appears through counsel or expressly waives counsel and elects to proceed *pro se* before trial can begin. This minimum period, which a defendant can waive in writing, allows defense counsel at least some time to prepare the case. A key issue is ascertaining when the thirty-day speedy trial clock starts ticking. For example, an arrest on one charge does not trigger the running of the time on another criminal offense, and a state arrest does not start the clock because the Speedy Trial Act is limited to those charged with federal crimes. If prosecutors add charges to an indictment, then the minimum time available to start trial is reset to the date of the additional charges.

On the back end, the Speedy Trial Act requires that the trial must begin within *seventy days* of an indictment or information being made public, or from the defendant's first appearance before the court, whichever is later. The outer limit is much more frequently litigated under the Act because the wheels of justice tend to move slowly, not quickly.

If the charge is dropped at the defendant's request and the defendant is later charged with the same crime, the speedy trial clock starts over. Similarly, if the charge is dismissed by a trial court and reinstated following an appeal, or if a defendant is to be tried again following a mistrial or order for a new trial, the seventy-day period begins again on the date the action occasioning the new trial becomes final.

B. Excluded Time

The Speedy Trial Act also contains a long list of periods of delay that the court excludes from the computation of the seventy-day period in which the trial must commence. These exclusions stop the clock rather than reset it, and are in the Act to ensure that it does not produce "assembly-line justice" that puts speed ahead of following proper procedures to ensure a reliable outcome to the case. Exclusions related to a defendant include:

- Delay resulting from other proceedings concerning the defendant, such as an examination to determine the mental competency or physical capacity;
- Delay due to the defendant's trial on other charges;
- Delay from an interlocutory appeal; and
- Delay resulting from any pretrial motion, although once the court takes the matter under advisement only thirty days can be excluded from the Speedy Trial Act calculation, even if the defendant is available for trial.

In addition, delays not directly related to the defendant may be excluded. For example, the period during which a co-defendant or essential witness is absent or unavailable is not counted toward the seventy-day limit.

C. Ends of Justice Exclusion

The Speedy Trial Act contains an open-ended basis for excluding time if the judge finds that the "ends of justice" require the delay in commencing trial. Delay caused by a continuance of the trial for this reason requires the trial court to set forth on the record the reasons for the ends-of-justice delay. The statute is clear that a court should not grant this type of continuance because of an overcrowded court docket, a lack of diligent preparation, or the prosecution's failure to have its witnesses available for trial absent extenuating circumstances.

In *Zedner v. United States*, 547 U.S. 489 (2006), the Supreme Court held that the Speedy Trial Act also does not permit a *defendant* to waive its protections in advance through a blanket consent. According to the Court, the Act provides specific factors for a court to consider in granting an ends-of-justice continuance, so that "[i]f a defendant could simply waive the application of the Act whenever he or she wanted more time, no defendant would ever need to put such considerations before the court under the rubric of an ends-of-justice exclusion." The Court noted that the Speedy Trial Act also protects society's interest in a prompt disposition of criminal charges, so the "public interest cannot be served ... if defendants may opt out of the Act entirely."

D. Remedies

The remedy for a violation of the Speedy Trial Act differs from that required for a violation of the Sixth Amendment speedy trial right. The constitutional violation mandates dismissal of the charges with prejudice, meaning the government cannot prosecute the charge at any time. A violation of the Speedy Trial Act's seventy-day limit gives the trial court the discretion to decide whether to dismiss the charges with or without prejudice. In determining what type of dismissal to order, the court should consider the seriousness of the offense, the facts and circumstances of the case which led to the dismissal, and the impact of a re-prosecution on the fair administration of justice. The *Zedner* Court explained the rationale of the dismissal without prejudice remedy as promoting "compliance with the Act without necessarily subverting important criminal prosecutions." Courts tend to order a dismissal without prejudice for a violation of the Speedy Trial Act unless it appears that there was serious prosecutorial negligence for not seeking a trial within the prescribed limits.

III. Pre-Indictment Delay

As noted above, the Sixth Amendment's speedy trial right does not apply to delay that occurs *before* a defendant is arrested or charged with a crime. The primary protection against having to defend against an overly stale criminal charge is the statute of limitations, which for most non-capital crimes is five years. The Supreme Court noted in *United States v. Marion*, 404 U.S. 307 (1971), that the limitations period in which the government must file charges provides "predictability by specifying a limit beyond which there is an irrebuttable presumption that a defendant's right to a fair trial would be prejudiced." For certain offenses, most notably murder, there is no statute of limitations, so it is possible to have a prosecution occur decades after the crime took place. For example, a defendant was convicted in 2005 for the murder of three young civil rights workers in Mississippi in 1964, and the Mississippi Supreme Court rejected the argument that the 41-year delay violated due process. *Killen v. State*, 958 So. 2d 172 (Miss. 2007).

A. Due Process

The Due Process Clause of the Fifth and Fourteenth Amendments also protects against oppressive delay before the government initiates a criminal prosecution. In *Marion*, the Supreme Court stated that the statute of limitations is not the only protection against pre-charge delay:

> [T]he Due Process Clause of the Fifth Amendment would require dismissal of the indictment if it were shown at trial that the pre-indictment delay in this case caused substantial prejudice to appellees' rights to a fair trial and that the delay was an intentional device to gain tactical advantage over the accused.

The scope of the due process protection is narrow, and a defendant must show actual prejudice. Even then, the Court noted, not all prejudice triggers relief because "[a]ctual prejudice to the defense of a criminal case may result from the shortest and most necessary delay; and no one suggests that every delay causing detriment to a defendant's case should abort a criminal prosecution."

B. Prejudice

Proof of actual prejudice is a prerequisite for a due process claim based on pre-indictment delay, but it does not make the claim automatically valid. The due process inquiry balances the reasons for the delay against the prejudice to the defendant. To prosecute a defendant following reasonable investigative delay does not deprive him of due process, even if his defense might have been somewhat prejudiced by the lapse of time.

In *United States v. Lovasco*, 431 U.S. 783 (1977), the Supreme Court found that even some prejudice to the defendant was insufficient if the prosecutor had good reason for delaying the filing of charges. The Court stated:

> [T]he Due Process Clause does not permit courts to abort criminal prosecutions simply because they disagree with a prosecutor's judgment as to when to seek an indictment. Judges are not free, in defining "due process," to impose on law enforcement officials our personal and private notions of fairness and to disregard the limits that bind judges in their judicial function.

The Court concluded that the prosecution's desire to amass additional evidence was proper, and that "prosecutors are under no duty to file charges as soon as probable cause exists but before they are satisfied they will be able to establish the suspect's guilt beyond a reasonable doubt."

Courts rarely dismiss charges due to government delay in filing them because of the high threshold required to show the prosecution acted improperly. While negligence can be a basis for finding a violation under the Sixth Amendment, a heavy caseload or other reasons usually will not be sufficient to establish *Marion*'s requirement that the prosecution acted intentionally to gain a tactical advantage through the delay. In demonstrating actual prejudice, courts require more than just claims that the memory of witnesses faded or they may be unavailable. For example, courts have found insufficient proof of prejudice from the death of a witness if it was not clear that the witness would have provided exculpatory testimony.

Checkpoints

- The *Barker v. Wingo* four-part test applies to delay after the filing of charges.

- The length of the delay must be presumptively prejudicial, generally understood as at least one year from arrest or filing of charges, to trigger the other parts of the test.

- The reason for the delay, defendant's assertion of the right, and prejudice from the delay are balanced if the delay is sufficient to trigger the speedy trial right analysis.

- The Speedy Trial Act supplements the constitutional protection by requiring a criminal trial within specified periods after the initiation of a criminal prosecution.

- The Act allows for time to be excluded from the calculation for specific reasons, and also if the "ends of justice" so require additional delay.

- The Due Process Clause prohibits the government from delaying the filing of criminal charges to gain an unfair advantage over the defendant.

Chapter 7

Right to Counsel

Roadmap

- Sixth Amendment right to counsel
- When the right to counsel attaches
- Limitations of the right to counsel
- What is included in the right to counsel
- Right of self-representation
- Ineffective assistance of counsel

I. Introduction

The Sixth Amendment provides that "[i]n all criminal prosecutions, the accused shall enjoy the right ... to have the Assistance of Counsel for his defence." But there are many questions that arise from this phrase, such as: 1) who has a right to counsel; 2) when does the right to counsel attach; 3) are there limitations to the right to counsel; 4) can one represent him or herself; and 5) what constitutes effective representation. These questions have been examined in a number of Supreme Court decisions. Rule 44 of the Federal Rules of Criminal Procedure provide that "[a] defendant who is unable to obtain counsel is entitled to have counsel appointed to represent the defendant at every stage of the proceeding from initial appearance through appeal, unless the defendant waives this right."

The right to counsel is also a component of the proper interrogation of an accused. A host of issues arise in the interrogation setting, including: when is there a right to counsel, can you question a defendant when counsel is not present, and when is the right to counsel appropriately waived. Discussion of these questions are covered in the chapter concerning interrogations and the Sixth Amendment. (See Vol. I, Chapter 15).

II. Who Has a Right to Counsel

Although the Sixth Amendment provides a clear right to counsel, several Supreme Court decisions led to the eventual recognition of this protection as a fundamental right applicable to the states in felony cases. The right to counsel has also been extended to misdemeanors, but only those with a sentence of incarceration. What constitutes incarceration has been discussed in several Court cases.

Unlike criminal cases, there is no automatic right to counsel for civil matters. Civil cases of juvenile delinquency and transfer of a prison inmate to a state hospital for mental treatment are examples of exceptions for when civil matters necessitate the appointment of counsel. Even though a civil contempt proceeding may result in incarceration, such as for non-payment of child support, the Supreme Court has held that the Due Process Clause of the Fourteenth Amendment does not "automatically" require the appointment of counsel. *Turner v. Rogers*, 131 S. Ct. 2507 (2011). Indigent defendants do, however, have a right to counsel in criminal contempt proceedings.

A. Pre-*Gideon* Right to Counsel

In *Powell v. Alabama (Scottsboro Boys Case)*, 287 U.S. 45 (1932), the Court held that due process required the appointment of counsel "in a capital case where the defendant is unable to employ counsel, and is incapable adequately of making his own defense because of ignorance, feeble-mindedness, illiteracy, or the like." Justice Sutherland examined the conviction of nine black youths convicted in Alabama of raping two white women. The Court noted that counsel for the defendants had not been designated until the morning of trial. The Court found that

> the ignorance and illiteracy of the defendants, their youth, the circumstances of public hostility, the imprisonment and the close surveillance of the defendants by the military forces, the fact their friends and families were all in other states and communication with them necessarily difficult, and above all that they stood in deadly peril of their lives—we think the failure of the trial court to give them reasonable time and opportunity to secure counsel was a clear denial of due process.

The *Powell* opinion called for the appointment of counsel for indigent defendants facing capital charges with unique circumstances such as seen in this case.

The Court extended *Powell*'s holding in *Johnson v. Zerbst*, 304 U.S. 458 (1938), where it held that the Sixth Amendment required counsel for indigent defendants who could be deprived of life or liberty in federal courts. In a non-capital case, the Court firmly noted that "[i]f the accused ... is not represented by counsel and has not competently and intelligently waived his constitutional right, the Sixth Amendment stands as a jurisdictional bar to a valid conviction and sentencing depriving him of his life or his liberty." At the heart of both the *Powell* and *Johnson v. Zerbst* decisions is the concept that the Sixth Amendment right to counsel protects the fundamental right to a fair trial.

The key element of *Johnson v. Zerbst*—the appointment of indigent defense counsel in federal felony cases—was not extended to the states when the Supreme Court decided *Betts v. Brady*, 316 U.S. 455 (1942). The Court in *Betts* held that a refusal to appoint counsel in state court for Betts was not so "offensive to the common and fundamental ideas of fairness" as to deny due process. Unlike *Powell*, *Betts* was not a capital case, and unlike *Johnson v. Zerbst*, *Betts* did not originate in a federal court. In *Betts*, the Court held that "[t]he Sixth Amendment of the national Constitution applies only to trials in federal courts."

B. *Gideon*—Right to Counsel Extended to States

The Supreme Court's landmark decision on the right to counsel is *Gideon v. Wainwright*, 372 U.S. 335 (1963), which held that the right to counsel extended to state cases. Clarence Earl Gideon was charged in the State of Florida with the felony of breaking into a poolroom with intent to commit a misdemeanor. Gideon appeared in the trial court without a lawyer and asked the court to appoint one for him. The court ruled that Florida only provided counsel when the case was a capital offense. After representing himself at trial, Gideon was convicted. The Supreme Court appointed counsel to represent Gideon in this appeal that would examine whether the case of *Betts*, which limited the Sixth Amendment right to counsel to federal courts alone, should be overturned. The Court noted that if the *Betts* case were followed then denial of counsel to Gideon was proper.

Justice Black, writing for the majority in *Gideon*, started by accepting the statement in *Betts* that fundamental rights in the Bill of Rights are "obligatory upon the States by the Fourteenth Amendment." But then the Court departed from *Betts* which had held that "the Sixth Amendment's guarantee of counsel is not one of these fundamental rights." The Court traced the history of the right to counsel under the Sixth Amendment and noted that the Court in *Betts* had departed from precedent such as *Powell*. *Gideon* reaffirmed the importance of the right to be represented by counsel, stating that the "government hires lawyers to prosecute and defendants who have the money hire lawyers to defend are the strongest indications of the wide-spread belief that lawyers in criminal courts are necessities, not luxuries." The Court further found that "[t]he right of one charged with crime to counsel may not be deemed fundamental and essential to fair trials in some countries, but it is in ours."

Although *Gideon* clearly mandated that states must appoint counsel for indigent defendants charged with felonies, there remains significant discussion as to whether the indigent defense system has satisfied this mandate. Underfunded defense systems continually raise issues of whether *Gideon's* promise has been met.

C. *Argersinger-Scott* — Actual Imprisonment Standard

Although *Gideon* provided a clear right to counsel for indigent defendants charged in state felonies, later cases faced the question of whether this right extended to misdemeanors. Questions also arose as to what types of sentences might require the appointment of counsel.

Argersinger v. Hamlin, 407 U.S. 25 (1972) extended *Gideon's* holding beyond felony cases, finding that "no person may be imprisoned for any offense, whether classified as petty, misdemeanor, or felony, unless he was represented by counsel at his trial." After being "[c]harged in Florida with carrying a concealed weapon, an offense punishable by imprisonment up to six months, a $1,000 fine, or both," the defendant was sentenced to 90 days in jail without the opportunity of appointed trial counsel. The Court noted that both *Powell* and *Gideon* involved felonies, but that "their rationale has relevance to any criminal trial, where an accused is deprived of his liberty." Justice Douglas stated that "the requirement of counsel may well be necessary for a fair trial even in a petty-offense prosecution."

Although *Argersinger* extended *Gideon* beyond felony prosecution, it limited the appointment of counsel to those cases where the defendant received an actual punishment of imprisonment. Thus, a defendant could be tried without counsel for a misdemeanor that authorized imprisonment as long as the court did not subject that individual to actual incarceration. This interpretation was clearly enunciated in *Scott v. Illinois*, 440 U.S. 367 (1979), a case involving an indigent defendant who was convicted of shoplifting and fined $50. The Illinois statute allowed for a $500 fine and up to one year in jail, and the defendant sought the appointment of counsel. The Court reaffirmed *Argersinger*, holding "that actual imprisonment is a penalty different in kind from fines or the mere threat of imprisonment." Absent imprisonment, there was no right to counsel.

The *Argersinger-Scott* cases that form an actual imprisonment standard led to issues of what is meant by the term "imprisonment." For example, in *Nichols v. United States*, 511 U.S. 738 (1994), the Court looked at whether the Sixth

Amendment "prohibits a sentencing court from considering a defendant's previous uncounseled misdemeanor conviction in sentencing him for a subsequent offense." The specific issue was whether a prior DUI conviction that resulted in no jail time could be used to enhance his sentence on federal felony drug charges, when he did not have counsel for the state misdemeanor DUI charge. Since no jail time was given on the DUI charge, the fact that he did not have counsel at that time did not constitute a deprivation of his rights when it was later used to enhance his federal drug conviction.

The Court again looked at the question of what constituted imprisonment in *Alabama v. Shelton*, 535 U.S. 654 (2002). Justice Ginsburg, writing for the majority, held that "a suspended sentence that may 'end up in the actual deprivation of a person's liberty' may not be imposed unless the defendant was accorded 'the guiding hand of counsel' in the prosecution for the crime charged." The defendant was sentenced to 30 days imprisonment, but the sentence was suspended and he was placed on two years' probation. Defendant Shelton, the Court stated, "is entitled to appointed counsel at the critical stage when his guilt or innocence of the charged crime is decided and his vulnerability to imprisonment is determined." The Court distinguished this decision from *Nichols* and another decision, *Gagnon v. Scarpelli*, 411 U.S. 778 (1973), in which the Court held that a defendant was not entitled to appointed counsel at a probation revocation hearing. A key difference with *Shelton* was that in both *Nichols* and *Gagnon* the accused was entitled to counsel when initially facing the felony charge. A defendant is entitled to counsel when facing the possibility of imprisonment or potential for imprisonment, but this right to counsel cannot be used to negate a sentencing enhancement or to include a right at a later probation revocation.

In addition to the constitutional guidelines provided by these cases, some states have statutes that pertain to the appointment of counsel for an indigent defendant accused of a crime. Although a state cannot provide a standard that falls below that of the Supreme Court, it can be more accommodating in the appointment of counsel. For example, Vermont allows for counsel to be appointed for indigent defendants accused of a "serious crime" which includes felonies and misdemeanors with imprisonment, but also includes imposed fines that exceed $1,000. *13 V.S.A. §§ 5201, 5206.*

III. Time Frame for the Right to Counsel

The Sixth Amendment right to counsel applies at "the initiation of adversary judicial criminal proceedings whether by way of formal charge, preliminary hearing, indictment, information, or arraignment." In *Rothgery v. Gillespie*

County, Tex., 554 U.S. 191 (2008), the Court held that the prosecutor did not have to be "aware of or involved in" the court hearing for the attachment of a right to counsel. The right attached at "the first appearance before a judicial officer at which a defendant is told of the formal accusation against him and restrictions are imposed on his liberty." The rule to take away from *Rothgery* is that the right to counsel attaches at the start of an "adversarial proceeding," and the accused is "entitled to the presence of appointed counsel during any 'critical stage' of the post-attachment proceedings."

The right to counsel under the Sixth Amendment is limited, however, to criminal trials. This includes the sentencing hearing, and when the sentencing is a deferred procedure or a revocation of probation, counsel is necessary. *Mempa v. Rhay*, 389 U.S. 128 (1967). Although there is no Sixth Amendment right to counsel for appeals, the Supreme Court has ruled that a denial of counsel on an initial appeal is a deprivation of equal protection and due process. *Douglas v. California*, 372 U.S. 353 (1963). This has not been extended to an indigent defendant that seeks counsel for a second-tier discretionary appeal or for a certiorari application to the Supreme Court. *Ross v. Moffitt*, 417 U.S. 600 (1974). States, however, often provide for counsel in post-conviction matters.

IV. Limitations, Conflicts, and Extensions of the Right to Counsel

The right to counsel includes the right to counsel of one's choice for the non-indigent defendant. Irrespective of effectiveness or ineffectiveness of counsel, a deprivation of the non-indigent's right to assistance of counsel of one's choosing is a Sixth Amendment violation that warrants an automatic reversal. *United States v. Gonzalez-Lopez*, 548 U.S. 140 (2006).

There are, however, some limits on this right to select counsel. As noted in *Wheat v. United States*, 486 U.S. 153 (1988), one does not have the right to be represented by "an advocate who is not a member of the bar." Nor does the accused have the right to be represented by counsel who has an actual conflict of interest. In *Wheat*, the Court stated that "the district court must be allowed substantial latitude in refusing waivers of conflicts of interest not only in those rare cases where an actual conflict may be demonstrated before trial, but in the more common cases where a potential for conflict exists which may or may not burgeon into an actual conflict as the trial progresses." A court evaluating this issue must "recognize a presumption in favor of [defendant's] counsel of choice, but that presumption may be overcome not only by a demonstration of actual conflict but by a showing of a serious potential for conflict."

Multiple representation of defendants can present challenges to the Sixth Amendment right to counsel. In *Holloway v. Arkansas*, 435 U.S. 475 (1978), the Supreme Court held that when defense counsel is forced to represent three co-defendants and objects because the defendants have divergent interests, it is grounds for an automatic reversal unless the trial court determines that there is no conflict. When there is no objection to the joint representation, and defense counsel suggests that the interests of the co-defendants are aligned, a defendant has to show "a conflict of interest actually affected the adequacy of his representation." *Cuyler v. Sullivan*, 446 U.S. 335 (1980). In this situation, the trial court has "no affirmative duty to inquire into the propriety of multiple representation." The *Sullivan* Court stated, "that the possibility of conflict is insufficient to impugn a criminal conviction. In order to demonstrate a violation of his Sixth Amendment rights, a defendant must establish that an actual conflict of interest adversely affected his lawyer's performance."

In *Mickens v. Taylor*, 535 U.S. 162 (2002), the Court looked at "what a defendant must show in order to demonstrate a Sixth Amendment violation where the trial court fails to inquire into a potential conflict of interest about which it knew or reasonably should have known." In this situation, a defendant needs to demonstrate that the conflict of interest "adversely affected counsel's performance."

Federal Rule of Criminal Procedure 44(c)(2) provides the court's responsibilities in cases of joint representation, stating:

> The court must promptly inquire about the propriety of joint representation and must personally advise each defendant of the right to the effective assistance of counsel, including separate representation. Unless there is good cause to believe that no conflict of interest is likely to arise, the court must take appropriate measures to protect each defendant's right to counsel.

There is no right to pay counsel with tainted funds as "[a] defendant has no Sixth Amendment right to spend another person's money." *Caplin & Drysdale*, 491 U.S. 617 (1989). In *United States v. Monsanto*, 491 U.S. 600 (1989), the Court found it constitutional to freeze an indicted defendant's assets if probable cause was present to believe that the assets would be subject to forfeiture, even when the defendant sought to use the funds to pay his or her attorney. More recently, in *Kaley v. United States*, 134 S. Ct. 1090 (2013), the Court held that defendants were not entitled to challenge the grand jury's probable cause finding that they committed the crime. A three-person dissent in *Kaley* was critical of the majority stating "the Court's opinion pays insufficient respect to the importance of an independent bar as a check on prosecutorial abuse and government overreaching." The dissent noted that "[g]ranting the Government the power to take away a defendant's chosen advocate strikes at the heart of that significant role."

In addition to a right to counsel, there is also concern about appointment of experts to assist the attorney. In *Ake v. Oklahoma*, 478 U.S. 68 (1968), a death penalty case, the Supreme Court found that due process required that when sanity was a significant issue of a case, an indigent defendant was entitled "access to a competent psychiatrist who will conduct an appropriate examination and assist in evaluation, preparation, and presentation of the defense." Since *Ake* state and federal cases have issued varying opinions when faced with the question of whether to provide the cost of a non-psychiatrist expert, such as a DNA expert. The key question is whether due process requires this assistance to assure the accused "a fair opportunity to present his defense" and "to participate meaningfully in [the] judicial proceeding."

V. Self-Representation

In some cases the accused asks to represent him or herself at trial. In *Faretta v. California*, 422 U.S. 806 (1975), the Court was faced with the issue of whether the accused "in a state criminal trial has a constitutional right to proceed without counsel when he voluntarily and intelligently elects to do so." Faretta, who was charged with theft in a California state case, requested that he be permitted to represent himself at trial. Although the trial court initially agreed to allow this self-representation, the judge later changed his position when he found that Faretta could not respond satisfactorily to the court's questions on the hearsay rule and "state law governing the challenge of potential jurors." At trial, the judge required the appointed public defender to conduct the trial and failed to allow Faretta to act as co-counsel.

The Supreme Court affirmed the trial court's ruling holding that Faretta did not have the right of self-representation. The Court, however, vacated and remanded his case. Justice Stewart, writing for the majority, noted that "[i]n forcing Faretta, under these circumstances, to accept against his will a state-appointed public defender, the California courts deprived him of his constitutional right to conduct his own defense." The Court noted that the "Sixth Amendment does not provide merely that a defense shall be made for the accused; it grants to the accused personally the right to make his defense." The Court stated, "it is one thing to hold that every defendant, rich or poor, has the right to the assistance of counsel, and quite another to say that a State may compel a defendant to accept a lawyer he does not want."

The Supreme Court's decision in *Faretta* was clear in noting the downside of self-representation. It stated that "[t]he right of self-representation is not a license to abuse the dignity of the courtroom," and the defendant who elects to proceed pro se cannot later claim that he or she was denied "effective assistance of counsel."

Two separate dissents of three justices, raised concerns about how self-representation emanated from the Sixth Amendment and the procedural problems that could accrue from allowing self-representation. Justice Blackmun, joined by Chief Justice Burger and Justice Rehnquist, stated "[i]f there is any truth to the old proverb that 'one who is his own lawyer has a fool for a client,' the Court by its opinion today now bestows a constitutional right on one to make a fool of himself."

In determining whether an accused individual can represent him or herself, courts routinely hold what has come to be known as a *Faretta* hearing. To represent oneself, "the accused must 'knowingly and intelligently' forgo those relinquished benefits." It is not necessary to "have the skill and experience of a lawyer in order competently and intelligently to choose self-representation," but the accused "should be made aware of the dangers and disadvantages of self-representation, so that the record will establish that 'he knows what he is doing and his choice is made with eyes open.'" A *Faretta* hearing will therefore attempt to discern if the defendant understands: a) the nature of the charges against him, b) the possible penalties, and c) the dangers and disadvantages of self-representation.

Although there is a right to choose between self-representation or representation by counsel, there is no right to have hybrid representation. "A defendant does not have a constitutional right to choreograph special appearances by counsel." *McKaskle v. Wiggins*, 465 U.S. 168 (1984). Courts, however, often use their discretion to appoint "standby counsel," to assist a pro se defendant should the need arise during trial. "Standby counsel" walks a fine line between making certain that the *Faretta* rights of the defendant are not infringed upon, and assisting the accused with presenting his or her defense.

In *McKaskle v. Wiggins*, the Court held that *Faretta* rights are "not infringed when standby counsel assists the pro se defendant in overcoming routine procedural evidentiary obstacles to the completion of some specific task, such as introducing evidence or objecting to testimony, that the defendant has clearly shown he wishes to complete." The Court further stated that, "[n]or are they infringed when counsel merely helps to ensure the defendant's compliance with basic rules of courtroom protocol and procedure." Once the *pro se* defendant allows substantial participation by the standby counsel, "at least until the defendant expressly and unambiguously renews his request that standby counsel be silenced," it is assumed he or she has allowed counsel to assist.

There are limits to the right of self-representation. For example, the right of self-representation does not include a right under federal law to the use of a law library. *Kane v. Garcia Espitia*, 546 U.S. 9 (2005). A State can also require counsel when a defendant is "found mentally competent to stand trial if represented by counsel but not mentally competent to conduct the trial" alone. *Indiana v. Edwards*, 554 U.S. 164 (2008).

Questions can arise when the defendant waives the right to counsel and enters a plea. In *Iowa v. Tovar*, 541 U.S. 77 (2004), the Supreme Court held that the Sixth Amendment does not require the trial court to warn a defendant that in waiving the right to an attorney he or she "will lose the opportunity to obtain an independent opinion on whether, under the facts and applicable law, it is wise to plead guilty." The Court held that it is only necessary that the "trial court informs the accused of the nature of the charges against him, of his right to be counseled regarding his plea, and of the range of allowable punishments attendant upon the entry of a guilty plea."

VI. Ineffective Assistance of Counsel

A Sixth Amendment right to counsel includes a right to effective representation. The bar of finding counsel ineffective, however, is not easy to meet. The seminal case on effective assistance of counsel is *Strickland v. Washington*, 466 U.S. 668 (1984), in which the Court looked at whether counsel at a sentencing hearing had provided effective assistance to the defendant. The defendant asserted six errors by counsel: that he "failed to move for a continuance to prepare for sentencing, to request a psychiatric report, to investigate and present character witnesses, to seek a presentence investigation report, to present meaningful arguments to the sentencing judge, and to investigate the medical examiner's reports or cross-examine the medical experts." The Court in *Strickland* stated:

> A convicted defendant's claim that counsel's assistance was so defective as to require reversal of a conviction or death sentence has two components. First, the defendant must show that counsel's performance was deficient. This requires showing that counsel made errors so serious that counsel was not functioning as the "counsel" guaranteed the defendant by the Sixth Amendment. Second, the defendant must show that the deficient performance prejudiced the defense. This requires showing that counsel's errors were so serious as to deprive the defendant of a fair trial, a trial whose result is reliable. Unless a de-

fendant makes both showings, it cannot be said that the conviction or death sentence resulted from a breakdown in the adversary process that renders the result unreliable.

Strickland's two-part test, whether counsel's representation "fell below an objective standard of reasonableness" and whether "there is a reasonable probability that, but for counsel's unprofessional errors, the result of the proceeding would have been different," serves as the key analysis for a finding of ineffective assistance of counsel. The Court held that counsel did not provide ineffective assistance.

In examining the first prong—constitutional deficiency—courts often look at the practice and expectations of the legal community as "[t]he proper measure of attorney performance remains simply reasonableness under prevailing professional norms." Certain aspects are considered basic: (1) "Counsel's function is to assist the defendant, and hence counsel owes the client a duty of loyalty, a duty to avoid conflicts of interest"; and (2) "Counsel also has a duty to bring to bear such skill and knowledge as will render the trial a reliable adversarial testing process."

Courts that review counsel's performance under the first prong of this test, to determine whether it was ineffective, are to be "highly deferential." That is, claims of reasonableness are to be "viewed as of the time of counsel's conduct" and "counsel is strongly presumed to have rendered adequate assistance and made all significant decisions in the exercise of reasonable professional judgment." Strategic decisions by counsel are not considered ineffective absent other circumstances. For example, in *Florida v. Nixon*, 543 U.S. 175 (2004), the Court held that a defense attorney's failure to secure the defendant's consent in conceding guilt at the guilt phase of a capital trial was not ineffective when the counsel had a "tenable strategy" that had been "disclosed to and discussed with the defendant."

Although strategic decisions may weigh against a finding of ineffectiveness, a court still needs to provide a *Strickland* inquiry that can be "probing and fact-specific." For example, when counsel presents some mitigation evidence, this does not "foreclose an inquiry into whether a facially deficient mitigation investigation might have prejudiced the defendant." *Sears v. Upton*, 561 U.S. 945 (2010). Likewise, a failure to investigate mitigating evidence that resulted in an inadequate investigation that prejudiced the defendant, can be found to be a basis for a finding of ineffective assistance of counsel. *Wiggins v. Smith*, 539 U.S. 510 (2003). So, too, the Court found ineffective assistance of counsel when defense counsel had an obligation in a death penalty case to look at mitigating evidence despite the defendant and his family saying that there was no mitigation evidence. *Rompilla v. Beard*, 545 U.S. 374 (2005).

In *Hinton v. Alabama*, 134 S. Ct. 1081 (2014), the Supreme Court held that the first prong of the *Strickland* test was met when counsel failed to request sufficient funds to hire an expert in a case. Counsel believed that he could not obtain a better expert for the $1,000 provided by the court and "that he was unable to obtain more than $1,000 to cover expert fees." Finding this belief wrong, the Court held that the failure to request additional funds was an "unreasonable performance under *Strickland*." Despite finding a deficient performance on the part of counsel, the Court remanded the case to the lower court to determine whether this performance was prejudicial.

In *Padilla v. Kentucky*, 559 U.S. 356 (2010), the Supreme Court considered whether a "lawful permanent resident of the United States for more than 40 years," who served in the military during the Vietnam War, had been denied effective assistance of counsel when his attorney told him not to worry about his immigration status in pleading guilty to "drug charges that made his deportation virtually mandatory." Writing for the majority, Justice Stevens held that "constitutionally competent counsel would have advised him" that this drug conviction could result in deportation. The Court refused to take the government's position that would have limited this holding to affirmative misadvice. The Court was concerned that this would "give counsel an incentive to remain silent on matters of great importance" and that it would deprive a "class of clients least able to represent themselves the most rudimentary advice on deportation." Despite the importance of having finality for plea agreements, the Court noted that defendants have a right to counsel, including effective assistance of counsel, during their plea negotiation. Effectiveness includes being informed if a "plea carries a risk of deportation." Although the Court held that Padilla's "counsel was constitutionally deficient," it remanded the case to determine whether the defendant had been prejudiced and was therefore entitled to relief. Thus, an examination of the second prong of the *Strickland* test would be required. *Padilla*, however, has been found to have no retroactive application. *Chaidez v. United States*, 133 S. Ct. 1103 (2013).

Concurring in *Padilla*, Justices Alito and Roberts found ineffectiveness under *Strickland* but limited the decision to holding that an attorney should not give misadvice and should advise the defendant that a criminal conviction could have "adverse immigration consequences." These justices disagreed with the Court in finding an obligation of the attorney to explain the immigration consequences. They were concerned that criminal defense attorneys might not be well versed in immigration law to provide expert immigration advice.

Dissenting in *Padilla*, Justices Scalia and Thomas advocated that the Sixth Amendment right to counsel did not include a duty "to advise about a conviction's collateral consequences." The dissenters stated that "[t]here is no basis in text or in principle to extend the constitutionally required advice regarding guilty pleas beyond those matters germane to the criminal prosecution at hand-to wit, the sentence that the plea will produce, the higher sentence that conviction after trial might entail, and the chances of such a conviction."

In each of these cases where there was a finding of ineffective assistance of counsel, the Court not only examined whether counsel's conduct fell below the proper level of reasonable performance, but also found that the second prong of *Strickland* had been met — prejudice to the defendant. For example, in *Rompilla v. Beard*, 545 U.S. 374 (2003), the failure to present mitigation fell below the reasonable standard for effective representation. Additionally, the Court noted that "[i]f the defense lawyers had looked in the file on Rompilla's prior conviction, it is uncontested they would have found a range of mitigation leads that no other source had opened up." The Court stated that this "might well have influenced the jury's appraisal" of his culpability and produced a different result in the sentence. This called for a reversal of the death sentence, with a retrial of the penalty phase or a stipulation to a life sentence.

That said, it is often difficult to prove prejudice under *Strickland*. In *Harrington v. Richter*, 131 S. Ct. 770 (2011), the Supreme Court held that "[i]n assessing prejudice under *Strickland*, the question is not whether a court can be certain counsel's performance had no effect on the outcome or whether it is possible a reasonable doubt might have been established if counsel acted differently." Rather, the Court stated that "*Strickland* asks whether it is 'reasonably likely' the result would have been different." It is necessary to show that "the likelihood of a different result must be substantial, not just conceivable." In judging this, deference should be accorded to the state court's decision on the merits, in this case the California Supreme Court.

Some cases, however, may automatically presume that prejudice exists. For example, a total lack of counsel, or circumstances like those in the *Powell* case may warrant an automatic finding of prejudice. There can also be a presumption of ineffectiveness, such as when counsel has an actual conflict of interest. But as noted in *United States v. Cronic*, 466 U.S. 648 (1984), a case decided on the same day as *Strickland*, it is not *per se* prejudice when counsel, who is inexperienced in criminal matters, is given only 25 days to prepare for trial.

The right to effective assistance of counsel is not limited to trial, and includes effective assistance of counsel prior to deciding whether to plead guilty. Thus, when counsel's advice on a plea falls below an appropriate standard of adequate assistance of counsel, and the defendant is prejudiced by the improper advice, there can be a Sixth Amendment violation of the right to counsel. *Lafler v. Cooper*, 132 S. Ct. 1376 (2012). Failure to communicate a plea offer to a client, when prejudice is demonstrated, also can be ineffective assistance of counsel. *Missouri v. Frye*, 132 S. Ct. 1399 (2012). So too, the Fourteenth Amendment's due process clause includes the right to effective assistance on a first appeal. *Evitts v. Lucey*, 469 U.S. 387 (1985).

In *Martinez v. Ryan*, 132 S. Ct. 1309 (2012), the Court examined the question of "whether ineffective assistance in an initial-review collateral proceeding on a claim of ineffective assistance at trial may provide cause for a procedural default in a federal habeas proceeding." The Court recognized a narrow exception to prior caselaw in finding that "[i]nadequate assistance of counsel at initial-review collateral proceedings may establish cause for a prisoner's procedural default of a claim of ineffective assistance at trial."

Checkpoints

- Indigent defendants have a right to counsel in both state and federal felony cases.

- There is a right to counsel in misdemeanor cases when there is actual imprisonment or when there is a suspended sentence that might result in imprisonment.

- The right to counsel attaches at adversarial judicial criminal proceedings.

- Denial of counsel on a first appeal is a deprivation of equal protection and due process.

- The right to counsel includes the right to counsel of one's choice for the non-indigent defendant, unless counsel has an actual conflict or the court believes there is a serious potential for a conflict.

- The right to counsel does not include the right to use tainted funds to pay counsel.

- In some cases, due process can include the right to have experts who can assist counsel in preparing the defendant's case.

- The right to counsel includes the right to self-representation.

- For self-representation, an accused needs to knowingly and intelligently waive representation and be apprised of the dangers and disadvantages of self-representation.

- Although there is no right to hybrid representation, courts sometimes appoint "standby counsel" to assist the accused who selects to represent him or herself.

- An accused is entitled to effective assistance of counsel.

- To determine whether counsel's representation is ineffective, the court looks at whether it fell below an objective standard of reasonableness and whether it was actually prejudicial to the defendant.

- Courts reviewing claims of ineffectiveness look at the conduct at the time it occurred with deference to counsel for strategic decisions.

- Deference should be given to the state court in deciding whether it is reasonably likely the result would have been different.

- Prejudice for an ineffectiveness claim can be presumed when counsel has an actual conflict of interest.

- When prejudice is found, it is ineffective assistance of counsel to fail to advise a defendant of a plea that is offered.

- When prejudice is found, it is ineffective assistance of counsel to provide incorrect information about whether to take a plea or to fail to properly advise a client that entering a plea could result in deportation.

Chapter 8

Discovery

I. Introduction

Pre-trial discovery is important to an adversarial system. It allows parties to properly prepare their case and removes the element of surprise at trial. Discovery can also lead to resolutions of cases without the necessity of trial. In the federal system, approximately 95% of cases are resolved by plea agreement, and plea agreements are equally pervasive in state systems. Seeing the government's evidence prior to trial can assist in fostering these plea agreements because knowing what the state can prove against the defendant can be a motivating factor for wanting to receive the benefit of a plea offer.

In contrast to the civil system, in most jurisdictions discovery is more limited in criminal cases. For one, the prosecution cannot take depositions from or demand a defendant to answer interrogatories. The Fifth Amendment right not to incriminate oneself would be violated if the defendant were forced to testify in this manner. Prosecutors do, however, have the power to obtain evidence though the use of subpoenas, search warrants, and police investigations. Discovery becomes particularly important to the defense because it allows the defendant to obtain the evidence accumulated by the prosecution in its investigation. After all, as noted by Justice Brennan in a landmark article, a trial should be a "quest for the truth" as opposed to a "sporting theory of justice."

Discovery, therefore, includes the constitutional obligations the prosecution owes to the defendant. Often these obligations emanate from the Constitution's Due Process Clause. Legislatures also provide discovery statutes that may specify what is discoverable, the method of discovery, timing, and remedies for non-compliance. There can also be discovery rules implemented by courts or rules committees, such as the Federal Rules of Criminal Procedure. Although the prosecution often has clear discovery obligations, those of the defense are usually less demanding.

There have been several recent discovery controversies in which the prosecution failed to fulfill its constitutional obligations to defendants. A failure of a former North Carolina district attorney to provide exculpatory discovery to Duke lacrosse players eventually resulted in the disbarment of the prosecutor. In the federal prosecution of former Senator Ted Stevens, discovery violations resulted in the dismissal of the case by the Department of Justice and institution of new oversight procedures and policies related to discovery. In the Michael Morton case, a defendant was wrongfully convicted and imprisoned for almost twenty-five years. Eventual DNA testing supported his innocence claim. The then-prosecutor, who was held to have failed to provide mitigating evidence to the defense, was held in contempt and sentenced to ten days in jail. This incident served as the basis for Texas passing the Michael Morton Act, a law that provides for more expansive discovery.

II. Constitutional Obligations

A. *Brady*—Obligation to Provide Exculpatory Material to the Defense

In *Brady v. Maryland*, 373 U.S. 83 (1963), the Supreme Court held that "suppression by the prosecution of evidence favorable to an accused upon request violates due process where the evidence is material either to guilt or to punishment, irrespective of the good faith or bad faith of the prosecution." Brady had asked the prosecution to provide his accomplice's statement made after his arrest. Although Brady was given several statements, he was not provided with one statement where his accomplice had admitted to the actual killing. This particular statement was important because Brady admitted involvement in the homicide, but claimed that it was his accomplice who had actually strangled the victim. The accomplice's statement confirming Brady's claim did not come to light until after trial, when Brady had been sentenced to death, and after that sentence was affirmed on appeal. The Supreme Court found this failure to provide the exculpatory statement to be a violation of Brady's Due Process rights under the Fourteenth Amendment.

Justice Douglas, writing for the majority in *Brady*, referred to the Court's prior holding in *Mooney v. Holohan*, 294 U.S. 103 (1935), in stressing the importance of a fair trial. He stated, "[s]ociety wins not only when the guilty are convicted but when criminal trials are fair." The Court stated, "[a] prosecution that withholds evidence on demand of an accused which if made available, would tend to exculpate him or reduce the penalty helps shape a trial that bears heavily on the defendant." The Court explained that this would "cast[] the prosecutor in the role of an architect of a proceeding that does not comport with standards of justice."

Despite this improper conduct in Brady that infringed on the fairness of the trial, the Court in *Brady* did not grant the defendant a new trial. Even if the accomplice's extra-judicial statement had been given to the defendant, it would not have resulted in a sentence below murder in the first degree. The Court said there was no basis for a retrial on the merits of the case. The Court, however, did affirm the holding of the Court of Appeals that had ruled that the defendant was entitled to a new hearing on punishment.

Courts looking at whether there is a *Brady* violation require the defendant to make three showings: 1) "[t]he evidence at issue must be favorable to the accused, either because it is exculpatory, or because it is impeaching; 2) that evidence must have been suppressed by the [government], either willfully or inadvertently; and 3) prejudice must have ensued." *Strickler v. Greene*, 527 U.S. 263 (1999).

Several issues arise from this test. First, is whether the accused needs to make a specific request for discoverable material. Second, is whether the discovery is going to be considered material. Finally, is a determination as to whether there is prejudice to the defendant because of the failure to disclose. Absent prejudice, there is no basis to reverse a conviction even though there has been a failure to provide the defendant with exculpatory material.

B. Materiality

Although *Brady* involved a case in which the defense made a specific request for materials, the duty to disclose is still required irrespective of whether the accused requested this information. It is, however, necessary that the discovery be both favorable to the defendant and "material either to guilt or to punishment." Two Supreme Court cases, *United States v. Agurs*, 427 U.S. 97 (1976), and *United States v. Bagley*, 473 U.S. 667 (1985), assist in understanding the materiality requirement of *Brady*.

In *Agurs*, the Court looked at three contexts where a *Brady* claim could arise: 1) where evidence introduced at trial, which had not been previously disclosed to the defense, included perjured testimony; 2) where the Government failed to provide specific exculpatory material that had been requested by the defense; and 3) where the Government failed to volunteer exculpatory evidence never requested, or requested only in a general way. In *Agurs*, the accused was charged with second degree murder for repeatedly stabbing the victim. The prosecution had failed to provide the defense with "certain background information" about the victim and the issue was whether this information "would have tended to support the argument that [the defendant] acted in self-defense." The key here was whether the defendant was denied due process rights under *Brady*. The Court looked at the significance of the failure of defense counsel to request this discovery material and the "standard by which the prosecution's failure to volunteer exculpatory material should be judged."

The Court in *Agurs* noted that in *Brady* the defense had made a specific request for the discovery material. The Court stated that "[w]hen the prosecutor receives a specific and relevant request, the failure to make any response is seldom, if ever, excusable." But the Court noted that in many cases the defense may be unaware of the discovery in the possession of the prosecutor. "[I]f the evidence is so clearly supportive of a claim of innocence that it gives the prosecution notice of a duty to produce, that duty should equally arise even if no request is made." The Court in *Agurs* held that "[t]he proper standard of materiality must reflect our overriding concern with the justice of the finding of guilt." If the evidence that is omitted "creates a reasonable doubt that did not otherwise exist, constitutional error has been committed." In *Agurs*, the arrest record had not been requested and there was no showing of any perjury. In this factual setting, failing to disclose to the defense the victim's record was found not to be a due process violation.

A second case also focused on how best to analyze materiality for a *Brady* determination. In *United States v. Bagley* the Court looked at disclosure of evidence that could have been used to show bias of government witnesses. *Bagley* abandoned the distinction between the second and third aspect outlined in *Agurs* (the specific-request and general or no request situations). The Supreme Court chose to reference the Court's prior decision in *Strickland v. Washington*, 466 U.S. 668 (1984), which was a case pertaining to whether counsel had been ineffective. In *Strickland* the Court examined whether there was "a reasonable probability that, but for counsel's unprofessional errors, the result of the proceeding would have been different." So, too, here the Court looked at whether the failure to provide the discovery material resulted in a reasonable probability that the result of the proceeding would have been different. Just as in *Strickland*, the *Bagley* Court said a "reasonable probability" is "a probability sufficient to undermine confidence in the outcome." The Court in *Bagley* believed that the *Strickland* approach could be used irrespective of whether the case was one with "no request," a "general request," or a "specific request." The Court stated that a prosecutor is not required to provide his or her "entire file to defense counsel, but only to disclose evidence favorable to the accused that, if suppressed, would deprive the defendant of a fair trial ..."

Materiality has been found when a prosecutor failed to provide statements from a witness that were the sole basis of the evidence against the defendant and when there were no other witnesses or physical evidence. *Smith v. Cain*, 132 S. Ct. 627 (2012). Some lower courts, however, have claimed that there is no *Brady* violation when the evidence is known to the defense. Referred to as the "due diligence" rule, this principle has not been adopted by all circuits.

Although a specific request for discovery sharpens a claim when there is deprivation of the requested discovery, a specific request is not required when the undisclosed evidence rises to a level that it would produce a different outcome in the trial or sentencing. In looking at the evidence to determine whether it is material, it is appropriate to examine this evidence "collectively, not item by item." Evidence that would "undermine confidence in the verdict" is considered material exculpatory evidence. *Kyles v. Whitley*, 514 U.S. 419 (1995).

Discovery that may be material for the defense may be problematic for the government to provide to the defendant. For example, in some cases the government may have concerns that providing this discovery will jeopardize the safety of their witnesses. In *Roviaro v. United States*, 353 U.S. 53 (1957), the Supreme Court examined whether the government needed to disclose the identity of undercover informants in a drug case. The Court stated, "[w]here the disclosure of an informer's identity, or of the contents of his communication, is relevant and helpful to the defense of an accused, or is essential to a fair determination of a cause, the privilege must give way. In these situations the trial court may require disclosure and, if the Government withholds the information, dismiss the action." The Court called for "balancing the public interest in protecting the flow of information against the individual's right to prepare his defense." In *Roviaro*, the Court found that the non-disclosure of the government's informant who was the "sole participant, other than the accused, in the transaction charged," was error.

Prosecutors not only have obligations to provide material exculpatory evidence, but they may also have a burden to correct discovery violations. In *Banks v. Dretke*, 540 U.S. 668 (2004), the Court held that "[w]hen police or prosecutors conceal significant exculpatory or impeaching material in the State's possession, it is ordinarily incumbent on the State to set the record straight." A key witness for the State was a paid informant but prosecutors failed to disclose this and failed to "disclose a pretrial transcript revealing that the other witness' trial testimony had been intensively coached by prosecutors and law enforcement officers."

Brady violations are sometimes the subject of civil actions brought against prosecutors. Post-conviction claims for DNA evidence can be pursued as a civil matter under 42 U.S.C. § 1983. *Skinner v. Switzer*, 131 S. Ct. 1289 (2011). A *Brady* violation, however, is insufficient for holding a district attorney's office liable under § 1983 when the claimed error is a "failure to train based on a single *Brady* violation." *Connick v. Thompson*, 131 S. Ct. 1350 (2011).

C. Impeachment Evidence

The duty to disclose evidence encompasses impeachment evidence as well as exculpatory evidence. *Giglio v. United States*, 405 U.S. 150 (1972). When the government's case depended almost entirely on a witness' testimony and the prosecutor failed to disclose that the witness would not be prosecuted if he cooperated with the government, this evidence is material irrespective of whether the individual prosecutor handling the case was aware of this promise. The credibility of this witness was important to this case so "evidence of any understanding or agreement as to a future prosecution would be relevant to his credibility and the jury was entitled to know of it."

D. Inadmissible Evidence

Evidence that may be helpful to the defense does not automatically establish a *Brady* violation just because the prosecution failed to provide it to the defense. For example, a failure to turn over polygraph results of two witnesses, despite the fact that one of the witnesses may have failed the polygraph test — something favorable to the defense — was not considered *Brady* misconduct because this evidence "could have had no direct effect on the outcome of trial." The polygraph results would have been inadmissible at trial under state law absent agreement of the parties. Therefore, the discovery deprivation did not change the trial result and was therefore not considered a *Brady* violation. *Wood v. Bartholomew*, 516 U.S. 1 (1995).

E. Pleas

The prosecutor's obligations are not as compelling when the defendant enters into a plea agreement. In *United States v. Ruiz*, 536 U.S. 622 (2002) the Court held that "impeachment [evidence] is special in relation to *a trial's fairness*, not in respect to whether a plea is *voluntary*." The Court in *Ruiz* held "that the Constitution does not require the Government to disclose material impeachment evidence prior to entering a plea agreement with a criminal defendant."

Angela Ruiz was offered a "fast track" plea agreement that would have significantly reduced her sentence on a case where immigration agents found 30 kilograms of marijuana in her luggage. The agreement specified that "any [known] information establishing the factual innocence of the defendant" "had been turned over to the defendant," and it acknowledged the Government's "continuing duty to provide such information." But the plea also required that the defendant "'waiv[e] the right' to receive 'impeachment information relating to any informants or other witnesses' as well as the right to receive information supporting any affirmative defense the defendant raises if the case goes to trial." The defendant refused this agreement, although she eventually pleaded guilty without the benefit of an agreement with the prosecutor. The government refused to recommend the sentence reduction that had been included in the agreement.

The *Ruiz* Court was concerned that if there was a constitutional requirement to provide impeachment evidence prior to the entry of a guilty plea, it "could seriously interfere with the Government's interest in securing those guilty pleas that are factually justified, desired by defendants, and help to secure the efficient administration of justice." If the government were forced to reveal this information it could mean revealing "the identities of cooperating informants, undercover investigators, or other prospective witnesses." The Court stated:

> It could require the Government to devote substantially more resources to trial preparation prior to plea bargaining, thereby depriving the plea-bargaining process of its main resource-saving advantages. Or it could lead the Government instead to abandon its heavy reliance upon plea bargaining in a vast number—90% or more—of federal criminal cases.

The Court held that the Constitution's due process requirement did not demand "so radical a change in the criminal justice process in order to achieve so comparatively small a constitutional benefit." *Ruiz* can be distinguished, however, from obligations to provide exculpatory *Brady* material prior to a defendant entering a plea.

F. Evidence Destruction

Although *Brady* requires disclosure of exculpatory evidence, there is no corresponding duty to preserve evidence. In *California v. Trombetta*, 467 U.S. 479 (1984), the Supreme Court examined two cases where the defendants were convicted of drunk driving charges. In both cases, the police used a breath-analysis (Intoxilyzer) device to check the alcohol concentration in the blood of the defendants. Both defendants scored above the legal limit allowed under California law. They argued that the State had failed to preserve the breath samples used in the test and the California Court of Appeals supported their argument and ordered a new trial without the Intoxilyzer evidence.

This decision, however, was reversed by the Supreme Court for three reasons. First the Court found that the officers had acted in "good faith and in accord with their normal practice." The Court noted that "California authorities in this case did not destroy respondents' breath samples in a calculated effort to circumvent the disclosure requirements established by *Brady v. Maryland* and its progeny." Second, even if the evidence had been preserved there was little chance that it would have exculpated the defendants. Thus, there was insufficient showing of materiality. Finally, the Court held that defendants had alternative means to demonstrate their innocence. For one, they could have tested the machine as well as the machines weekly calibration results. They also could have cross-examined the officers who performed the test to assure that it had been administered properly. Thus, the Court in *Trombetta* found no due process violation and held that there is no requirement "that law enforcement agencies preserve breath samples in order to introduce the results of breath-analysis tests at trial."

Four years later in *Arizona v. Youngblood*, 488 U.S. 51 (1988), the Court examined whether a defendant was denied due process when the police failed to preserve evidence that might have been useful to him. The defendant was charged with child molestation, sexual assault, and kidnapping, but the state "failed to preserve semen samples from the victim's body and clothing." The Court noted that the evidence could have been more useful to the defendant in his trial than the evidence destroyed in the *Trombetta* case. Despite this finding by the Court, however, the majority held that "unless a criminal defendant can show bad faith on the part of the police, failure to preserve potentially useful evidence does not constitute a denial of due process of law." The Court stated:

> We think that requiring a defendant to show bad faith on the part of the police both limits the extent of the police's obligation to preserve evidence to reasonable bounds and confines it to that class of cases where the interests of justice most clearly require it, *i.e.*, those cases in which the police themselves by their conduct indicate that the evidence could form a basis for exonerating the defendant.

Although there is no constitutional requirement to preserve evidence, states may provide statutory obligations regarding the preservation of evidence. For example, Virginia has a statute pertaining to the storage, preservation and retention of human biological evidence in felony cases that in part provides:

> [n]otwithstanding any provision of law or rule of court, upon motion of a person convicted of a felony but not sentenced to death or his attorney of record to the circuit court that entered the judgment for the offense, the court shall order the storage, preservation, and retention of specifically identified human biological evidence or representative samples collected or obtained in the case for a period of up to 15 years from the time of conviction, unless the court determines, in its discretion, that the evidence should be retained for a longer period of time.

VA. CODE ANN. § 19.2-270.4:1. In the federal system, 18 U.S.C. § 3600A(a) provides that "[n]otwithstanding any other provision of law, the Government shall preserve biological evidence that was secured in the investigation or prosecution of a Federal offense, if a defendant is under a sentence of imprisonment for such offense."

G. Witness Statements

In 1957, the Supreme Court in *Jencks v. United States*, 353 U.S. 657 (1957), held that the defendant who is on trial in a federal criminal prosecution is entitled, for impeachment purposes, to relevant and competent statements of a government witness that are in possession of the government if the evidence pertains to the activities that the witness has testified about during the trial. Jencks was indicted for violating the false statement statute for allegations that he falsely swore in an affidavit that he was not "a member of the Communist Party or affiliated with such Party." Two paid government witnesses testified against him at trial without first allowing the defendant the right to inspect and use the government statements for cross-examination. The Supreme Court reversed the conviction, holding that a "preliminary foundation of inconsistency" was not necessary because the two witnesses provided a "sufficient foundation" that their reports were of the events and activities related in their testimony.

There was significant concern after the *Jencks* decision because it failed to provide when such statements needed to be provided to the defense. Obviously, the government was concerned about the safety of its witnesses and what effect disclosure of their statements would have on these witnesses.

Congress almost immediately passed 18 U.S.C. § 3500, known as the Jencks Act, that provided that witness statements would not be the "subject of subpoena, discovery, or inspection until said witness has testified on direct examination in the trial of the case." Federal Rule of Criminal Procedure 26.2 reaffirmed the necessity to turn witness statements over only after the witness had testified. It provided that both the prosecution and defense had this discovery obligation. In reality, most federal prosecutors provide *Jencks* material in advance of when it is necessitated by statute and rule. For example, some jurisdictions will provide this material ten days before trial, others three days, and others the evening before the witness testifies. The benefit of providing it in advance is that it will alleviate the need for a continuance to be granted for the party to review the prior witness statements.

Questions have arisen as to what gets provided pursuant to Rule 26.2. In this regard "statement" is defined in this Rule to include written statements adopted or approved by the witness, "a substantially verbatim, contemporaneously recorded recital of the witness's oral statement that is contained in any recording or any transcription of a recording," or witness statements to a grand jury. The Rule's requirement to produce statements within the attorney's "possession" has been given a broad definition to include statements held by government attorneys other than the ones handling the case, and also any agents of the office. It has even been extended to statements held by local police and nonfederal investigators when there is a joint federal-state investigation.

H. Ethical Obligations

Brady obligations for prosecutors are replicated in the *ABA Model Rules of Professional Conduct*. Rule 3.8 provides that prosecutors in a criminal case shall "make timely disclosure to the defense of all evidence or information known to the prosecutor that tends to negate the guilt of the accused or mitigates the offense, and, in connection with sentencing, disclose to the defense and to the tribunal all unprivileged mitigating information known to the prosecutor, except when the prosecutor is relieved of this responsibility by a protective order of the tribunal."

III. Statutory and Rule Obligations

Typically states have statutes or court rules that control the method, timing, and specifics of discovery. In the federal system there are both statutes and court rules that may apply to discovery production, such as previously seen with the Jencks Act and later Federal Rule of Criminal Procedure 26.2. Another example is Federal Rule of Criminal Procedure 15, which provides that depositions may be taken in "exceptional circumstances." Federal courts also permit the taking of depositions "in the interest of justice." States may also allow for depositions in criminal cases. For example, in Nebraska both the prosecutor and defense counsel can request the taking of a deposition in felony and certain misdemeanor cases. Absent the witness being the defendant, the court can order the taking of the deposition "when it finds the testimony of the witness" to "be material or relevant" or "of assistance to the parties in the preparation of their respective cases." NEB. REV. ST. § 29-1917.

A key discovery rule in the federal system is found in Federal Rule of Criminal Procedure, Rule 16. This Rule provides specifics on government and defense discovery obligations. Oftentimes, the defense needs to request the discovery to make government production mandatory. Thus, upon defendant's request, the government must disclose defendant's oral statements, written or recorded statements, prior record, and the government needs to permit the defendant:

> to inspect and to copy or photograph books, papers, documents, data, photographs, tangible objects, buildings or places, or copies or portions of any of these items, if the item is within the government's possession, custody, or control and: 1) the item is material to preparing the defense; 2) the government intends to use the item in its case-in-chief at trial; or 3) the items was obtained from or belongs to the defendant.

There are also requirements for reports of examinations and tests and expert witnesses to be turned over. Rule 16 does not authorize discovery of attorney-client material or work-product items of the prosecution. It also does not include grand jury proceedings as discoverable, except as allowed by other rules, such as Rule 6(e). Rule 16 also includes the discovery obligations of the defense. These are usually triggered when the defense has requested some discovery from the government.

Rule 16 provides for continuing discovery obligations and also provides the available remedies for non-compliance. These include specific orders to comply with the discovery request, continuances, prohibition from introduction of the undisclosed evidence, and other orders that the court determines are just under the circumstances.

In *Taylor v. Illinois*, 484 U.S. 400 (1988), the defense was precluded from presenting a witness due to a failure to comply with a pretrial discovery request. The Court held that a sanction of refusing to allow the witness to testify was "not absolutely prohibited by the Compulsory Process Clause of the Sixth Amendment." The Court found no constitutional violation based on the specific facts of this case. The Court stated, "[m]ore is at stake than possible prejudice to the prosecution. We are also concerned with the impact of this kind of conduct on the integrity of the judicial process itself. The trial judge found that the discovery violation in this case was both willful and blatant."

A strong dissent by Justice Brennan stated:

> Criminal discovery is not a game. It is integral to the quest for truth and the fair adjudication of guilt or innocence. Violations of discovery rules thus cannot go uncorrected or undeterred without undermining the truthseeking process. The question in this case, however, is not whether discovery rules should be enforced but whether the need to correct and deter discovery violations requires a sanction that itself distorts the truthseeking process by excluding material evidence of innocence in a criminal case.

A failure to receive discovery is not the only problem faced by defense counsel. There can also be a problem when too much discovery is received. With increased computerization and document cases in the white collar area, defense counsel can be faced with receiving a warehouse full of evidence. In such cases, requests can be made for the material to be provided in a searchable format or for specific items to be identified.

IV. Reciprocal Discovery

The government has no constitutional right to receive discovery from the defense. There are federal and state statutes and rules that call for reciprocal discovery, that includes discovery from the defense to the prosecution. Discovery from the defense is limited by the Constitution, usually the self-incrimination provisions that cannot compel a defendant to testify against him or herself. Additionally, because the prosecution has the burden of proof in a case, the defense may be uncertain of what, if any, defense will be provided until after the prosecution has met its burden.

One area that has generated a strong disclosure obligation imposed on the defense is with respect to alibi notices. A defendant who intends to present an alibi defense may be required by statute to give notice to the prosecution of that intent and provide details concerning the witnesses who will testify as to the whereabouts of the defendant at the time of the crime.

In *Williams v. Florida*, 399 U.S. 78 (1970), the Court looked at two issues, a Sixth Amendment jury issue and whether the Florida alibi-notice statute deprived the defendant of his constitutional right not to incriminate himself. Williams filed a pre-trial motion for a protective order asking to be excused from filing an alibi notice in advance of trial that would furnish the prosecuting attorney with information "as to the place where he claims to have been and with the names and addresses of the alibi witnesses he intends to use." The Court denied this motion that was premised upon his Fifth and Fourteenth Amendment rights under the Constitution.

After his subsequent conviction and life sentence, the Court noted that Florida's alibi statute was reciprocal with continuing duties for both the prosecution and defense. The Court said, "[t]he threatened sanction for failure to comply is the exclusion at trial of the defendant's alibi evidence — except for his own testimony — or, in the case of the State, the exclusion of the State's evidence offered in rebuttal of the alibi." The Court did not accept the defense's argument, stating that "the notice-of-alibi rule by itself in no way affected [defendant's] crucial decision to call alibi witnesses or added to the legitimate pressures leading to that course of action." The only real effect here was that it accelerated when the defense would need to disclose this information. The Court declined to hold that the "privilege against compulsory self-incrimination guarantees the defendant the right to surprise the State with an alibi defense."

Chief Justice Burger, concurring in the opinion, noted how a notice-of-alibi could lead to dispositions of cases when the prosecutor re-examines their evidence in light of an alibi notice and decides to perhaps dismiss the case. It could also lead to expedited plea agreements as each side re-examines their case in light of this discovery.

Justice Black, joined by Justice Douglas, issued a sharp dissent to the Court's ruling on allowing the notice-of-alibi. The notice-of-alibi rule is a constitutional violation "because it requires a defendant to disclose information to the State so that the State can use that information to destroy him." The dissenting justices stated:

> The defendant, under our Constitution, need not do anything at all to defend himself, and certainly he cannot be required to help convict himself. Rather he has an absolute, unqualified right to compel the State to investigate its own case, find its own witnesses, prove its own facts, and convince the jury through its own resources. Throughout the process the defendant has a fundamental right to remain silent, in effect challenging the State at every point to: 'Prove it!'

Three years later, the Supreme Court decided *Wardius v. Oregon*, 412 U.S. 470 (1973), resolving the unanswered question from *Williams* of the enforceability of an alibi notice when the State does not require reciprocal discovery. The Court held that "the Due Process Clause of the Fourteenth Amendment forbids enforcement of alibi rules unless reciprocal discovery rights are given to criminal defendants." The defendant's conviction was reversed because the Oregon statute failed to provide for reciprocal discovery.

Federal Rule of Criminal Procedure 12.1 provides the rules regarding notice of alibi in the federal system. The government can request that the defendant notify of an intended alibi defense. But "[t]he request must state the time, date, and place of the alleged offense." The defendant has 14 days to respond to this request, and the defendant's notice has to include "each specific place where the defendant claims to have been at the time of the alleged offense; and the name, address, and telephone number of each alibi witness on whom the defendant intends to rely." The government then has an obligation to respond to this information with certain other information. The Rule provides for continuing disclosure duties when new information is learned by either party. Courts, however, can make exceptions, and the Rule also provides that a failure to comply with the disclosure requirements can result in the exclusion of the testimony.

There are also other specific reciprocal discovery and notice obligations targeted to the defense. For example, under Federal Rule of Criminal Procedure 12.2, there is a requirement for the defense to file a notice telling of its intent to present an insanity defense at trial. There is also a requirement under Federal Rule of Criminal Procedure 12.3 that if "a defendant intends to assert a defense of actual or believed exercise of public authority on behalf of a law enforcement agency or federal intelligence agency at the time of the alleged offense, the defendant must so notify an attorney for the government."

Checkpoints

- Discovery is important to assure the defendant a fair trial.
- Due process requires prosecutors to provide the defense with exculpatory material evidence as to guilt or punishment.
- A defendant does not need to make a specific request for exculpatory discovery evidence that is material.
- Evidence is material if there is a reasonable probability that it would have changed the outcome of the case.
- Materiality is examined collectively, not item by item.
- A prejudicial failure to disclose material exculpatory evidence to the defendant is a violation of the Constitution's Due Process Clause.
- A prosecutor is not required to provide his or her entire file to the defense counsel, but only to disclose evidence favorable to the accused that if suppressed would deprive the defendant of a fair trial.
- Informant evidence requires balancing the public interest in protecting the flow of information against the individual's right to prepare his or her defense.
- Prosecutors have the burden to correct discovery violations.
- The duty to disclose evidence encompasses impeachment evidence as well as exculpatory evidence.
- There is no duty to disclose evidence that would be inadmissible at trial.
- Discovery obligations may not be as stringent when a defendant pleads guilty.
- Absent a statute requiring the preservation of evidence, there is no constitutional requirement to do so.
- In the federal system, witness statements need to be provided to counsel to allow for impeachment on cross-examination.
- Ethics rules require prosecutors to provide exculpatory evidence to the defense.
- Statutes or rules may require reciprocal discovery, such as the requirement to provide notice-of-alibi.
- A failure to comply with a discovery order can result in several possible remedies, including a court precluding a witness who had not been revealed from testifying.

Chapter 9

The Plea Bargaining Process

Roadmap

- What is a plea agreement
- Rationale for plea agreements
- Types of pleas
- Victims' rights
- Requirements for entering a guilty plea
- Constitutional rights waived on entry of a guilty plea
- Voluntary and intelligent waiver of rights
- Effective assistance of counsel in waiving constitutional rights
- The process of entering a plea
- Discovery rights for pleas
- Contract law applied to plea agreements
- Withdrawal of a plea

I. Introduction

A. Benefits of Plea Agreements

In a high percentage of criminal cases, approximately 95% in the federal system, the prosecution and defense reach an agreement in which the defendant will enter a plea of guilty and usually receive the benefit of reduced charges or a recommendation for a lesser sentence. There are strong advantages to both sides to proceed with a plea agreement.

For the prosecutor, the plea offers finality to the process. It also provides efficiency in having cases quickly processed in the system. Limited financial resources often preclude prosecutors from trying all of their cases. It would also be unmanageable to the court system if prosecutors went to trial on every criminal case charged. In addition to having a quicker resolution of criminal cases, a plea eliminates the risk of a lesser result at trial, or an acquittal. Prosecutors may also use the plea bargaining process to offer a defendant reduced charges or a lower sentence in return for cooperation in providing testimony or evidence against accomplices or others who have been charged criminally or might be in the future.

For the defense there are additional advantages to a plea agreement. Pleas often mean the prosecutor will dismiss some of the pending charges, or prospective charges might not be brought. It can also entail a recommendation to the court that the defendant receive a reduced sentence. The agreement eliminates the risk of an unknown result, such as a guilty finding on all counts, which might occur if the defendant goes to trial. Assuring certainty in the result and a lower sentence are the most common reasons for a defendant to want to enter a plea of guilty through a plea agreement. For example, in the federal system a defendant can receive a downward sentencing adjustment for acceptance of responsibility. There can, however, be other motivations, such as an assurance that other family members will not be indicted. It is controversial whether this practice of offering pleas that avoid charging family members should be used by prosecutors.

B. Constitutional Validity of Pleas

Plea bargaining has both constitutional and oftentimes statutory constraints. Changing a "not guilty" plea to a plea of "guilty" requires the accused to waive certain rights and also requires an acknowledgment of committing the crime. In *Brady v. United States*, 397 U.S. 742 (1970), the Court recognized pleas as an acceptable route for resolving cases. The defendant, facing a possible death sentence, elected to change his plea to guilty. His change of plea came after becoming aware that his co-defendant, who had plead guilty, was going to testify against him at his trial. Hearing this, he decided not to go to trial and to enter a guilty plea. When he subsequently challenged the plea because of a change in the law that prohibited imposing a death sentence for the offense he was charged with, the Court held that "[t]he voluntariness of Brady's plea can be determined only by considering all of the relevant circumstances surrounding it." In this case, the defendant faced the possibility of a heavier sentence if he went to trial. Entering a guilty plea merely "to avoid the possibility of a death penalty" does not render a plea invalid. The Court noted:

> We find no requirement in the Constitution that a defendant must be permitted to disown his solemn admissions in open court that he committed the act with which he is charged simply because it later devel-

ops that the State would have had a weaker case than the defendant had thought or that the maximum penalty then assumed applicable has been held inapplicable in subsequent judicial decisions.

In *Brady* the Court recognized that the defendant's plea may have been entered to avoid the possibility of a death sentence. But as long as the plea was truthful and was "voluntarily and intelligently" made, it would be held acceptable. The Court found that "[w]aivers of constitutional rights not only must be voluntary but must be knowing, intelligent acts done with sufficient awareness of the relevant circumstances and likely consequences."

C. Types of Pleas

Defendants usually enter either a plea of guilty, with or without a plea agreement, or not guilty. In some instances, the defendant may enter a plea of "*nolo contendere,*" often referred to as a plea of "no contest." This plea has the result of a court entering a guilty finding without the defendant affirmatively admitting to the conduct. A defendant might enter such a plea when he or she does not want to go to trial but also does not want the admission of guilt on the record. In some cases, entering a plea of *nolo contendere* is done to protect the defendant from having an admission that might be used in a collateral civil action, such as when a defendant has a traffic ticket that resulted from an accident that caused injury to individuals. The defendant might not want to go to trial on the traffic violation, yet may also not want a guilty admission to be used against him or her in a later civil action resulting from the accident. For those jurisdictions that allow for a *nolo contendere* plea, it allows the court to make the finding of guilt with the defendant accepting this finding, but not admitting to the criminal act.

It is also possible to have conditional pleas, deferred prosecutions, or agreements for non-prosecutions. With conditional pleas, the defendant enters a plea of guilty but reserves the right to raise an issue or several points on appeal and if successful in the appeal then the guilty plea will be discarded. This scenario often arises when a defendant wishes to preserve an issue for appeal, but if the ruling on that issue were negative, he or she does not want to proceed to trial.

With a "deferred prosecution agreement," a court withholds entering a conviction while the defendant performs certain activities, such as community service, or a period of time passes without the defendant engaging in additional criminal conduct. For example, a defendant may enter a plea of guilty, but the court might hold it without entering it on the record for three years and if the defendant has no criminal activity during that time, the court or prosecutor would then dismiss the original charges. This process is often used in the juvenile context when there is a desire to excuse youthful conduct. It allows the court to have a possible criminal conviction hanging over the head of the defendant, while also protecting him or her from having a criminal record that could hurt the youthful offender later in life.

Deferred prosecution agreements have recently been used in the corporate criminal context. Corporations agree to certain terms and conditions such as providing discovery to prosecutors as to who in the corporation was committing the criminal acts or agreeing to have a monitor oversee compliance operations in the corporation. The corporation will usually also pay a civil fine. The benefit of a deferred prosecution agreement to the defendant is that it does not receive the consequences of having a criminal conviction entered against the corporation unless it fails to abide by the terms within the agreement.

Non-prosecution agreements, in contrast, are agreements prior to the filing of the charges that outline an agreement to engage in certain conduct, such as a corporation hiring an independent monitor to oversee activities in the organization in order to assure that criminal conduct does not continue to occur. With a non-prosecution agreement, there is no filing of criminal charges if the defendant abides by the terms of the agreement. Because no charges are filed, the agreement is usually processed without court intervention.

D. Victim's Rights

Victim participation in the plea bargaining process has increased with states passing statutes that require a prosecutor to consult with victims either during the plea process or prior to offering or accepting an agreement. For example, in Mississippi, a "victim has the right to be present at any proceeding at which a negotiated plea for the person accused of committing the criminal offense against the victim will be presented to the court." MISS. CODE ANN. § 99-43-27.

Mississippi statutes also provide that a court cannot accept a plea agreement unless the prosecutor assures the court that "reasonable efforts were made to confer with the victim," and "reasonable efforts were made to give the victim notice of the plea proceeding, including the offense to which the defendant will plead guilty, the date that the plea will be presented to the court, the terms of any sentence agreed to as part of the negotiated plea, and that the victim has the right to be present." MISS. CODE ANN. § 99-43-27. In some instances there have been state constitutional amendments to provide victim rights. For example, in Indiana, a 1996 state constitutional amendment provided that "[v]ictims of crime, as defined by law, shall have the right to be treated with fairness, dignity, and respect throughout the criminal justice process; and, ..., to be informed of and present during public hearings and to confer with the prosecution, to the extent that exercising these rights does not infringe upon the constitutional rights of the accused." IND. CONST. ART. 1, § 13.

Crime victims' rights are also found in the federal system. For example, 18 U.S.C. § 3771(a)(4) allows victims to be heard at public proceedings "involving release, plea, sentencing, or any parole proceeding." Federal Rule of Criminal Procedure 60 also provides for victim's rights, including the right to be heard on release, a plea, or sentencing.

II. The Process

A. Constitutional Requirements

1. *Waiving Rights*—Boykin v. Alabama

A requisite of a constitutionally valid plea agreement is that the defendant knowingly waives certain rights. The landmark Supreme Court decision of *Boykin v. Alabama*, 395 U.S. 238 (1969), outlines the constitutional requirements for a plea. In *Boykin*, the defendant pled guilty at his arraignment to five indictments alleging robbery. The trial court did not ask the defendant any questions pertaining to this plea, but pursuant to Alabama law had the jury hear the case for purposes of setting punishment. When instructing the jury, the judge told them the defendant pleaded guilty to five instances of robbery, and the jury then returned a sentence of death for the defendant. Although the defense raised the issue of whether a sentence of death was cruel and unusual punishment for a crime of robbery, the Alabama Supreme Court, on its own initiative, decided to look at the plea bargaining process used in this case. In a split decision, the Alabama Supreme Court affirmed the lower court's decision.

The Supreme Court in *Boykin* decided to use the analysis for Sixth Amendment right to counsel cases as its analogy for what should be required for a valid plea agreement. Just as "[t]he record must show, or there must be an allegation and evidence which show, that an accused was offered counsel but intelligently and understandingly rejected the offer" to have a proper waiver for a plea, it needs to be determined "whether a guilty plea is voluntarily made." The Court stated that you cannot assume a waiver of three important rights on a silent record. These rights are: 1) "the privilege against compulsory self-incrimination guaranteed by the Fifth Amendment and applicable to the States by reason of the Fourteenth" Amendment; 2) "the right to trial by jury" and 3) "the right to confront one's accusers." The Court reversed the convictions in *Boykin* because the record did not disclose "that the defendant voluntarily and understandingly entered his pleas of guilty." From the *Boykin* case one understands that for a valid plea it is necessary to have a record showing that the defendant voluntarily and understandingly waivered his or her constitutional rights.

What happens when a court uses a prior conviction that was obtained pursuant to a plea agreement to increase a defendant's sentence for the current offense? Although *Boykin* required a record showing a valid waiver of rights, states may shift the burden from the prosecution to the defendant to prove an impropriety of a plea when the prior guilty finding is being used as part of a recidivist enhancement. In this context, the government does not have the exclusive burden to prove that there has been adherence to *Boykin*. In *Parke v. Raley*, 506 U.S. 20 (1992), the Supreme Court held that in the circumstances of using a prior guilty plea conviction for purposes of increasing the sentence of a defendant on a new charge, there is a "presumption of regularity" for the prior plea hearings, thus a presumption that the plea was entered correctly. Thus, in *Parke v. Raley,* the Court found that a Kentucky burden-shifting rule did not violate due process when a recidivist defendant had the burden of production when claiming a *Boykin* violation occurred in prior guilty pleas.

A defendant also does not lose Fifth Amendment Self-Incrimination rights at sentencing just by pleading guilty. Not only does a plea not affect a defendant's right against self-incrimination, but a court cannot draw an adverse inference from the defendant's silence at the sentencing hearing that is using the plea. *Mitchell v. United States*, 526 U.S. 314 (1999).

2. Voluntariness

Cases after *Boykin* have examined what constitutes a voluntary waiver of rights. One component to a voluntary waiver is that the accused be made aware of charges against him or her. In *Henderson v. Morgan*, 426 U.S. 637 (1976), the Supreme Court examined "whether a defendant may enter a voluntary plea of guilty to a charge of second-degree murder without being informed that intent to cause the death of his victim was an element of the offense." In this case, the defendant had been charged with first-degree murder. Although he was found competent to stand trial, the Court noted his low intelligence level. The defendant entered a plea to second-degree murder and at the plea colloquy he acknowledged that he was accused of killing the victim in this case and that he was waiving his right to jury trial. There was no discussion, however, that he understood for such a plea he needed to have intended to cause the death of the victim. At sentencing, the defendant stated that he "meant no harm" to the deceased. Despite this statement, the trial court accepted the plea. The Supreme Court rejected this being a voluntary plea, finding that the defendant "did not receive adequate notice of the offense to which he pleaded guilty." The Court, therefore, affirmed the lower court finding that the "conviction was entered without due process of law."

It is also necessary that the accused be competent. A plea entered by a defendant who does not understand the charges against him or her, is not viable as it is not made in a voluntary and intelligent manner.

3. Ineffective Assistance of Counsel

Voluntariness requires that the accused have effective assistance of counsel. In assessing whether counsel was competent, courts use the test enunciated in *Strickland v. Washington* (See Chapter 7). In assessing counsel's advice with respect to a plea, courts look at whether counsel's advice "was within the range of competence demanded of attorneys in criminal cases." *McMann v. Richardson*, 397 U.S. 759 (1970). In *Hill v. Lockhart*, 474 U.S. 52 (1985), the defendant pled guilty to first-degree murder and theft of property. He argued that his court-appointed attorney had not advised "him that as a second offender, he was required to serve one-half of his sentence before becoming eligible for parole." Writing for the Court's majority, Justice Rehnquist used the *Strickland* test and found that the defendant had failed to show "prejudice" that would meet this test. In *Burt v. Titlow*, 134 S. Ct. 10 (2013), the Court held that "[w]hen a state prisoner asks a federal court to set aside a sentence due to ineffective assistance of counsel during plea bargaining, ... the federal court uses[s] a 'doubly deferential' standard of review that gives both the state court and the defense attorney the benefit of the doubt."

Effective assistance of counsel requires that defense counsel communicate a prosecutor's written plea offer, prior to the offer expiring. In *Missouri v. Frye*, 132 S. Ct. 1399 (2012), the Court noted that "ninety seven percent of federal convictions and ninety-four percent of state convictions are the result of guilty pleas." As such, "criminal defendants require effective counsel during plea negotiations." Frye had been charged with driving with a revoked license and had been convicted for this offense on three prior occasions, which made this a felony case in Missouri. The prosecutor offered two possible pleas, one of which would have reduced the charged to a misdemeanor. The plea offer had a time limit within which the defendant could accept one of them. The defendant eventually pleaded guilty, and on a post-conviction motion he argued that he had not received the offers from his defense counsel.

The Court in *Frye* noted that "[a]s a general rule, defense counsel has the duty to communicate formal offers from the prosecution to accept a plea on terms and conditions that may be favorable to the accused." When there is a failure to convey a plea offer, the court needs to determine if there has been prejudice. In *Missouri v. Frye*, the Court remanded to the state court to determine if there was prejudice. The Court stated that "if Frye fails to show a reasonable probability the prosecutor would have adhered to the agreement, there is no *Strickland* prejudice. Likewise, if the trial court could have refused to accept the plea agreement, and if Frye fails to show a reasonable probability the trial court would have accepted the plea, there is no *Strickland* prejudice." In the *Frye* case the Court noted that Frye had a new offense for driving without a license so "there was reason to doubt that the prosecution would have adhered to the agreement or that the trial court would have accepted it." In *Padilla v. Kentucky*, 559 U.S. 356 (2010), the Supreme Court considered whether there was a denial of effective assistance of counsel when the defendant's attorney told him not to worry about his immigration status in pleading guilty to "drug charges that made his deportation virtually mandatory." In this case, Justice Stevens stated that "constitutionally competent counsel would have advised him" that this drug conviction could result in deportation. The Court did, however, remand the case to determine if there was prejudice to the defendant. The Court in *Chaidez v. United States*, 133 S. Ct. 1103 (2013) ruled that *Padilla* does not apply retroactively.

The remedy when there has been a finding of ineffective assistance on a plea is to have the prosecutor reoffer the plea agreement. If the defendant accepts the plea, the "state trial court can then exercise its discretion in determining whether to vacate the convictions and resentence [the defendant] pursuant to the plea agreement, to vacate only some of the convictions and resentence [the defendant] accordingly, or to leave the convictions and sentence from trial undisturbed." *Lafler v. Cooper*, 132 S. Ct. 1376 (2012).

Although there is a requirement for effective assistance of counsel at a plea hearing–a critical stage of the trial–a defendant can waive counsel. *Iowa v. Tovar*, 541 U.S. 77 (2004). This requires that the defendant be warned of the dangers of proceeding without counsel and a determination that the accused knowingly and intelligently waived his or her right to counsel.

4. Discovery

Although there is no constitutional requirement that the accused receive exculpatory material prior to pleading guilty, it is imperative that a prosecutor provide exculpatory evidence to the accused in a timely manner. There is also an ethical rule for attorneys that mandates that, absent a court order relieving the prosecutor of the obligation, the prosecutor needs to make "timely disclosure to the defense of all evidence or information known to the prosecutor that tends to negate the guilt of the accused or mitigates the offense, and, in connection with sentencing, disclose to the defense and to the tribunal all unprivileged mitigating information known to the prosecutor." ABA MODEL RULES OF PROFESSIONAL CONDUCT, RULE 3.8.

In *United States v. Ruiz*, 536 U.S. 622 (2002) the Court held that receipt of impeachment evidence goes to the "fairness of a trial," and not to the voluntariness of a plea. (See Chapter 8). As such, plea agreements may be upheld when the defendant fails to receive impeachment evidence prior to entering his or her guilty plea.

5. Induced Pleas

Courts have needed to resolve situations when prosecutors have threatened increased charges if a defendant fails to accept a plea agreement or enter a plea to the existing charges (see Chapter 3). In *Bordenkircher v. Hayes*, 434 U.S. 357 (1978), the Court examined a situation where the prosecutor had offered the defendant a recommended five year sentence and said that if the defendant failed to plead guilty "he would return to the grand jury to seek an indictment under the Kentucky Habitual Criminal Act," which would mean that the defendant would be facing charges with a possible sentence of life imprisonment. The defendant rejected the plea opportunity and the prosecutor moved forward with the threat by increasing the charges. The defendant was found guilty after a jury trial and sentenced to life imprisonment. The Supreme Court started by noting that the prosecutor stated the intent to bring the greater charge at the beginning of the plea negotiations, making this scenario no different than if the grand jury had indicted the defendant at the outset with the greater recidivist charge.

The Supreme Court reversed the appellate court's finding of prosecutorial vindictiveness. The Court found that these facts were distinguishable from those in its prior decision in *Blackledge v. Perry*, 417 U.S. 21 (1974), where it held that it was improper for a prosecutor to increase charges when a defendant invoked appellate rights. The Court in *Bordenkircher v. Hayes* stated that "[w]hile confronting a defendant with the risk of more severe punishment clearly may have a 'discouraging effect on the defendant's assertion of his trial rights, the imposition of these difficult choices [is] an inevitable'—and permissible—'attribute of any legitimate system which tolerates and encourages the negotiation of pleas.'"

Two separate dissents were written in this case. In the first, by Justice Blackmun and joined by Justices Brennan and Marshall, the dissenting justices cited to the Court's decision in *North Carolina v. Pearce*, 395 U.S. 711 (1969) which held that "vindictiveness against a defendant for having successfully attacked his first conviction must play no part in the sentence he receives after a new trial." This dissenting opinion expressed the view that there is "little difference between vindictiveness" after a conviction and "vindictiveness in the 'give-and-take negotiation common in plea bargaining.'" Also dissenting was Justice Powell who stated that "[i]n this case, the prosecutor's actions denied [the defendant] due process because their admitted purpose was to discourage and then to penalize with unique severity his exercise of constitutional rights."

6. Admission of Facts

There is no constitutional requirement that the defendant admit to facts for acceptance of a plea. There is a need, however, for a factual basis for the plea.

Some jurisdictions allow for an "*Alford* plea" when the defendant is pleading guilty to the charge, but is not admitting the underlying facts that form the crime. In *North Carolina v. Alford*, 400 U.S. 25 (1970), the Court held that "[a]n individual accused of [a] crime may voluntarily, knowingly, and understandingly consent to the imposition of a prison sentence even if he is unwilling or unable to admit his participation in the acts constituting the crime." Justice White, writing for the Court in *Alford*, noted that there is no "material difference between a plea that refuses to admit commission of the criminal act and a plea containing a protestation of innocence when [] a defendant intelligently concludes that his interests require entry of a guilty plea and the record before the judge contains strong evidence of actual guilt."

There are two qualifications to a court accepting an *Alford* plea: first, that a factual basis is provided for the plea; and second, that there must be strong evidence of guilt against the defendant. In Alford's case, the evidence was strong and he had pled guilty to avoid a death sentence. This was considered to be a valid plea.

B. Rule 11

Federal Rule of Criminal Procedure 11 provides the plea process in the federal system. It allows for pleas of not guilty, guilty, and with the court's consent *nolo cotendere*. Before accepting a *nolo contendere* plea a "court must consider the parties' views and the public interest in the effective administration of justice." It also allows for a conditional plea so that a defendant can present an issue that he or she had an adverse determination of in a pretrial motion, to an appellate tribunal. When a defendant remains silent and fails to enter a plea, the court is instructed to enter a plea of not guilty.

As previously noted, a high percentage of cases are resolved via a plea agreement. These agreements are between the prosecution and defense without judge participation. When a judge participates in a plea negotiation in violation of Federal Rule of Criminal Procedure 11(c)(1), that instructs that "the court must not participate in [plea] discussion," it is considered "harmless error if it does not affect substantial rights." *United States v. Davila*, 133 S. Ct. 2139 (2013). Absent good cause, pleas are presented in open court and include a specification as to the benefits that the defendant will receive and the obligation of the government under the agreement. For example, the agreement may provide for a plea to Count I, with a dismissal of Counts II and III, and include a recommendation of a specific sentencing range. Under some provisions of Rule 11(c)(3)(B) "the defendant has no right to withdraw the plea if the court does not follow the recommendation or request," and the court is bound to notify the defendant of this possibility. Other agreements may bind the judge. A judge that rejects such a plea must notify the parties, advise the defendant that he or she is not required to follow the plea, and provide an opportunity for the accused to withdraw the plea. The court also needs to "advise the defendant personally that if the plea is not withdrawn, the court may dispose of the case less favorably toward the defendant than the plea agreement contemplated." Plea agreement proceedings need to "be recorded by a court reporter or by a suitable recording device."

Prior to accepting a plea there is colloquy between the court and the defendant in open court that assures that the defendant is waiving his or her rights knowingly and voluntarily. The judge needs to make certain that the plea "did not result from force, threats, or promises (other than promises in a plea agreement)." Prior to accepting the defendant's plea, the judge needs to address fourteen items that the defendant is waiving. These are:

1) Statements given by the defendant under oath can be used against the defendant in a perjury or false statement prosecution;
2) The right to plead not guilty;
3) The right to a jury trial;
4) The right to counsel;
5) The right not to incriminate oneself and the right to compulsory process;
6) Waiver of rights on acceptance of plea;
7) Nature of the charges against the defendant;
8) The maximum penalty;
9) Any mandatory minimum penalty that applies;
10) Any applicable forfeiture;
11) Court's authority to order restitution;
12) Court's obligation to impose a special assessment;

13) Court's obligation to calculate under the sentencing guidelines and to sentence using sentencing factors under section 3553(a); and
14) Waiver of appellate rights and collateral attacks;
15) That, if convicted, a defendant who is not a United States citizen may be removed from the United States, denied citizenship, and denied admission to the United States in the future.

The court also needs to determine the factual basis for the plea. Although it is required that the court determine if there is any applicable forfeiture, a factual basis for the plea does not necessitate that the court delve into the factual basis for the stipulated forfeiture of assets that the parties may have agreed to as part of the plea agreement. *Libretti v. United States*, 516 U.S. 29 (1995).

One issue that sometimes arises is whether the plea negotiation can be used later as evidence against the defendant, or alternatively, as what sentence the prosecutor might have been offering to the defendant. Rule 11 references the Federal Rules of Evidence, Rule 410, as to the admissibility or inadmissibility of pleas and plea discussions. The Supreme Court in *United States v. Mezzanatto*, 513 U.S. 196 (1995), held that the defendant can waive the plea-statement Rules. The Court stated that "there is no reason to believe that allowing negotiation as to waiver of the plea-statement Rules will bring plea bargaining to a grinding halt; it may well have the opposite effect."

Rule 11 covers other important matters. For example, it provides for the withdrawal of pleas. This rule also accounts for situations when there is not strict compliance with the rule's provisions. Absent it affecting substantial rights, a variance from the mandates of the rule will be harmless error. A defendant has an obligation to object when he or she thinks there is a Rule 11 error, and a failure to do so requires the defendant to then show a plain error to obtain relief from the plea entered. *United States v. Vonn*, 535 U.S. 55 (2002).

III. Broken Promises

Contract law controls how to resolve issues that arise when one party fails to abide by the plea agreement reached by the parties. Yet contract law is modified to fit the criminal law context. For example, normally in contract law there are two parties reaching an agreement. In the criminal setting, a judge plays a role in accepting or rejecting the agreement and in providing oversight to the process. Likewise, the defendant's constitutional rights can override a contractual obligation. So too, the government's power is far greater than the defendant's in the negotiation of a plea agreement.

The landmark decision for use of contract principles with plea agreements is found in the case of *Santobello v. New York*, 404 U.S. 257 (1971). In *Santobello*, the state had agreed to make no sentencing recommendation on a plea to gambling crimes. The issue before the Supreme Court was "whether the State's failure to keep a commitment concerning the sentence recommendation on a guilty plea required a new trial." The Court said that whether "the breach of agreement was inadvertent does not lessen its impact." "[S]taff lawyers in a prosecutor's office have the burden of 'letting the left hand know what the right hand is doing' or has done." This point was emphasized by Justice Douglas in his concurrence when he stated, "[t]he staff of the prosecution is a unit and each member must be presumed to know the commitments made by any other member."

The Court valued promises and agreements reached by the parties and said those agreements needed to be fulfilled. As such, the judgment entered by the trial court was vacated and the case was remanded to the state court. In his concurrence, Justice Douglas wrote that in "choosing a remedy, [] a court ought to accord a defendant's preference considerable, if not controlling, weight...."

Santobello set the groundwork for court's using contract law to consider breaches and interpretations of plea agreements. Cases have included using contract law to modify the agreement, to determine whether there has been substantial performance, and even using the parol evidence rule in contract law when a party adds an oral promise to a written agreement. The parol evidence rule precludes the use of extrinsic evidence that goes beyond the walls of the contract.

In some cases, courts look to interpret the plea agreement to determine if the prosecution has defaulted in its promises. In *United States v. Benchimol*, 471 U.S. 453 (1985), the Supreme Court examined whether prosecutors defaulted on a plea when the prosecutor failed to explain the reasons for the plea and failed to endorse it "enthusiastically." The defendant agreed to plead guilty and the plea called for the government to recommend probation with restitution. Although the government corrected at sentencing a probation report that stated that the government would stand silent, the prosecutor failed to explain the reasons for the lenient sentence. The Supreme Court held that the prosecutor had not defaulted on the agreement as one cannot imply as a matter of law that prosecutors need to explain the reasons for the sentencing recommendation in the plea agreement.

When the prosecution breaches a plea agreement, it is necessary for defense counsel to object. A failure to properly preserve the error may subject the defendant to "plain error" review. Puckett v. United States, 556 U.S. 129 (2009).

Applying contract law to plea agreements is not exclusive to promises alleged to be broken by the prosecution. Courts have also had to resolve plea agreement breaches by the defense. In *Ricketts v. Adamson*, 483 U.S. 1 (1987), the Supreme Court was faced with the issue of whether a defendant could be prosecuted for first-degree murder after he breached a plea agreement that provided for a lesser offense. In this case he had not only pleaded guilty to the lesser offense, but had been sentenced and had started serving that sentence. The defendant, as part of his plea, had agreed to testify against others on trial for this murder. A failure to abide by the agreement rendered it "null and void." The defendant did, in fact, testify against two individuals who were initially convicted. But when their convictions were overturned and the case sent back for retrial he took the Fifth Amendment when called to testify at their trial. Upon refusing to testify at this second trial, the defendant was confronted with his plea agreement and thereafter the State filed a new charge against him for first-degree murder. The Ninth Circuit Court of Appeals found this to be a double jeopardy violation and granted defendant's writ of habeas corpus. In reversing, the Supreme Court noted that "both parties bargained for and received substantial benefits." The majority found that the defendant's agreement extended to having to testify on a retrial. The Court stated that "permitting the State to enforce the agreement the parties actually made does not violate the Double Jeopardy Clause."

A four-person dissent in *Adamson* questioned whether the defendant had actually breached the agreement. The dissenters looked at whether it was reasonable to interpret a requirement for the defendant to testify to apply to not only the initial trials, but also retrials. Without a breach, the dissent noted, there would be no double jeopardy violation.

IV. Plea Withdrawals

Just as people change their minds about many different subjects, defendants entering into plea agreements sometimes change their minds. In the federal system, Rule 11 outlines the procedure for the defendant who decides to withdraw his or her plea. A plea of guilty or *nolo contendere* can be withdrawn by the defendant prior to its acceptance and no reason needs to be given. After acceptance of a plea, but prior to sentencing, it can be withdrawn if the court rejects the plea or if a "defendant can show a fair and just reason for requesting the withdrawal." Rule 11(d) notes, however, that "[a]fter the court imposes sentence, the defendant may not withdraw a plea of guilty or *nolo contendere*, and the plea may be set aside only on direct appeal or collateral attack."

In *United States v. Hyde*, 520 U.S. 670 (1997), the defendant plead guilty to four counts, with the government then dismissing four counts and agreeing not to bring additional charges related to defendant's fraudulent conduct. The court determined that the defendant's plea was "knowingly, voluntarily, and intelligently" made. The trial court also determined that there was a factual basis for this plea. The trial court accepted the plea but then deferred decision on whether to accept the plea *agreement* entered into between the parties. During the period that the court had the plea agreement under advisement, the defendant attempted to withdraw the plea that he had entered. Whether the defendant had the right to withdraw his plea during this period became the issue on appeal.

The Court of Appeals in *Hyde* ruled that a defendant had the right to withdraw a plea when a court defers its ruling on plea acceptance. The Supreme Court, however, reversed holding that withdrawal of his plea required a showing of a "fair and just reason." Thus, the Court was unwilling to allow for an automatic withdrawal once a defendant had entered a guilty plea.

If the withdrawal is prior to the court's acceptance of the plea, there is no issue that that defendant has this right. The defendant is not the only party that can withdraw a plea prior to its entry in court. When a prosecutor withdraws a plea offer that has been accepted by the defendant, there is no due process violation to the defendant if he or she later pleads to a higher sentence. In *Mabry v. Johnson*, 467 U.S. 504 (1984), the defendant's acceptance of a plea that would allow for a concurrent sentence could not be enforced when the prosecutor later stated "that a mistake had been made and withdrew the offer." This was all done prior to a court acceptance of the proposed plea. The prosecutor then offered the same term of years to the defendant—21 years—but changed the offer so that the sentence would be served consecutively to the defendant's other sentences; thus, increasing the defendant's actual prison time. The defendant eventually accepted this new plea, but raised the issue in a habeas corpus relief petition as to whether he had a constitutional right to specific performance on the first plea offered that was later withdrawn by prosecutors. The Court, in rejecting the defendant's argument, noted that due process challenges look at whether the plea was voluntarily and intelligently made. It held that the plea the defendant did accept was not the result of "governmental deception." The Court stated that the defendant's "inability to enforce the prosecutor's offer is without constitutional significance."

Checkpoints

- A high percentage of cases in both the federal and state systems are resolved through a plea bargain.

- Eliminating risk, finality, and efficiency are strong arguments for a prosecutor to plead cases.

- Reduced sentence, dismissal of charges, and eliminating an unknown risk at trial are strong arguments for a defendant to enter a plea of guilty.

- Plea agreements are an acceptable manner to resolve a criminal matter.

- A defendant may enter a *"nolo contendere"* plea, a plea of "no contest," when they want the case resolved but do not want an admission of guilt on record.

- A defendant may enter a conditional plea, a guilty plea conditioned on the ability to remove it, in order to preserve an issue for appeal.

- Deferred prosecution agreements allow a matter to continue for a period of time to assure that the defendant will not engage in continued criminal activity or for the purpose of having the defendant perform certain acts for the prosecution.

- Many states have statutes or constitutional amendments that afford victim's rights in the plea process.

- Entering a guilty plea waives the privilege against compulsory self-incrimination, the right to trial by jury, and the right to confront one's accusers.

- Defendants entering a guilty plea must do so voluntarily and understandingly.

- Waiving rights to enter a guilty plea requires that the accused have effective assistance of counsel.

- Failing to convey a plea offer is ineffective assistance of counsel that is subject to *Strickland* analysis to determine if the defendant was prejudiced.

- A defendant has the right to self-representation on a plea.

- Prosecutorial threats to increase charges if there is a failure to plead guilty does not violate due process.

- A guilty plea can be upheld despite the defendant's refusal to admit guilt when there is strong evidence against the accused.

- Federal Rule of Criminal Procedure, Rule 11, provides the plea process for federal courts.

- Rule 11 provides the specific warnings that the federal court needs to give to a defendant prior to a plea being entered to assure that the accused acted knowingly and voluntarily in waiving their rights.

- Contract law is used to determine the rights of parties with plea agreements.

- Withdrawal of a plea depends on the timing of when it occurs, with it allowed prior to acceptance of the plea and more constrained thereafter.

- Both the prosecution and defense may need to consider withdrawals of pleas by the other party.

Chapter 10

Criminal Jury Trials

Roadmap

- Constitutional basis for jury trials
- Crimes entitled to jury trials
- What constitutes a jury
- Decision-making by a jury
- Waiver of trial by jury
- Jury selection
- *Voir dire*
- Challenges to jurors
- Restrictions on peremptory challenges
- Qualifications for jury service

I. Introduction

Central to the judicial system in the United States is the right to a jury trial in criminal cases. The use of jury trials in the criminal justice process can be traced back to English law. The U.S. Constitutional right to a "jury trial is granted to criminal defendants in order to prevent oppression by the Government." *Duncan v. Louisiana*, 391 U.S. 145 (1968). There are many questions that remain when one examines the jury trial right. For example, what crimes entitle a defendant the right to have a jury trial? How many people are needed to constitute a jury? Does the vote of the jury have to be unanimous? What decisions does a jury make and what decisions are matters of law for the court to resolve? Can a defendant waive his or her right to trial by jury, and how does one determine if the waiver is proper?

In addition to determining the scope of jury rights in criminal cases, there are also questions that arise in picking a jury. For example, who can serve on a jury? What is considered a fair jury? How many peremptory strikes are the prosecution and defense entitled to, and what restrictions exist on eliminating jurors from sitting on a case? And finally, are death penalty cases different, calling for a different jury selection process? These issues are covered in this chapter.

II. Constitutional Right to Trial by Jury

A. Constitutional Basis

The right to trial by jury is found in two places in the U.S. Constitution. It is located in Article III, Section 2 of the Constitution, which provides that "[t]he Trial of all Crimes, except in Cases of Impeachment, shall be by Jury ..." It is also included in the Sixth Amendment, which provides in part that "[i]n all criminal prosecutions, the accused shall enjoy the right to a speedy and public trial, by an impartial jury of the State and district wherein the crime shall have been committed ..."

The landmark decision extending the right to trial by jury to the states is *Duncan v. Louisiana.* Gary Duncan, the defendant, had requested a trial by jury for a charge of simple battery that accrued from an incident with conflicting testimony. Duncan was attempting to get his African-American cousins to leave an encounter with several Caucasian youths. Some onlookers at the scene claimed that Duncan had slapped one of the Caucasian youths, while others at the scene said that he merely touched him. Duncan was denied a trial by jury, with the state claiming that the Louisiana Constitution only granted jury trials when the punishable sentence was death or hard labor. Duncan was convicted of simple battery in Louisiana, a misdemeanor with a penalty of up to two years imprisonment. The trial court sentenced him to sixty days and a fine. The Louisiana Supreme Court upheld the lower court's decision that he was not entitled to a jury trial.

In an opinion authored by Justice White, the Court noted that many constitutional rights had been incorporated to the States via the Fourteenth Amendment. These included the rights of free speech, press and religion under the First Amendment, rights against unreasonable searches and seizures under the Fourth Amendment, and rights to counsel under the Sixth Amendment. The test, the Court noted, was whether the right was a "fundamental right, essential to a fair trial." The Court traced the history of the right to trial by jury, finding that "[t]he deep commitment of the Nation to the right of jury trial in serious criminal cases as a defense against arbitrary law enforcement qualifies for protection under the Due Process Clause of the Fourteenth Amendment, and must therefore be respected by the States." The Court stated "that the Fourteenth Amendment guarantees a right of jury trial in all criminal cases which—were they to be tried in a federal court—would come within the Sixth Amendment's guarantee."

Finding the right to trial by jury applicable to the States for "serious" crimes, the Court in *Duncan* next examined whether it applied to this defendant who was convicted of a simple battery. Justice White wrote that the line between "serious" and "petty" offenses did not need to be decided with this case because a crime punishable by two years in prison, which is what the defendant faced when going to trial, was "a serious crime and not a petty offense."

Although the Court decided the case by finding "the right to trial by jury" from the Sixth Amendment applicable to the States, Justice White did not advocate for complete incorporation of the Bill of Rights, a position taken by Justices Black and Douglas in their concurring opinion. Instead Justice White used what has been called "selective incorporation" because the Court was picking particular rights applicable to the States via the Fourteenth Amendment, but not saying that all rights within the Bill of Rights would apply to the States. Justices Black and Douglas questioned the selective approach to incorporation and called for full incorporation of the Bill of Rights to the States.

In addition to a concurring opinion by Justices Black and Douglas, a concurrence by Justice Fortas emphasized the limited right to jury trial being provided by this decision. He wrote to ensure that the decision did not mean that all the "particulars of according that right must be uniform." He stated all the "bag and baggage" that comes with the Sixth Amendment jury trial right did not come with this decision. Thus, he wanted to make clear that rights to "unanimous verdicts or a jury of 12 upon the States" would not be assumed as being fundamental and obligatory on the States by this decision's finding of the right to a jury trial applicable to the States.

A strong dissent by Justices Harlan and Stewart advocated against "fastening on the States federal notions of criminal justice." They criticized the Court's holding stating:

> Today's Court still remains unwilling to accept the total incorporationists' view of the history of the Fourteenth Amendment. This, if accepted, would afford a cogent reason for applying the Sixth Amendment to the States. The Court is also, apparently, unwilling to face the task of determining whether denial of trial by jury in the situation before us, or in other situations, is fundamentally unfair. Consequently, the Court has compromised on the ease of the incorporationist position, without its internal logic. It has simply as-

sumed that the question before us is whether the Jury Trial Clause of the Sixth Amendment should be incorporated into the Fourteenth, jot-for-jot and case-for-case, or ignored. Then the Court merely declares that the clause in question is 'in' rather than 'out.'

The dissenters were not persuaded that there had been "unfairness" in this case or in the "yet unbounded category of cases" tried to a court in Louisiana.

B. Scope of Right — Who Is Entitled to a Jury Trial

The right to jury trial is triggered when the offense is "serious" as opposed to "petty." *Duncan v. Louisiana.* Those crimes that are designated as "petty" can be tried without a jury. But what makes an offense fit this "serious" category, and where is the line between these offenses and petty ones are questions that have been considered in several Supreme Court decisions.

Baldwin v. New York, 399 U.S. 66 (1970), was a key case that prompted the Supreme Court to examine this issue. The defendant had been denied a jury trial for the crime of "jostling" (criminalizing conduct one would engage in if they were pickpocketing), a Class A misdemeanor in New York that had a maximum sentence of one year imprisonment. Looking for an objective criteria for deciding the issue of whether this was a petty offense, the Court decided that the most relevant criteria was the "severity of the maximum authorized penalty." Prior cases had determined that a maximum sentence of two years would be classified as serious. The Court in *Baldwin* took it a step further, however, saying that "no offense can be deemed 'petty' for purposes of the right to trial by jury where imprisonment for more than six months is authorized." The Court did not, however, say that everything under six months would be considered "petty" offenses.

In setting a line at greater than six months for not being petty offenses, the Court rejected the state's position that the line should be one year — the then-existing line in New York between felonies and misdemeanors. The Court chose instead to look to the federal system's approach at the time of this decision, which was that petty offenses were those punishable by not more than six months imprisonment and a $500 fine.

The Supreme Court refined the delineation between "serious" and "petty" offenses in *Blanton v. City of North Las Vegas, Nevada*, 489 U.S. 538 (1989), when the Court examined the question of whether there was a constitutional right to trial by jury for a charge of driving under the influence (DUI). In *Blanton*, two first-time DUI offenders were denied rights to trial by jury. A DUI conviction in Nevada at this time carried a host of different possible penalties:

2 days to 6 months imprisonment, 48 hours of community service in clothing designating the person as a DUI offender, and a fine from $200 to $1,000. The defendant also suffered a loss of his or her driver's license for 90 days, with the possibility of a restricted license for work after 45 days. An additional consequence of a DUI conviction was that the defendant was required to attend alcohol abuse education classes at his or her own expense. Repeat offenders suffered increased penalties including a year loss of license for a second time offender and a minimum term of one year imprisonment for a third time offender.

The Supreme Court in *Blanton* found no denial of constitutional rights since the maximum term of incarceration that the defendants faced was six months and the maximum possible fine was $1,000. Although the *Blanton* Court, like the *Baldwin* Court, was not willing to say that everything under six months is automatically a "petty" offense, it did say that this would be the presumption. One would be entitled to a jury trial even though the sentence was below 6 months "in the rare situation where a legislature packs an offense it deems 'serious' with onerous penalties that nonetheless 'do not puncture the 6-month incarceration line.'" The Court was not persuaded by the increased penalties for repeat offenders under Nevada law as this was not the penalty facing these two defendants. Nor was the Court willing to call it "serious" because of the additional penalties of loss of a driver's license, attendance at an alcohol abuse school, a $1,000 fine, or community service which involved wearing clothing that let others know the defendant was convicted of DUI.

The Supreme Court again examined the effect of collateral penalties of a conviction on the right to jury trial in *United States v. Nachtigal*, 507 U.S. 1 (1993). The defendant was charged with DUI in a national park, which carried a penalty of up to six months imprisonment and a fine of up to $5,000, with an alternative penalty for the imprisonment or probation of up to five years. The Court also had the option to add conditions to this probationary period.

The Court in *Nachtigal* was not willing to provide this defendant with a jury trial. The Court used the *Blanton* analysis that a charged offense carrying a maximum penalty of up to six months would be "presumptively" considered a "petty" offense. The Court was not persuaded to remove it from the "petty" offense category just because the fine was higher and there was an extended probation alternative. Nor did the fact that a judge could add probation conditions to the sentence sway the Supreme Court to say it was anything but "petty."

What happens when the defendant faces multiple petty offenses — will this require a jury trial if the aggregate prison term for all the offenses exceeds six months? In *Lewis v. United States*, 518 U.S. 322 (1996), the defendant, a postal worker, was charged with taking the contents of mail. He was charged with two counts of obstructing the mail, and each count carried a maximum sentence of six months. The defendant's request for a jury trial was denied with the trial judge saying that she did not intend to give the defendant a sentence in excess of six months. The Supreme Court agreed with this decision denying the defendant a jury trial.

Justice O'Connor, writing the Court's opinion in *Lewis,* stated, "[n]o jury trial right exists where a defendant is prosecuted for multiple petty offenses." She also stated that "[t]he Sixth Amendment's guarantee of the right to a jury trial does not extend to petty offenses, and its scope does not change where a defendant faces a potential aggregate prison term in excess of six months for petty offenses charged." One rationale provided for this holding is that even if the aggregation allowed for a jury trial, if the total time for the offenses exceeded 6 months, the prosecution could circumvent such a ruling by charging a defendant with two separate charges.

Justices Kennedy and Breyer concurred in *Lewis,* saying that the defendant could not have received in excess of six months here, so they agreed with Justice O'Connor's opinion that there was no right to a jury trial. They were, however, critical of her opinion that allowed offenses to be tried without a jury when the aggregate of the charges might bring imprisonment to a defendant in excess of six months.

These two justices reminded the Court of its holding in *Codispoti v. Pennsylvania,* 418 U.S. 506 (1974), where a defendant who was convicted of seven contempt charges was sentenced to individual terms under six months, but terms that were to run consecutively for a total of 39 months. In *Codispoti,* the Court held that a jury trial was required. The concurring justices did not agree that *Codispoti* should be distinguished because of the crime being of special concern — contempt, and there being no statutory maximum for contempt. Justices Kennedy and Breyer noted in *Lewis* that the underlying purpose of having a jury is a liberty interest — to protect individuals from government power. This protection is needed when a "judge in a single case sends a defendant to prison for years." But they also noted that a jury trial was not needed "when all possibility for a sentence longer than six months has been foreclosed."

C. Jury Composition — Size of Jury

There is a grand jury (see Chapter 2) that hears evidence to determine if indictments should be issued. There is also the petit jury, or trial jury. One issue that arises with respect to trial juries is how many individuals need to sit on the jury to satisfy the defendant's constitutional right to a trial by jury. Most states have a 12-person jury. There is, however, no U.S. constitutional requirement for states to use a 12-person jury in a criminal prosecution.

In *Williams v. Florida*, 399 U.S. 78 (1970), the defendant filed a pretrial motion asking for a 12-person jury as opposed to a 6-person jury, which was used in all but capital cases in Florida. Defendant's motion was denied and following his conviction for robbery, he was sentenced to life imprisonment. One of the issues he raised on appeal was whether his Sixth Amendment rights were denied because of the failure to have a 12-person jury. The Supreme Court held "that the 12-man panel is not a necessary ingredient of 'trial by jury.'" The Court noted the accidental history that appeared to lead to a number of 12 for juries. The Sixth Amendment, it found, only required that there be a sufficient size for deliberation, a number sufficient to avoid government oppression, and enough members to have a representative cross-section of the community. The Court also noted that there was no evidence showing a diminished reliability of jury verdicts with 6-person juries. Thus, it concluded that Florida did not violate the defendant's rights by having a 6-person as opposed to 12-person jury. Dissenting on this issue was Justice Marshall, who advocated that before a person can be sent away for the rest of his or her life, the individual should be provided a jury of 12 people.

When Georgia tried to go below a 6-person jury, a different result was seen. In *Ballew v. Georgia*, 435 U.S. 223 (1978), the defendant, a manager of an adult theater, had a two-count misdemeanor obscenity charge brought against him. The defendant requested a 12-person jury, but the trial court used a 5-person jury, which was acceptable for misdemeanor cases under the Georgia Constitution. The Supreme Court in *Ballew* noted that in the *Williams* case the Court had not ruled on whether it was permissible to have a jury below six persons. The Court reflected on data that raised doubts about the group deliberative method and the accuracy of the results with smaller jury panels. It noted that this could work to the detriment of the defense, as there would be less likelihood of hung juries. There was also more of a chance of excluding minority representation in the community with a smaller jury. The Court stated:

> We readily admit that we do not pretend to discern a clear line between six members and five. But the assembled data raise substantial doubt about the reliability and appropriate representation of panels smaller than six. Because of the fundamental importance of the jury trial to the American system of criminal justice, any further reduction that promotes inaccurate and possibly biased decisionmaking, that causes untoward differences in verdicts, and that prevents juries from truly representing their communities, attains constitutional significance.

The Court was unwilling to allow Georgia's unanimity requirement as a justification of the constitutional deprivation in having a 5-person jury. The cost-saving of a State by having a lesser number of jurors was also an insufficient excuse for the Court to allow reducing the jury size below six persons. In the end, the Court in *Ballew* found that a 5-person jury deprived the defendant of his jury trial right under the Sixth and Fourteenth Amendments.

Although states may have juries below twelve individuals, the federal system will not tolerate this approach, absent special circumstances. Federal Rule of Criminal Procedure 23(c) requires a twelve-person jury. That said, it also allows the parties to stipulate prior to a jury decision to a smaller jury or the court can allow the case to proceed with fewer than twelve if it "finds it necessary to excuse a juror for good cause after the trial begins." Once the jury begins deliberations, "the court may permit a jury of 11 persons to return a verdict, even without a stipulation by the parties, if the court finds good cause to excuse a juror."

D. Jury Decisions — Jury Unanimity

In addition to questions of how many jurors are necessary to meet the Sixth Amendment's right to a jury trial, there are also questions of whether the vote of the jury needs to be unanimous. In most states and in the federal system, unanimous juries are the norm. There is, however, caselaw that holds that there is no constitutional obligation for a unanimous jury decision. This question is not simplistic as it also requires consideration of what aspects of the case might warrant unanimity.

On the same day the Court issued two cases pertaining to unanimity for state criminal jury trials: *Apodaca v. Oregon*, 406 U.S. 404 (1972) and *Johnson v. Louisiana*, 406 U.S. 356 (1972). Reconciling the varying opinions in these two cases can be difficult, but it is important to note that both cases involved 12-person juries. The Court elucidated further on this issue in a later Louisiana case, *Burch v. Louisiana*, 441 U.S. 130 (1979), a case with only six jurors.

In *Apodaca v. Oregon*, the Court looked at whether States were required to have a unanimous jury. Oregon allowed verdicts of 10-2 in all cases except those with verdicts for first degree murder, which required unanimity in the jurors' verdict of guilty. Three defendants tried in Oregon raised the question of unanimity in that two had jury votes of 11-1 and the third had a 10-2 vote.

In finding that unanimity was not required by the Sixth Amendment's right to jury trial, the Court in *Apodaca* noted that unanimity, like the number of members of a jury, had no constitutional significance. The Court rejected the defendant's argument that unanimity was needed to reinforce the reasonable doubt standard in criminal cases. The Court also rejected the defendant's argument that unanimity was important for having a fair cross-section on the jury. Justice White, writing for the plurality, stated, "[w]e simply find no proof for the notion that a majority will disregard its instructions and cast its votes for guilt or innocence based on prejudice rather than the evidence."

Justice Powell's concurring opinion was written to express his difference in reasoning from Justice White's in *Apodaca*, a case coming from Oregon. He believed that not "all of the elements of jury trial within the meaning of the Sixth Amendment are necessarily embodied in or incorporated into the Due Process Clause of the Fourteenth Amendment." Thus, although unanimity was required for federal jury trials, this provision was not incorporated into the Fourteenth Amendment and therefore States were not bound to have unanimous juries. In contrast, a four-justice dissent argued that a "unanimous verdict is an essential element of a Sixth Amendment jury trial."

The Court also looked at the Louisiana scheme in a case where there was a 9-3 verdict issued by a 12-person jury. In *Johnson v. Louisiana*, the Court found that jury unanimity was not warranted for upholding the reasonable doubt standard. The Court also examined an equal protection claim as Louisiana required unanimous verdicts in capital cases and those with only five members on the jury, while not requiring it for other cases such as the one before this Court. Finding that there was a rational basis for this difference, the Court rejected this equal protection claim.

Justice Blackmon wrote a concurring opinion, applicable to both the *Johnson* and *Apodaca* cases, to express his view that although the scheme was not against the U.S. Constitution, he did not endorse such a system. It should be noted, as was pointed out by the dissent in *Johnson*, that the *Johnson* case was tried prior to the Court's ruling in *Duncan*, thus the Sixth Amendment had yet to have been found applicable to the States. This aspect differed from the facts of the *Apodaca* case. But the dissenters in *Johnson* still advocated for unanimity by saying that the Fourteenth Amendment provided a basis for a right to trial by jury and this right included a unanimous jury.

In *Burch v. Louisiana*, the Court again examined the Louisiana jury scheme. This time the defendants were an individual and a corporation, who were convicted by a non-unanimous 6-person jury for two counts of crimes that alleged the exhibiting of two obscene motion pictures. The crime required a jury trial as it was not a petty offense.

The Court in *Burch* noted that only two states allowed a 6-person jury not to be unanimous. It then rejected the State's argument for non-unanimous 6-person juries that was premised on this procedure providing a more efficient system with time-savings and less hung juries. These benefits the Court felt were "speculative." The Court stated,

More importantly, we think that when a State has reduced the size of its juries to the minimum number of jurors permitted by the Constitution, the additional authorization of nonunanimous verdicts by such juries sufficiently threatens the constitutional principles that led to the establishment of the size threshold that any countervailing interest of the State should yield.

A dissent argued that this case should not return for retrial, but rather the convictions should be reversed.

The federal system requires that the jury verdict must be unanimous. *Federal Rules of Criminal Procedure, Rule 31(a)*. The importance of unanimity is seen in that a party has the right to ask the court to poll the jurors individually prior to their being released. "If the poll reveals a lack of unanimity, the court may direct the jury to deliberate further or may declare a mistrial and discharge the jury." *Federal Rules of Criminal Procedure, Rule 31(d)*.

E. Waiver of Jury

Can a defendant waive the right to trial by jury just as a defendant can waive a right to counsel? (See Chapter 7). State constitutions, statutes, and court rules typically resolve what is necessary for a defendant to waive the right to jury trial in order to have the case adjudicated by the court in a bench trial. Who has to consent to this waiver is one point of difference among different jurisdictions. For example, in New Jersey, the judge and defendant need to consent, but the prosecutor merely gets notice. Judge Handler, in his dissenting opinion in *State v. Dunne*, 590 A.2d 1144 (N.J. 1991), noted the array of different approaches taken by states when it comes to defendants being allowed to waive the right to a jury trial.

Federal Rule of Criminal Procedure, Rule 23(a) provides that to waive a jury trial in the federal system, for those entitled to have one, three things are required. First, the defendant has to waive a jury trial and it must be in writing. Second, the government needs to consent. Finally, the court needs to approve the request to have a bench trial. If any of these three are not met, the case proceeds with a jury.

This was challenged by a defendant who wanted to proceed with a bench trial in a federal case in which he had thirty charges of mail fraud. In *Singer v. United States*, 380 U.S. 24 (1965), the defendant was accused of using the "mails to dupe amateur songwriters into sending him money for the marketing of their songs." The defendant waived a jury trial and the court was willing to accept this waiver. The government refused, and the defendant was later convicted on twenty-nine of the thirty counts. On appeal he argued "that a defendant in a federal criminal case has not only an unconditional constitutional right" "to a trial by jury, but also a correlative right to have his case decided by a judge alone if he considers such a trial to be to his advantage." He contested the federal criminal procedure rule that placed restrictions on his right to waive a jury trial. The Supreme Court rejected his argument:

> We can find no evidence that the common law recognized that defendants had the right to choose between court and jury trial. Although instances of waiver of jury trial can be found in certain of the colonies prior to the adoption of the Constitution, they were isolated instances occurring pursuant to colonial 'constitutions' or statutes and were clear departures from the common law. There is no indication that the colonists considered the ability to waive a jury trial to be of equal importance to the right to demand one. Having found that the Constitution neither confers nor recognizes a right of criminal defendants to have their cases tried before a judge alone, we also conclude that Rule 23(a) sets forth a reasonable procedure governing attempted waivers of jury trials.

The right to trial by jury can be waived in some circumstances, such as when the accused waives the right and the government consents. This may occur when a juror becomes ill and the defendant agrees to proceed with a lesser number of jurors. *Patton v. United States*, 281 U.S. 276 (1930). Federal Rules of Criminal Procedure outline methods of stipulating to a lesser number of jurors.

If a case does proceed without a jury, the trial court is required to make a finding of guilty or not guilty. Additionally, a party can request prior to a "finding of guilty or not guilty" to have the court "state its specific findings of fact in open court or in a written decision or opinion." *Federal Rules of Criminal Procedure, Rule 23 (c)*.

F. Questions of Fact and Law

Absent a waiver, the Sixth Amendment jury trial right includes the right of the jury to make a finding of guilt beyond a reasonable doubt on the elements of the crime charged. *Sullivan v. Louisiana*, 508 U.S. 275 (1993). In *United States v. Gaudin*, 515 U.S. 506 (1995), the Supreme Court looked at whether the element of materiality in a case against a defendant charged with making a false material statement to a federal agency under 18 U.S.C. § 1001 was a question of law or fact. Justice Scalia, writing for the majority, held that "materiality" is a question that a jury should decide. He wrote that there is no historical consistency that supports questions of materiality in perjury cases being questions for the judge to decide. Thus, a trial court that removed this question from the province of the jury infringed on the defendant's jury trial right.

But a failure to allow a jury to decide such a question may not always result in a reversal as the Court may find the error to be harmless error. In *Neder v. United States*, 527 U.S. 1 (1999), the Supreme Court held that such an error does not equate to "such defects as the complete deprivation of counsel or trial before a biased judge," and thus courts can examine this error using a harmless error approach. Thus, in a case with an element of materiality in the crime charged, a failure to instruct the jury on this element may not necessarily result in a reversal of the conviction.

Some issues raise unique questions as to whether they are issues within the province of the jury. This has been a source of concern with several decisions in the sentencing area.

In *Apprendi v. New Jersey*, 530 U.S. 466 (2000), the Supreme Court held that "[o]ther than the fact of a prior conviction, any fact that increases the penalty for a crime beyond the prescribed statutory maximum must be submitted to a jury, and proved beyond a reasonable doubt." In *Apprendi*, the defendant faced a five to ten year sentence for violation of a New Jersey statute of possession of a firearm for an unlawful purpose. New Jersey also had a hate crime statute that allowed for an extended sentence between ten and twenty years when the defendant committed the crime "with a purpose to intimidate an individual or group of individuals because of race, color, gender, handicap, religion, sexual orientation or ethnicity." The defendant received a twelve year sentence on one of the counts as a result of the trial judge finding that the defendant acted with racial bias. The issue before the Court was whether the violation of the hate crime statute authorizing the increased penalty, required a jury.

The Court in *Apprendi* noted that judges have discretion to evaluate factors within the statutory range. Likewise, increasing a sentence because of prior convictions is within the judge's power. But in a 5–4 decision the Court held that it was a jury decision to decide other issues that would increase a penalty above the statutory maximum.

In addition to having the power to increase a sentence based on prior convictions, trial judges also can determine facts that would allow imposition of a consecutive, as opposed to a concurrent, sentence. In *Oregon v. Ice*, 555 U.S. 160 (2009), the Supreme Court held that its decision was faithful to the principles in *Apprendi* because upholding this "Oregon statute that assigns to judges a decision that has not traditionally belonged to the jury is faithful to that aim."

Other Supreme Court decisions have reinforced the principle espoused in *Apprendi*. For example, in *Ring v. Arizona*, 536 U.S. 584 (2002), the Supreme

Court held improper an Arizona statute that allowed the judge in a capital case to solely determine whether aggravating factors warranted imposition of the death penalty. The Court held this was a violation of the defendant's Sixth Amendment right to a jury trial.

Likewise, in *Blakely v. Washington*, 542 U.S. 296 (2004), a case where the defendant had plead guilty to a crime with a maximum sentence of 53 months, but then received a sentence of 90 months because the state court found that the defendant had acted with "deliberate cruelty," the Supreme Court held that not having the jury determine this issue was a violation of the defendant's Sixth Amendment rights to trial by jury. Because these factors had not been admitted to in the plea agreement, the defendant was entitled to have them decided by a jury prior to receiving an increased sentence of more than three years.

The cases of *Apprendi, Ring*, and *Blakely*, although involving state sentencing schemes, apply equally in the federal system. In *United States v. Booker*, 543 U.S. 220 (2005), the Court held that the right to a jury trial needs to be considered when using the federal sentencing guidelines. (See Chapter 14). "Any fact that, by law, increases the penalty for a crime is an 'element' that must be submitted to the jury and found beyond a reasonable doubt," and this includes mandatory minimum sentences which increase the penalty for a crime. *Alleyne v. United States*, 133 S. Ct. 1251 (2013). When a sentence is modified, however, pursuant to a federal statute that allows a defendant to receive the benefit of a reduced sentence when the sentencing range is lowered by the Sentencing Commission and the "reduction is consistent with" applicable policy statements, this re-sentencing does not trigger the Sixth Amendment. *Dillon v. United States*, 560 U.S. 817 (2010).

Jury verdicts are granted enormous respect in the criminal justice process. They will not be "upset by speculation or inquiry," even when a verdict can be the "result of compromise, or [ ] a mistake on the part of the jury." *Dunn v. United States*, 284 U.S. 390 (1932).

III. Jury Selection

A. Generally

Jury selection entails two parts: 1) calling the venire (*i.e.* all prospective jurors), and 2) selection of the specific jurors for a case from the venire. The venire needs to provide a "fair cross-section of the community." To select jurors from the pool assembled, the prospective jurors are questioned in a process called *voir dire*. The attorneys then have the ability to strike jurors without ex-

pressing reasons, by exercising peremptory challenges and having them excluded from the case. There are a limited number of peremptory challenges
afforded to each party, as well as restrictions to using these strikes in a discriminatory manner. Jurors can also be removed for cause when they are in-
eligible by statute to serve on a jury or when they cannot fairly decide the case.
Death penalty cases present unique concerns in determining whether a juror
can decide the case fairly.

B. Venire

The venire provides the pool of jurors used to select the specific jurors for
the trial. Courts have held that the Sixth Amendment right to trial by jury includes the right to have a fair cross-section from which to select a jury. This prohibits the systematic exclusion of cognizable groups from the jury selection
process. As was stated in *Ballard v. United States*, 329 U.S. 187 (1946), this
"does not mean, of course, that every jury must contain representatives of all
the economic, social, religious, racial, political and geographical groups of the
community; frequently such complete representation would be impossible.
But it does mean that prospective jurors shall be selected by court officials
without systematic and intentional exclusion of any of these groups."

Early cases challenged the exclusion of specific groups premised on violations of equal protection. Thus, the Supreme Court did not allow a process
that excluded African Americans from sitting as jurors. *Strauder v. West Virginia*,
100 U.S. 303 (1879). The Court also used its supervisory powers to correct the
intentional and systematic exclusion of women from the panel of grand and petit
jurors. *Ballard*.

More recently, challenges to the venire have shifted the focus to the Sixth
Amendment right to jury as applied to the states via the Fourteenth Amendment. The landmark decision in this regard is *Taylor v. Louisiana*, 419 U.S. 522
(1975), in which the Supreme Court rejected a Louisiana law that largely excluded women from "jury service unless she had previously filed a written declaration of her desire to be subject to jury service."

Billy J. Taylor, a male, challenged the venire claiming he was deprived of
his constitutional right to "a fair trial by jury of a representative segment of
the community." The parties stipulated that although 53% of the individuals
eligible for jury service were woman, only 10% were actually available for the
venire, and that of the 175 individuals selected for his venire, there were no women.
The Supreme Court held women, as a class, could not be given automatic exemptions based solely on sex "if the consequence is that criminal jury venires
are almost totally male."

In ascertaining what is a fair cross-section, the Court in *Taylor* noted that "[c]ommunities differ at different times and places. What is a fair cross section at one time or place is not necessarily a fair cross-section at another time or a different place." The Court was clear that there was "no requirement that petit juries actually chosen must mirror the community and reflect the various distinctive groups in the population." The Court also noted that its decision did not preclude States from having qualifications for its jurors and also having exemptions.

Exemptions were a focus of the Court's decision in *Duren v. Missouri*, 439 U.S. 357 (1979), as women could request to be exempt from serving on a jury in Missouri. The defendant argued that his right to a fair-cross section of his community was denied by this automatic jury exemption given to women. The Court provided a three-prong test:

> In order to establish a prima facie violation of the fair-cross-section requirement, the defendant must show (1) that the group alleged to be excluded is a 'distinctive' group in the community; (2) that the representation of this group in venires from which juries are selected is not fair and reasonable in relation to the number of such persons in the community; and (3) that this underrepresentation is due to systematic exclusion of the group in the jury-selection process.

Because of the "gross discrepancy between the percentage of women in jury venires and the percentage of women in the community," the Court found that "women were not fairly represented in the source from which petit juries were drawn" in this county. Finding the underrepresentation to be systematic, the Court noted that the burden shifted to the state to show a justification for exempting women. The Court in *Duren* noted that "most occupational and other reasonable exemptions may inevitably involve some degree of overinclusiveness or underinclusiveness." That said, the Court was clear that "any category expressly limited to a group in the community of sufficient magnitude and distinctiveness so as to be within the fair-cross-section requirement—such as women– runs the danger of resulting in underrepresentation sufficient to constitute a prima facie violation of that constitutional requirement."

Justice Rehnquist, who dissented in *Duren*, expressed strong concerns about the ramifications of the decision on society in finding what a fair cross-section entails. He noted that there was no showing that this defendant had suffered unfair or prejudicial treatment.

Federal statutes set forth the jury selection process for federal courts. 28 U.S.C.§ 1861 et. seq. It offers guidance of what will be considered a fair-cross section for purposes of federal law. It states that "[i]t is the policy of the United States that all litigants in Federal courts entitled to trial by jury shall have the right to grand and petit juries selected at random from a fair cross section of the community in the district or division wherein the court convenes." Discrimination from jury duty is prohibited when premised upon "race, color, religion, sex, national origin, or economic status." 28 U.S.C. § 1862. There is also a statute on the method for challenging compliance with the selection procedures. 28 U.S.C. § 1867.

C. *Voir Dire*

The process of picking jurors assembled from the pool to serve on the trial jury is done by questioning the prospective jurors in a process called *voir dire*. There is no uniform method among the states and different federal districts for how to conduct *voir dire*. The *voir dire* process allows each side to learn more information about the prospective jurors in order to determine who they wish to exclude as possible jurors. It also allows the court to ascertain if any prospective jurors are biased and need to be excluded for cause.

In *Mu'Min v. Virginia*, 500 U.S. 415 (1991), a high-publicity death penalty case, the defendant argued that his Sixth Amendment jury trial rights were violated when the judge refused to question prospective jurors on news reports they had heard about the case. The defense wanted individual jury questioning and also submitted sixty-four proposed questions for jurors to be asked on *voir dire*. The trial court refused this defense request, although it did question jurors in panels of four. The trial court also asked questions to ascertain whether a prospective juror was biased against the defendant. The jurors "[a]ll swore that they could enter the jury box with an open mind and wait until the entire case was presented before reaching a conclusion as to guilt or innocence." The court also asked follow-up questions to see who the prospective juror might have had conversations with concerning the case. As a result of the trial court's questioning of prospective jurors, several jurors were dismissed for various reasons, including a juror "who equivocated as to whether she could enter the jury box with an open mind."

Reviewing the trial court's *voir dire* procedure, the majority of the Supreme Court in *Mu'Min* held that there is no constitutional requirement that jurors be asked questions about the content of the pre-trial publicity that they came into contact with, and that the *voir dire* in this case was constitutionally sufficient. (See Chapter 11). The Court distinguished *voir dire* issues in federal cases, which are subject to the Court's supervisory power, from state cases which are limited to constitutional proscriptions. That said, trial courts have much discretion in how *voir dire* is conducted.

One area where oversight has been provided relates to when questions regarding racial bias can be asked in *voir dire*. If there are "special circumstances" showing that racial issues are "inextricably bound up with the conduct of the trial" or the case involves "a violent crime and where the defendant and the victim are members of different racial or ethnic groups," federal trial courts need to grant a defendant's request to inquire as to whether prospective jurors have racial or ethnic bias. A "failure to honor his request … will be reversible error only where the circumstances of the case indicate that there is a reasonable possibility that racial or ethnic prejudice might have influenced the jury." *Rosales-Lopez v. United States*, 451 U.S. 182 (1981).

In a state death penalty case where a defendant was alleged to have committed an interracial crime, the Supreme Court held that the defendant was entitled to have potential jurors questioned concerning racial prejudice. *Turner v. Murray*, 476 U.S. 28 (1986). In Turner the Court discussed *Ristaino v. Ross*, 424 U.S. 589 (1976), stating that "[t]he mere fact that petitioner is black and his victim white does not constitute a 'special circumstance' of constitutional proportions." But what distinguished *Turner* from *Ristaino* was that *Turner* involved capital punishment. "Because of the range of discretion entrusted to a jury in a capital sentencing hearing, there is a unique opportunity for racial prejudice to operate but remain undetected." As such, the Court held "that a capital defendant accused of an interracial crime is entitled to have prospective jurors informed of the race of the victim and questioned on the issue of racial bias." The Court in *Turner* emphasized the "finality of the death sentence" in vacating the defendant's death sentence, although noting that the defendant did not have to be retried on guilt.

Federal Rules of Criminal Procedure, Rule 24(a) provides the method for *voir dire* in the federal system. Much discretion is left with the court, as it allows the court to ask the questions, or to permit the attorneys to ask the questions. If the court conducts the *voir dire*, then it is necessary that the attorneys be allowed follow-up questions or be allowed to "submit further questions that the court may ask." Irrespective of whether the court asks the questions for the attorneys or allows the attorneys to ask the questions, the court has discretion to determine that the questions are proper.

D. Peremptory Challenges

1. Description

Each side is allowed to strike some jurors without explanation. In describing peremptory challenges, the Supreme Court in *Swain v. Alabama*, 380 U.S. 202 (1965), stated:

The essential nature of the peremptory challenge is that it is one exercised without a reason stated, without inquiry and without being subject to the court's control. While challenges for cause permit rejection of jurors on a narrowly specified, provable and legally cognizable basis of partiality, the peremptory permits rejection for a real or imagined partiality that is less easily designated or demonstrable.

There are, however, some restrictions that are mandated in the striking of jurors. The Supreme Court has been vocal in prohibiting some forms of discriminatory peremptory strikes.

2. Procedures

Federal Rules of Criminal Procedure, Rule 24(b) specifies the number of peremptory challenges allowed in federal trials. The court has discretion when there are multiple defendants to provide additional peremptory challenges. The court also has discretion with multiple defendants to permit "the defendants to exercise those challenges separately or jointly."

Rule 24(b) provides that if the case involves a possible death penalty then each side is allowed twenty peremptory challenges. Other felony cases get six peremptory challenges for the government and ten for "the defendant or defendants jointly" "when the defendant is charged with a crime punishable by imprisonment of more than one year." The parties each have three peremptory strikes for misdemeanors, crimes "punishable by fine, imprisonment of one year or less, or both."

Alternate jurors are routinely picked to allow for circumstances when a juror needs to be excused during trial or deliberations. This can be as a result of the inability of the juror to continue his or her service or because of a disqualification. The federal rules permit impaneling up to six alternate jurors to account for these situations. Rule 24(c)(4) accounts for the procedure of allowing additional peremptory challenges dependent upon the number of alternates being selected.

States provide comparable rules on the peremptory challenge process. For example, the Alaska Rules of Criminal Procedure provide that parties get ten peremptory challenges for offenses above a year, three for those punishable by imprisonment for not more than one year, or by a fine, or both. Additionally, when there are multiple defendants, the court can grant additional peremptory challenges. *Alaska Rules of Criminal Procedure, Rule 24.* But the number of peremptory challenges that will be allowed is a decision for state legislators and rules committees. The Supreme Court has made it clear that "[t]he right to exercise peremptory challenges in state court is determined by state law." In *Rivera v. Illinois*, 556 U.S. 148 (2009), the Court stated that, "[t]his Court has 'long recognized' that 'peremptory challenges' are not of federal constitutional dimension."

3. Batson v. Kentucky

The landmark decision regarding the unconstitutionality of discriminatory peremptory challenges was *Batson v. Kentucky*, 476 U.S. 79 (1986). Prior to *Batson*, in *Swain v. Alabama*, the Supreme Court examined a defendant's claim of "invidious discrimination in the selection of jurors." The Court noted that blacks were not totally excluded from the jury panels and that there was insufficient proof of invidious discrimination, despite the fact that no black juror had ever served on a petit jury in that county. A huge evidentiary burden was placed on a defendant trying to prove a denial of equal protection. *Batson* lifted that burden.

In *Batson*, a black man was convicted of second-degree burglary and receipt of stolen goods. The prosecutor in selecting a jury peremptorily struck all blacks, leaving the defendant with a completely white jury. The defendant challenged the jury selection as a violation of rights under the Sixth Amendment and also under equal protection. The trial court denied the defendant's challenge to the jury stating that parties could peremptorily "strike anybody they want to."

Justice Powell, writing for the Supreme Court, noted that "[t]he harm from discriminatory jury selection extends beyond that inflicted on the defendant and the excluded juror to touch the entire community." He stated that "[s]election procedures that purposefully exclude black persons from juries undermine public confidence in the fairness of our system of justice." The Court recognized the "crippling burden of proof" enunciated in *Swain* and went on to "reject this evidentiary formulation as inconsistent with standards that have been developed since *Swain* for assessing a prima facie case under the Equal Protection Clause."

Batson set forth a three part process for reviewing whether a peremptory challenge was discriminatory: 1) the defendant needs to make a prima facie case of discrimination; 2) the burden then shifts to the state to provide a "neutral explanation" for the challenges; 3) the trial court then determines "if the defendant has established purposeful discrimination." In implementing this process, the opinion notes that "the trial court should consider all relevant circumstances." The prosecutor's rationale for striking a juror does not need to reach the level of a strike for cause, but he or she cannot "strike black veniremen on the assumption that they will be biased in a particular case simply because the defendant is black." Although the Court rejected the use of peremptory challenges to discriminate against black jurors, the case was remanded to allow the prosecutor to "come forward with a neutral explanation" for striking black jurors. The Court noted that a failure to do so calls for the conviction to be reversed.

Several concurring opinions were filed in this case and two justices dissented. Of particular note is a concurring opinion by Justice Marshall, who stated that the decision in *Batson* would not end "racial discrimination that peremptories inject into the jury-selection process." He said "that goal can be accomplished only by eliminating peremptory challenges entirely."

4. Post-Batson *Cases*

Post-*Batson* cases expand on the principles enunciated by the Court. In *Powers v. Ohio*, 499 U.S. 400 (1991), the Supreme Court held that a white criminal defendant could raise a *Batson* claim when a prosecutor improperly excluded an African American from the jury. In another case, *Edmondson v. Leesville Concrete Co.*, 500 U.S. 614 (1991), the Court found that racial discriminatory use of peremptory challenges applied not only to criminal cases, but also extended to civil cases. In *Georgia v. McCollum*, 505 U.S. 42 (1992), the Court took it one step further in holding that *Batson*'s principles applied not only to the State's use of its peremptory strikes, but also those of defense. Thus, a defendant cannot engage in purposeful racial discrimination in using his or her peremptory strikes.

In *Hernandez v. New York*, 500 U.S. 352 (1991), the Supreme Court considered a claim that a prosecutor used peremptory challenges to exclude Latinos. The Court found the use of the *Batson* analysis appropriate to this case, but then held that here the prosecutor offered a sufficient race-neutral basis for his peremptory challenges.

Batson was extended beyond race in *J.E.B. v. Alabama ex rel. T.B.*, 511 U.S. 127 (1994), when the Court stated that "gender, like race, is an unconstitutional proxy for juror competence and impartiality." The Court noted that "[d]iscrimination in jury selection, whether based on race or on gender, causes harm to the litigants, the community, and the individual jurors who are wrongfully excluded from participation in the judicial process."

Claims are sometimes made that the reasons given for a particular peremptory strike are pretextual in nature, and that the counsel is merely providing a race-neutral reason to exclude a juror. In *Felkner v. Jackson*, 131 S. Ct. 1305 (2011) the Court noted that *Batson* issues "turn[] largely on an 'evaluation of credibility.'" In this regard, the Court said that the trial court should be given "great deference." This is in large part because the trial judge is best able to evaluate the juror's demeanor. *Snyder v. Louisiana*, 552 U.S. 472 (2008). For example, a prosecutor's explanation that he struck a juror because of "long, unkempt hair, a mustache, and a beard — is race neutral and satisfies the prosecution's step two burden of articulating a nondiscriminatory reason for the strike." *Purkett v. Elem*, 514 U.S. 765 (1995).

In *Miller-El v. Drekte*, 545 U.S. 231 (2005), however, the Supreme Court granted federal habeas relief, refusing to accept the state court's finding of nonpretextual strikes excusing ten of the eleven black jurors. The Court said that when it was shown by "clear and convincing evidence" that the state's court findings were incorrect, relief is warranted. The Court stated that "[i]f the stated reason [by the prosecutor for his or her strike] does not hold up, its pretextual significance does not fade because a trial judge, or an appeals court, can imagine a reason that might not have been shown up as false."

In both *Snyder v. Louisiana*, and *Miller-El v. Drekte*, the Supreme Court reversed premised on a *Batson* violation. When a state trial judge acting in good faith, however, incorrectly rules on a peremptory challenge claim, this error does not automatically rise to the level of there being a denial of due process. In *Rivera v. Illinois*, 556 U.S. 148 (2009), the Supreme Court noted that "[b]ecause peremptory challenges are within the States' province to grant or withhold, the mistaken denial of a state-provided peremptory challenge does not, without more, violate the Federal Constitution." The Court in this case was concerned that "[t]o hold that a one-time, good-faith misapplication of *Batson* violates due process would likely discourage trial courts and prosecutors from policing a criminal defendant's discriminatory use of peremptory challenges."

E. Juror Qualifications and Challenges for Cause

States often outline a list of criteria that serve as disqualifying factors for serving on a jury. These can be found in state statutes or court rules that are adopted by the jurisdiction. For example, in Iowa there are sixteen factors that serve as the basis for challenges for cause for either the prosecution or defense. These include reasons such as the prospective juror having a prior felony conviction, "unsoundness of mind," being the individual who provided bail to the defendant, indicted for a like offense, or having been a witness for or against the defendant in a prior hearing. *I.C.A., Rule 2.18.*

A State may specify that a person can be removed for cause if he or she "is biased for or against a party or attorney" or "has opinions or conscientious scruples which would improperly influence the person's verdict." *Alaska Rules of Criminal Procedure, Rule 24.* It is also common to exclude individuals with a relation to the parties. So for example, *Utah Rules of Criminal Procedure, Rule 18* provides a challenge for cause when there is "[c]onsanguinity or affinity within the fourth degree to the person alleged to be injured by the offense charged, or on whose complaint the prosecution was instituted." Some states will exclude jurors who cannot read or write. See Tex. Code Crim. Pro. art. 35.16 (a).

A federal statute also provides for qualifications for jury service. Individuals are qualified unless the person

> "1) is not a citizen of the United States eighteen years old who has resided for a period of tne year within the judicial district; 2) is unable to read, write, and understand the English language with a degree of proficiency sufficient to fill out satisfactorily the juror qualification form; 3) is unable to speak the English language; 4) is incapable, by reason of mental or physical infirmity, to render satisfactory jury service; or 5) has a charge pending against him for the commission of , or has been convicted in a State or Federal court of record of, a crime punishable by imprisonment for more than one year and his civil rights have not been restored." 28 U.S.C. § 1865.

According to the Sixth Amendment, a defendant is provided a trial "by an impartial jury." Judges are given wide discretion in deciding when a juror lacks impartiality and should be excused for cause. 28 U.S.C. § 1870. The Sixth Amendment does not provide a specific test for determining the impartiality of the jury. *Frazier v. United States*, 335 U.S. 497 (1948). Judges or counsel routinely question jurors to determine if they can be impartial. Upon finding a juror who cannot be impartial, the juror is usually excused for cause. There is no limit to the number of jurors that can be excused for cause.

F. Capital Punishment Cases

Capital cases present unique considerations when parties attempt to secure an impartial jury. As previously noted, in capital cases where the defendant is accused of an interracial crime, he or she is entitled in the *voir dire* of prospective jurors to inform them of the race of the victim and question them on racial bias. (*See supra* Part III, C— *Voir Dire*).

When the death penalty is a possible punishment, the case is bifurcated with the jury first determining whether the accused is guilty, and if this first stage is met, the jury then determines whether the punishment should be death. Because of this extraordinary penalty, jurors are questioned during the *voir dire* as to their ability to be impartial in a death determination. This process is used to produce a "death-qualified" jury. Some justices have been enormously critical of this process, such as Justice Stevens, who argues that "obtaining a 'death qualified jury' is really a procedure that has the purpose and effect of obtaining a jury that is biased in favor of conviction." *Baze v. Rees*, 553 U.S. 35 (2008) (J. Stevens, concurring).

Several cases are used to produce the test of whether jurors excluded for cause—for being in favor of or against the death penalty—justify their removal. First in the line of cases is *Witherspoon v. Illinois*, 391 U.S. 510 (1968). In *Witherspoon*, the Supreme Court examined a trial court's excusing for cause forty-seven prospective jurors of a ninety-six person venire, all of whom had voiced general objections to the death penalty. The Court found this to be a violation of defendant's rights under the Sixth and Fourteenth Amendments of the U.S. Constitution because merely being opposed to the death penalty, or indicating that in some cases they would refuse to recommend a death sentence, is not sufficient for excluding a prospective juror. The Court held that a juror only had to "be willing to *consider* all of the penalties provided by state law, and that he not be irrevocably committed, before the trial has begun, to vote against the penalty of death regardless of the facts and circumstances that might emerge in the course of the proceedings." The *Witherspoon* test, used by later courts, is found in a footnote in the opinion where it states that jurors can be excluded for cause if they make it:

> unmistakably clear (1) that they would *automatically* vote against the imposition of capital punishment without regard to any evidence that might be developed at the trial of the case before them, or (2) that their attitude toward the death penalty would prevent them from making an impartial decision as to the defendant's *guilt*.

Jurors properly excluded are sometimes referred to as "*Witherspoon*-excludables."

In *Adams v. Texas*, 448 U.S. 38 (1980), the Court referenced the *Witherspoon* test as the foundation for holding that it was unconstitutional to exclude "members of the venire from jury service because they were unable to take an oath that the mandatory penalty of death or imprisonment for life would not 'affect [their] deliberations on any issue of fact.'" In *Lockett v. Ohio*, 438 U.S. 586 (1978), the Court found no violation of the *Witherspoon* test when jurors were excluded who "made it 'unmistakably clear' that they could not be trusted to 'abide by existing law' and 'to follow conscientiously the instructions' of the trial judge."

The *Witherspoon* test was critically examined in *Wainwright v. Witt*, 469 U.S. 412 (1985), in which the Supreme Court started by saying that the *Witherspoon* doctrine is "best understood in the context of its facts." Convicted of first-degree murder in Florida, and facing death, the defendant argued on appeal that several prospective jurors had been improperly excluded for cause by the trial court. In *Witt*, the Court adopted the test from *Adams, supra*, that the "standard is whether juror's views would 'prevent or substantially impair the performance of his duties as a juror in accordance with his instructions and his oath.'" *Witt* also endorsed the view that deference should be given to the trial court in making this decision. Four principles, therefore, developed as the *Witherspoon-Witt* test and are captured in a later case as:

> First, a criminal defendant has the right to an impartial jury drawn from a venire that has not been tilted in favor of capital punishment by selective prosecutorial challenges for cause. Second, the State has a strong interest in having jurors who are able to apply capital punishment within the framework state law prescribes. Third, to balance these interests, a juror who is substantially impaired in his or her ability to impose the death penalty under the state-law framework can be excused for cause. but if the juror is not substantially impaired, removal for cause is impermissible. Fourth, in determining whether the removal of a potential juror would vindicate the State's interest without violating the defendant's right, the trial court makes a judgment based in part on the demeanor of the juror, a judgment owed deference by reviewing courts. (Citations Omitted). *Uttecht v. Brown*, 551 U.S. 1 (2007).

A reverse-*Witherspoon* scenario was seen in *Morgan v. Illinois*, 504 U.S. 719 (1992), where the issue was what happens when a juror would automatically impose the death penalty upon conviction. The Court held that a juror who is unwilling to consider aggravating and mitigating factors prior to deciding whether to impose a sentence of death can be challenged for cause as the juror fails to meet the "requirement of impartiality embodied in the Due Process Clause of the Fourteenth Amendment." The Court in *Morgan* noted how important it was to allow a defendant in a capital case the right to inquire whether jurors would automatically impose a sentence of death. Questions that merely asked jurors whether they would "follow the law" or be "fair" were insufficient to capture whether the juror could truly be impartial on this important sentencing issue.

A joint trial, where one defendant is eligible to receive a sentence of death and the other defendant is not facing a possible death sentence, raises the issue of what happens when a death-qualified jury is selected. Does this deprive the non-death penalty defendant from a jury that is a fair cross-section in his or her community? In *Buchanan v. Kentucky*, 483 U.S. 402 (1987), the Court held that this did not violate the defendant's Sixth Amendment rights. "'*Witherspoon*-excludables' are not a distinctive group for fair-cross section purposes."

Checkpoints

- The jury trial right traces to English law and serves to protect citizens from government oppression.

- The Constitution and its Sixth Amendment provide for a right to trial by jury.

- Some Supreme Court justices advocate for complete incorporation of all the Bill of Rights being applied to the States, while others use a selective incorporation.

- The Constitutional right to trial by jury applies to the States.

- The right to trial by jury applies to "serious" offenses and is not required with "petty" offenses.

- A serious crime is one that is punishable in excess of six months imprisonment.

- A crime under six months is presumed to be petty, but in rare instances when a legislature adds significant collateral consequences to the punishment, it might be held to require a jury trial.

- Multiple petty offenses, that when aggregated, might be punishable above six months, do not necessarily make the case subject to a jury trial.

- Absent special circumstances, the federal system requires a 12-person jury for criminal cases, but States can have a lower number of members on the jury as long as it does not go below six persons.

- Although the federal system requires unanimity by the jury, a state can have a lesser unanimity requirement, but unanimity will be required if the jury is a 6-person jury or less.

- Although States vary on what is required for a waiver of the right to jury trial, in the federal system written waiver by the defendant, consent by the government and court approval is required.

- A defendant in the federal system has no automatic right to waiver of a jury trial if the government fails to consent to a waiver.

- Bench trials in the federal system require the court to make specific findings of fact in open court or enter a written decision.

- The right to a jury trial includes the right of the jury to decide whether the prosecution proved the elements of the crime charged beyond a reasonable doubt.

- Facts that increase the maximum punishment of a defendant must be either agreed to through a plea agreement or decided by a jury.

- The Sixth Amendment right to trial by jury is not implicated when a judge decides to give consecutive, as opposed to concurrent, sentences or when a sentence is increased because of a defendant's prior convictions.

- The Sixth Amendment right to trial by jury affords the defendant with a jury venire that represents a fair cross-section of the community.

- To show a violation of the fair-cross-section requirement, the defendant needs to show that the excluded group is a "distinctive" group, that the representation from this group in the venire is not fair and reasonable in relation to the number of such persons in the community, and that the underrepresentation is due to systematic exclusion of the group in the jury-selection process.

- Jurors are questioned in a process called *voir dire* to determine if they can be impartial jurors and to allow counsel the ability to strike jurors peremptorily.

- Specific *voir dire* questions may be warranted when there are "special circumstances" that find that racial issues are "inextricably bound up with the conduct of the trial" or the case involves "a violent crime and where the defendant and the victim are members of different racial or ethnic groups."

- In a capital case where the defendant is accused of an interracial crime, the defendant is entitled in the *voir dire* of prospective jurors to inform them of the race of the victim and question them on racial bias.

- With some exceptions, peremptory challenges permit the parties to strike prospective jurors without providing an explanation.

- Once a party challenging peremptory strikes based upon racial or gender discrimination makes a prima facie showing of discrimination, the burden shifts to the striking party to provide a "neutral explanation" for the challenges, which is then evaluated by the court to determine if there was purposeful discrimination.

- Deference is given to the trial court in assessing whether the party's reason for peremptorily striking a juror was improper, but clear and convincing evidence of the invalidity of this reason warrants correction by the higher court.

- When a state trial judge, acting in good faith, incorrectly rules on a peremptory challenge claim, this error does not automatically rise to the level of there being a denial of due process.

- Jurisdictions usually have statutes or court rules that specify juror qualifications, such as being able to understand the English language.

- A juror who cannot be impartial may be eliminated by the court for cause, and judges are given wide discretion to evaluate the impartiality of the juror.

- In death cases, jurors cannot be excluded merely because they are opposed to the death penalty.

- In obtaining a death-qualified jury, jurors can be excluded if their views would prevent or substantially impair them from the performance of their duties as jurors in accordance with the law — if they could consider only death or only non-death as a punishment.

- In a death penalty case, defendants are allowed to inquire of jurors beyond questions of whether they can be fair or follow the law.

Chapter 11

The Media and Fair Trials

Roadmap

- Fair trial versus free press conflict in media trial coverage
- First, Sixth, and Fourteenth Amendment constitutional regulation of this conflict
- Ethical constraints on lawyers dealing with the press
- Remedies for potential prejudice from media coverage: *voir dire*, change of venue, and jury instructions

---

This chapter addresses the occasional conflict between two rights: that of the media, lawyers, and clients to free speech versus that of the accused to a fair trial. The First Amendment guarantees the right to free speech and a free press. Especially in high-profile trials, the media seek to cover them much like sporting events, gaining audience size by playing up the more salacious aspects of the case. Even before trial, from the time of arrest, media coverage can be intense, motivated by the search for profit for media producers and recognition for reporters. The problem is magnified by the rise of the internet and the associated number of specialized blogs and social networking sites. Media coverage of criminal cases spreads rapidly. Law enforcement, including the prosecution, may want to seek out media attention, both for self-interested reasons and for the legitimate purpose of keeping the public informed of the operation of the criminal justice system. Prosecutors and the police may also reach out to seek the public's help in capturing fleeing felons or to alert the public to criminal dangers. Furthermore, the natural motivations of adversaries to seek advantage may lead prosecutors and police to try to educate the public — the potential jury pool — early on about the state's theory of the case. These same adversarial motivations may prompt defense counsel to spread its own case theory via the media.

These media contacts, however, pose substantial dangers to the accused's due process right to a fair trial and Sixth Amendment right to trial by an impartial jury. Early in a case, law enforcement has the most information about events. It is, therefore, to those agencies that the media turn. Incautious comments by law enforcement can make an accused look guilty in the eyes of the public. Those early impressions prove to have remarkable staying power, limiting the defense's ability to respond effectively. Additionally, press fear-mongering thus anti-defendant coverage, tends to sell better than a more balanced approach. Jurors chosen from the public may thus already have made up their mind that the defendant is guilty, effectively denying the presumption of innocence. Even worse, jurors may still consciously believe they can be fair when a large bloc of social science evidence — albeit not uncontested — suggests that they cannot. Yet seeking jurors totally ignorant about a high-profile case may be hard and it is not clear that the jury system should search solely for citizens so uninterested in public affairs that they are unaware of major events capturing the nation's (or the locality's) attention. Moreover, even when jurors cannot remember being exposed to media coverage, they often are affected by the general anti-defendant atmosphere that such coverage promotes.

Correspondingly, in a media-driven culture, defense counsel seek out the press too, sometimes in an effort to counterbalance law enforcement statements or to correct media error, other times to seek their own advantage with the potential jury pool, to promote other client goals (such as protecting business reputation), or even to foster defense counsel's own career ambitions. Yet if the state cannot respond to defense counsel statements that it sees as inaccurate or unfair, society may itself be denied trial fairness. The judge in such instances thus faces a dilemma: How to protect the accused's and society's right to a fair trial without unduly impinging on the media's and parties' right to free speech? Answering this question is this chapter's main goal. But it is not the chapter's only goal because the fair trial/free press tension also raises other related constitutional and ethical issues that this chapter will also address. Both constitutional and ethical concerns require considering what remedies, if any, are available short of silencing the press where trial fairness is endangered. These remedies, also discussed in this chapter, include change of venue motions, improved *voir dire*, and cautionary jury instructions.

I. Fair Trial versus Free Press:
The Major Constitutional Issues

A. Background

Like most constitutional rights, the rights to free speech and to a free press are not absolute. Instead, they must sometimes bow to countervailing considerations. The Supreme Court applies various balancing tests based upon the type of speech involved. Here we mention the two most important of these tests. "Core" First Amendment speech, such as political speech, is subject to "strict scrutiny," meaning that free speech rights may be limited only to serve compelling state interests and only via the alternatives that are least restrictive of those rights. Outside the core, such as occurs with much commercial speech, various forms of mid-level scrutiny apply. Middle level scrutiny generally means that speech limitations survive constitutional challenge if there are "substantial" countervailing state interests, there being no requirement of choosing the least restrictive alternatives. Variations on these tests, sometimes explicitly stated and in other instances merely implicit in the Court's analysis, play a crucial role in the fair trial/free press constitutional law cases to be discussed below.

In these cases, several preliminary points must be noted about how the Court engages in interest-balancing. First, the size of the state interest in regulation can vary with the speaker and the context. Thus, elected prosecutors and candidates running for office are arguably engaged in truly core political speech of the greatest interest to voters. Defense counsel, on the other hand, rarely play such an overtly political role. Yet in some cases the client's cause — perhaps an abortion opponent arrested on criminal trespassing charges — also raise overt political issues. The press, as the "Fourth Estate" playing special social roles, including monitoring governmental abuses, may likewise make a claim to special protection. Correspondingly, lawyers, though they speak on behalf of clients, have dual obligations. Defense lawyers must competently — the old phrase was "zealously" — represent their clients. But they are also "officers of the court," having some obligations to the system of justice. Prosecutors, though partly adversaries, are also obligated to "do justice" and serve "the People," including victims, communities, and even accused offenders. The combined public and private roles played by lawyers may thus affect their free speech rights, even when speaking on behalf of clients, sometimes subjecting them to more regulation than their clients themselves or the press.

Second, trial judges have a variety of tools at their disposal to resolve the fair trial/free press tension. "Gag orders" imposed on the press entirely silencing them from covering a case are the most restrictive, and almost never upheld. But there are many other less restrictive options, including gagging the lawyers, giving cautionary jury instructions, aggressively using *voir dire* to screen out biased jurors, and even changing the trial venue to a less emotionally-invested location. Some sort of remedy is important not only to avoid inflaming the jury's emotions but also to protect it from hearing evidence inadmissible at trial. Trial fairness depends upon jurors deciding guilt based solely on evidence that the adversaries have deemed important and that the court has found reliable enough to provide a basis for decision. Publicity should not offer the opportunity for an end run around the rules of evidence. Nor should publicity subtly or overtly pressure jurors into one verdict rather than another.

Third, media coverage can do damage to trial fairness in ways that do not turn on its impact on the jury. Publicity may result in pressures for judges to slant rulings to avoid an unpopular verdict. The trial judge herself may be tainted by the publicity in a way that affects the quality of her rulings. At a minimum, the judge may be exposed to one version of events by the media before the opposing party has an opportunity to challenge that story. Judges and lawyers may also both shed decorum to "play to the camera," getting their fifteen minutes of fame. Witnesses may fear coming forward if it means being thrust into the public eye. When they do come forward, they may consciously or subconsciously mold their testimony to conform with media depictions of the crime. Some potential jurors may even seek to sit on the jury to advance their own interests in publicity or selling their story to the press.

Fourth, there has recently been much attention paid to the problem of convicting the innocent. But even an acquittal does not undo all the harm an accused may face from unfair, or even fair, press coverage. The primary harm can be to reputation, which is no small injury. Customers and stock purchasers can shun a business accused of, or its officers charged with, a crime such as fraud. By the time of an acquittal, the company may be bankrupt. Employers may harbor suspicions about an accused despite his acquittal, making it hard for him to find a job. The emotional drain of even temporary damage to reputation — such as lost trust of family and friends — can be enormous. Even a convicted defendant, however, may face more stigma than he deserves, creating pressure for an unduly harsh sentence or resulting in social ostracism even after he has paid his debt to society. Reputational injuries, not solely trial accuracy and fairness injuries, thus loom in the background, as do often unacknowledged concerns about participants' privacy.

A final caution. The relevant case law has a lengthy precedential history, and there are a host of lower court cases developing the standards discussed here further. This chapter is meant merely to provide a snap shot of current law as embodied in the most important Supreme Court opinions and in the American Bar Association (ABA) codes of ethics.

B. Gag Orders

1. The Press

Where the press is involved, the United States Supreme Court has weighed the balance between media coverage and fair trial rights heavily in favor of the media, all but prohibiting gag orders silencing pre- or post-trial coverage of a case. The first of two seminal relevant modern cases, *Sheppard v. Maxwell*, 384 U.S. 333 (1966), illustrates the point.

a. *Sheppard v. Maxwell*

Marilyn Sheppard, the wife of Cleveland surgeon Sam Sheppard, was found bludgeoned to death at her home in 1954. Dr. Sheppard was charged with, and ultimately convicted of, the murder. Before Sheppard's arrest, and during the investigation, law enforcement had fed local newspapers stories about Sheppard's reluctance to help police or take a lie detector test. A front page editorial insisted that Sheppard was "getting away with murder." Other editorials asked why Sheppard was not yet in jail or urged authorities to "Quit Stalling—Bring Him In." When the trial began, newspapers published photographs of prospective jurors and their names and addresses, resulting in numerous sources contacting them by letter or phone. All but one of the jurors ultimately chosen to hear the case admitted familiarity with press coverage. Meanwhile, the press reported witness accounts never presented at trial. Nor were jurors sequestered during trial, and the trial judge merely "suggest[ed]" that they avoid further press exposure. A "carnival atmosphere" prevailed at the trial, with the courtroom packed with reporters. As Justice Clark later put it, "The fact is that bedlam reigned at the courthouse during the trial and newsmen took over practically the entire courtroom, hounding most of the participants in the trial, especially Sheppard."

The Court overturned Sheppard's conviction because of the "massive, pervasive and prejudicial publicity that attended his prosecution." The Court thus granted Sheppard habeas relief for denial of his right to a fair trial. Yet there was no evidence that the most highly prejudicial publicity had in fact reached the jury. That evidentiary dearth resulted from the trial judge's denying most defense requests to interview the jurors. But, under the circumstances, the Court simply assumed that prejudicial material reached jurors' eyes and ears.

Nevertheless, the Court stressed that nothing in its opinion was meant to prohibit the press from reporting on matters observed in the courtroom. The tone of the Court's opinion shied away from any suggestion that gagging the press would ever be permissible. The media was the "handmaiden" of systemic fairness, for the press "guards against the miscarriage of justice by subjecting the police, prosecutors, and judicial processes to extensive public scrutiny and criticism."

Safeguarding trial fairness thus rested with the trial court. But, the *Sheppard* Court explained, the trial court had numerous tools at its disposal to promote a fair trial. Notably, gag orders could be issued against trial participants. Thus, "the trial court might well have proscribed extrajudicial statements by any lawyer, party, witness, or court official which divulged prejudicial matters. . . ." References to Sheppard's refusal to take a lie-detector test, his alleged statements to police, and opinions about his guilt would have been among the sorts of statements that could have been prohibited. But, noted the Court, an array of less extreme alternative options was also available, including intense *voir dire*, jury sequestration, continuances to allow community anger to soften, and even a change of trial venue.

b. *Nebraska Press Association v. Stuart*

In *Nebraska Press Association v. Stuart*, 427 U.S. 539 (1976), the Court overturned a gag order prohibiting media publication of confessions or statements against interest purportedly made by the defendant. The defendant had been charged with murdering a ten-year-old girl and a number of her family members in a farming community of only 850 people. The Court adopted a "clear and present danger to the administration of justice" test — an analysis arguably often associated with strict scrutiny — for justifying gag orders (which are generally disfavored as "prior restraints" on speech). The Court seemed at first to suggest, however, that this version of the clear and present danger test was a relatively lenient one, not requiring an imminent danger to justice, yet permitting suppression if the evil feared from pretrial publicity was sufficiently large, though its occurrence be quite improbable.

But the Court articulated several details of this test that set a high hurdle for meeting it: first, a court must conclude that pervasive, intense pretrial publicity that might impair a fair trial *will occur* absent suppression; second, that less restrictive alternatives will be inadequate to protect the defendant's rights; and third, that the gag order will succeed in halting prejudicial publicity. The Court found the risk of massive prejudicial publicity in the grisly case before it in a small farming community nevertheless to fall short of meeting these three requirements. Although this was not a per se bar on gag orders, it was a "virtual death knell," for if the risk to a fair trial did not outweigh free press concerns under those egregious facts, it is hard to see when fair trial rights would ever prevail. Moreover, as it did in *Sheppard*, the Court in *Nebraska Press Association* reaffirmed, rather than rejected, the importance of the availability of less restrictive options, like venue change or jury instructions, "to mitigate the effects of pretrial publicity."

2. Defense Counsel

Where lawyers' speech, rather than that of the press, is involved, however, the Court has suggested that even more aggressive measures can be taken to avoid infringing upon the accused's fair trial rights, including, under certain circumstances, gagging the attorneys. The press, of course, is likely to object to silencing lawyers, a primary source of relevant information about a case, thus indirectly silencing the press itself. But the Court has not seemed troubled by these entreaties because of the special role of lawyers in our adversary system.

a. *Florida Bar v. Went For It, Inc.*: Officers of the Court

In *Florida Bar v. Went For It, Inc.*, 515 U.S. 618 (1995), the Court seemed to embrace implicitly the special role that lawyers play in our system of justice, upholding a Florida bar rule prohibiting personal injury lawyers from sending targeted direct-mail solicitations to victims and their relatives for thirty days following an accident. The Florida Bar's brief to the Court was more explicit on this point than the Court's opinion itself. Although *Went For It, Inc.* did not involve pretrial publicity, the bar's brief in that case discussed the "officer of the court" rationale for regulating lawyers' speech in such a way as to set the stage for better understanding that rationale's function in cases in the precise setting that is the subject of this chapter.

The bar argued that the Court "has historically recognized that the exercise of free expression is subject to reasonable limitations when the nature of such exercise is detrimental to, or inconsistent with, the mission of the public institution within which the expression is exercised," offering examples from public employment, penal institutions, the armed forces, and educational institutions. Indeed, the bar noted, the Court itself recognized that "lawyers are essential to the primary government function of administering justice, and have historically been 'officers of the courts.'" The bar recognized that this was part of lawyers' dual role as self-employed businesspeople *and* "assistants to the court in the search of a just solution to disputes." The bar then concluded:

> While lawyers are not public employees, the analogy is valid. As "officers of the court" lawyers perform an essential role in the administration of justice. Courts have always recognized that a lawyer's speech within the courtroom is subject to considerable judicial oversight in order to protect the integrity of the judicial process. The fact that advertising the availability of legal services takes place outside the courtroom is of little consequence in this context. Such advertising deals solely with an essential aspect of the administration of the public function. To the extent that it may adversely affect the mission of the judicial system, the State has no less interest in its regulation than it does in any employment situation.... The public's perception of, and

confidence in, its system of justice and those who administer it is critical to the stability of a democratic society.

The Court in *Went For It, Inc* applied an intermediate level of scrutiny governing commercial speech that was first set forth in *Central Hudson Gas & Electric Corp. v. Public Service Commission*, 447 U.S. 557 (1980). Under that rule, speech that is misleading or concerns unlawful activity is protected only if: (1) the government asserts a substantial interest; (2) the government demonstrates that the protection of commercial speech directly and materially advances that interest; and (3) the regulation is narrowly drawn. The *Went For It, Inc.* Court's explanation of the meaning of these three prongs helps set the stage for understanding how the Court weighs defense free speech rights, defense counsel obligations to serve as an officer of the court, and systemic fairness.

The Court emphasized that, unlike under rational basis review, the Court would consider only the interests articulated by the state. It would not presuppose others. However, the Court had "little trouble" crediting the Bar's asserted interest in protecting the "privacy and tranquility of personal injury victims and their loved ones" by prohibiting mail solicitations to accident victims within thirty days of the accident. These interests mattered because they were factors relevant to the Bar's "paramount" interest in "curbing activities that negatively affect the administration of justice." The harm to the legal profession's reputation from what the bar described as conduct "universally … deplorable and beneath common decency because of its intrusion upon the special vulnerability of … victims or their families" was likely to have such a negative effect.

The Court found *Central Hudson's* second prong—advancing of the government's interest in a direct and material way—was met as well in *Went For It, Inc.* In doing so, however, the Court emphasized that the state cannot meet its burden by "mere speculation and conjecture." Rather, the government must demonstrate that "the harms it recites are real and that its restriction will in fact alleviate them to a material degree." The state met its burden by its extensive and unrebutted empirical data, consisting of a 106-page summary of the bar's two-year study of lawyer advertising and solicitation. The study contained both statistical data, including surveys of Florida adults about their views on direct mail advertising, a subset of whom actually received such advertising, and anecdotal data "noteworthy for its breadth and detail." The majority rejected the dissent's complaints of methodological flaws in the study, specifically, that there were few indications of the sample size or selection procedure and no copies of the actual surveys employed. The five-member majority determined that case law did not require that empirical data be accompanied by a "surfeit of background information." Indeed, the Court noted, in other First Amendment contexts, applying a compelling state interest standard, studies and anecdotes pertaining to different localities altogether were found to be adequate. In one case, even history, consensus and simple common sense were sufficient.

Significantly, the Court distinguished *Shapero v. Kentucky Bar Association*, 486 U.S. 466 (1980), where the Court held that the First Amendment was violated with a categorical prohibition on lawyers who solicit legal business for pecuniary gain by sending truthful and non-deceptive letters to potential clients. The *Went For It* Court distinguished *Shapero* partly because the state had never sought to justify its flat letter-solicitation prohibition on privacy grounds, had not offered empirical evidence of undue influence and overreaching — apparently the only interest the state did identify — or invasion of privacy, and involved a broad ban on all direct-mail solicitations, regardless of time or recipient, unlike the thirty day delay rule in *Went For It*. The *Went For It* Court also emphasized that the case before it, unlike *Shapero*, involved targeted letters to victims or relatives "while wounds are still open," a "willful or knowing affront to or invasion of the tranquility of bereaved or injured individuals that ... simply does not cause the same kind of reputational harm to the profession unearthed by the Florida Bar's study."

The Court also distinguished *Bolger v. Youngs Drug Products Corp.*, 463 U.S. 60 (1985), in which the Court rejected the federal government's "paternalistic" effort to ban potentially offensive direct mail advertisements for contraceptives. The *Went For It* situation differed because continuing "outrage and irritation" came from the mere receipt of letter solicitations by aggrieved families, even if the letters were never read. On the other hand, in *Bolger* the injury came from reading the letters, and recipients could simply avert their eyes or throw the offending literature in the trash. Moreover, unlike in *Bolger*, the *Went For It* rule was concerned not with "'offense' in the abstract ... but with the demonstrable detrimental effects that such 'offense' has on the profession it regulates."

Although not expressly mentioning the "officer of the court" rationale relied upon by the Bar, the Court's emphasis on each lawyer's need sometimes to subordinate his commercial speech interests to the interests of the community that may be harmed resonates with the Bar's argument about the special obligations of attorneys to the justice system. The Court did require some empirical or extensive anecdotal evidence to support the state's purported interests in regulation, but the support could be far from perfect. Privacy invasion mattered too, justifying stronger restrictions on lawyers' speech where individual privacy interests might be injured. Moreover, that a particular method of lawyer communication was postponed, rather than entirely banned, mattered to the Court too. Granted, *Went for It* arose in a civil setting outside the risks of ill effects on a trial that are raised by pretrial publicity in criminal cases. Nevertheless, *Went for It* might suggest that the Court views much lawyer speech as primarily commercial in nature, meriting only middle scrutiny of state regulatory efforts, even in other contexts. Furthermore, pretrial publicity raises risks of privacy invasion to individuals in high-profile cases that may be more severe than those involved in *Went for It*—especially for criminal defendants whose lost privacy may wound their reputations severely and risk their conviction based upon juror preconceptions. Moreover, though lawyer speech about a criminal case might be delayed far longer than in *Went for It*, the speech is nevertheless not entirely barred, as the many lawyer-authored books on specific criminal cases illustrate.

b. *Gentile v. State Bar*

Gentile v. State Bar, 501 U.S. 1030 (1991), unlike *Went for It, Inc.*, specifically involved pretrial publicity. There, Dominic Gentile held a press conference about a case within hours after his client had been indicted on criminal charges. Gentile's counsel made a prepared statement to the press in which he said that his client was innocent and that there was far more evidence that a Detective Scholl had committed the crime than had the defendant. Counsel further accused the prosecutor and police department of using the prosecution to cover up Detective Scholl's crimes. Defense counsel additionally declared that at least several of the "victims" were drug dealers and money launderers. The State Bar of Nevada had a rule in force similar to the then-operative version of Rule 3.6 of the ABA's *Model Rules of Professional Conduct* that governed what lawyers could tell the press about pending cases. After a hearing, the State Bar Disciplinary Board recommended a private reprimand, finding a Rule 3.6 violation. This conclusion was approved on appeal to the Nevada Supreme Court, but reversed by the United States Supreme Court.

While the Court held that the discipline imposed did violate the First Amendment, the Court held that this was so because the state's "safe harbor" provision in its Rule 3.6 equivalent permitted the speech in question, and, if it did not (as the state supreme court held), then it violated constitutional bars on undue vagueness and selective enforcement.

But the Court strongly suggested that, had Rule 3.6 been more clearly drafted, it would have upheld the regulation. Moreover, it would have done so because of the special obligations of lawyers to the justice system that limits their free speech rights. While there were various opinions in *Gentile*, five members of the Court agreed that the state may regulate speech by lawyers representing clients in pending cases more readily than it may regulate the press. Moreover, these five members did so because they concluded that lawyers are different, serving a special role.

Thus, Chief Justice Rehnquist, in an opinion for the Court, stressed "that lawyers in pending cases [are] subject to ethical restrictions, on speech to which an ordinary citizen would not be." Indeed, he concluded, "[e]ven in an area far from the courtroom and the pendency of a case," lawyers are not protected to the same extent as those individuals in other professions. This was so because a lawyer is "an officer of the court, and, like the court itself, an instrument … of justice." Thus the speech of "lawyers in pending cases may be regulated under a less demanding standard than that established for regulation of the press."

Justice O'Connor reaffirmed these principles in her concurrence. But on this point Justices Marshall, Blackmun, Stevens, and Kennedy disagreed in dissent, concluding that the speech at issue was critical of the government and thus lay "at the very center of the First Amendment." Furthermore, five Justices concluded that the core provision of Nevada's Rule 3.6 equivalent, which prohibited lawyer speech that created a "substantial likelihood" of "material prejudice" at trial, met this more deferential First Amendment test.

The rationale for this deference to the Rule 3.6 drafters was, once again, that lawyers, as officers of the court, have a "fiduciary responsibility not to engage in public debate that will redound to the detriment of the parties or … the fair administration of justice." The Rule 3.6 equivalent's "substantial likelihood" test was, the Court concluded, designed precisely to "protect the integrity and fairness of [the s]tate's judicial system." Moreover, the limitations the rule imposed were narrow and necessary to achieve the state goals of avoiding improper influence on the likely outcome of the trial and avoiding tainting or prejudicing the jury venire. The Court found that the state had an adequate interest even if an untainted jury panel could ultimately be found.

The Court found the tailoring sufficiently narrow, even though other options to protect a fair trial were available, such as sensitive *voir dire* or a change of venue. The Court concluded that these methods impose "serious costs" on the state and litigants, a substantial harm the state can legitimately avoid. The Court found narrow tailoring even though it admitted that other options like *voir dire* might have completely avoided any impact of the publicity on the trial outcome in particular cases, without the need to muzzle the lawyers or the parties. This is not the kind of "narrow tailoring" associated with a compelling state interest analysis. It is more like requiring "less restrictive" than "least restrictive" alternatives, a form of middle scrutiny.

Furthermore, the Court found a "substantial government interest," even though the defense attorney sought to counteract allegedly prejudicial statements first made to the press *by prosecutors*. The defense attorney responded in the media (1) in order to protect his client's reputation and (2) because the defense had information that the prosecution lacked. The Court also found it significant that the lawyers' comments were merely postponed until after trial—effectively a time, place, and manner restriction—an observation that could potentially be understood as permitting limiting lawyers' speech *only* to protect trial fairness, a reading that would therefore allow statements damaging trial participants' reputations.

Despite the Court's strong defense of the state's regulatory authority over the lawyer's speech in *Gentile*, the Court ultimately held that the discipline imposed there violated the Constitution because the state's safe harbor provision was unduly vague. But the *Gentile* Court's logic provided ample ground for upholding better-drafted restrictions on lawyers' speech as a means to promote fair trials untainted by pretrial media coverage. Indeed, the ABA redrafted Rule 3.6 in light of *Gentile* to achieve just this goal, a point discussed in greater detail later in this chapter.

Moreover, although the Court found inadequate defense counsel's asserted justification for his statements in *Gentile* that they were an act of self-defense needed in part to restore the damage done to his client's reputation by the prosecutor, that conclusion is best understood as an application of the principle that two wrongs do not make a right. It should not be read as condoning the prosecutor's reputation-wounding statements themselves or minimizing the weight of protecting against reputational harm as a justification for limiting or gagging prosecutors' public statements. To the contrary, the prosecutor, unlike defense counsel, has a "duty to do justice." Whatever this highly-contested term means, at the very least it includes taking steps to affirmatively provide the accused with a fair trial and certainly includes avoiding efforts to deny the accused such a trial. It also includes protecting against excessive and broader harms, such as undue harm to reputation, as is explained in more depth shortly. This greater burden of responsibility is imposed on the prosecutor because of the enormous power he wields on behalf of the state against the usually weaker defendant. *See* MODEL CODE OF PROF'L RESPONSIBILITY EC 7-13 (1980) ("duty to seek justice"); MODEL RULES OF PROF'L CONDUCT R. 3.8 ("Minister of Justice").

C. Elected Nature of Most Prosecutors: A First Amendment Wrinkle?

1. Elected Judge Analogy

In *Republican Party of Minnesota v. White*, 536 U.S. 765 (2002), the Court held unconstitutional under the First Amendment Minnesota's state constitutional prohibition against candidates for judicial office, including sitting judges, announcing their views on disputed legal or political issues (Minnesota's so-called "announce clause"). The Minnesota Supreme Court limited the apparently broad meaning of the announce clause, declaring it to reach only disputed issues likely to come before the candidate were he to be elected a judge. Comments on past judicial decisions were, therefore, permissible, though a candidate's public insistence on ignoring the stare decisis effect of such decisions was banned.

Gregory Wersal withdrew from his 1996 campaign for a judgeship after a complaint was filed against him for, among other things, distributing literature criticizing Minnesota Supreme Court abortion, crime, and welfare decisions. When he ran again in 1998, he sought an advisory opinion from the Lawyers Professional Responsibility Board on whether it planned to enforce the announce clause. When Wersal received an equivocal answer, he filed suit in federal district court, along with other plaintiffs, seeking a declaration of the announce clause's unconstitutionality as violative of free speech under the First Amendment. Upon the filing of cross-motions for summary judgment, the district court held against the plaintiffs, concluding that the announce clause was indeed constitutional. The Supreme Court reversed.

The Court concluded that the announce clause permitted content discrimination against speech at the core of First Amendment protections, and therefore subjected it to strict scrutiny. But the Court found that the clause, even as narrowly interpreted by Minnesota's Supreme Court, was not narrowly tailored to serve the allegedly compelling state interests of preserving the actual and apparent impartiality of the state judiciary. There were, said the Court, three possible meanings of "impartiality" in this context. First, according to the Court, impartiality might mean a lack of preconception in favor of a particular view of the law. But such a goal, insisted the Court, is "neither possible nor desirable"; impossible psychologically and undesirable because it would reflect a "complete *tabula rasa*," hardly the sort of learned mind sought in a judicial candidate. To pretend otherwise—to lie—for the sake of creating a false appearance of this sort of impartiality cannot constitute a compelling interest.

A second meaning of impartiality might be "open-mindedness," a willingness to remain open to persuasion, at least in a pending case, even on legal questions for which the judge holds a preconceived position. The Court concluded, however, that the state had not met its burden under the strict scrutiny test of establishing that campaign statements of positions are uniquely destructive of open-mindedness. The Court noted that candidate *promises* to take a particular action were banned by separate state laws, but such promises were not before it, and it simply was not persuaded that non-promissory statements of legal and policy positions would in effect psychologically operate as promises committing the former candidate to action once sitting on the judge's bench.

The third sense of impartiality examined by the Court was bias for or against a particular *party* to the proceeding, the correct position being that the judge who hears a case should "apply the law to … [one party] in the same way he applies it to any other party." On this point too, however, the Court declared:

> We think it plain that the announce clause is not narrowly tailored to serve impartiality (or the appearance of impartiality) in this sense. Indeed, the clause is barely tailored to serve that interest *at all*, in as much as it does not restrict speech for or against particular *parties*, but rather speech for or against particular *issues*. To be sure, when a case arises that turns on a legal issue on which the judge (as a candidate) had taken a particular stand, the party taking the opposite stand is likely to lose. But not because of any bias against that party, or favoritism toward the other party. *Any* party taking that position is just as likely to lose. The judge is applying the law (as he sees it) evenhandedly.

The Court rejected any rigid distinction between judicial and legislative elections in a country, like ours, where courts can "make" common law, set aside laws enacted by the legislature, and alter the shape of state constitutions. Accordingly, any abridgement of the right to speak in the electioneering context turns First Amendment jurisprudence upside down, for "[d]ebate on the qualifications of candidates is 'at the core of our electoral process and of the First Amendment freedoms,'" and it is "'simply not the function of government to select which issues are worth discussing or debating in the course of a political campaign.'"

2. Elected Prosecutors

It can be argued that elected prosecutors' speech is indistinguishable in any relevant way from judicial speech. Like judges in lower court cases, prosecutors are always running for office. If their speech ends up endangering the right to a fair trial in a particular case, less-restrictive procedural remedies, like a change of venue, might be necessary. But silencing the prosecutors' speech in the first place is unwise absent the most unusual and compelling of circumstances. Prosecutors' speech about ongoing cases can serve a valuable public function because the investigation or prosecution is often important on issues of public policy. As the Supreme Court has explained, "it would be difficult to single out any aspect of government of higher ... importance to the people than the manner in which criminal trials are conducted." *Richmond Newspapers, Inc. v. Virginia,* 448 U.S. 555, 575 (1980). Prosecutors also might have an obligation to keep the public informed about criminal matters. Furthermore, the prosecutor is an advocate, who may need to make public statements to counteract those of the defense or to respond to media statements unfairly biasing the jury pool against the state's case.

II. Ethical Constraints

A. Prosecutors' Special Obligations

The ABA recognizes the prosecutor's special responsibilities concerning communicating with the media in Rule 3.8(f) of the Model Rules of Professional Conduct. That rule mandates that, with one exception, prosecutors must "refrain from making extrajudicial comments that have a substantial likelihood of heightening public condemnation of the accused." The one exception from this mandate is for statements that are *necessary* to inform the public of the nature and extent of the prosecutor's action and that serve a legitimate law enforcement purpose. Moreover, the prosecutor has an affirmative obligation to exercise reasonable care to "prevent investigators, law enforcement personnel, employees or other persons assisting or associated with the prosecutor in a criminal case from making an extrajudicial statement that the prosecutor would be prohibited from making under Rule 3.6 [governing media statements by all lawyers] or this rule."

Because Rule 3.8(f) refers to avoiding heightening "public condemnation" of the accused, rather than merely to preventing prejudice in a potential adjudicatory proceeding, the Rule's text may be read as guarding against harm to the accused's reputation as an important interest distinct from ensuring a fair trial. Comment 5 to Rule 3.8 indeed explains that paragraph (f) of that rule "supplements" Rule 3.6's protections against pretrial publicity biasing potential jurors because "[i]n the context of a criminal prosecution, a prosecutor's extrajudicial statement can create the *additional problem* of increasing public condemnation of the accused." Note too that the rule requires the prosecutor to make a probability judgment: is there a *substantial* likelihood that the prosecutor's statements will heighten public condemnation of the accused? *See* MODEL RULES OF PROF'L CONDUCT R. 3.8(f) & cmt. 5

Commentators have critiqued Rule 3.8(f) as only sporadically enforced. Moreover, it does not expressly address what some believe is the greater need for gag orders to prevent reputational injury than to prevent injury to a fair trial. Fair trials can arguably be protected against prejudicial publicity by the various tools discussed above: jury instructions, jury selection procedures, delay to let passions cool, and venue change. But these remedies are all focused on trial fairness, not fairness to an accused's reputation. Constitutional law in the area likewise tends to emphasize trial fairness as the primary concern to be balanced against free speech. But there simply are no tools to prevent reputational damage separate and apart from tools available only at trial.

B. All Lawyers

1. Content of Statements to the Press

ABA Model Rule of Professional Conduct 3.6 applies to all lawyers, not merely prosecutors, and, unlike the prosecutor-specific rule, focuses on trial fairness. Rule 3.6(a) declares a general prohibition on any lawyer who currently is or has participated in investigating or litigating a matter from making a certain type of extrajudicial statement. Specifically, lawyers "shall not" make such statements where the lawyer "knows or reasonably should know" that they will be "disseminated by means of public communication and will have a substantial likelihood of materially prejudicing an adjudicative proceeding in the matter." Note that a negligence standard is sufficient to support sanctions. It is enough that the lawyer "reasonably should know" that he has raised the prohibited risk. But this risk must not be a minor one. Rather, it must raise a "substantial likelihood" of the feared harm to trial fairness. Furthermore, the harm to trial fairness is defined as "materially prejudicing an adjudicative proceeding." Although the term "materially prejudicing" is not defined, it seems to suggest one changing, or at least raising a significant risk (a "substantial likelihood") of changing, the trial's outcome. The word "prejudice" itself, moreover, seems to suggest unfairness or inappropriateness. Yet this is vague guidance. Comment 5 to the Rule thus seeks to add clarity by specifying six types of statement content that are "more likely than not to have a material prejudicial effect on a proceeding, particularly when they refer to … a criminal matter, or any other proceeding that could result in incarceration." These six risky subject matter statements are those relating to:

(1) the character, credibility, reputation, or criminal record of a party, suspect in a criminal investigation or witness, or the identity of a witness,
or the expected testimony of a party or witness;

(2) in a criminal case or proceeding that could result in incarceration, the
possibility of a guilty plea to the offense or the existence or contents of
any confession, admission, or statement given by the defendant or suspect or that person's refusal or failure to make a statement;

(3) the performance or results of any examination or test or the refusal or
failure of a person to submit to an examination or test, or the identity
or nature of the physical evidence expected to be presented;

(4) any opinion as to the guilt or innocence of a defendant or suspect in a
criminal case or proceeding that could result in incarceration;

(5) information that the lawyer knows or reasonably should know is likely
to be inadmissible as evidence in a trial and that would, if disclosed,
create a substantial risk of prejudicing an impartial trial; or

(6) the fact that a defendant has been charged with a crime, unless there is
included therein a statement explaining that the charge is merely an accusation and that the defendant is presumed innocent until and unless
proven guilty.

Comment 7 stresses that "[c]riminal jury trials will be the most sensitive to
extrajudicial speech," apparently meaning more sensitive than bench trials or
civil trials, though material prejudice is possible in those instances as well.
Note too that the rule is limited to commentary by lawyers involved in investigating or litigating the case and their associates. The Rules' drafters' rationale was stated in comment 3 to the Rule: "Recognizing that the public value of
informed commentary is great and the likelihood of prejudice to a proceeding
by the commentary of a lawyer who is not involved in the proceeding is small,
the rule applies only to lawyers who are, or who have been involved in the investigation or litigation of a case, and their associates."

Remember that *Gentile* approved of the substantial likelihood test now in
Rule 3.6 and that was in the rule there before the Court. But the Court in *Gentile* thought that that test in isolation raised undue vagueness problems. To address those problems, the ABA both added the Rule's comment 5, just discussed,
and added to the Rule's text itself a subsection (b) specifying what things a
lawyer can safely say to the media, in effect creating a safe harbor. Those safe
harbors include revealing the following information:

(1) the claim, offense or defense involved and, except when prohibited by
law, the identity of the persons involved;

(2) information contained in a public record;

(3) that an investigation of a matter is in progress;

(4) the scheduling or result of any step in litigation;

(5) a request for assistance in obtaining evidence and information necessary thereto;

(6) a warning of danger concerning the behavior of a person involved, when
there is reason to believe that there exists the likelihood of substantial harm
to an individual or to the public interest; and

(7) in a criminal case, in addition to subparagraphs (1) through (6):

(i)   the identity, residence, occupation, and family of the accused;

(ii)   if the accused has not been apprehended, information necessary to aid in apprehension of that person;

(iii)   the time and place of arrest; and

(iv)   the identity of investigating and arresting officers or agencies
and the length of the investigation.

This is not an exhaustive list of permissible statements, but a lawyer can be
confident that anything on the list is indeed permissible.

Rule 3.6 addresses a right of fair response when an adversary, a member of
the press, or anyone else has made an unfairly prejudicial statement to the
media. The theory seems to be that a partial remedy for speech-inflicted injury
is more speech correcting or fairly countering the injurious speech. More
specifically, Rule 3.6(c) permits a lawyer to make a statement "that a reasonable lawyer would believe is required to protect a client from the substantial undue
prejudicial effect of recent publicity not initiated by the lawyer or the lawyer's
client." Note the implicit contributory fault concept: a client cannot make an
unduly prejudicial statement to open the door for his lawyer's then making
statements she otherwise could not. The offending statements must come from
some source other than the lawyer or her client. Only then is the right to fair
response to statements creating substantial unduly prejudicial effects triggered.
To avoid this exception's swallowing the rule, Rule 3.6(c) also limits responding statements to "such information as is necessary to mitigate the recent adverse publicity."

Special confidentiality rules may also limit lawyers' speech, for example, in
juvenile, domestic relations, and mental disability proceedings. Rule 3.4 (c),
prohibiting knowingly disobeying "an obligation under the rules of a tribunal," governs such confidentiality restrictions. The only exception recognized
by Rule 3.4(c) is "for an open refusal [to comply with a tribunal's rules] based
on an assertion that no valid obligation exists."

Lawyers may not circumvent these rules by turning to other lawyers in their
offices who are not involved in investigating or trying the case. Thus Rule 3.6

(d) declares that "No lawyer associated in a firm or government agency with a lawyer subject to paragraph (a) shall make a statement prohibited by paragraph (a)."

Finally, Comment 1 to Rule 3.6 stresses that some limitations on lawyer speech are necessary to avoid circumventing the rules of evidence and of trial decorum, particularly in jury trials. But the comment likewise stresses the important free speech concerns: the public's right to know about safety threats and efforts to combat them, its "legitimate interest in the conduct of legal proceedings, particularly in matters of general public concern," and the "direct significance in debate and deliberation over questions of public policy" of the subject matter of legal proceedings.

2. Client Media Campaigns

Sometimes clients insist on conducting their own media campaigns. A businessman might, for example, be more worried about the ill effects of media coverage on his livelihood than his likely conviction and sentence for a first offense. If a lawyer becomes involved in such a campaign, either in deciding whether the client should wage it and, if so, what should be said and how, the lawyer is arguably bound by the codes of ethics. In other words, the lawyer should not be able to use the client to say what the lawyer cannot. Moreover, the lawyer's advice might best be limited to statements that can affect trial outcomes and fairness. If a lawyer is involved in waging such a campaign, furthermore, the lawyer must do so competently. But strictly legal training may not be sufficient for a lawyer to behave competently in this area. The lawyer likely should, by training and experience, be familiar with the science and artistry of media communication. Many lawyers, concerned that they do not have sufficient expertise on their own, retain media consultants, either to aid the client in his own campaign or to aid the lawyer in deciding what he or she should say to the press. Media consultants are, however, expensive, and some lawyers feel that the ethical dangers and risks to the client of media contact outweigh the benefits. Lawyers will also often advise clients simply not to discuss the case with anyone, including the press, though not all lawyers agree in every case, and not all clients do what their lawyers advise. *See, e.g., State v. Grossberg*, 705 A.2d 608 (Del. Super. Ct. 1997) (holding that a lawyer preparing his client and witnesses for a media appearance in a pending case cannot advise them to comment on areas prohibited to him were he the one to speak).

3. Lawyer Media Contracts

ABA Model Rule of Professional Responsibility 1.8(d) reads as follows: "Prior to the conclusion of representation of a client, a lawyer shall not make or negotiate an agreement giving the lawyer literary or media rights to a portrayal or account based in substantial part on information relating to the representation." Yet this rule alone is no guarantee of a lawyer's ethical behavior. Even after the lawyer's representation is concluded, lawyer media deals risk revealing confidential information. Moreover, a lawyer expected later to cash in with the media may exercise muddled judgment, even while representing a client. That conflict of interest may be hard to overcome, because the potential financial rewards may distort the lawyer's judgement about important issues, such as whether to accept a plea offer when that might lessen the media value of the case. Comment 9 to Rule 1.8(d) thus cautions lawyers to be careful to guard against such conflicts: "[m]easures suitable in the representation of the client may detract from the publication value of an account of the representation." Nevertheless, insists this commentary, it is the client's interests, not the lawyer's financial needs, that must prevail.

III. Remedies for Prejudicial Media Coverage

Whether unfairly prejudicial information reaches jurors through the media because of the media's own investigative efforts or because of attorney comments, a remedy is required to protect the Sixth Amendment right to an impartial jury and the Fifth and Fourteenth Amendment due process rights to fundamentally fair trial procedures. As discussed in Part I, the Court has been reluctant to impose gag orders on the media, partly because the Court assumes that there are a variety of remedial devices, including in particular *voir dire*, cautionary jury instructions, and change of venue motions. This chapter portion is devoted to exploring the effectiveness of these remedies in practice and some hints for trial and appellate practitioners.

A. *Voir Dire*

In *Mu'Min v. Virginia*, 500 U.S. 415 (1991), the Court squarely addressed the degree of detail the court must exercise in questioning potential jurors on *voir dire* to avoid sitting a partial jury in a high-profile case. There Mu'Min, while an inmate serving a 48-year sentence for murder, allegedly committed a murder and robbery of a carpet store owner when Mu'Min temporarily escaped from a work detail during his lunch break. The case received extensive news coverage, including criticizing various government officials' conduct as responsible for the escape. But the publicity included reports that Mu'Min had confessed to killing his victim with a steel spike, once in the neck, once in the chest; that he had contemplated raping her; that he had escaped for previous criminal forays on several occasions; and that government officials were already convinced of his guilt. The trial court denied a motion for change of venue. The trial judge denied a defense motion for individual *voir dire*, preferring collective questioning but agreeing to break the venire into panels of four, where necessary, for further questioning about trial publicity. The court also rejected defendant's request, via motion, that the court ask jurors who had seen news items the specific content of what they had seen.

Twenty-six jurors were questioned as a group. The trial judge asked group members who had acquired any information about the case from any source to identify themselves. But the court did not inquire of those who responded about what was the specific source of their information. Those prospective jurors were asked whether they could still be impartial, whether whatever information they received would affect their impartiality, whether they could enter the jury box with an open mind and wait until hearing the entire case before reaching a fixed opinion, and whether anything they had learned from other sources would prevent them from having an open mind until all the evidence was completed, if they were seated as jurors. The court denied the defense's motion to dismiss all sixteen prospective jurors who admitted having been exposed to information about the case, then denied the defense's renewed motion for a change of venue. The court did dismiss for cause one of the sixteen jurors because he said that he could not be impartial. The court conducted further *voir dire* in panels of four, asking any juror who had received information about the case whether he or she had formed an opinion about guilt and, if so, whether the juror could still be impartial. If a juror said that he or she had discussed the case with anyone, the court asked with whom and whether the juror could still be impartial. One juror was dismissed because of her feelings toward Muslims, another because of her refusal to impose a death sentence if the defendant is found guilty, a third because of his insistence on imposing the death penalty if the defendant is found guilty. The trial judge also dismissed *sua sponte* a prospective juror who equivocated about her impartiality. The prosecution and the defense each exercised six peremptory challenges. Of the twelve jurors seated, eight had read or heard something about the case, but none of the eight admitted to forming an opinion about guilt or to holding any bias. That jury convicted Mu'Min of capital murder and recommended a death sentence.

The Supreme Court affirmed the conviction. The Court conceded that more detailed questioning of each juror about the content of the media or other information to which the juror was exposed might have enabled defense counsel to make more informed use of peremptory challenges. But there is no constitutional right to such challenges, noted the Court. The Court further conceded that more detail about media content might aid the trial court's credibility determination whether jurors were being truthful. But that these questions would be more helpful does not alone render the trial fundamentally unfair in their absence. Whether questions about media content might force jurors to reevaluate their answers that they could be impartial was, in the Court's view, "speculative." Furthermore, group questioning, even in small groups of four, would be counterproductive as one prospective juror's summary of media content would then expose other prospective jurors to that content. But individual questioning of certain jurors might make them feel as if they were on trial, a by no means dispositive but certainly a relevant point. Moreover, judges traditionally have wide discretion in conducting *voir dire* for media bias. That deference, explained the Court, makes sense because the judge "sits in the locale where the publicity is said to have had its effect and brings to his evaluation of any such claim his own perception of the depth and extent of news stories that might influence a juror." The Court cautioned that the trial judge must not impute his perceptions to the prospective jurors but suggested that judicial perceptions aid the trial judge in better evaluating media's impact on jurors and in deciding "how detailed an inquiry to make of the members of the jury venire."

A trial judge's finding of juror impartiality is, therefore, reversible only for "manifest error."

In some cases, the Court agreed, a "wave of public passion" can be so great as to raise a presumption of prejudice in a community of particular characteristics, including size. But, in the Court's view, the nature of the publicity here — much of which focused on wrongdoing by corrections officials — in a metropolitan area of over three million people did not fit into that presumptive category. Moreover, the *voir dire* here was far from perfunctory. Four questions were asked of the group on pretrial publicity's effects and follow up questions were asked in panels of four. The trial judge found this procedure sufficient for him to make credibility determinations. Additionally, this questioning did result in the dismissal of some jurors. Further questioning about the specific content of the media to which the prospective jurors were each exposed was thus not required.

Justice O'Connor, in her concurring opinion, emphasized that the defense attached to their motion for a change of venue 47 newspaper articles, thus making the trial judge aware of the full range of information to which potential jurors could have been exposed. Having this information well-armed the trial court to make prospective juror credibility determinations. Content questioning would merely "repeat what the judge already knew" but might have been helpful in assessing credibility based upon the questioned individual's tone of voice or demeanor. But that such questioning might be marginally more useful does not make it a requirement of the Sixth Amendment.

Social science calls into question the wisdom of the Court's decision and of Justice O'Connor's concurrence. Much of that science reveals that prospective jurors do not always reveal their views fully or honestly, especially in open court group questioning. Moreover, many jurors do not know their own ability to be impartial under many circumstances of media exposure. Much of the process causing prejudice occurs unconsciously or preconsciously. Prospective jurors often tend as well to minimize their media exposure or its effects on them.

Justice Marshall, joined by Justices Blackmun and Stevens, in dissent, expressed views consistent with this social science. Marshall emphasized that the type of information reported in this case — a confession, gruesome details about the killing's being done with a steel spike, the defendant's alleged prior escapes to commit other crimes, and the conviction of officials in the defendant's guilt — were particularly inflammatory. Furthermore, explained Justice Marshall, a prospective juror's own assurances of impartiality are simply not trustworthy because he " 'may have an interest in concealing his own bias ... [or] may be unaware of it,' " quoting Justice O'Connor's opinion in *Smith v. Phillips*, 455 U.S. 209 (1982). A juror's natural human pride alone may interfere with the juror's freely admitting to himself or others that he cannot be fair. Indeed, insisted Justice Marshall, the cursory *voir dire* here was inconsistent with the "*searching* questioning of potential jurors ... to screen out those with fixed opinions as to guilt or innocence" that the Court demanded in *Nebraska Press Association*, discussed above.

In Justice Marshall's view, content questioning is required whenever a juror admits to media exposure for three reasons. First, some content is so inflammatory as to create a strong presumption that a prospective juror's claim of impartiality should not be believed. Second, the question of impartiality is itself a mixed question of law and fact. A prospective juror may thus not fully understand what impartiality means. Content questioning enables the judge to gather the facts needed to make the partly legal decision whether a juror can be impartial. Third, content exposure details are necessary to accurate judicial fact finding; "the precise content of ... publicity constitutes contextual information essential to an accurate assessment of whether the prospective juror's profession of impartiality is believable." Justice Marshall also rejected the argument that content-questioning would be unduly burdensome on trial courts, noting that it has worked well where it or analogous procedures have been used. Finally, Marshall found O'Connor's point that the trial judge was well-informed about the content of the media messages irrelevant to whether the prospective jurors were aware of that content and rendered partial by it. In Marshall's view, the particular content expressed by the media in the case before the Court was so inflammatory that the Court should hold that it was prejudicial as a matter of law.

Justice Kennedy dissented on an entirely different ground. He emphasized that total juror ignorance of a case is not required. But he also stressed that deference to trial judge decisions in this area is based on the expectation that the trial judge will conduct a sufficient *voir dire*. The problem for Justice Kennedy in this case was that the questions were phrased in such a way that a potential juror's silence in the face of each relevant question was taken as an implied assertion that the juror lacked bias or prejudice. Allowing prospective jurors simply to say nothing in a group setting does not provide the trial judge adequate information on which to judge their credibility.

The Court's most recent pronouncement on the adequacy of *voir dire* in preventing pretrial publicity from producing an unfair trial came in *Skilling v. United States*, 561 U.S. 358 (2010). Skilling was first President, then chief operating officer, and finally the chief executive officer of Enron Corporation. Skilling faced criminal charges arising out of Enron's collapse into bankruptcy. Skilling had unsuccessfully sought a change of venue based on pretrial publicity. The trial judge denied Skilling's counsel's motion for attorney-led *voir dire*, concluding that judge-led *voir dire* was more likely to promote more forthcoming responses from potential jurors. But the court permitted counsel to ask follow-up questions and, after general *voir dire*, permitted individual *voir dire* concerning exposure to, and the effect of, publicity. Once the selected jurors took their oath, the court instructed them not to discuss the case or follow media examining it. Skilling was convicted of nineteen of the charged counts but acquitted of another nine charges.

On appeal, Skilling raised several objections about the quality of the *voir dire*. It lasted just five hours and, he alleged, "'[m]ost of the court's questions were conclusory[,] high-level, and failed adequately to probe juror's true feelings,' and the court 'consistently took jurors at their word once they claimed they could be fair, no matter what other indications of bias were present.'" Skilling also argued that the comments of several seated jurors relevant to the impact of publicity on them showed that they could not have, and in fact did not, treat Skilling fairly. The Court rejected each of these contentions.

The five hours of the judge's questioning did not, concluded the Court, adequately reflect the true scope of the *voir dire*. The trial judge initially screened venire members with a "comprehensive questionnaire drafted in large part by Skilling." That questionnaire prompted successful for-cause strikes against a number of potential jurors and "served as a springboard for further questions put to remaining members of the array." Furthermore, "[a]t Skilling's urging, the court examined each prospective juror individually, thus preventing the spread of any prejudicial information to other venire members." The court promoted candor by initially conducting *voir dire* itself and by admonishing members of the array that there were no right and wrong answers to the questions. The parties were allowed to ask follow-up questions, an opportunity Skilling's counsel did not take with more than half the venire because, he admitted, the court and other counsel had adequately covered the relevant issues. Eleven of the seated jurors had no connection to Enron, the twelfth having only an "insubstantial" connection, and fourteen jurors and alternates "specifically stated they had paid scant attention to Enron-related news." None of the seated jurors checked the "yes" box of the questionnaire inquiry whether they had an opinion about Skilling. Although some of those seated expressed sympathy for Enron's alleged victims or saw greed as at the root of its collapse, none expressed animus toward Skilling.

Nor, explained the Court, was the current case anything like one relied upon by Skilling: *Irvin v. Dowd*, 366 U.S. 717 (1961). In *Dowd*, the media reported that the defendant had an adult arson and several juvenile convictions, was found AWOL by a court-martial, faced a lineup and lie-detector test, had been placed at the crime scene, and confessed to the six charged murders and to twenty-four burglaries. The media further reported characterizations of Irvin as "remorseless and without conscience," "a parole violator and fraudulent check artist," and the object of a sheriff's promise to devote his life to seeing Irvin executed. The reporting newspapers reached 95% of the dwellings in the tiny county of 30,000 residents where the trial took place, while radio and television reports about the case "blanketed that county." Many of the prospective jurors had opinions about guilt, and eight of the twelve seated jurors said, during *voir dire*, that they thought Irvin guilty. Under these circumstances, the Supreme Court found actual prejudice despite jurors' claims that they could be impartial.

But, said the Court in *Skilling*, "news stories about Enron contained nothing resembling the horrifying information rife in reports about Irvin's rampage of robberies and murders." Moreover, many of the media reports in Houston, an enormous city of millions of residents, reached a much smaller percentage of the population than was true in Irvin. Importantly, also unlike in *Irvin*, the *Skilling* judge seated jurors who "uniformly disclaimed having ever formed an opinion about the case." That the jurors ultimately acquitted Skilling of nine of the charges facing him was, to the Court, further evidence of the jurors' fairness.

The Court in *Skilling* furthermore rebutted the claim that the trial judge simply accepted prospective jurors' word that they could be impartial. To the contrary, the court asked follow-up questions "to uncover concealed bias," doing so face-to-face, thus being able to judge credibility. Coupling these information sources with the responses to the comprehensive questionnaire "gave the court a sturdy foundation to assess fitness for jury service."

Finally, the Court did not find actual bias by any of the seated jurors. Skilling, concluded the Court, identified juror comments during *voir dire* taken in isolation. When those comments were taken in context, however, they revealed that the seated jurors were indeed fair. For example, though one juror saw Enron's greed as triggering its bankruptcy, he said he had "no idea" whether Skilling had crossed the line to becoming a crook. Another, though angry about the effect of Enron's collapse on her retirement account, said that she "did not 'personally blame' Skilling." Nor, having paid little attention to media accounts, could she know whether he was probably guilty. The Court found similar contextual indicators for each of the remaining seated jurors whose fairness Skilling challenged. Said the Court, "Taking account of the full record, rather than incomplete exchanges culled from it, we find no cause to upset the lower court's judgment that Skilling's jury met th[e] measure" of rendering a verdict based on the evidence rather than on earlier impressions. "Jurors," the Court further explained, "need not enter the box with empty heads in order to determine the facts impartially."

B. Cautionary Jury Instructions

Much social science suggests that cautionary instructions have little impact on overcoming prejudice induced by media coverage. In experimental mock trial studies, jurors seem incapable of obeying instructions to ignore whatever they may have heard in the press. At least two explanations are offered for this phenomenon. First, humans tend to make quick judgments based upon initial information exposure, judgments that prove hardily resistant to change in the face of later contrary information. Second, there seems to be a "backfire effect" in which jurors resent the limitations that instructions seek to impose on juror freedom. In a sense they rebel, paying even more attention to the information.

C. Change of Venue

1. Basic Principles

The unamended Constitution's text requires criminal trials ordinarily to occur "in the State where the ... Crimes ... have been committed." The Sixth

Amendment added the requirement that a criminal jury trial must occur in the "State and district wherein the crime shall have been committed." The Sixth Amendment also ensures criminal defendants trial by an impartial jury, such impartiality also being considered a mandate of due process. There is a potential conflict between the impartial jury mandate and the local trial mandate when publicity renders the local jury pool unlikely to be capable of impartiality. Consequently, the Supreme Court has held that the "Constitution's place-of-trial prescriptions ... do not impede transfer of the proceeding to a different district at the defendant's request if extraordinary local prejudice will prevent a fair trial—a 'basic requirement of due process.'" *Skilling v. United States*, 561 U.S. 358 (2010).

Federal Rule of Criminal Procedure 21(a) mandates a transfer of the location for trial "for prejudice." This mandatory change of venue provision applies only under the following circumstances: "Upon the defendant's motion, the court must transfer the proceedings against that defendant to another district if the court is satisfied that so great a prejudice against the defendant exists in the transferring district that the defendant cannot obtain a fair and impartial trial there." Rule 21(b) also provides for *discretionary* venue change "for the convenience of the parties, any victim, and the witnesses, and in the interest of justice." It is the mandatory provision of Rule 21(a) that matters most, however, when a change of venue is sought based upon a defendant's fear of being denied a fair trial because of the exposure of the jury pool in the original venue to unfairly prejudicial publicity. Venue transfer motions on those grounds also necessarily implicate constitutional issues of a fair trial versus a free press. In such motions, the defense seeks to show that the publicity is so "widespread, inflammatory, adverse, and prejudicial as to raise a substantial doubt that defendants can obtain a fair trial." *Dewberry v. State*, 4 S.W.3d 735, 735 (Tex. Crim. App. 1999). The prosecution, on the other hand, tries to prove that the publicity is "factual, informative, and accurate." *State v. Means*, 547 N.W.2d 615, 622 (Iowa Ct. App. 1996). At least five factors are relevant in this proof process: (1) the nature, extent, and likely impact of the publicity; (2) the size and demographic characteristics of the potential venues; (3) the nature and gravity of the offense; (4) victim and defendant-specific perceptions; (5) and government-sponsored publicity.

a. Nature, Extent, and Likely Impact of Publicity

If the rate of dismissing jurors for cause during *voir dire* is high, that can be an indication that the current venue is a difficult one in which to grant a defendant a fair trial. It would be helpful in making this case to engage in content-based questioning similar to that which in *Mu'Min* the Court held was not required as part of voir dire.

One of the central common pieces of evidence on media impact, however, is the public opinion survey. These surveys are conducted by experts in psychology or statistics. It is important to remember that the judgment is a *relative* one of degrees of risk of partiality. Surveys may reveal that the numbers of persons exposed to media stories about a particular case and those aware of particularly inflammatory facts who have closed their minds to innocence are high in the current trial location, low — but not zero — in the proposed new location. Zero risk in any venue is not realistic. The nature of the coverage matters too. Some crimes have their highest profile only in the area where the crime occurred, other crimes get true national coverage. In the latter cases, it will be harder to find a fair venue but, once again, courts look at the question, explicitly or implicitly, as one of comparative, not absolute, fairness.

The content of the stories matters too. Some coverage is more gruesome than other coverage. Moreover, coverage of the items that the ethics rules largely prohibit lawyers from revealing to the press is fairly well-correlated with the sort of coverage that is most damaging to trial fairness. Submitting with the motion a collection of relevant news stories and a content analysis of them performed by an expert can help to convey effectively to the court the content, degree of dissemination, and likely impact of the stories.

One illustrative case on the content question is *Rideau v. Louisiana*, 373 U.S. 723 (1963). Rideau had kidnapped several employees, and killed one, during a robbery. Rideau's confession to police was taped and broadcast three times on local television stations to an audience ranging up to about a third of the population of a relatively small community. Rideau's venue transfer motion was denied, and he was convicted. The Supreme Court reversed. "What the people [in the community] saw on their television sets," noted the Court, "was Rideau, in jail, flanked by the sheriff and two state troopers, admitting in detail the commission of the robbery, kidnapping, and murder." The Court continued: "To the tens of thousands of people who saw and heard it, [the interrogation] in a very real sense was Rideau's trial — at which he pleaded guilty." That reality rendered the later trial mere "kangaroo court proceedings."

b. Size and Demographic Composition

Smaller jurisdictions are more easily inundated by media coverage. They are also more likely to foster the kind of gossip that magnifies the negative impact of such coverage. In smaller jurisdictions, the jury pool will tend to be more cohesive, which may be attributable to lower migration into the community, greater knowledge about the crime due to less criminal activity in the area, and a narrower range of views among the population. Size mattered, for example, in *Rideau*, where television reports blanketed much of a local parish of only 150,000 people. Although a defendant is not entitled to a jury of a particular racial or gender composition, some state statutes require courts to consider the relative racial composition of the current and proposed venues as one factor in deciding a change of venue motion.

c. Nature and Gravity of the Offense

The most serious crimes garner the most intense news coverage. Rapes are more attention-grabbing than petty thefts, murders of more salacious interest than minor assaults. Some judges address this problem by allowing trial delay to permit community tempers to cool. If the crimes are serious enough, it is not clear whether such delays succeed in sufficiently improving trial fairness, and it is hard to know how much of a delay is sufficient.

d. Victim and Defendant-Specific Concerns

A defendant who is a movie or sports star will generate massive publicity at times for that reason alone. Politicians' alleged wrongs similarly spark intense public interest. Likewise, victims are sometimes already public figures. Even when they are not, local statutes, procedures, or customs may require the trial judge to consider the emotional and financial impact of the venue change on the victim and his or her family. Concerns about monetary, travel, and emotional costs to the victim cannot outweigh the defendant's constitutional rights, yet those concerns will often play a *sub silentio* role in the court's assessment of the nature and extent of those rights.

e. Government-Sponsored Publicity

Inflammatory statements by government attorneys are arguably particularly likely to influence potential jurors. Government lawyers carry the veneer of speaking for the People. Their words may thus be given especially heavy weight. Courts sometimes consider this concern in ruling on venue motions, especially where the government lawyers' speech seems to have been made in violation of ethics codes.

2. Skilling v. United States

In *Skilling v. United States*, 561 U.S. 358 (2010), the Court addressed a defendant's claim that denial of his change of venue motions on grounds of harmful pretrial publicity was in error. Skilling faced criminal charges arising from his leadership role in the recently-collapsed Enron Corporation. Skilling had made two change of venue motions. In support of the first one, he submitted hundreds of news reports about Enron's collapse, combined with expert affidavits portraying the Houston community's attitudes toward the event relative to the attitudes of other venues. The second motion was made after prospective jurors answered a detailed survey about their attitudes. Skilling argued that the survey revealed pervasive bias and that new reports of a guilty plea in another Enron-related prosecution further tainted the local community. The district court denied both motions on the ground that Skilling had not established that the publicity or community bias raised a presumption of inherent jury prejudice. The Supreme Court agreed.

"Prominence does not necessarily produce prejudice, and juror *impartiality*, we have reiterated, does not require *ignorance*," said the Court. Houston had a diverse 4.5 million person jury pool, making "the suggestion that 12 impartial individuals could not be empaneled ... hard to sustain." Furthermore, though "not kind," the news stories about Skilling lacked a confession or "other blatantly prejudicial information of the type readers or viewers could not reasonably be expected to shut from sight." Additionally, four years had passed between Enron's bankruptcy and the trial, ample time for passions to cool. "Although reporters covered Enron-related news throughout this period, the decibel-level of media attention diminished somewhat in the years following Enron's collapse." Moreover, the jurors, though convicting Skilling of a number of charges, acquitted him of nine of them, providing confidence that the trial judge's conclusion that no presumption of prejudice was warranted was correct. The sheer size and negative tone of news coverage and the sheer number of victims were insufficient to justify such a presumption. The information that made its way into the media was neither vivid nor unforgettable. As to the related defendant's guilty plea, the district court had delayed proceedings two weeks to lessen its impact and added questioning about it to *voir dire*, with only two venire members remembering it, neither ultimately being empaneled. "Although publicity about a codefendant's guilty plea calls for an inquiry to guard against actual prejudice, it does not ordinarily—and, we are satisfied, it did not here—warrant an automatic presumption of prejudice."

Skilling illustrates many of the factors considered in venue motions, including particularly, the nature of the media content, the size and diversity of the local community, the gravity of the offense, and the relative communal awareness of the defendant's public reputation. *Skilling* also illustrates typical defense tactics in change of venue cases, most importantly, collecting news reports and relying upon social scientists conducting local studies of the relative community attitudes.

D. The Cumulative Remedies Hypothesis

Much of the social science discussed above looks at the impact of each remedy, in its current form, on overcoming the effects of prejudicial publicity. But some authors claim that it is possible to improve each remedy (for example, to improve the quality of cautionary instructions) so that, cumulatively, using all the various remedies at once should be sufficient to bring us close to guaranteeing a fair trial. The cumulative remedies hypothesis remains controversial, however, and further study will be required before the dispute is resolved.

Checkpoints

- The Due Process Clauses guarantee criminal defendants a right to a fair trial.

- The Sixth Amendment guarantees criminal defendants the right to trial before an impartial jury.

- Media coverage of a criminal trial may bias the jury in favor of a conviction, thus potentially violating the rights to a fair trial before an impartial jury.

- Gag orders silencing the press, however, raise First Amendment free speech issues and thus will rarely be granted, and then only if publication poses a clear and present danger to the administration of justice. This test will be met only if:

  - Pervasive, intense pretrial publicity *will* occur absent suppression of the speech;

  - Less restrictive alternatives will be inadequate to protect the defendant's rights; and

  - The gag order will succeed in halting prejudicial publicity.

- Less restrictive alternatives include:

  - Gagging prosecutors and defense counsel;

  - Aggressive *voir dire* to exclude biased persons from the jury;

  - Cautionary jury instructions; and

  - Change of venue.

- Whether *voir dire* is adequate to overcome prejudicial publicity is a case-specific question but will include such factors as the content of the questions, the availability of individual questioning of potential jurors about exposure to publicity and whether it affected each juror's ability to be fair, and the tone and demeanor of each such person in answering relevant questions.

- Jury instructions can caution jurors to decide only based upon the evidence presented at trial and not based upon media coverage, but social science raises doubts about the efficacy of such instructions.

- Change of venue motions in federal court are governed by Fed. R. Crim. P. 21 and include several factors in deciding whether publicity was so "widespread, inflammatory, adverse, and prejudicial as to raise a substantial doubt that defendants can obtain a fair trial," a test sometimes also phrased as whether the publicity raises a presumption of prejudice without venue transfer.

- The relevant factors for a change of venue motion are:

  - The nature, extent, and likely impact of the publicity;

  - The size and demographic composition of the community;

  - The nature and gravity of the offense;

  - Victim and defendant-specific concerns; and

- The nature and extent in particular of government-sponsored speech, especially by the prosecutor.
- Model Rule of Professional Conduct 3.8(f) generally mandates that prosecutors "refrain from making extrajudicial comments that have a substantial likelihood of heightening public condemnation of the accused."
- Model Rule of Professional Conduct 3.6 prohibits each lawyer involved in investigating or litigating a matter from making extrajudicial statements that she knows or reasonably should know will be "disseminated by means of public communication and will have a substantial likelihood of materially prejudicing an adjudicative proceeding in the matter."
- Other ethical rules govern client media campaigns and lawyer media contracts.

Chapter 12

Presenting Evidence

Roadmap

- The Confrontation Clause and Hearsay
- The *Bruton* Rule and Joint Trials
- The Compulsory Process Clause
- The Alternative-Perpetrator Defense
- Immunity Orders and Agreements

I. The Confrontation Clause

The Sixth Amendment to the Constitution guarantees the accused the right to "confront" the "witnesses" against him. The right secured by the Confrontation Clause applies only in criminal cases. The right primarily has been understood by the Supreme Court as protecting the defense's opportunity for effective cross-examination at trial; the secondary purpose has been understood as promoting face-to-face witness examination. These protections create two significant ancillary considerations: the admissibility of hearsay evidence at trial, and the use of screens or other techniques to protect testifying children from seeing the accused at trial.

A. Hearsay and the Rule of *Crawford*

1. Background

Hearsay, as defined in most evidence codes, is a statement made out-of-court that is later offered by someone other than the speaker as proof of the truth of the matter asserted in the court proceeding. While not a simple evidentiary concept, at this juncture, it is enough to know that the person testifying on the stand, the *witness,* does not have firsthand knowledge of the thing about which they are testifying; their knowledge is based on the out of court statement of another person, the *declarant*. Each jurisdiction's rules of evidence will be the first mechanism for governing the admissibility of hearsay. However, much hearsay is admissible under those rules, even when the hearsay *declarant* is available to themselves testify at trial. For this reason, hearsay admissible under state or federal evidentiary rules may sometimes be rendered inadmissible by the Confrontation Clause, which generally requires that *witnesses* be produced for cross-examination.

For many years, the Supreme Court followed a reliability approach to the admissibility of hearsay under the Confrontation Clause. Under that approach, admissible hearsay had to have adequate "indicia of reliability" to satisfy the constitutional requirement. Such indicia could be shown in two ways: first, by the evidence fitting into a "firmly rooted" (traditional or historically old) hearsay exception; second, by displaying "particularized guarantees of trustworthiness" even if not firmly rooted. Several academics criticized this Confrontation Clause admissibility model. That protection, they maintained, was historically focused not simply on whether evidence was trustworthy but rather on whether such trustworthiness could be tested in a particular fashion, *i.e.*, by cross-examination. Other guarantees of trustworthiness were, thus, irrelevant.

2. *"Testimonial" Evidence Overview: The* Crawford *Rule*

In *Crawford v. Washington*, 541 U.S. 36 (2004), the Supreme Court accepted this critique and overturned the reliability approach to confrontation. The new approach in *Crawford* bars admission of all *testimonial* hearsay unless the defense has an opportunity at or before the trial to cross-examine the hearsay declarant on the statement in question.

Crawford itself involved a self-defense claim raised by Michael Crawford, charged with the stabbing of Kenneth Lee. Crawford told police that he confronted Lee because he had raped Crawford's wife, Sylvia. Crawford insisted that during the fray, Lee pulled out a weapon and cut Crawford's hand, so Crawford stabbed Lee in self-defense. However, in a tape-recorded statement, Sylvia instead told the police that she did not see a weapon in Lee's hands before the stabbing. Sylvia refused to testify at trial, raising the state's protection of marital privilege. Accordingly, the state succeeded in admitting the tape recording over Crawford's Confrontation Clause objection under the hearsay exception for declarations made against the speaker's own interest (Sylvia had admitted to facilitating the assault). The jury convicted Crawford.

The Court reversed, finding Sylvia's tape-recorded statement to be testimonial and, therefore, barred by the Confrontation Clause absent the opportunity to cross-examine her.

In coming to its decision, the Court relied on its reading of the relevant history of the Confrontation Clause: aimed at protecting against the civil law's abuses and their early encroachment upon common law practice. These abuses included witness examination outside the presence of counsel, even of the accused. The Court also found the historical meaning of "witnesses" to be those who "bear testimony," and "testimony" to be "'[a] solemn declaration or affirmation made for the purpose of establishing or proving some fact." Although the Court refused to offer a comprehensive definition of when hearsay thus qualifies as *testimonial*, it gave these five examples of what comes within that term:

- affidavits;
- statements given to police officers in the course of custodial interrogations;
- depositions;
- courtroom testimony; and
- "statements that were made under circumstances that would lead an objective witness reasonably to believe that the statement would be available for use at a later trial."

The central Confrontation Clause issue in most cases is whether a hearsay statement qualifies as "testimonial" under one of these, or perhaps some other, definition—the list was apparently not meant to be exhaustive. *Crawford* lauded the testimonial approach not only for being more consistent with the historical understanding of the Confrontation Clause, but also because it believed that this approach would be more predictable than the vague reliability approach. The Court denounced the reliability approach as the discredited "*Roberts* legacy," named after the case first adopting the reliability standard, *Ohio v. Roberts*, 448 U.S. 56 (1980).

"In sum," said the majority in a 5-4 opinion written by Justice Scalia, "even if the Sixth Amendment is not solely concerned with testimonial hearsay, that is its primary object, and interrogations by law enforcement officers fall squarely within that class." The Court stated,

> We use the term "interrogation" in its colloquial, rather than any technical legal, sense. Just as various definitions of "testimonial" exist, one can imagine various definitions of "interrogation," and we need not select among them in this case. Sylvia's recorded statement, knowingly given in response to structured police questioning, qualifies under any conceivable definition.

3. Police "Interrogation" Elaborated

a. 911 Calls

In two consolidated cases, *Davis v. Washington* and *Hammon v. Indiana*, 547 U.S. 813 (2006), the Supreme Court clarified the meaning of "interrogation" (one of the potential types of "testimonial" statements) in the context of 911 calls. The Court also resolved a question left unanswered in *Crawford*: whether the Confrontation Clause *only* protects against "testimonial" hearsay or whether the *Roberts* approach might still survive to exclude some non-testimonial but unreliable hearsay. *Davis* gave a clear answer: the *Roberts* approach is dead.

The Court summarized the rule it crafted in *Davis* and *Hammon* thus:

> Statements are non-testimonial when made in the course of police interrogation under circumstances objectively indicating that the primary purpose of the interrogation is to enable police assistance to meet an ongoing emergency. They are testimonial when the circumstances objectively indicate that there is no such ongoing emergency, and that the primary purpose of the interrogation is to establish or prove past events potentially relevant to later criminal prosecution.

(i) Emergencies: The Davis Rule

In *Davis v. Washington*, a 911 operator answered a call, which terminated before anyone spoke. The operator returned the call, and Michelle McCottry answered. McCottry revealed that she was being abused by her ex-boyfriend, Adrian Davis. She alleged that Davis was "jumpin' on [her] again," using his fists, and that he had just ran out the door, leaving in a car with someone else. She gave the operator more information identifying Davis. Police arrived within minutes, where they found fresh injuries on McCottry's face and forearm, and observed her "frantic efforts to gather her belongings and her children so that they could leave the residence." At Davis's trial for felony violation of a no-contact order, McCottry failed to appear to testify. Accordingly, the prosecution played the tape of the 911 call for the jury, which convicted Davis.

In reviewing the admission of this evidence, initially, the Supreme Court noted that, although most of the American cases applying the Confrontation Clause or its state constitutional or common law counterparts were of the "most formal sort—sworn testimony in judicial proceedings or formal depositions under oath," the English origins of the Clause were not limited merely to prior in-court testimony and formal depositions. The Court stated,

[W]e do not think it conceivable that the protections of the Confrontation Clause can readily be evaded by having a note-taking policeman *recite* the unsworn hearsay testimony of the declarant instead of having the declarant sign a deposition. Indeed, if there is one point for which no case — English or early American, state or federal — can be cited, that is it.

Despite its reluctance to narrow the scope of the Confrontation Clause's protections, the Court still found that the noted portions of the 911 tape were not testimonial in nature because the recorded statements were made to seek help in dealing with an emergency.

Although less formal inquiries than depositions or signed affidavits, including police questioning, might thus be testimonial, just what constitutes an "interrogation" for these purposes needed to be clarified. The Court answered that what it had in mind in *Crawford* were "interrogations solely directed at establishing the facts of a past crime, in order to identify (or provide evidence to convict) the perpetrator." The product of such an interrogation is testimonial. "[Testimony] is, in the terms of the 1828 American dictionary quoted in *Crawford*," explained the *Davis* Court, "'[a] solemn declaration or affirmation made for the purpose of establishing or proving some fact.'" 911 calls do not ordinarily fit this definition. McCottry was speaking about "events *as they actually happened*," not about past occurrences, and "any reasonable listener would recognize that McCottry (unlike Sylvia Crawford) was facing an ongoing emergency," thus making her words "a call for help against a bona fide physical threat." Moreover,

the difference in the level of formality between the two interviews is striking. Crawford was responding calmly, at the station house, to a series of questions, with the officer-interrogator taping and making notes of her answers; McCottry's frantic answers were provided over the phone, in an environment that was not tranquil, or even (as far as any reasonable 911 operator could make out) safe.

Accordingly, concluded the Court, the *objective* purpose of McCottry's 911 call was to gain aid in meeting an ongoing emergency, thus not being "testimonial." The Court concluded,

She simply was not acting as a *witness*; she was not *testifying*. What she said was not "a weaker substitute for live testimony" at trial, like Lord Cobham's statements in *Raleigh's Case* or Sylvia Crawford's statements in *Crawford*. In each of those cases, the *ex parte* actors and the evidentiary products of the *ex parte* communications aligned perfectly with their courtroom analogues. McCottry's emergency statement does not. No "witness" goes into court to proclaim an emergency and seek help.

The Court recognized several caveats to its holding. First, conversations like 911 calls that begin as calls for help might *evolve* into testimonial statements whose primary purpose is to re-create past events. In *Davis*, the operator continued asking questions after the emergency ended when the defendant had fled. Those statements might well resemble "structured police questioning" of the kind involved in *Crawford*. Statements of that kind might need to be redacted. The task of distinguishing between the testimonial and non-testimonial portions of the 911 call would not be beyond police or trial court competence. To the contrary, "police officers can and will distinguish almost instinctively between questions necessary to secure their own safety or the safety of the public and questions designed solely to elicit testimonial statements."

Second, simply because a statement is made other than in response to an interrogation does not necessarily mean that the statement is non-testimonial. "The Framers were no more willing to exempt from cross-examination volunteered testimony or answers to open-ended questions than they were to exempt answers to detailed interrogation." Indeed, noted the Court, "[p]art of the evidence against Sir Walter Raleigh [in his trial that was so important to the Confrontation Clause's history] was a letter from Lord Cobham that was plainly not the result of sustained questioning." For example, a statement not obtained from interrogation might fit into one of the other four of the five examples of testimonial statements given in *Crawford*, although, arguably, the Court implicitly found that not to be the case in *Davis*.

Third, the Court re-interpreted some of its pre-*Crawford* Confrontation Clause case law as examples illustrating *non*-testimonial statements. In particular, statements unwittingly made to a government informant were found to be non-testimonial. *See Bourjaily v. United States*, 483 U.S. 171 (1987). Similarly, statements made from one prisoner to another were non-testimonial. *See Dutton v. Evans*, 400 U.S. 74 (1970).

Finally, even testimonial statements might be admissible if they resulted from certain wrongful conduct by the defendant other than the mere commission of the crime with which he is charged. This "forfeiture doctrine" is discussed later in this chapter.

(ii) Reconstructing the Past: Hammon

In *Hammon v. Indiana*, police responded to a domestic disturbance call at the home of Amy and Hershel Hammon. Police, upon arrival, separated Amy from Hershel, questioned Amy, and had her sign the following battery affi-davit: "Broke our furnace and shoved me down to the floor into the broken glass. Hit me in chest and threw me down. Broke our lamps and phone. Tore up my van where I couldn't leave the house. Attacked my daughter." No phys-ical disturbance occurred during the time of the police presence.

Amy failed to appear at trial. One of the officers read the affidavit to the jury. Over defense objections, the trial judge admitted the affidavit under the present-sense impression (arguably incorrectly) and excited utterance (arguably correctly) exceptions to the hearsay rule.

The Supreme Court concluded that the trial court's admission of Amy's af-fidavit was erroneous. The affidavit's creation arose from an objective purpose to re-create past events, not to address an ongoing emergency, thus making the affidavit testimonial. Unlike *Davis,* there "was no emergency in progress; the interrogating officer testified that he had heard no arguments or crashing and saw no one throw or break anything...." Indeed, upon their arrival, Amy told the police "that things were fine, and there was no immediate threat to her person." By the time the officer questioned Amy for the second time — the time that resulted in the affidavit — the inquiry was about what had already happened rather than what was still happening.

The Court conceded that the statements in *Crawford* were more formal. They followed *Miranda* warnings, were tape-recorded, and occurred at the station-house. But none of these factors were essential to their status as testimonial:

> What we called the "striking resemblance" of the *Crawford* statement to civil law *ex parte* examinations is shared by Amy's statement here. Both declarants were actively separated from the defendant — officers forcibly prevented Hershel from participating in the interrogation. Both statements deliberately recounted, in response to police ques-tioning, how potentially criminal past events began and progressed. And both took place some time after the events described were over. Such statements under official interrogation are an obvious substitute for live testimony, because they do precisely *what a witness does* on direct examination; they are inherently testimonial.

The Court also responded to Justice Thomas's argument in dissent which as-serted that the Court, in treating Amy's statements as testimonial, had gone well beyond the primary abuse at which the Confrontation Clause aimed: formal depositions like those taken by the Marian magistrates. These were magistrates authorized by the Marian statutes to take ex parte statements from the accused and others. The Court asserted,

We do not dispute that formality is essential to testimonial utterance. But we no longer have examining Marian magistrates; and we do have, as our 18th century forebears did not, examining police officers who perform investigative and testimonial functions once performed by examining Marian magistrates. It imports sufficient formality, in our view, that lies to such officers are criminal offenses. Restricting the Confrontation Clause to the precise forms against which it was originally directed is a recipe for its extinction.

b. Figuring Out "Primary Purpose": *Michigan v. Bryant*

Michigan v. Bryant, 131 S. Ct. 1143 (2011), has complicated—some would even say obfuscated—the analysis of "primary purpose," at least where that purpose concerns the difference between a non-testimonial emergency and a testimonial reconstruction of past events. In *Bryant*, police responding to a radio dispatch late one evening found Anthony Covington lying in a gas station parking lot with an abdominal gunshot wound. He was in great pain and spoke with difficulty. In response to police questioning, Covington said that "Rick" shot him after the victim had a conversation with Richard Bryant through the back door of Bryant's house. Covington recognized Bryant's voice, and when he turned to leave, he was shot through the door. He drove away and ended up in the lot where police found him. Between five to ten minutes from the police officer's conversation with Covington, emergency medical services arrived and transported him to the hospital, where he died a few hours later. A jury convicted Bryant of second-degree murder and related charges after the police testified at trial about their conversation with Covington. The conversation was apparently admitted under the excited utterance exception to the hearsay rule.

The Supreme Court held that Covington's statements were non-testimonial. The Court described the issue before it as determining for the first time whether *Davis* "extends beyond an initial victim to a potential threat to the responding police and the public at large." The Court responded to this question in the affirmative, and, thus, apparently expanding the meaning of an emergency. In doing so, however, the Court also re-crafted the "primary purpose" inquiry in several ways.

First, the Court seemed to revive the *Roberts* reliability inquiry, at least as a factor in determining primary purpose. Thus, the Court explained: "In making the primary purpose determination, standard rules of hearsay, designed to identify some statements as reliable, will be relevant." In particular, the excited utterance exception is justified as promoting reliability because the declarant is too emotionally stimulated to lie. However, an emergency acts in a similar fashion, focusing the excited individual on responding to that emergency rather than on re-creating past facts.

Second, the medical condition of the declarant matters. It "sheds light on the ability of the victim to have any purpose at all in responding to police questions and on the likelihood that any purpose formed would necessarily be a testimonial one." The declarant's medical condition, particularly when he is the victim of the crime, also helps first responders "judge the existence and magnitude of a continuing threat to the victim, themselves, and the public."

Third, the presence of a weapon also matters. In *Hammon*, the defendant's only weapons were his fists, so separating him from his wife was sufficient to end the danger. But where, as in *Bryant*, the attack consisted of using a gun on the victim, a danger to the public still existed. The Court seemed to put the burden on the defense of showing that the danger had passed by the time of police questioning. Because Covington did not tell the police whether the threat was limited to him, and because Bryant might have been determined to finish the job he had started, the end of the violent act did not necessarily mean the end of the emergency. Indeed, the lack of knowledge of Bryant's whereabouts created reason enough for the police to worry. The mere existence of an emergency did not, alone, establish whether the primary purpose of that interrogation was to meet such an emergency, but it surely merited significant weight.

Fourth, location and informality were important. The location—an exposed public area—added to the sense of emergency. Moreover, the situation was "fluid and somewhat confused," with various officers arriving at different times and many asking questions. Those questions were largely of the type designed to enable the police to assess the potential danger to the police, the public, and the victim. Such informality suggested a primary purpose to address an ongoing emergency, for the "circumstances lacked the formality that would have alerted Covington to or focused him on the possible future prosecutorial use of his statements."

Fifth, the Court rejected determining purpose from the perspective of either the police or the declarant alone. Police and victims both suffer from mixed motives. Police act both as first responders and criminal investigators. "Their dual responsibilities may mean that they act with different motives simultaneously or in quick succession." Victims may want the threat to end but may also envision the assailant's prosecution. Alternatively, a victim may respond reflexively, having no real purpose at all, or may be so debilitated by injury as to be unable to think clearly enough to understand just what is the primary purpose of police inquiries. Accordingly, the Court adopted a "combined approach" considering, "[i]n addition to the circumstances in which an encounter occurs, the statements and actions of both the declarant and interrogators" to "provide objective evidence of the primary purpose of the interrogation." The objective evidence of "the interrogation," rather than of law enforcement or declarant, governed. Perhaps this approach was complex, conceded the Court, but "accuracy" superseded "simplicity." The combination of circumstances before the Court demonstrated that the primary objective purpose of Covington's interrogation was to deal with an ongoing emergency.

Justice Scalia, in a dissenting opinion joined by Justice Ginsburg, encapsulated the sort of critique of *Bryant* that many commentators quickly embraced. That critique focused on the ambiguity created by the majority's position. Justice Scalia found the Court's account, where the police interrogated Covington primarily to protect him and others from a murderer-on-the-loose, was "so transparently false that professing to believe it demeans this institution." For Justice Scalia, it was the declarant's intent alone that counted:

> In-court testimony is more than a narrative of past events; it is a solemn declaration made in the course of a criminal trial. For an out-of-court statement to qualify as testimonial, the declarant must intend the statement to be a solemn declaration rather than an unconsidered or offhand remark; and he must make the statement with the understanding that it may be used to invoke the coercive machinery of the State against the accused.... That is what distinguishes a narrative told to a friend over dinner from a statement to the police.... The hidden purpose of an interrogator cannot substitute for the declarant's intentional solemnity or his understanding of how his words may be used.
>
> Only a declarant-focused inquiry could work in every conceivable fact pattern, according to Justice Scalia. The interrogator's actions and identity matter, but only insofar as they shed light on the declarant's intentions.

Nor did Justice Scalia worry that the specter of a severely injured victim's intentions being ambiguous or nonexistent would make his audience's actions and context the only determinable options. To the contrary, the *Crawford* inquiry partly turns on "the actions and statements of a declarant's audience only because they shape the declarant's perception of why his audience is listening and therefore influence *his purpose* in making the declaration." If the declarant is so badly injured that he is incapable of perceiving his own purposes, then he also cannot perceive why his interrogators are interested in what he has to say. Consequently, the interrogators' actions become less, not more, relevant. Furthermore, to consider the mixed motives of *both* the police and the declarant multiplies the difficulties of divining primary purpose relative to the simpler question posed and answered by focusing on the victim's perspective alone.

Justice Scalia worried too that the Court's approach left judges free to pick whatever perspective they wished. Thus, judges could pick the police's perspective where they tricked a declarant into giving a statement against a sympathetic defendant. By contrast, judges could pick the declarant's perspective, declaring "damning hearsay nontestimonial," when that perspective favors the result that the judges want. In short, judges remain free to do whatever they deem fairest under the circumstances, a "malleable" approach suffering the same vices as did the discredited reliability approach. Under these circumstances, "the guarantee of confrontation is no guarantee at all."

Justice Scalia was also troubled by the Court's "revisionist narrative" scheme reintroducing reliability as a Confrontation Clause jurisprudence guide, at least in the context of real and faux emergencies. Indeed, Justice Scalia saw the Court as implicitly importing the excited utterance exception into the Constitution. Reliability, insisted Justice Scalia, is irrelevant to whether statements are testimonial.

4. Forensic Evidence

a. *Melendez-Diaz v. Massachusetts*

In *Melendez-Diaz v. Massachusetts*, 557 U.S. 305 (2009), a Massachusetts court admitted into evidence the affidavits of forensic lab analysts who concluded that a substance seized by the police was cocaine. The Supreme Court held that forensic lab affidavits are no different from most other affidavits that would be offered in criminal cases: ex parte testimony under oath for the purpose of taking the place of live testimony at trial. Accordingly, because the reports were testimonial affidavits, the documents were inadmissible absent an opportunity for cross-examination.

The Court rejected arguments that forensic lab analysts were not "conventional witnesses because they observed neither the crime itself nor human action connected to it." The same might be true of a police report documenting post-crime law enforcement investigation, yet those police reports are indeed testimonial. Further, the fact that witnesses, including lab analysts, purportedly *volunteer* statements rather than respond to police investigation is irrelevant. The statements remain solemn declarations that an objective witness would reasonably believe would be available for later use at trial.

The Court rejected with particular force the argument that "neutral scientific testing" is so reliable that live cross-examination is unnecessary. The Court cautioned that that argument was "little more than an invitation to return to our overruled decision in *Roberts*, which held that evidence with particularized guarantees of trustworthiness was admissible notwithstanding the Confrontation Clause."

Furthermore, the Court made plain that if it was to revert to the foregone *Roberts* approach, forensic evidence would not even pass that lower-threshold test because it is not uniquely trustworthy. Most forensic evidence labs are administered by the police or other law enforcement agencies. Laboratory administrators report to the heads of these agencies. Quoting a National Academy of Sciences (NAS) report on forensic evidence, the Court explained: "Because forensic scientists often are driven in their work by a need to answer a particular question related to the issues of a particular case, they sometimes face pressure to sacrifice appropriate methodology for the sake of expediency." Consequently, a "forensic analyst responding to a request from a law enforcement official may feel pressure—or have an incentive—to alter the evidence in a manner favorable to the prosecution." Cross-examination may reveal fraudulent analysis and, as with any expert witness, may reveal deficiencies in the analyst's training or judgment. Again citing the NAS report, the Court noted that forensic science disciplines differ in reliability, error rates, and degree of acceptance in the scientific community.

The Court, too, was not persuaded that the forensic report's status as a business or official record changed the analysis. Some such records implicate the Confrontation Clause, some do not. But records, like those here, *created* "for the sole purpose of providing evidence against a defendant" are testimonial in nature. Indeed, because their *sole* purpose was to provide evidence in a criminal trial, the Court questioned whether they were admissible business or official records at all, even under evidence codes like the Federal Rules of Evidence. The Court did concede that history created an exception to Confrontation Clause mandates for clerks' certificates authenticating official records. But the affidavits in question did far more than simply attest to the authenticity of a writing; instead, the affidavits created testimony central to the substantive claim against the defendant.

The Court found it similarly irrelevant to the Confrontation Clause analysis the fact that the defense is entitled to summon witnesses to challenge the forensic analysis. Even though the Compulsory Process Clause of the Sixth Amendment secures the right of defendants to subpoena witnesses, the Court pointed out, such witnesses might not be available or might simply fail to appear. More importantly, "the Confrontation Clause imposes a burden on the prosecution to present its witnesses, not on the defendant to bring those witnesses into court. Its value to the defendant," the Court emphasized, "is not replaced by a system in which the prosecution presents its evidence via *ex parte* affidavits and waits for the defendant to subpoena the affiants if he chooses."

Finally, the Court rejected the idea that countervailing concerns, such as the "necessities of trial and the adversary process," could outweigh the demands of confrontation. The Confrontation Clause, like the right to trial by jury and to the privilege against self-incrimination, "is binding, and we may not disregard it at our convenience." In any event, the Court doubted the dire predictions by the dissent of trials overwhelmed by the burden of presenting live forensic analyst testimony and of crime labs crippled by the need to testify rather than keeping up with lab work. That was not the experience, said the Court, of states already following a live-analyst-testimony rule. Moreover, most cases result in guilty pleas anyway, and most defense counsel will not demand producing forensic analysts where the latter have done a good job. Forcing them to testify would merely strengthen the prosecutor's case.

On the question of defense demands for producing the analysts, the Court noted that burden-shifting statutes, such as notice-and-demand statutes, would likely be consistent with the Confrontation Clause. Such statutes require the prosecution to notify the defense of the intent to use an analyst's report at trial. The defense then has a specified period of time in which to object and demand live testimony. But, explained the Court, defendants must always object to evidence, with these statutes merely governing when and how the objection is to be made. Just as it is consistent with the Compulsory Process Clause to require the defense to announce in advance its intention to present certain witnesses at trial, so is it consistent with the Confrontation Clause to object to certain prosecution evidence before trial.

b. *Bullcoming v. New Mexico*

In *Bullcoming v. New Mexico*, 131 S. Ct. 2705 (2011), the Supreme Court faced the question whether the prosecution's successful effort to admit a laboratory report in an aggravated drunk driving case, combined with calling a lab technician who was not the one who performed the relevant scientific test, was consistent with *Crawford*. The Court held that it was not. More specifically, the state successfully admitted a certification from a forensic analyst who performed a gas chromatograph test, purportedly showing that Bullcoming's blood alcohol level at the time he was driving was well over the legal limit. Caylor, the lab analyst who did the test, certified that he checked to ensure that the forensic report and sample numbers matched, performed a test on Bullcoming's blood sample, followed all proper procedures, and that no circumstance affected the integrity of the sample or the validity of the analysis. He further reported the machine's readout. The prosecution called a different analyst, Razatos, at the jury trial, explaining to the court that Caylor was on unpaid leave. Razatos testified as an expert witness, explaining the procedures ordinarily followed and the meaning of the results. The Supreme Court concluded that the certificate was testimonial, and thus inadmissible, because it was essentially indistinguishable from *Melendez-Diaz*. Although the certificate was not notarized, it was sufficiently formal, and thus constituted a testimonial statement.

The Court further concluded that there was ample need for cross-examination of Caylor that could not be met by cross-examining Razatos. Caylor's representations in the certificate involved more than mere authentication or the simple reporting of a machine readout. Instead, the certificate's representations "relat[ed] to past events and human actions not revealed in raw, machine-produced data," which require the opportunity for cross examination. Additionally, Razatos, who was neither involved in performing the gas chromatograph test nor observed it, admitted at trial that he had no way to know whether Caylor followed proper protocols. Razatos could not "expose any lapses or lies" by Caylor, nor could he testify as to "Caylor's proficiency, the care he took in performing his work," or why he was placed on unpaid leave. Cross-examining Caylor could have resolved these questions, as well as revealed any evasiveness or dishonesty.

The Court also refused to accept the argument that Razatos's testimony, given his expertise with gas chromatographs, was sufficiently reliable. The Confrontation Clause protects cross-examination partly because it improves reliability. But the Clause does not protect reliability itself. "Accordingly, the analysts who write reports that the prosecution introduces must be made available for confrontation even if they possess 'the scientific acumen of Mme. Curie and the veracity of Mother Teresa.'" Nevertheless, the Court noted that the reliability of the testimony was in question. The process of acquiring these blood alcohol results was imperfect. For example, in the neighboring state of Colorado, one forensics lab produced 206 inaccurate blood alcohol results over three years. So even if reliability was a definitive factor in determining the admissibility of the testimony, such reliability was absent here.

Four Justices dissented: Chief Justice Roberts, and Justices Kennedy, Breyer, and Alito. Their dissent can fairly be characterized as calling into question at least *Melendez-Diaz*, and perhaps *Crawford* itself. The dissent emphasized what it perceived to be the routine nature of Caylor's certificate, the reliability likely inherent in the test, and the sufficiency of Razatos's testimony to allow testing of reliability at trial. The defense also read the data on the impact of *Melendez-Diaz* differently, arguing that it had imposed a severe burden on the prosecution.

Melendez-Diaz did not have the sweeping effect of removing forensic reports from the courtroom. Most states have notice-and-demand statutes allowing admission of forensic reports unless the defense demands production of the lab analyst. In most cases, the defense will not want to demand a live witness whose testimony would merely highlight cold conclusions otherwise stated in a report. Most cases also involve guilty pleas rather than trials, so no witnesses are produced. Furthermore, the data suggest that *Melendez-Diaz* has not appreciably increased the number of analysts called to testify at trials.

c. *Williams v. Illinois*

The scope of *Bullcoming* was further analyzed in *Williams v. Illinois*, 132 S. Ct. 2221 (2012), on the issue of whether the Confrontation Clause was violated when an expert prosecution witness relied upon a scientific report prepared by another analyst, but where the report itself was not admitted into evidence for the truth of the matter asserted. The government's expert testified in a bench trial that she conducted a test of the defendant's DNA herself and found that it matched the DNA taken from a rape victim that, after analysis by a different technician, provided the genetic profile of the perpetrator. In comparing the two sets of results, the expert concluded that the defendant was the person identified in the DNA sample taken from the victim. The first DNA report was not admitted into evidence, and the expert relied on it only to the extent that it allowed her to conduct her own analysis of whether the defendant was involved in the crime. The expert admitted on cross-examination to not having any role in the DNA test of the sample taken from the victim, stating "that she trusted Cellmark to do reliable work because it was an accredited lab, but she admitted she had not seen any of the calibrations or work that Cellmark had done in deducing a male DNA profile from the vaginal swabs."

The case revolved around the expert's reference to the first DNA test in response to a question from the prosecutor, on which she relied for her conclusion that the defendant's DNA matched that of the perpetrator of the rape. In an opinion for a plurality of the justice, Justice Alito pointed out that "[i]t has long been accepted that an expert witness may voice an opinion based on facts concerning the events at issue in a particular case even if the expert lacks first-hand knowledge of those facts." Although an expert cannot disclose inadmissible evidence in a jury trial, the prosecution of Williams was in a bench trial, and so "[w]hen the judge sits as the trier of fact, it is presumed that the judge will understand the limited reason for the disclosure of the underlying inadmissible information and will not rely on that information for any improper purpose."

The plurality found no violation of the defendant's confrontation right. Justice Alito noted that it would have been acceptable under the Confrontation Clause for her to answer the following question: "Was there a computer match generated of the male DNA profile *produced by Cellmark* to a male DNA profile that had been identified as having originated from Sandy Williams?" (italics in original). But the question actually answered was "Was there a computer match generated of the male DNA profile *found in semen from the vaginal swabs of*

[L.J.] to a male DNA profile that had been identified as having originated from Sandy Williams?" (italics in original). By making a direct reference to the DNA evidence, that meant the expert was conveying information about the prior lab test and not simply providing her own opinion. Had this been a jury trial, then the reference could have been used to find the defendant was the perpetrator; but this was a bench trial, so "we must assume that the trial judge understood that the portion of [the expert's] testimony ... was not admissible to prove the truth of the matter asserted."

The Confrontation Clause did not apply because "[t]he correctness of this expert opinion, which the defense was able to test on cross-examination, was not in any way dependent on the origin of the samples from which the profiles were derived." The reference to the earlier DNA test was not to offer it into evidence but "to show that the expert's reasoning was not illogical, and that the weight of the expert's opinion does not depend on factual premises unsupported by other evidence in the record—not to prove the truth of the underlying facts." The plurality found there was no hearsay admitted into evidence by the expert's reference to the earlier test, so "if the trial judge in this case did not rely on the statement in question for its truth, there is simply no way around the proviso in *Crawford* that the Confrontation Clause applies only to out-of-court statements that are 'use[d]' to 'establis[h] the truth of the matter asserted.'"

The plurality asserted that its analysis was consistent with *Melendez-Diaz* and *Bullcoming*, because in those cases the forensic reports were offered for the truth of their conclusions that helped establish the defendant's guilt, while the expert's reference to the DNA test "was not to be considered for its truth but only for the 'distinctive and limited purpose' of seeing whether it matched something else." The plurality explained that there are four safeguards to prevent abuses from having an expert testify about information that would not otherwise be admissible under the Confrontation Clause:

- "trial courts can screen out experts who would act as mere conduits for hearsay by strictly enforcing the requirement that experts display some genuine scientific, technical, or other specialized knowledge";
- Federal Rule of Evidence 703 generally precludes experts from disclosing inadmissible evidence to a jury;
- "trial judges may and, under most circumstances, must, instruct the jury that out-of-court statements cannot be accepted for their truth, and that an expert's opinion is only as good as the independent evidence that establishes its underlying premises"; and
- "if the prosecution cannot muster any independent admissible evidence to prove the foundational facts that are essential to the relevance of the

expert's testimony, then the expert's testimony cannot be given any weight by the trier of fact."

After concluding the Confrontation Clause did not apply to the expert's testimony, the plurality then explained why there was no constitutional violation *even if* the reference to the prior DNA test was hearsay offered for the truth of the matter asserted, an act that might appear to trigger *Crawford*. Justice Alito evinced his hostility to *Crawford*'s analysis by explaining that its approach to hearsay arose only when the offending evidence had two characteristics: "(a) they involved out-of-court statements having the primary purpose of accusing a targeted individual of engaging in criminal conduct and (b) they involved formalized statements such as affidavits, depositions, prior testimony, or confessions." The plurality noted that one exception to this approach was *Hammon*, which did not have the same measure of formality but did involve an out-of-court statement whose "primary purpose" was to target someone engaged in criminal conduct. The prior DNA test in *Williams* did not come within *Crawford*'s prohibition because "its primary purpose was to catch a dangerous rapist who was still at large, not to obtain evidence for use against petitioner, who was neither in custody nor under suspicion at that time." The plurality justified its position by noting that "technicians who prepare a DNA profile generally have no way of knowing whether it will turn out to be incriminating or exonerating — or both," so they would not be accusing anyone of wrongdoing.

Justices Thomas and Breyer concurred in the judgment on the ground that the expert's reference to the prior DNA test was not "testimonial" within the meaning of *Crawford*, although each offered a different rationale for reaching that conclusion. Justice Kagan wrote the dissenting opinion, arguing that "[t]he plurality's first rationale endorses a prosecutorial dodge; its second relies on distinguishing indistinguishable forensic reports." The dissent claimed that the expert's "testimony is functionally identical to the 'surrogate testimony' that New Mexico proffered in *Bullcoming*, which did nothing to cure the problem identified in *Melendez–Diaz* (which, for its part, straightforwardly applied our decision in *Crawford*)."

The plurality in *Williams* took a very constrained view of what types of out-of-court statements violate the Confrontation Clause rights of a defendant. This approach seeks to cabin *Crawford* to a fairly narrow, albeit important, range of evidence that directly points to a defendant's guilt and has a measure of formality to it, at least such as that involved in police investigative questioning that is not in response to an immediate emergency situation. Both *Williams* and *Bryant* show that the Supreme Court remains divided on the scope of the Confrontation Clause and its application once the fairly straightforward circumstances of *Crawford*, *Melendez-Diaz*, and *Bullcoming* are left behind.

5. Forfeiture

The concept of "forfeiture by wrongdoing" appears in Federal Rule of Evidence 804(b)(6). That provision creates a hearsay exception for an unavailable witness's statement when offered at trial "against a party that wrongfully caused — or acquiesced in wrongfully causing — the declarant's unavailability as a witness, and did so intending that result." Wrongdoing to keep a witness off the stand at trial may include threats, bribes, or lies. If the statement would otherwise be inadmissible under the hearsay rule, Rule 804(b)(6) renders the statement nevertheless admissible. The theory is one of fairness and deterrence: a party who tries to keep a witness off the stand and then objects to the witness's statements as hearsay "forfeits" his right to object to the hearsay. Like the parent-murderer who seeks mercy because he is an orphan, the acquiescing party's objection will fall on willfully deaf judicial ears.

The Supreme Court has embraced a similar doctrine in the area of confrontation. Specifically, the Court has held that a defendant who purposely and successfully acts to render a witness unavailable to testify at trial forfeits any Confrontation Clause objections to hearsay statements by that witness. In *Davis v. Washington*, 547 U.S. 813 (2006), the Court said in *dicta* that "when defendants seek to undermine the judicial process by procuring or coercing silence from witnesses and victims, the Sixth Amendment does not require courts to acquiesce." Thus, a defendant need not assist the prosecution in proving guilt, but "they *do* have the duty to refrain from acting in ways that destroy the integrity of the criminal-trial system." Accordingly, quoting its *Crawford* opinion, the Court reiterated that "the rule of forfeiture by wrongdoing ... extinguishes confrontation claims on essentially equitable grounds."

The *Davis* Court took no position on the standards for demonstrating forfeiture. But the Court did cite with approval the use of a preponderance of evidence burden on the state, which most courts follow when considering the admission of hearsay under Federal Rule of Evidence 804(b)(6). The Court also suggested that hearsay might be admissible at the foundational hearing before the trial judge to determine whether forfeiture occurred, as would also be true under Rule 804(b)(6). The Court remanded the case for Indiana's courts to determine whether forfeiture by wrongdoing occurred in *Davis's* companion case of *Hammon*.

In *Giles v. California*, 554 U.S. 353 (2008), the Court squarely confronted the forfeiture question. Dwayne Giles had shot dead his ex-girlfriend, Brenda Avie, shooting her six times. Giles claimed self-defense. Prosecutors successfully introduced at trial a statement Avie had made to the police three weeks before the shooting. Giles, said Avie, accused her of having an affair, choked her, punched her in the face and head, held a folding knife near her, and threatened to kill her if he found her cheating. The trial judge admitted the statements under a California law permitting admission of hearsay statements describing threatened or actual infliction of physical injury on a declarant unavailable at trial where the judge finds the statements to be trustworthy. A jury convicted Giles of first-degree murder, and two California courts, on grounds of forfeiture, rejected Confrontation Clause challenges.

The Supreme Court acknowledged that both history and precedent supported a Confrontation Clause exception for forfeiture by wrongdoing. Those same sources, however, limited the exception to cases where "the defendant engaged in conduct *designed* to prevent the witness from testifying...." The exception thus did not extend to the typical murder case (absent a dying declaration, which is also excepted from the Confrontation Clause), where the defendant rendered the witness unavailable to testify but did not engage in the criminal act *for the purpose* of preventing such testimony.

The Court in *Giles* rejected an argument for extending the forfeiture exception based on the equitable maxim that "a defendant should not be permitted to benefit from his own wrong." Applying that maxim to a murder case would require a trial judge to determine, *before trial*, that the defendant was in fact guilty of the crime. Such an approach "does not sit well with the right to trial by jury. It is akin, one might say, 'to dispensing with jury trial because a defendant is obviously guilty.'"

The Court described Federal Rule of Evidence 804(b)(6) as codifying the forfeiture doctrine. The Court noted that every commentator agreed that the intent mentioned in the Rule "means the exception applies only if the defendant has in mind the particular purpose of making the witness unavailable." The majority likewise rejected the dissent's argument that the objectives of the forfeiture doctrine required reading it broadly, even if history and precedent did not require doing so. Once again, the Court rejected the idea that its role was to extrapolate from underlying Sixth Amendment values, enforcing only rules that, in the Court's opinion, serve those values. The Sixth Amendment sought fairness through confrontation, and nothing in its text or history suggested that the judiciary could develop open-ended exceptions to the Clause's confrontation mandate.

The Court was unconvinced by the dissent's argument that the majority's rule would wreak havoc with domestic violence cases. First, noted the Court, only testimonial statements would be excluded. "Statements to friends and neighbors about abuse and intimidation, and statements to physicians in the course of receiving treatment would be excluded, if at all, only by hearsay rules, [under] which [jurisdictions] are free to adopt the dissent's version of forfeiture by wrongdoing."

Second, in many instances domestic violence will be aimed at isolating the victim from outside help, including engaging in conduct "designed to prevent testimony to police officers or cooperation in criminal prosecutions." Where such facts are proven, forfeiture would apply. Because the state courts considered the defendant's purpose to discourage the declarant's testimony irrelevant, the state courts erred. The Court thus remanded the case for further proceedings.

It is worth noting that Justices Souter and Ginsburg concurred in most of the majority's opinion, but they refused to find any claim that history was dispositive. Justices Thomas and Alito concurred on forfeiture grounds, but noted their conclusion that the hearsay statement in question should not have been considered testimonial in the first place. Justice Thomas in particular insisted that a more "formalized dialogue" would be required for the Confrontation Clause to apply.

6. Crawford *and the Rules of Evidence*

It is clear that the forfeiture by wrongdoing and dying declaration exceptions to the hearsay rule, as they are recited in the Federal Rules of Evidence and most state evidence codes, survive confrontation challenges because they fit into exceptions to the Confrontation Clause's mandate. Most business records, and even most public records, for example, are prepared primarily so that the organization or public agency can get its daily work done. These ordinary business records would thus not seem to be testimonial, though at least one Justice apparently views the Court as having reserved judgment on the question. But when such records are prepared for the *purpose* of providing evidence at a criminal trial, the records should be considered testimonial.

Statements made to police, even if admitted as excited utterances, will face case-specific scrutiny to determine whether they were made to address ongoing emergencies (Confrontation Clause inapplicable) or resulted from police interrogation (Confrontation Clause applicable). Present sense impressions, because they must be made as an event is observed or immediately thereafter, are generally unlikely to be made to the police or where a reasonable person would expect they may be used in court. If made to the police, that would usually occur during a 911 call while a crime is ongoing, thus more likely the product of an ongoing emergency rather than from interrogation.

Expert opinions, whether in public or business records, if offered by law enforcement, police forensics labs, or experts hired by the prosecution to testify at trial, would be testimonial. That they are testimonial is a different question from whether the expert's reliance on other testimonial opinions violates the Confrontation Clause, which the Supreme Court found did not violate the Constitution in *Williams v. Illinois*, 132 S. Ct. 2221 (2012). The prior reported testimony exception almost by definition involves testimonial hearsay because it involves earlier statements made under oath for eventual potential use at a trial. But that exception also requires that the person against whom it is now offered had an earlier opportunity for cross-examination, thus frequently meeting the dictates of the *Crawford* rule. Statements against a declarant's pecuniary or proprietary interest would not necessarily be testimonial. But statements against the declarant's penal interest again seem also definitively testimonial, because the risk that they will be used to convict the declarant of the crime is precisely what makes the statement against the speaker's interest. But there may be situations in which one conspirator is acknowledging a course of criminal conduct to another member of the criminal confederation, which is unlikely to be viewed at testimonial.

Generalizations like these seem to be fair inferences from the Court's case law thus far. But lower court decisions must always be consulted because case-specific factual differences often matter.

B. Co-Defendant Statements

1. Bruton v. United States

Bruton v. United States, 391 U.S. 123 (1968), addressed the situation where a guilt-establishing statement by one of two (or more) jointly-tried co-defendants implicates another co-defendant, and the declarant does not take the stand to testify at trial. In that situation, the declarant is unavailable to be cross-examined by his non-confessing co-defendant at trial because the Fifth Amendment privilege against self-incrimination precludes calling a co-defendant to testify unless the person voluntarily waives the right to not testify. Such a deprival of cross examination appears to be a clear Confrontation Clause violation. But what if the Supreme Court instructed the jury to use the statement only against the declarant, not the other co-defendant referenced in the statement? Would not that cure any Confrontation Clause violation, rendering the situation the same as one in which no statement had been admitted in the first place? The Court answered that question with a resounding "no."

In *Bruton*, a postal inspector testified at the joint trial of Evans and Bruton that Evans confessed to the inspector to committing an armed robbery along with an unnamed accomplice. Both Bruton and Evans appealed their convictions. The appellate court reversed Evans's conviction on the ground the statement was inadmissible. But it did not reverse Bruton's conviction because the jury had been instructed only to consider Evans's confession against him, not Bruton's.

The Supreme Court reversed. Jury instructions to disregard evidence or limit its use might sometimes be successful for other issues in a case; but given the enormous persuasive power of confessions, the Court concluded that jurors could not be expected "to perform the overwhelming task" of considering a confession by one of two jointly-tried co-defendants implicating the other *only* in gauging the confessor's guilt:

> [T]here are some contexts in which the risk that a jury will not, or cannot, follow instructions is so great, and the consequences of failure so vital to the defendant, that the practical and human limitations of the jury system cannot be ignored.... Such a context is presented here, where the powerfully incriminating extrajudicial statements of a co-defendant, who stands side-by-side with the defendant, are deliberately spread before the jury in a joint trial. Not only are the incriminations devastating to the defendant, but their credibility is inevitably suspect, a fact recognized when accomplices do take the stand and the jury is instructed to weigh their testimony carefully given the unrecognized motivations to shift blame to others. The unreliability of such evidence is intolerably compounded when the alleged accomplice, as here, does not testify and cannot be tested by cross-examination.

The "substantial threats" posed to confrontation rights by the admissibility of Evans's statement at his joint trial with Bruton was sufficient to establish a Confrontation Clause violation.

2. Richardson v. Marsh

In *Richardson v. Marsh*, 481 U.S. 200 (1987), the Supreme Court refused to extend *Bruton* to a situation in which the co-defendant's confession redacted not only the defendant's name but any reference to her existence. Three individuals — Williams, Martin, and Marsh — were charged with assaulting Cynthia Knighton and murdering her four-year-old son and aunt. At the joint trial of two of the defendants, Williams and Marsh, Knighton testified that when the three defendants appeared at her home, one with a gun, she and her son had tried to flee. But defendant Marsh grabbed Knighton and held her until the two other defendants returned, apparently having gone upstairs to look for money. Marsh also periodically peered out a peephole. When Williams and Martin returned from the apparent search, one of them gave a paper grocery bag (perhaps containing money) to Marsh. The two other co-defendants forced the victims into the basement, shooting them, with only Knighton surviving.

A police officer next testified to Williams' statement, which was redacted to omit any reference not only to Marsh, but to anyone other than Williams and Martin. The statement also described a pre-robbery conversation in which Martin supposedly said that he would have to kill the victims. The court admonished the jury at that time not to use the confession against Marsh.

Marsh also testified, claiming that she accompanied Martin to the home to borrow money. Marsh had lost money with which Martin had meant to buy drugs. Marsh suggested borrowing from a man from whom she had borrowed in the past. Marsh testified to surprise when Martin pulled a gun, insisting she did not feel free to leave and was too scared to try. She admitted that Martin gave her a grocery bag, but claimed she left the house without the bag and had no idea that Williams and Martin planned a robbery and murder.

The prosecutor, in his closing argument, linked Marsh to a portion of Williams' confession, despite having just told the jury not to use Williams' confession against Marsh. The trial judge again instructed the jury not to use Williams' confession against Marsh. Nevertheless, that jury convicted Marsh of two counts of felony murder and one count of assault to commit murder.

The Court found no Confrontation Clause violation. It concluded that *Bruton* created a narrow exception to the assumption that jurors follow instructions. *Bruton* applied, said the Court, only to the narrow circumstance in which a "facially incriminating" confession of a non-testifying co-defendant is introduced at their joint trial. But here the confession did not *expressly* implicate Marsh as an accomplice. Indeed, the confession never even mentioned the existence of Marsh or a third accomplice. The confession became incriminating "only when linked with evidence introduced later at trial [by] the defendant's own testimony." A confession requiring such inferential linkage is far less vivid than direct testimony that "'the defendant helped me commit the crime....'" In the latter circumstance, a jury is far less likely to fail to heed a judge's instruction to limit application of the confession to its declarant.

The Court suggested that even in *Bruton* itself, adequate redaction may have been sufficient. In any event, extending *Bruton* to cases like *Marsh* would impose a severe burden on the criminal justice system for little reason. Joint trials are common and promote efficiency, especially with large conspiracies. Requiring witnesses to testify repeatedly at numerous trials against individual defendants would be burdensome, even traumatizing. Such an approach would unfairly favor later-tried defendants, who know what evidence was offered at earlier trials, and would avoid the "scandal and inequity of inconsistent verdicts." Joint trials also enable "more accurate assessment of relative culpability-advantages, which sometimes operate to the defendant's benefit." Barring use of co-defendant confessions entirely is not feasible because they are essential to convicting those who violate the law.

Nevertheless, the Court remanded the case for consideration of whether the prosecutor's effort to "undo the effect of the limiting instruction by urging the jury to use Williams' confession in evaluating respondent's case" undermined Confrontation Clause precepts. The Court expressed doubt, however, whether that issue had been properly preserved by the defendant. If it was not preserved, or if it was but did not affect the jury's reasoning, presumably, under the Court's rule articulated in *Marsh*, her conviction would stand.

3. Gray v. Maryland

In another case that hinged on whether redacted information might avoid a Confrontation Clause violation, *Gray v. Maryland*, 523 U.S. 185 (1998), the Supreme Court found an inartful redaction insufficient to escape *Bruton*'s strictures. There, Anthony Bell confessed to beating Stacey Williams to death, aided by Kevin Gray and "Tank" Valandingham. Bell and Gray were jointly tried for murder. At trial, a police detective read Bell's confession, inserting the word "deleted" or "deletion" whenever Gray or Tank's name appeared. After he finished, the prosecutor asked, "[A]fter he gave you that information, you subsequently were able to arrest Mr. Kevin Gray; is that correct?" The state also succeeded in admitting the written copy of the confessions, with blanks separated by commas replacing Gray and Tank's names. Gray testified, denying his participation, and other witnesses testified that all three men (Gray, Tank, and Bell) and three others participated in the murder. The trial judge cautioned the jury not to use the confession against Gray, but the jury apparently connected both Gray and Bell to the statement.

The Court saw the case before it as closer to *Bruton* than *Richardson*. The jury was likely to react similarly to this confession and an unredacted one, and would do so even absent the prosecutor's expressly linking the confession to Gray, as occurred here:

> Consider a simplified but typical example, a confession that reads, "I, Bob Smith, along with Sam Jones, robbed the bank." To replace the words "Sam Jones" with an obvious blank will not likely fool anyone. A juror somewhat familiar with the criminal law would know immediately that the blank, in the phrase, "I, Bob Smith, along with _____, robbed the bank," refers to defendant Jones. A juror who does not know the law and who therefore wonders to whom the blank might refer need only lift his eyes to Jones sitting at counsel table, to find what will

seem the obvious answer, at least if the juror hears the judge's instruction not to consider the confession as evidence against Jones, for that instruction will provide an obvious reason for the blank.

The Court noted that a "more sophisticated juror, wondering if the blank refers to someone else, might also wonder how, if it did, the prosecutor could argue the confession is reliable, for the prosecutor, after all, has been arguing that Jones, not someone else, helped Smith commit the crime."

Indeed, by encouraging juror speculation, the redaction might lead jurors to over-emphasize the confession. Furthermore, a confession saying "blank and a defendant" committed a crime functions grammatically the same as one filling in the blank with a name. Jurors will naturally, therefore, fill in the blank themselves. Accordingly, redacted confessions of a form like that in *Gray* will generally be inadmissible, though the Court suggested that this might not always be true. There might be confessions in which a link to the defendant is less transparent, thus not posing the same dangers.

The Court also clarified *Richardson's* reference to confessions that rely on inferences to incriminate a defendant. *Richardson* was not meant to exclude from *Bruton's* scope all confessions raising inferences. Rather, *Richardson* turned on the *kind of* inference: one making a confession incriminating only when linked to the defendant via other evidence introduced at trial. But inferences from redacted statements referring to someone else, often obviously the defendant, and which involve inferences that a jury ordinarily could make immediately, even were the confession the very first item introduced at trial," flout the Confrontation Clause's mandate. This rule does not, insisted the Court, implicate *Richardson's* policy concerns either because properly-redacted confessions, like that in *Richardson,* are normally easily crafted. Severance of defendants for trial is not required.

d. *Crawford's* Impact on *Bruton*

Recall that *Crawford* apparently limited the Confrontation Clause to "testimonial" statements. It might follow, therefore, that *Bruton's* rule does not extend to nontestimonial statements, such as many of those statements made to a friend, lover, or confidential informant in privacy. Such statements are nontestimonial because they are made without the declarant's objective expectation that the statement will be used in court. Most courts addressing the question have indeed so held, though there is a split.

C. Manner of Presenting Testimony: Confrontation Clause Concerns

There is a line of Confrontation Clause case law that concerns not merely the opportunity for witness cross-examination but further the adequacy of that opportunity. This same line of cases also addresses whether the Confrontation Clause protects face-to-face confrontation. For example, where certain vulnerable victims, such as children or sexual assault victims, are involved, the alleged victim directly facing the accused may be emotionally disturbing to the victim. Seeing the alleged assailant's eyes merely feet away may cause the accuser to be so distraught as to be unable to testify. Prosecutors experimented with screens blocking the alleged victim's view of the accused or with closed-circuit television, in which the accused is in another room, able to observe the witness while the witness is unable in turn to observe the accused. The issue is whether these sorts of devices violate the Confrontation Clause.

1. Witness Screens

In *Coy v. Iowa*, 487 U.S. 1012 (1988), the defendant was charged with sexually assaulting two thirteen-year-old girls. Pursuant to a state statute authorizing the procedure, the trial court granted a prosecution motion to have a large screen placed between each of the girls and the defendant during the former's testimony. The screen enabled the defendant to see the witnesses dimly through the screen, but they could not see him at all. State courts rejected the Confrontation Clause and due process challenges to this procedure, but the Supreme Court reversed, remanding the case to the lower courts for a harmless error analysis.

The Court concluded that the Confrontation Clause includes protection for *face-to-face* encounters between the accused and his accusers. Moreover, concluded the Court, face-to-face encounters can promote more reliable testimony. "The face-to-face presence may, unfortunately, upset the truthful rape victim or abused child; but by the same token it may confound and undo the false accuser, or reveal the child coached by a malevolent adult. It is a truism that constitutional protections have costs."

The Court acknowledged that it had, in the past, permitted balancing rights implied from the Confrontation Clause against other interests. But, concluded the Court, that is "not the same as holding that we can identify exceptions, in light of other important interests, to the irreducible meaning of the Clause: 'a right to *meet face to face* all those who appear and give evidence *at trial*'" (italics in orginal). Nevertheless, it left for another day whether exceptions might sometimes exist, though noting that, if they do exist, they could apply only "when necessary to further an important public policy." The Court rejected the state's claim that this case presented just such a situation:

> The State maintains that such necessity is established here by the statute, which creates a legislatively imposed presumption of trauma. Our cases suggest, however, that even as exceptions from the normal implications of the Confrontation Clause, as opposed to its most literal application, something more than the type of generalized finding underlying such a statute is needed when the exception is not "firmly ... rooted in our jurisprudence...." The exception created in the Iowa statute, which was passed in 1985, could hardly be viewed as firmly rooted. Since there have been no individualized findings that these particular witnesses needed special protection, the judgment here could not be sustained by any conceivable exception.

Justice O'Connor, joined by Justice White, concurred. Justice O'Connor emphasized that child abuse was a powerful competing interest, particularly suggesting that two-way closed circuit television systems for protecting children from seeing their alleged abusers might survive constitutional muster. Justice O'Connor described the Court as creating a mere "preference" for face-to-face confrontation. Justices Blackmun and Rehnquist dissented from this insistence on a case-specific inquiry. "[L]egislative exceptions to the Confrontation Clause of general applicability are commonplace," they concluded.

2. Closed-Circuit Television

The Supreme Court in *Maryland v. Craig*, 497 U.S. 836 (1990), squarely addressed—and approved—taking a child's testimony through closed circuit television, outside the courtroom and the immediate presence of the defendant and the jury, where a finding of necessity was previously made. Defense counsel, who, along with the prosecutor, accompanied the child during the out-of-court questioning, was in constant electronic communication with the defendant. The Court approved the procedure despite the child's being unable to see the defendant during the examination:

> We find it significant ... that Maryland's procedure preserves all of the other elements of the confrontation right: The child witness must be competent to testify and must testify under oath; the defendant retains full opportunity for contemporaneous cross-examination; and the judge, jury, and defendant are able to view (albeit by video monitor) the demeanor (and body) of the witness as he or she testifies. Although we are mindful of the many subtle effects face-to-face con-

frontation may have on an adversary criminal proceeding, the presence of these other elements of confrontation — oath, cross-examination, and observation of the witness' demeanor — adequately ensures that the testimony is both reliable and subject to rigorous adversarial testing in a manner functionally equivalent to that accorded live, in-person testimony. These safeguards of reliability and adversariness render the use of such a procedure a far cry from the undisputed prohibition of the Confrontation Clause: trial by an ex parte affidavit or inquisition.

In *Craig*, the Court's justification for upholding the closed circuit procedure was partly that the child would suffer "trauma" from seeing her assailant. The Court was unclear about *why* the trauma mattered. There is language in the *Craig* opinion suggesting that the trauma showing permitted the Court to engage in interest balancing, which it had previously declined to do: preventing psychological harm to the child was simply more important than the defendant's right to eyeball-to-eyeball contact with his accuser. Thus, the Court found that the "important public policy" in protecting the "physical and psychological well-being of child abuse victims" was sufficiently important to "outweigh," in the case before it, the defendant's right to face his accuser in court, given that reliability was otherwise being assured.

In other constitutional evidence doctrine cases, the Court has recognized the need for interest balancing. As discussed above, it is unclear whether such interest-balancing under the Confrontation Clause survives *Crawford* and *Bullcoming*, which seem to suggest it does not, though the multiple opinions in *Bullcoming* raise some confusion on the point. Furthermore, even if those decisions stand for a rejection of interest-balancing, they occurred in the hearsay context in which there was no opportunity for cross-examination. It is uncertain whether the same approach would prevail in the face-to-face aspect of the Confrontation Clause, in which cross-examination does occur but the manner in which that happens is contested.

The costs just discussed are *internal* ones that affect the participants to the individual trial alone, particularly child victims' psychological trauma from seeing the accused. But external costs that go well beyond the impact on just the individual trial participants can stem from victim cross-examination when there are virtually no limits on the manner in which it is conducted. For example, cross-examination of adult rape victims at trial to demonstrate that the person was "asking for it" arguably imposes substantial external social costs: heightened subordination of women as a group, their lowered social status and reduced autonomy, and their exclusion from real participation in trials as institutions of self-government. These costs are imposed on the rape victim individually but are also systemic costs imposed on society as a whole.

Indeed, although the Court worried in *Craig* about proof of trauma to the individual child, it understood that the procedure followed in *Craig* was created by the legislature to address a portion of the broader social problems created by child abuse. Thirty-seven state legislatures, the Court noted, had created special trial procedures for abused children. The Court saw these procedures as stemming from "the State's traditional and 'transcendent' interest in protecting the welfare of children" and from the "growing body of academic literature documenting the psychological trauma suffered by child abuse victims who must testify in court."

An alternative way to read *Craig's* trauma requirement, however, is that trauma mattered because it undermined testimonial reliability. Under this reading, the state must show that trauma would render the child's testimony unreliable. For example, a minor victim might distort his or her testimony because of having been threatened by the defendant or being overwhelmed by guilt. Alternatively, the child might feel intimidated or be easily confused. If reliability is the touchstone, then *Craig* did not "balance away" the right to face-to-face contact. Rather, the right never existed in the first place because its exercise under the circumstances would have defeated the Confrontation Clause's function in enhancing testimonial reliability.

Craig did indeed require trauma caused by the child's *seeing the accused*, not simply the ordinary trauma from testifying. Moreover, the Court at one point noted:

> [T]he use of Maryland's special procedure ... *adequately ensures the accuracy of the testimony* and preserves the adversary nature of the trial. [Citations omitted.] Indeed, where face-to-face confrontation causes significant emotional distress in a child witness, there is evidence that such confrontation would *in fact disserve the Confrontation Clause's truth-seeking goal. See, e.g.,* [Justice Blackmun's dissenting opinion *in Coy*]: (face-to-face confrontation "may so overwhelm the child as to prevent the possibility of effective testimony, *thereby undermining the truth-finding function* of the trial itself").

Whether this reading survives *Crawford* is also open to question. *Crawford* rejected an understanding of the Confrontation Clause as broadly protecting evidentiary reliability. Rather, the Clause protects reliability via the method of cross-examination. But *Craig's* logic is not necessarily inconsistent with this perspective. *Craig* might be seen as raising a case-specific situation in which full-blown, face-to-face cross-examination distorts evidentiary reliability rather than raising any serious prospect of promoting it. In such an unusual circumstance, special procedures might arguably be required merely to ensure that the manner of cross-examination achieves its social goal. One flaw in such an argument, however, is that the Confrontation Clause protects a right of the defendant, not of the state. The reliability distortions involved in *Craig* harm the state alone. Still, the defendant may be seen as having a right only to cross-examination in a manner that serves confrontation's constitutional purposes. Where cross undermines those purposes, his right simply would not exist. There would thus be no bar to the state implementing procedures to restore cross to its proper function. Due process might also arguably embrace a similar approach.

A federal statute, 18 U.S.C. § 3509, and a number of states provide for child witnesses to testify by 2-way closed circuit television in sexual abuse cases. The federal law permits this means of testifying in the following circumstances:

(i)   The child is unable to testify because of fear.
(ii)   There is a substantial likelihood, established by expert testimony, that the child would suffer emotional trauma from testifying.
(iii) The child suffers a mental or other infirmity.
(iv)   Conduct by defendant or defense counsel causes the child to be unable to continue testifying.

Four states have adopted the Uniform Child Witness Testimony by Alternative Methods Act, which generally follows the requirements set forth in *Craig* for having a child testify outside the direct presence of the defendant.

D. Cross-Examination's Function and Adequacy Generally

The purpose of cross-examination is to "augment accuracy in the fact-finding process by ensuring the defendant an effective means to test adverse evidence." *Ohio v. Roberts*, 448 U.S. 56 (1980). This is not a guarantee of actual effectiveness. Rather, all that is guaranteed is a realistic and fair chance of calling a witness's credibility into question. Cross-examination functions to promote accuracy by "affording the trier of fact a satisfactory basis for evaluating the truth...."

The Supreme Court has found that a wide range of obstacles to defense questioning does not necessarily prevent adequate cross-examination. Thus, it did not matter under the Confrontation Clause that the state failed to produce medical records that a defense attorney deemed essential to his adequately examining a child sexual assault victim. *Pennsylvania v. Ritchie*, 480 U.S. 39 (1987). Nor did it matter that a prosecution expert forgot the basis of his opinion. *Delaware v. Fensterer*, 474 U.S. 15 (1985). In yet another case, an assault victim identified the defendant from a photospread. At trial, however, the victim simply could not remember whether police or others had suggested that the victim identify the defendant. *United States v. Owens*, 484 U.S. 554 (1988).

II. The Compulsory Process Clause

A. Background

1. Connection to the Rules of Evidence

The Sixth Amendment to the United States Constitution guarantees the defendant's right "to have compulsory process for obtaining witnesses in his favor." On its face, this Compulsory Process Clause seems to guarantee merely the defendant's right to subpoena witnesses to attend trial. However, such a right would be a hollow one if state rules of evidence could then prevent the witnesses from testifying. The Clause has thus been interpreted to require state evidentiary rules, at least sometimes, to bow to the defendant's need for the evidence. The courts have provided far less clarity, however, for distinguishing between those situations where state evidence rules prevail and those that do not. Because of this lack of clarity, making sense of the case law can be aided first by better understanding debates about the Clause's meaning.

2. Debates about the Clause

a. Promoting Evidentiary Reliability

One way of making the distinction between constitutionally valid and invalid evidence rules under the Compulsory Process Clause might be to inquire into the extent to which state evidentiary rules promote evidentiary reliability. Interpreting the Clause as demanding the admission of unreliable evidence would undermine truth-finding. It would seem odd to require admitting evidence that leads the jury astray. Some case law, indeed, seems to embody this concern with reliability. Reliability concerns have been especially robust when categorical evidence rules exclude entire classes of evidence. Courts sometimes override such rules when evidence within the class is nevertheless reliable in an individual case.

b. Prosecutorial Control

Reliability is clearly not the sole — nor perhaps even the primary — concern of the Constitution. Both structurally and historically, the criminal procedure provisions were designed to limit government power. The Compulsory Process

Clause does this by guaranteeing the defendant's right to present evidence supporting an entirely different narrative from that of the state. The Clause also enables the defense to expose holes in the prosecution's version of events by challenging their witnesses' credibility, completeness, and perspective. Furthermore, the Clause can expose governmental lies, incompetence, and abuses of power. The defense should not itself be free to cause trial havoc with misleading, speculative, or fraudulent evidence; but under this government-monitoring approach, the standard for the admissibility of defense evidence should be low: evidence that changes the probabilities, however slightly, of a fact of consequence being true. Under this view, a disparity in the application of evidence rules—higher admissibility burdens on the prosecution than on the defense—makes perfect sense, for it is the prosecutor's power, not the defendant's, that needs to be restrained.

This prosecutorial control model further subverts a reliability focus because of its malleability and weakness. So long as states can craft plausible reliability justifications for their evidentiary rules, they can exclude defense evidence. Of course, the force of this critique depends on whether a state-deferential "rational basis" test or a more vigorous "strict scrutiny" test is applied. Still, defenders of this model argue that the Clause contemplates ensuring reliability via a particular mechanism: namely, the adversarial process. The ability for cross-examination, prosecution rebuttal, and jury instructions to test the defense's trustworthiness is a sufficient guarantee of reliability.

c. Links to the Confrontation Clause

This adversarial approach resonates with modern Confrontation Clause jurisprudence of *Crawford*, which abandoned any independent inquiry into the reliability of prosecutorial evidence in determining whether it complied with the Constitution. Rather, the Clause was seen as guaranteeing the right to cross-examination as a way of testing evidentiary reliability, though cross-examination has other virtues as well; for example, in revealing and limiting governmental abuses. The two Clauses thus are siblings, both appearing in the Sixth Amendment and both relying on the central guarantees of the American adversarial system. If this is so, however, perhaps the two Clauses should mirror each other more precisely. Remember that the Confrontation Clause protects only "testimonial" evidence. The Compulsory Process Clause, some commentators have suggested, should likewise be limited to such evidence. Doing so would, however, vastly narrow the Clause's potentially broad reach.

d. Links to Due Process

The narrowed reach of the Compulsory Process Clause under an approach limiting it to testimonial evidence might be reversed by the Due Process Clause's embrace of the beyond a reasonable doubt standard. Non-testimonial defense evidence that may fairly be seen as raising a reasonable doubt should thus be admissible under due process.

The due process link need not, however, be limited to the beyond a reasonable doubt standard. Due process guarantees "fundamentally fair" procedures in an American adversarial system of ordered liberty. It might, therefore, be argued that due process requires the defense to have fair access to evidence in its favor, no matter what the Compulsory Process Clause requires. But this approach creates its own problems. The Court generally interprets free-standing due process criminal procedural guarantees in a way that is far less robust than more specific constitutional provisions. Due process "fairness" is arguably more maleable than more specific guarantees, the presence of fairness too variable to the eye of the beholder. Furthermore, the Court generally prefers to rely on more specific over more general criminal procedural guarantees when the former are available. The Court has nevertheless muddied the waters by sometimes finding a "right to present a defense" as inherent in the combination of Compulsory Process and Due Process Clause guarantees. Critics have complained that this introduction of due process concepts into the right has necessarily watered it down.

e. Interest-Balancing

Yet another problem arises when deciding whether compulsory process protections should be absolute — save for the meeting of some minimal evidentiary threshold — or should be balanced against countervailing concerns, constitutional or otherwise. The Compulsory Process Clause's potentially broad scope seems to necessitate such balancing. It has been utilized in numerous cases to override claims of psychotherapist-patient, executive, and other forms of privileges. Defendants have sought to apply it to admit arguably untrustworthy scientific and other expert testimony, hearsay without applicable exceptions, and otherwise inadmissible character evidence. To recognize a broad scope for the Compulsory Process Clause would allow it to potentially gut virtually all state evidentiary rules, at least as applied to the defense. Moreover, argue some commentators, tolerating such a high level of anti-prosecution evidentiary disparity might impose a high cost in lost public respect for the justice system and free too many of the guilty. Balancing helps limit the Compulsory Process Clause's otherwise unmanageable reach.

B. *The Court's Case Law*

This survey of varied perspectives has been necessitated by the Court's ambiguous, sparse, and often factually-limited precedent on compulsory process. Each of the concerns just discussed—disparity, innocence, freeing the guilty, reliability, respect for adversarial processes versus fearing them, and balancing—can be found in *some* of the Court's cases. This background thus helps in navigating a dense precedential thicket.

1. Washington v. Texas

The Supreme Court's first modern treatment of the Compulsory Process Clause occurred in *Washington v. Texas*, 388 U.S. 14 (1967). That case also first incorporated the Clause against the states as a fundamentally fair procedure contained within the Fourteenth Amendment's Due Process Clause.

In *Washington,* the defendant and several other young men, including one Charles Fuller, headed to the home of Washington's ex-girlfriend. Fuller had with him a shotgun. Washington, motivated by jealousy of the girl's new boyfriend, and the other young men, threw bricks at the house. When the residents came out to investigate, Washington or Fuller fired the shotgun, killing the ex-girlfriend's new boyfriend. The group fled, with Fuller carrying the shotgun.

At Washington's trial, he sought to call Fuller to the stand. Fuller had already been convicted and sentenced to 50 years' imprisonment for murdering the boyfriend. Washington insisted that Fuller would testify that Washington tried to persuade Fuller to leave without shooting, but that Fuller had insisted on killing, firing the fatal shot. Two Texas statutes prohibited one of several co-participants charged with or convicted of the same crime from testifying on another co-participant's behalf. But the statute did not bar any co-participant from testifying *for the state.* Washington was thus convicted without the jury hearing Fuller's testimony.

The Court found the Sixth Amendment's Compulsory Process Clause fundamental to a fair trial because "[t]he right to offer the testimony of witnesses, and to compel their attendance, if necessary, is in plain terms the right to present a defense...." But that right ensures the defendant can present his own "version of the facts as well as the prosecution's to the jury so it may decide where the truth lies." Moreover, the Court linked the Compulsory Process Clause to its already-incorporated protection for face-to-face confrontation. "Just as an accused has the right to confront the prosecution's witnesses for the purpose of challenging their testimony, he has the right to present his own witnesses to establish a defense. This right is a fundamental element of due process of law."

The Court found the Compulsory Process Clause to be designed to overcome common law disabilities on the right of the defendant to call witnesses on his own behalf. Moreover, said the Court, it could "hardly be doubted" that the Clause would be violated if a state barred all defense testimony. The Court concluded it "is difficult to see how the Constitution is any less violated by arbitrary rules that prevent whole categories of defense witnesses from testifying on the basis of prior assumptions that presume them unworthy of belief."

The accomplice-testimony-disqualification requirement was just such an arbitrary rule. The state had argued that the rule rationally identified a group particularly likely to commit perjury. But the exceptions to the rule belied this justification. Thus the prosecution could call accomplices when "common sense" suggests that they are even more likely to lie for the state than for the defense, especially where the accomplices are awaiting trial or sentencing, thus wanting to remain in the state's good graces. "To think that criminals will lie to save their fellows, but not to obtain favors from the prosecution for themselves is indeed to clothe the criminal class with more nobility than one might expect to find in the public at large." A second exception permitted an acquitted defendant to testify for "his comrade, secure in the knowledge that he could incriminate himself as freely as he liked in his testimony, since he could not again be prosecuted for the same offense." However, testimony under such circumstances raises a graver risk of perjury than does pro-defense testimony from an accomplice still awaiting trial. Such a result "arbitrarily" applied a testimonial bar only to the defense, not the prosecution, and only where the risks to trial accuracy were, relatively speaking, at their lowest. Barring Washington from calling a witness capable of testifying to "relevant and material" evidence based upon personal knowledge under such circumstances could not be justified. The Court held that "[t]he Framers of the Constitution did not intend to commit the futile act of giving to a defendant the right to secure attendance of witnesses whose testimony he had no right to use," and found that the defense should have been permitted to call its witness.

2. Chambers v. Mississippi

Six years later, the Supreme Court revisited the Compulsory Process Clause right in *Chambers v. Mississippi*, 410 U.S. 284 (1973). There, a melee started when a large crowd gathered around police attempting to make an arrest. Officer Liberty was shot during the commotion, eventually dying from his wounds. Before dying, however, he fired his riot gun into an alley from which the shots apparently came, hitting Leon Chambers, who fell to the ground, appearing to the officers to be dead. Chambers lived and was charged with Officer Liberty's murder. Another man, Gable McDonald, however, had also been in the crowd. McDonald confessed to Chambers' attorneys to having been Officer Liberty's real killer. McDonald signed a transcription of the confession, and the police jailed him for the murder. But at the preliminary hearing McDonald recanted, insisting that a Reverend Stokes encouraged McDonald to lie so that they could share in the proceeds of a lawsuit that Chambers would bring against the city.

Chambers called McDonald at trial to lay a successful foundation for admitting his confession. The state, on cross-examination, had McDonald repeat his recantation story told at his preliminary hearing. But the court refused Chamber's request to cross-examine McDonald as a hostile witness, finding McDonald to be non-hostile and relying on the state's evidence rule generally prohibiting a party's cross-examining its own witnesses on the ground that a party "vouches" for the witnesses he calls. The court also denied Chamber's motion to call three separate witnesses, each of whom would testify that on each of three separate occasions, McDonald had respectively admitted committing the murder to each of them. The court excluded their testimony on hearsay grounds. That left Chambers with calling one witness who testified that he saw McDonald shoot Liberty and a second witness who testified that he saw McDonald with a pistol in his hand immediately after the shooting. Chambers was also able to prove that he was never found with a gun at the scene and that most of the officers never saw him shoot Liberty. One officer testified unequivocally, however, that he saw Chambers fire the shots.

The Court first found a denial of Confrontation Clause rights in the application of the witness-voucher rule. That rule operated both to bar cross-examination about McDonald's three prior oral confessions and to undermine his claimed renunciation of his confession. Moreover, the rule rested on a flat presumption that a party vouches for the credibility of witnesses he calls rather than making a case-specific inquiry concerning that question. Additionally, the presumption was inconsistent with the realities of modern criminal practice, in which a defendant must take his witnesses as he finds them. The prosecution's theory was that there was a single shooter, and McDonald's recantation sought to finger Chambers as that one offender, thus being "adverse" to the defense. While the right to cross-examination must sometimes bow to countervailing considerations, this was not such a case.

The violation of Chamber's rights was compounded, concluded the Court, by a violation of Chamber's right to present a defense by Mississippi's version of the hearsay rules' barring three witnesses from testifying to McDonald's multiple oral confessions. Those confessions might seem to fit under the declaration-against-interest exception to the hearsay bar. But Mississippi's version of that exception did not apply to statements, like McDonald's confessions, that were against the declarant's *penal* interest. The purported justification for not extending the exception to such statements is the risk that confessors to crime "are often motivated by extraneous considerations and, therefore, not as inherently reliable as statements against pecuniary or proprietary interest." The Court did not decide whether that assumption of unreliability might sometimes be true. But it did decide that the assumption had no basis in the case before it.

To the contrary, the Court found that the hearsay statements in question bore "considerable assurance of their reliability." First, McDonald made spontaneous confessions close in time to the murder to close acquaintances. Second, much other evidence corroborated those confessions: his sworn written statement; a witness who testified to seeing him with a gun after the shooting; an eyewitness who testified to seeing him shoot; proof of his pre-shooting ownership of a .22 caliber revolver like the weapon involved in the murder; and his post-shooting purchase of a different weapon. Moreover, the three independent confessions corroborated each other. Third, McDonald had everything to lose and nothing even arguably to gain by his confessions. Fourth, he was present at trial and could have been cross-examined by the state on all these matters.

Accordingly, concluded the Court, the rejected hearsay "bore persuasive assurances of trustworthiness, and this was within the basic rationale of the exception for declarations against interest." The hearsay was also "critical" to the defense, leaving the case "far less persuasive" in its absence. Given that the rights involved "directly affect[ed] the ascertainment of guilt," the "hearsay rule may not be applied mechanically to defeat the ends of justice." In so holding, the Court emphasized that it was establishing "no new principles of constitutional law." Similarly, its holding did not "signal any diminution in the respect traditionally accorded to the States in the establishment and implementation of their own criminal trial rules and procedures." Instead, its holding was limited to the "facts and circumstances of this case...."

Despite this disclaimer, *Chambers* seemed at the time to embrace robust scrutiny of evidentiary reliability as a facet of compulsory process inquiry. *Chambers* also suggested that categorical prohibitions on evidence on grounds of unreliability could not consistently stand if those grounds were absent in a particular case.

3. Crane v. Kentucky

In *Crane v. Kentucky*, 476 U.S. 683 (1986), a sixteen-year-old boy, arrested for a robbery, purportedly spontaneously confessed to a host of other crimes, including a murder. Crane moved to suppress the confession as involuntarily given in violation of the Fifth and Fourteenth Amendment's Due Process Clauses. The trial judge denied that motion. But the trial judge granted a motion to bar the defense from offering any witness testimony concerning the length, manner, and other circumstances of the confession other than to indicate inconsistencies in this confession. The trial judge's position was that such evidence went solely to the confession's voluntariness — a question solely for the court — not its truthfulness.

That ruling was extremely troublesome for the defense's case. There was no physical evidence linking Crane to the crime, the confession being the primary means for doing so. Moreover, Crane maintained that he had been questioned for a protracted period in a windowless room by up to six officers who refused his repeated requests to call his mother and badgered him into a false confession.

Upon review, the Supreme Court rejected the idea that evidence of the voluntariness and credibility of confessions involve "conceptually distinct and mutually exclusive categories." To prevent interrogation techniques that are offensive to a civilized justice system, the requirement of due process bars statements not freely and voluntarily given. But that a confession is voluntary "does not undercut the defendant's traditional prerogative to challenge the confession's *reliability* during the course of the trial." Moreover, much of the same evidence that is relevant to voluntariness may also be relevant to confession accuracy, the latter question being for the jury. As the Court explained,

> [T]he physical and psychological environment that yielded the confession can also be of substantial relevance to the ultimate factual issue of the defendant's guilt or innocence. Confessions, even those that have been found to be voluntary, are not conclusive of guilt. And, as with any other part of the prosecutor's case, a confession may be shown to be "insufficiently corroborated or otherwise ... unworthy of belief." ... Indeed, stripped of the power to describe to the jury the circumstances that prompted his confession, the defendant is effectively disabled from answering the one question every rational juror needs answered: If the defendant is innocent, why did he previously admit his guilt?

The trial judge's ruling thus violated the defendant's right to "a meaningful opportunity to present a complete defense," whether that right is rooted in Due Process, Compulsory Process, or Confrontation. "We break no new ground," said the Court, in declaring the opportunity to be heard, a fundamental right. But that opportunity would be hollow if the "State were permitted to exclude competent, reliable evidence bearing on the credibility of a confession when such evidence is central to the defendant's claim of innocence." Absent valid state justification, blanket exclusion of such exculpatory evidence denied defendant the opportunity to subject the prosecutor's case to "'meaningful adversarial testing.'" Such testing was particularly important in the "peculiar circumstances of this case" where a defendant linked to a crime primarily by his confession "sought to paint a picture of a young, uneducated boy who was kept against his will in a small, windowless room for a protracted period until he confessed to every unsolved crime in the county, including the one for which he now stands convicted." In so holding, however, the Court repeated its "traditional reluctance to impose constitutional constraints on ordinary evidentiary rulings by state trial courts" and the unquestioned "power of States to exclude evidence through the application of evidentiary rules that themselves serve the interests of fairness and reliability." The Court thus insisted on the case-specific nature of its decision.

That reluctance to constrain evidentiary rulings was re-emphasized in *Nevada v. Jackson*, 133 S. Ct. 1990 (2013), a *per curiam* opinion overturning the grant of habeas corpus relief on the ground that the defendant was not afforded a sufficient opportunity to present evidence. There the Court stated, "Only rarely have we held that the right to present a complete defense was violated by the exclusion of defense evidence under a state rule of evidence."

4. Taylor v. Illinois

In *Taylor v. Illinois*, 484 U.S. 400 (1988), the Supreme Court rejected the argument that total preclusion of a defense witness from testifying as a sanction for a defense discovery violation was a per se violation of the Compulsory Process Clause. Taylor had been charged with murdering Jack Bridges, firing one shot in his back while he was trying to flee. On the second day of trial, defense counsel for the first time identified Alfred Wormley as a witness for the defense. Defense counsel offered an excuse for the late notification: he was unable previously to locate the witness. The voir dire of Wormley the next day revealed that he had not seen the incident itself but had, before its occurrence, seen Bridges and his brother with two guns in a blanket. Bridges then said they were "after" the defendant. Wormley further testified that he subsequently ran into the defendant and warned him that Bridges and his brother had weapons. But under cross-examination, Wormley admitted that he had not met the defendant until four months ago — over two years after the incident. Furthermore, he had spoken to defense counsel one week before trial started. Rather than find the witness was not telling the truth, which would be a permissible

ground to exclude the testimony, the trial judge barred the witness as a sanction for the attorney's breach of the discovery rules.

The Court did find in favor of the defendant in the present case, holding that
the Compulsory Process Clause appropriately governed what sanctions can be
imposed for discovery violations. But the Court declined to broaden its holding, rejecting Taylor's argument that the Clause always prohibited total witness preclusion as a sanction. Granted, explained the Court, less extreme
remedies like a continuance or a mistrial might be available. But under the appropriate circumstances, the harsher preclusion sanction may be necessary.
Specifically, if defense counsel's explanation reveals that the late witness identification was willful, motivated by the desire for tactical advantage that would
minimize the prosecutor's effectiveness on cross-examination and ability to
rebut the defense witness's testimony, preclusion is entirely consistent with the
Clause's purposes.

The Court offered several reasons justifying its newly-articulated rule. Unlike most constitutional criminal procedure guarantees, the Compulsory Process
Clause does not automatically become active but requires *deliberately planned
affirmative defense conduct*. Regulating the timing and means by which such conduct occurs, especially given that it might never occur, thus not triggering the
Clause, merely helps to further the Clause's central purpose: "to vindicate the
principle that the 'ends of criminal justice would be defeated if judgments were
to be founded on a partial or speculative presentation of the facts.'" Pretrial
discovery of an opposing witnesses' identity serves precisely the same purpose.
Reasonably early discovery "minimizes the risk that a judgment will be predicated on incomplete, misleading, or even deliberately fabricated testimony."

Discovery rules protect not only the prosecution but the "broader public
interest in a full and truthful disclosure of critical facts." Proper discovery reduces the risk that false testimony will be believed, and defendants willing to
produce false testimony relevant to trial may be equally willing to lie about the
reasons for apparent discovery abuse. Those clients may mislead honest attorneys, but there are also "occasions when an attorney assumes that the duty
of loyalty to the client outweighs elementary obligations to the court." In short,
countervailing public interests sometimes outweigh the benefits of a rigid application of the Clause in a particular case.

The Court made several assumptions. Notably, it found that evidence undis-
covered until after trial has begun is unlikely to affect the trial outcome. It also
assumed that "there is something suspect about a defense witness who is not
identified until after the 11th hour has passed." Particularly where there is a
pattern of such violations "explicable only on the assumption that the violations were designed to conceal a plan to present fabricated evidence, it would

be entirely appropriate to exclude the tainted evidence regardless of whether other sanctions would also be merited."

The Court also rejected defense's argument that the prosecution suffered no prejudice because it had the opportunity to question Wormley on *voir dire*. The Court and the public, not only the prosecutor, have an interest in "protecting the trial process from the pollution of perjured testimony." By focusing on the rights of other participants in the trial process, it was easier for the Court to limit the impact of the Compulsory Process Clause.

The Court was likewise unpersuaded by defense's argument that it would be "unfair to visit the sins of the lawyer upon ... [the] client." The adversary process, the Court emphasized, can function effectively *only* if the lawyer has full authority to make most tactical decisions concerning trial management.

> [G]iven the protections afforded by the attorney-client privilege and the fact that extreme cases may involve unscrupulous conduct by both the client and the lawyer, it would be highly impracticable to require an investigation into their relative responsibilities before applying the sanction of preclusion. In responding to discovery, the client has a duty to be candid and forthcoming with the lawyer, and when the lawyer responds, he or she speaks for the client.

The Court had no trouble concluding that the rules and rationales that it articulated governed Taylor's case. The very different stories told by Taylor's lawyer (alleging that he did not locate the witness until after the trial began) and the witness himself (testifying that he spoke to the lawyer the Wednesday of the week before trial) supported an inference of willful misconduct. Moreover, the witness's story seemed hard to believe, given that he claimed to have warned the defendant that Bridges was gunning for him yet admitted not meeting the defendant until two years later. Under these circumstances, preclusion made sense. The Court cautioned: "Whenever a lawyer makes use of the sword provided by the Compulsory Process Clause, there is some risk that he may wound his own client."

5. Rock v. Arkansas

Rock v. Arkansas, 483 U.S. 44 (1987), involved a manslaughter charge against Vickie Lorene Rock for killing her husband. Rock had trouble remembering details, so her attorney sent her to a hypnotist. Rock explained what she remembered about the events to the hypnotist before being hypnotized. After two hypnosis sessions, Rock now remembered additional details: that she had her thumb on the hammer, but no finger on the trigger, and that the gun discharged when her husband grabbed her arm while they were scuffling. A gun expert therefore examined the .22 and found it defective, prone to fire when hit or dropped even when the trigger had not been squeezed. Rock's defense was thus that the killing was accidental.

The trial judge granted the prosecutor's motion to exclude hypnotically refreshed testimony, applying a *per se* rule excluding such evidence. Rock was allowed to testify only to her vague pre-hypnosis memory of events, though her gun expert's testimony was admitted. She was convicted, sentenced to ten years' imprisonment. The Supreme Court later held that application of this *per se* rule of exclusion violated Rock's right to present a defense under the particular facts of the case.

The Court was especially disturbed that the blanket limit on the testimony of "the most important witness for the defense in many criminal cases": the defendant. Central to compulsory process "is an accused's right to present his own version of events in his own words." Indeed, that principle was a corollary of the Fifth Amendment privilege against self-incrimination. That privilege permits the defendant to remain silent until she voluntarily chooses to speak in her own defense. But once she chooses to speak, she may not arbitrarily be denied the right to do so, particularly given "the conviction of our time" that truth is ordinarily better served by the jury hearing evidence than not, leaving it to determine credibility and weight. Just as she may not be arbitrarily denied the right to speak at all, so she may not arbitrarily be limited in conveying material portions of her testimony.

The Court conceded, however, that in appropriate cases the right to present a defense must bow to other legitimate interests. "But restrictions of a defendant's right to testify may not be arbitrary or disproportionate to the purposes they are designed to serve." The *per se* rule was a disproportionate one to serve the goal of promoting reliable evidence because it did not permit a defendant to show that, given the reasons for the hypnosis, "the circumstances under which it took place, or any independent verification of the information it produced," the hypnotically-refreshed testimony was sufficiently reliable in a particular case.

The Court cautioned that the state would be free to establish guidelines to assess the reliability of hypnotically-refreshed testimony in a specific case. It further suggested that exclusion in a particular case may be acceptable upon a showing of unreliability under those circumstances. But the state had "not shown that hypnotically enhanced testimony is always so untrustworthy and so immune to the traditional means of evaluating credibility that it should disable a defendant from presenting her version of the events for which she is on trial."

6. United States v. Scheffer

In *United States v. Scheffer*, 523 U.S. 303 (1998), the Supreme Court held that the *per se* exclusion of polygraph evidence from a general court-martial did not violate the right to present a defense. The polygraph examiner, administering the test at the request of the Air Force, concluded that the defendant was not deceptive. The defendant sought to admit the polygraph evidence at trial to buttress his testimony that he did not *knowingly* use drugs. But the polygraph results were excluded under Military Rule of Evidence 707, which flatly barred admitting anyone's polygraph results. The court martial convicted defendant on all counts.

The Supreme Court once again emphasized that the right to present evidence must sometimes bow to countervailing concerns, of which promoting evidentiary reliability was an important one. But the Court also declared that it had found exclusion of evidence arbitrary or disproportionate only when infringing "upon a weighty interest of the accused." The Court found that the state had three legitimate interests in a rule of *per se* exclusion, yet any infringements on the accused's interests were not "weighty."

First, there was no scientific consensus on the reliability of polygraph evidence, with much evidence that it was unreliable. Consequently, per se exclusion served the state's interest in promoting admission of only reliable evidence at trial. In *Rock*, of course, the Court had used the absence of scientific consensus on reliability as a ground for *rejecting* per se rules of exclusion of hypnotically-refreshed recall, requiring a defendant to be free to argue that such recall was reliable in a particular case. The *Scheffer* majority, however, acknowledged no such conflict with *Rock*. To the contrary, and in direct contradiction of *Rock*, the Court considered the difficulty of knowing in a particular case whether a polygraph was reliable as a reason to favor wholesale exclusion over individual-case inquiry.

Second, polygraph evidence differed from other expert evidence. Most experts testify to factual matters outside juror knowledge. However, polygraph operators testify to whether a witness is or is not credible, a function at the heart of the jury's role. The polygraph's "aura of infallibility," cloaked in scientific clothing, might lead jurors to abandon their duty independently to judge credibility.

Third, collateral case-specific litigation over a particular polygraph operator's qualifications, use of appropriate questions, efforts to avoid suspect countermeasures to defeat the exam, and testing the quality of interpretation of the results would consume time and resources on a collateral matter. That would distract the fact finder from its duty to judge guilt or innocence. Again, the Court in *Rock* apparently viewed creating investigative resources to evaluate the case-specific reliability of the evidence as central to the defendant's right to present a defense. Again, the *Scheffer* Court mentioned no inconsistency on this point with *Rock*.

Instead, *Scheffer* distinguished *Rock.* The rule there barred the *defendant herself* from fully testifying, an interest *Scheffer* saw as particularly important. Additionally, in *Rock*, the ban on hypnotically-refreshed testimony "deprived the jury of the testimony of the only witness who was at the scene and had first-hand knowledge of the facts." But the rule in *Scheffer* barred neither the defendant nor any other defense witness from testifying about case facts. The rule barred only expert opinion intended merely to bolster Scheffer's own testimony. Scheffer was otherwise free to present his entire alternative theory of the case. Accordingly, unlike in *Rock*, the rule in *Scheffer* implicated no weighty defense interest.

While purporting to apply *Rock's* arbitrary or disproportionate test, *Scheffer* arguably turned that test on its head. If a state can exclude an entire category of defense evidence based on claims of the evidence's unreliability where no empirical evidence demonstrated that unreliability, it is difficult to imagine what sorts of evidence would be mandated to be at least considered for admissibility in a specific case under the defendant's purported right to present a defense. Would only firm proof of the *reliability* of an entire category of evidence permit a defendant to insist on its being offered? On the other hand, perhaps *Scheffer's* result can be explained by the polygraph's usurpation of the jury's role and the equal application of the *per se* bar to both prosecution and defense. Alternatively, *Scheffer* might reflect merely greater caution in cabining the potential scope of the principles articulated in earlier cases. Finally, *Scheffer* might simply be precisely an instance of the cautious, case-by-case analysis the Court purported to embrace in its other cases, resting the result merely on the combination of particular circumstances and signaling no change of greater significance.

C. The Alternative Perpetrator Defense

One common type of evidence that can be central to a defense is that a third-party or "alternative perpetrator" did the crime. Offering evidence of an alternative perpetrator differs from presenting an alibi, which seeks merely to prove that the defendant did not commit the crime because he was not present at its location when it occurred. But an alternative perpetrator defense goes further, seeking to convince the jury not only that this defendant did not commit the crime but that a specific other third party did so.

Courts generally refuse to admit such evidence if it is weak, worrying that it will merely distract the jury from focusing on the central issues in the case before it. On the other hand, where such evidence is of significant strength, it may go to show that an innocent person is on trial. Courts have adopted variously stated tests to balance these competing concerns, but many of the dominant tests have the same gist: evidence of third-party guilt is admissible only if there is a direct connection between the evidence offered and the third party's guilt. Restated, the alternative perpetrator evidence must not be speculative but must, instead, tend directly to establish an act by the third party in furtherance of the charged crime.

A second, arguably less-demanding, approach asks only whether the proffered evidence is capable of raising a reasonable doubt as to the defendant's guilt. A third test asks whether the proffered evidence has a "legitimate tendency" to prove the third-party's guilt. A fourth approach simply balances the probative value of the evidence against the risks of its causing unfair prejudice, confusion of the issues, or a waste of time.

Indeed, in *Chambers v. Mississippi*, in which the defendant was prohibited from offering evidence that another man, McDonald, had committed the crime and had confessed to doing so, this involved alternative perpetrator evidence. *Chambers's* striking down that exclusion raised the hopes of some commentators that state courts would ease application of their tests for admitting evidence of third-party guilt. But that did not happen. Recently, however, the Supreme Court returned to the question of the constitutionality of third-party guilt evidence.

In *Holmes v. South Carolina*, 547 U.S. 319 (2006), the defendant, Bobby Lee Holmes, was convicted by a jury of raping, robbing, and murdering an 86-year-old woman. The prosecution's case included DNA evidence showing a mix of Holmes's and the victim's blood on her tank top as well as showing his DNA in her underwear. The state also introduced evidence of fibers found on the victim's nightgown and other locations consistent with fibers in Holmes's sweatshirt and blue jeans and of his palm prints found near the door knob and the interior of the front door of the victim's house. The state further introduced evidence that Holmes had been seen near the victim's house shortly before the crime.

Holmes's defense challenged the forensic evidence, claiming it was contaminated and that the police had tried to frame him. But Holmes also sought to offer evidence that not he but a third party, Jimmy McCaw White, committed the crime. At a pretrial hearing, Holmes offered numerous witnesses to support this argument. Several witnesses placed White in the victim's neighborhood the morning of the murder, with, more importantly, four other witnesses testifying that White either explicitly or tacitly acknowledged to them having committed the crime. Thus, one witness testified that he asked White whether the "word on the street" that White did the crime was true. The witness recounted that White responded simply that he liked older women, that he "did what they say he did," and that he "had no regrets about it at all." Another witness, incarcerated with White, testified that White also admitted to this witness to having committed the crime and that police officers had asked the witness to testify falsely against Holmes. White too testified at the pretrial hearing, but he denied admitting the crime to anyone and offered a tenuous alibi, as it was refuted by another witness.

The trial court excluded all this third-party guilt evidence, concluding that it merely cast "bare suspicion upon another." The South Carolina Supreme Court agreed, applying this test: "[W]here there is strong evidence of an appellant's guilt, especially where there is strong forensic evidence, the proffered evidence about a third party's guilt does not raise a reasonable inference as to the appellant's own innocence." Given the strong forensic evidence against Holmes, his proffered evidence of third-party guilt did not raise a reasonable inference of his innocence and was therefore properly excluded from trial.

The Supreme Court noted that well-established evidence rules excluding defense evidence on the grounds that its probative value is substantially outweighed by countervailing concerns, such as unfair prejudice or confusing the jury, often serve legitimate purposes that are proportionate to the end being served. Accordingly, such rules do not infringe upon the defendant's constitutional right to present a defense. Rules commonly seen in many states exclude third-party perpetrator evidence brought in an effort to raise a reasonable doubt as to the defendant's guilt where such evidence: (a) only raises a conjectural inference of third party guilt; (b) casts bare suspicion on the third party; or, (c) establishes a speculative or remote connection to the crime. Such rules once governed in South Carolina. But the state court had "radically changed and extended" this traditional rule. Its new rule focused not on weighing probative value against unfair prejudice but solely on the strength of the prosecution's case. If the prosecution's case "is strong enough, the evidence of third-party guilt is excluded even if that evidence, viewed independently, would have great probative value and even if it would not pose an undue risk of harassment, prejudice, or confusion of the issues."

In reversing the conviction, the Supreme Court found the state's one-sided approach unjustifiable. That approach ignored defense challenges to the credibility and reliability of prosecution evidence. Holmes had vigorously challenged the forensic evidence as mishandled and resulting from a "deliberate plot to frame petitioner...." The state court concluded that these attacks did "not entirely 'eviscerate'" the state's case, credibility being a question of weight for the jury, rather than of admissibility for the judge. The purpose of the traditional exclusionary rule concerning third-party-perpetrator evidence is to focus the trial on its central issues, rather than permitting distraction by evidence having only a "very weak logical connection" to those issues. But the state court's current approach turns on the flawed logic that assumes that strong evidence that a defendant is the sole perpetrator necessarily means that any "evidence of third-party guilt must be weak." That logic is flawed because "the true strength of the prosecution's proof cannot be assessed without considering challenges to the reliability of the prosecution's evidence." The Court elaborated:

> Just because the prosecution's evidence, *if credited*, would provide strong support for a guilty verdict, it does not follow that evidence of third-party guilt has only a weak logical connection to the central issues in the case. And where the credibility of the prosecution's witnesses or the reliability of its evidence is not conceded, the strength of the prosecution's case cannot be assessed without making the sort of factual findings that have traditionally been reserved for the trier of fact and that the South Carolina courts did not purport to make in this case.

The South Carolina court's conclusion was no more justifiable than its converse, namely that Holmes' evidence of White as the real perpetrator, if believed, squarely proves that White, not Holmes, did the crime, so the state should be barred from presenting evidence of Holmes's guilt. No one had suggested that the state should be so barred, and there was no justification for treating the defense less generously than the prosecution.

The South Carolina court's rule was thus arbitrary because the strength of one party's case raises no logical conclusions about the strength of the other party's rebuttal case. Such an arbitrary rule did not rationally serve the end of focusing the trial's attention solely on its main issue, thereby violating the defendant's right to have a meaningful opportunity to present a complete defense. Consequently, the Court vacated the South Carolina Supreme Court's judgment, remanding for proceedings consistent with its opinion.

III. Immunity Orders and Agreements

A. Background

1. Compelled Testimonial Communications

The Fifth Amendment privilege against self-incrimination protects an accused against being compelled to be a witness against himself (see Chapter 13). That privilege is limited to "testimonial communications" rather than physical evidence because only such communications involve "witnessing." A testimonial communication can roughly be understood as conduct intending to express a message. Most often, such conduct is embodied in words, whether written or oral, but some conduct is intended to send word-like messages, though no words are in fact used. An example is the act of producing documents requested under a subpoena. The mere act of responding to the subpoena's command to produce certain specified writings is the equivalent of saying, "Yes, these documents exist, and, yes, these are the documents you requested." This "act of production" is usually a testimonial communication. *Fisher v. United States*, 425 U.S. 391 (1976). The Fifth Amendment privilege does not, however, exclude all such testimonial communications from trial. Rather, the privilege applies only to such communications that are "compelled," but one way to compel a communication is via a subpoena *testificundum* (a court order to testify) or a subpoena *duces tecum* (a court order to produce certain documents).

2. A Link in a Chain and Motions to Quash

The privilege exists, however, only when it provides a link in a chain to a criminal prosecution. The question is whether "the claimant is confronted by substantial and real, and not merely trifling or imaginary, hazards of incrimination." *United States v. Apfelbaum*, 445 U.S. 115 (1980). A witness granted immunity no longer faces a substantial and real risk of prosecution for his compelled communications, in effect losing the privilege's protection or, as it is more often phrased, being granted an adequate substitute for the privilege because it gets the individual what he really wants from the privilege: protection from exposure to criminal prosecution. At least this is the theory behind immunity; though, in practice, we will see that an accused can still face substantial risk of later use of his words or testimonial actions in a later criminal trial.

The grant of immunity means that a witness cannot refuse to testify on the ground that it will tend to incriminate him. A prosecutor wanting to obtain testimony from reluctant witnesses before an investigating or indicting grand jury might, therefore, seek an immunity order for certain witnesses. Once such an order is granted, the witness is issued a subpoena (a type of court order), and if the witness refuses to testify, appear, or produce documents, then the witness may be held in contempt (civil or criminal) for violating the order to testify. A witness believing that he or she has good reason not to testify must file a motion to quash the subpoena in advance of the date on which the person is required to respond. If the witness can show some flaw in the immunity order or some other ground for declaring the subpoena illegal, for example, it violates freedom of speech by seeking the sources relied upon by a newspaper reporter, those issues may be raised at the hearing on the motion to quash.

3. Transactional, Use, and Derivative Use Immunity

There are two types of immunity: statutory and negotiated. Statutory immunity must be granted by a court and can usually only be obtained at the prosecutor's request. For state or federal statutory immunity legislation to be sufficient to create a substitute for the privilege, the legislation must guarantee either "transactional immunity" or "use and derivative use" immunity. *See* 18 U.S.C. § 6001–6005. Transactional immunity grants the speaker immunity from being prosecuted for the "transactions"—that is, the offenses relating to the compelled testimony. Use immunity prevents the speaker's statements from being used against him at a later criminal trial. But use immunity alone is constitutionally inadequate because it does not prevent use of the fruits of those statements against him.

For example, a defendant might in a statement confess to having committed a charged act of fraud. But in that same statement he might tell the police where to find the documents demonstrating his fraud. Those documents are the "fruit" of his statement: but for his statement, the documents would not have been discovered. Use immunity would bar admitting at a criminal trial his confession to the fraud charge. But it would not bar admitting at trial the documents to which he directed the police, thus likely leading to his conviction of fraud anyway. For this reason, only granting him use and *derivative* use immunity—thus preventing use of the documents, too—is an adequate substitute for the privilege.

Note that statutory immunity protects against use of the statements or their fruits for a crime *already* committed. If the individual's confession is made under oath in court, he can thus face perjury charges if he lies, even if he testifies pursuant to a statutory immunity order. A person testifying under an immunity grant cannot, however, be compelled to testify again without a later immunity order for that subsequent testimony, partly because differences between the two accounts might expose the speaker to a substantial risk of a perjury prosecution. *Pillsbury Co. v. Conboy*, 459 U.S. 248 (1983).

Negotiated or contractual immunity consists of whatever immunity can be negotiated between the prosecution and the defense. Prosecutors will generally resist the broad protections of transactional immunity, agreeing only to a grant at best of use and derivative use immunity. Principles of contract law largely control enforcement of the agreement.

These simple observations raise difficult complexities discussed further below. A few points are worth noting preliminarily, however. Importantly, use and derivative use immunity do not bar the use of fruits discovered by sources independent from the defendant's own compelled words. Defendants might fear that prosecutors can too easily claim that the identity of witnesses or documents provided by a defendant's statements were also obtained by "independent" sources, suspecting that, in truth, those sources never would have been found without the defendant's words. To avoid such problems, the Supreme Court declared in *Kastigar v. United States*, 406 U.S. 441 (1972), the following: "[O]nce a defendant demonstrates that he has testified under a ... grant of immunity, to matters related to the [subsequent] prosecution, the [prosecuting] authorities have the burden of showing that their evidence is not tainted by establishing that they had an independent, legitimate source for the disputed evidence." Indeed, "this imposes on the prosecution the affirmative duty to prove that the evidence it proposes to use is derived from a legitimate source wholly independent of the compelled testimony." That duty ensures that "the compelled testimony can in no way lead to the infliction of criminal penalties."

Kastigar further declared that proving an independent source was a "heavy burden." Nevertheless, lower courts have required proving the independent source merely by a preponderance of the evidence, *see United States v. Hampton*, 775 F.2d 1479 (11th Cir. 1985), though some courts instead impose a clear and convincing burden. But meeting even the lower burden can prove difficult. Thus, after Oliver North testified before Congress in the infamous Iran-Contra scandal under a grant of use and derivative use immunity, prosecutors opened a criminal investigation. They made what many considered extraordinary efforts to seal off their criminal investigation from the congressional one. The government convicted North, but that conviction was overturned on appeal on the ground that prosecutors failed sufficiently to prove that the evidence they used at the criminal trial was truly obtained independently from the congressional statements made by North. In part, the appellate court reasoned that the extensive television coverage of North's statements at the congressional hearings likely subtly affected the testimony of the prosecution's witnesses at the criminal trial.

B. Negotiated Immunity

1. Witnesses, Subjects, and Targets

A person with information relevant to an inquiry is a "witness," a term usually used to identify someone whom the prosecutor does not believe to face criminal liability. *See* U.S. Dept. of Justice, U.S. Attorney's Manual §9-11.151. With witnesses, because they are believed to have relevant information but not suspected of being personally involved in criminality, the risk to a client from testifying may initially seem small. But a witness designation provides only limited security for defense counsel. After the witness testifies, the state is free to change that designation. Indeed, other witness's testimony may create reason to alter that designation.

The Department of Justice describes a "target" as "a person as to whom the prosecutor or the grand jury has substantial evidence linking him or her to commission of a crime and who, in the judgment of the prosecutor, is a putative defendant." Sometimes a corporation can be a target without its employees involved in the illegal conduct being in that category and vice-versa. The target designation is a clear warning sign of grave client danger in testifying.

"Subjects" are the third type of individuals identified by the Department of Justice. They rest in a sort of definitional limbo between witnesses and targets. The good news for defense counsel is that subjects are not yet targets. The bad news is that they can become targets.

Whichever designation the Department of Justice has provided, defense counsel must conduct an independent investigation to gauge likely criminal liability. Where such liability is real, defense counsel will recommend that a witness raise the privilege, refusing to respond to questions before a grand jury. On the other hand, the mere fact that prosecutors subpoena a client tells the defense lawyer that prosecutors need something from that person: information. That gives defense counsel some power to try to negotiate a favorable outcome.

Favorable outcomes can be of various types. One favorable outcome is obtaining use and derivative use immunity to protect against undue exposure to criminal prosecution. By cooperating with prosecutors subject to such an agreement, the witness hopes to obtain prosecutors' good graces, further diminishing the chances of becoming a target. Another kind of favorable outcome occurs when defense counsel believes that the risk of criminal liability exposure is high and that the potential that prosecutors will gather enough evidence on their own to pursue prosecuting the client is also high. In that case, defense counsel might combine an immunity agreement with a guilty plea: an agreement to aid the state by testifying truthfully at trial in exchange for either immunity or a plea to a lesser charge or some combination.

2. Prosecutor Concerns

A grant of immunity, especially early in a case, carries grave risks for the prosecutor. The *Kastigar* burden may prevent a prosecutor as a practical matter from pursuing a case against a witness given use and derivative use immunity. A prosecutor believing that someone is a mere witness may get stung by granting him or her immunity only later to discover that the person was a central player in a criminal conspiracy. A prosecutor will not, therefore, simply accept defense counsel's word as to the role of the client in a crime or whether the client has access to information truly valuable to the prosecution that it may not be able to obtain on its own.

Prosecutors thus usually reject "blind" immunity grants, instead insisting on at least a defense counsel proffer of what the client will say. But prosecutors are usually not satisfied by such proffers alone. They want to question the client personally to determine the level of culpability and whether the person is credible.

3. Defense Concerns

Non-immunized statements may expose the client to criminal prosecution. Defense counsel will thus often seek "proffer protection" or limited immunity, ideally at least use and derivative use immunity for the client's statements made during the proffer interview. But United States Attorneys often are unwilling to do more than provide a letter declaring that statements made by the witness at the proffer session cannot be used against the interviewee in the government's case-in-chief at any later criminal trial. These letters also usually provide that leads derived from the statements can be used, as may the statements themselves on cross-examination to impeach the speaker should he testify at his own later trial. In other words, the prosecutor usually agrees only to use but not derivative use immunity of proffer-interview statements. The risk of client harm is thus worth accepting only if the defense lawyer believes there is a significant chance of convincing the prosecution ultimately to grant full use and derivative use immunity for testimony given at trial and statements made during any trial preparation sessions with the prosecution. If a criminal conspiracy spans several jurisdictions, raising risks of prosecution by one or more states, the immunity binds only the parties to it. A client would, thus, not have true use immunity protection without getting all relevant prosecutors' offices to sign off on an agreement. A defense lawyer should also at a minimum seek immunity for the act of producing any documents. If the government is likely to seek a guilty plea rather than offer immunity, then the proffer can be a means to establish cooperation that results in a substantially reduced punishment

Though not binding law, the United States Attorney's Manual does set office policy. Defense appeals to policy can affect a prosecutor's decisions. One section prohibits prosecuting a witness who has testified pursuant to a compulsion order, such as before a grand jury, for offenses first disclosed in — or closely related to — that testimony without the express prior permission of the Attorney General of the United States; permission that is hard to get and is not routinely sought. Moreover, "[t]he request to prosecute should indicate the circumstances justifying prosecution and the method by which the government will be able to establish that the evidence it will use against the witness will meet the government's burden under *Kastigar v. United States*, 406 U.S. 441 (1972)." Testifying before a grand jury pursuant to an immunity order therefore brings with it policy-appeal benefits as well as strictly legal ones — albeit benefits that must always be weighed against the costs.

This discussion of immunity orders and negotiated immunity agreements has obvious links to the discussions of plea negotiations in Chapters 9 and grand jury investigations in Chapter 2. Often, immunity negotiations, at a minimum concerning the proffer session, are a prerequisite to reaching a plea deal.

Checkpoints

- The Confrontation Clause primarily protects the opportunity of the accused for effective cross-examination of witnesses.

- Under the rule of *Crawford v. Washington*, "testimonial" hearsay is barred from trial unless the accused has an opportunity before or at trial to cross-examine the declarant on the statement.

- The Supreme Court has been ambiguous about the meaning of "testimonial," but has suggested instances where hearsay might be testimonial: (1) affidavits; (2) statements given to police officers in the course of custodial interrogations; (3) depositions; (4) courtroom testimony; and (5) "statements that were made under circumstances that would lead an objective witness reasonably to believe that the statement would be available for use at a later trial."

- "Custodial interrogations" includes backward-looking questioning to recreate past events but does not include statements made from a police effort to resolve an ongoing emergency, the latter statements thus not being "testimonial," therefore not protected by the Confrontation Clause.

- Whether an interrogation is backward-looking or addressing an ongoing emergency is a question of objective purpose but does not turn on the intentions of either the police or the declarant alone but rather of the situation.

- Forensic lab reports are the equivalent of *ex parte* affidavits and are considered testimonial so that the author of the report must be called to testify.

- An expert witness's reference to a scientific report is not "testimonial" regarding the contents of that report.

- A criminal defendant can forfeit a Confrontation Clause hearsay objection if the declarant's unavailability was purposely caused by the defendant to prevent the person from testifying, such as might be accomplished by witness threats or bribery.

- The "*Bruton* rule" prohibits admitting into evidence at a joint trial of co-defendants a statement by one co-defendant implicating the other in the crime because jury instructions to consider the confession only against the defendant actually making it are considered inadequate.

- Admission of a defendant's statement implicating another defendant can violate the Confrontation Clause because the co-defendant has no automatic right to cross-examine the defendant who made the incriminating statement because that person has a constitutional right not to testify.

- The *Bruton* rule does not apply to a statement that redacted not only the defendant's name but any reference to his existence.

- A redacted statement that includes mere deletions, such as references to co-defendants as "blank," violates *Bruton* because it suggests that another person was involved, and the jury may readily conclude that that person was a co-defendant.

- The *Bruton* rule does not apply when (1) the co-defendant who made the statement testifies at trial; (2) the trials are severed; (3) separate juries are provided for each defendant; (4) it is a bench trial rather than a jury trial.
- The Confrontation Clause protects the right to "face-to-face" confrontation, so a statute flatly permitting child witnesses in a sexual abuse case to testify behind a screen or from another room through a remote video feed to save them the distress of seeing his face was unconstitutional.
- A procedure permitting the use of closed-circuit television is permissible upon a case-specific finding in a child sexual assault case that it is necessary for the children to be able to testify.
- The Compulsory Process Clause entitles criminal defendants to call witnesses to testify on their behalf.
- The Court has struck down a number of rules that exclude entire classes of witness testimony on behalf of the defense, though often suggesting that it will uphold case-specific judgments to exclude testimony where it would not be reliable.
- The "alternative perpetrator defense" argues that a third party, not the defendant, committed the crime, so that the Compulsory Process Clause was violated by prohibiting a defendant from offering evidence of a third party's guilt on the ground that the prosecution's case was so strong that any evidence of third party guilt would be too speculative.
- A substitute for the Fifth Amendment's privilege against self-incrimination is either transactional immunity or use plus derivative use immunity.
- Transactional immunity protects a defendant from being prosecuted for the offense about which the person testifies.
- Use/derivative use immunity prevents using a defendant's own statement against the person along with the fruits attributable to the statement, such as physical evidence discovered by being mentioned in the statement.

Chapter 13

Adjudicating Guilt

Roadmap

- Defendant's right to be present at trial
- Waiver of the right to be present by absence or conduct
- Defendant's appearance in shackles, jail clothing, or under medication
- Defendant's right to testify or to remain silent
- The rule of "no comment" on defendant's decision not to testify
- Jury instructions on the presumption of innocence and prosecution's burden of proof
- Instructions on the jury's power to nullify
- "Dynamite" instructions to deadlocked juries
- General and special verdicts
- Special verdicts in death penalty cases
- Inconsistent verdicts

I. Introduction

Several special rules that arise during criminal trials will be addressed in this chapter. These concern, first, the defendant's right to be present at trial and to choose whether or not to testify without incurring any prejudice from remaining silent, and second, the handling of jury instructions and jury verdicts.

II. The Defendant's Right to Be Present

A. Proceedings to Which the Right Applies

A criminal defendant has the right to be present during trial—a right that encompasses all critical stages of the proceedings. *Illinois v. Allen*, 397 U.S. 337 (1970). While the right has a basis in the Confrontation Clause of the Sixth

Amendment, it also has roots in notions of due process. As a result, it is not restricted to situations in which the defendant actually is confronting witnesses or in which evidence against him or her is being introduced; rather, it extends to all trial-related proceedings to which the defendant's presence "has a relation, reasonably substantial, to the fullness of his opportunity to defend against the charge." *United States v. Gagnon*, 470 U.S. 522 (1985).

In *Gagnon*, the proceeding at issue was a meeting in the judge's chambers with a juror who had noticed the defendant sketching pictures of the jurors. The judge explained to the juror that the defendant would cease sketching, asked whether other jurors were aware of the sketching, and inquired into the juror's ability to continue impartially. The defendant was not present during the meeting (although his counsel was), and the Court upheld the conviction, finding that his presence there did not affect his "opportunity to defend against the charge" because it involved a minor occurrence and the defendant would not have done or gained anything had he been present.

In *Kentucky v. Stincer*, 482 U.S. 730 (1987), the defendant challenged the fact that he was not present during a pretrial proceeding to determine the testimonial competence of two young children offered as witnesses by the prosecution in a sexual abuse case. The Court found no violation of Stincer's rights because the questions asked of the witnesses during that proceeding did not involve the substantive issues of the case. As a result, his absence from the pretrial proceeding did not affect his ability to assist his counsel (who had been present at the pretrial proceeding) in cross-examining the witnesses.

B. Harmless Error Analysis

If a defendant's right to be present was violated during trial, a reviewing court on direct appeal must examine the record to determine whether the violation was harmless beyond a reasonable doubt under the standard articulated in *Chapman v. California*, 386 U.S. 18 (1967). *Rushen v. Spain*, 464 U.S. 114 (1983). (See Chapter 16).

C. Waiver of the Right

1. Waiver by Absence

Defendants may forego their right to be present during trial by engaging in voluntary, knowing and intelligent waivers. In appropriate situations, waivers by conduct will be found if defendants absent themselves voluntarily from trial. *Diaz v. United States*, 223 U.S. 442 (1912). The waiver-by-conduct rule will apply, for example, when a defendant who was present at the outset of the trial flees at some point during trial. In such a circumstance, the proceedings can continue, with the defendant tried *"in absentia."*

Proceeding *in absentia* is problematic when the defendant fails to show up for any stage of the trial. Does her absence indicate her voluntary choice to forego the right to be present, or does it reflect instead her misunderstanding about the date and time of trial, her inability (financial or otherwise) to get to the courthouse, or her ignorance of the consequences of absence? If she has not yet been in front of the trial court, her absence can be ambiguous. The Supreme Court has suggested, although not yet decided, that a trial *in absentia* in such a situation would violate the defendant's right to be present. *Crosby v. United States*, 506 U.S. 255 (1993).

This approach is reflected in Federal Rule of Criminal Procedure 43, which permits a federal trial court to find waiver only when the defendant voluntarily absents himself *after* the trial has begun: "A defendant who was initially present at trial ... waives the right to be present ... when the defendant is voluntarily absent after the trial has begun, regardless of whether the court informed the defendant of an obligation to remain during trial." The Court in *Crosby* confirmed that if a federal defendant flees or otherwise does not attend from the outset, then under Rule 43 he cannot be found to have waived his right to be present for the remainder of the proceedings.

Some jurisdictions impose other limits on the type of proceedings that can be conducted *in absentia*. The most common limitation requires the defendant's presence at sentencing. The Supreme Court has not addressed this issue, but Rule 43 permits a federal trial court to proceed with sentencing *in absentia* in a noncapital case, if the defendant is "voluntarily absent." If a defendant is facing a potential sentence of death, then the person must be present for the sentencing phase of the case.

2. Waiver by Disruptive Conduct

Sometimes defendants engage in such obstreperous conduct during trial that the proceedings literally are brought to a halt. Both the Constitution and Rule 43 permit a trial court to find waiver-by-conduct in this situation, ordering the defendant removed so that the trial can continue in his or her absence. The Supreme Court explained in *Illinois v. Allen*, 397 U.S. 337 (1970), that "a defendant can lose his right to be present at trial if, after he has been warned by the judge that he will be removed if he continues his disruptive behavior, he nevertheless insists on conducting himself in a manner so disorderly, disruptive, and disrespectful of the court that his trial cannot be carried on with him in the courtroom." The trial court also is permitted to attempt to coerce the defendant's cooperation by citing him with contempt or even having him physically retrained in the courtroom. A decision to continue trial outside the defendant's presence is not a final determination that the person cannot participate for the rest of the proceeding, and careful trial judges will seek assurances from the defendant that he will cooperate to permit a return to the courtroom, as was done in *Allen.*

D. The Manner in Which Defendant Is Present

1. Shackles and Jail Clothing

There are constitutional implications to the defendant's physical appearance before the jury. Defendants may not be routinely shackled in front of juries; instead, shackling is permitted only upon a showing of special need having to do with a particular defendant. *Deck v. Missouri,* 544 U.S. 622 (2005). Similarly, defendants cannot be compelled to wear jail clothing in the courtroom absent a showing of special need. *Estelle v. Williams,* 425 U.S. 501 (1976). The concern animating these rules is that the jury would associate the shackles and jail clothing with guilt and would prejudge the defendant. By contrast, the presence of law enforcement personnel in the courtroom is not so "inherently prejudicial" as to require a showing of special need. *Holbrook v. Flynn,* 475 U.S. 560 (1986).

2. Forced Medication

A related concern surrounds the forcible medication of the defendant during trial. Due process permits criminal cases to go forward only against those defendants who are competent to stand trial—those who have "sufficient present ability to consult with [their] lawyer[s] with a reasonable degree of rational understanding" and "a rational as well as factual understanding of the proceedings." *Dusky v. United States,* 362 U.S. 402 (1960). Antipsychotic drugs may successfully render a mentally ill defendant competent to stand trial under this standard, but they also may affect his demeanor at trial. An altered demeanor may reduce the effectiveness of a defense such as insanity by making the defendant appear rational and controlled. Or, drugs may make a defendant appear robotic and unfeeling, thus potentially prejudicing the jury. They also may affect a defendant's ability to assist his or her attorney. Despite these concerns, courts may, in rare circumstances, compel defendants to take antipsychotic drugs in order to procure their participation at trial.

In *Sell v. United States,* 539 U.S. 166 (2003), the Supreme Court articulated a four-factor test that requires trial courts first to determine:

1. the importance of the government's interest in prosecution;

2. whether forcible medication will further the government's interest while ensuring a fair trial;

3. whether forcible medication is necessary to achieve the government's interest, or whether less intrusive treatments or drugs may suffice; and

4. whether the proposed drugs are medically appropriate.

Even where compelled medication is ordered, there may be opportunities to reduce the likelihood of prejudice to the defendant. In *Riggins v. United States*, 504 U.S. 127 (1992), the Supreme Court suggested that the defendant might introduce expert testimony to describe his pre-medicated demeanor and explain the impact of the drugs on his present demeanor. In addition, the trial court may deliver a cautionary instruction to the jury.

III. Defendant's Right to Testify or to Remain Silent

Chapter 12 explains the complex issues underlying the Sixth Amendment's Compulsory Process Clause, including discussion of the defendant's right to offer his or her own testimony. This chapter will briefly review that right and its flip-side—the defendant's right to remain silent—before setting out Supreme Court rules governing prosecutorial or judicial comment on the defendant's exercise of those rights.

A. The Rights in General

Criminal defendants traditionally were barred from testifying on their own behalf, as were all parties to litigation in the common law era, on the theory that the testimony of interested persons was inherently untrustworthy. In the nineteenth century, however, states began permitting criminal defendants to testify in order to "advance[] both the detection of guilt and the protection of innocence," *Rock v. Arkansas*, 483 U.S. 44 (1987). By the time the Supreme Court decided *Rock*, nearly all states had enacted statutes permitting defendants to testify. In *Rock*, the Court enshrined the right of defendants to testify as a constitutionally mandated one. Rooted in both the Sixth Amendment's Compulsory Process Clause and in due process, the right is incorporated against the states through the Bill of Rights. The defendant also has a right *not* to testify, based on the 5th Amendment right against self-incrimination. *Griffin v. California*, 380 U.S. 609 (1965).

B. Prohibition against Burdening the Exercise of Rights

There are situations in which penalizing the defendant's decision to remain silent violates the constitution. In *Griffin*, a murder defendant elected not to testify at his trial and appealed his conviction after the prosecutor, during closing argument, drew the jury's attention to his silence:

> The defendant certainly knows whether Essie Mae had this beat up appearance at the time he left her apartment and went down the alley with her.... He would know that. He would know how she got down the alley. He would know how the blood got on the bottom of the concrete steps. He would know how long he was with her in that box. He would know how her wig got off. He would know whether he beat her or mistreated her. He would know whether he walked away from that place cool as a cucumber when he saw Mr. Villasenor because he was conscious of his own guilt and wanted to get away from that damaged or injured woman. These things he has not seen fit to take the stand and deny or explain. And in the whole world, if anybody would know, this defendant would know. Essie Mae is dead, she can't tell you her side of the story. The defendant won't.

Aggravating the situation was one of the trial court's instructions, which permitted the jury to draw adverse inferences from the defendant's decision not to testify:

> As to any evidence or facts against him which the defendant can reasonably be expected to deny or explain because of facts within his knowledge, if he does not testify or if, though he does testify, he fails to deny or explain such evidence, the jury may take that failure into consideration as tending to indicate the truth of such evidence and as indicating that among the inferences that may be reasonably drawn therefrom those unfavorable to the defendant are the more probable.

The Supreme Court disapproved both the prosecution's argument and the trial court's instruction, establishing what is known as the "no comment" rule. It explained that adverse comment on the refusal to testify "is a remnant of the inquisitorial system of criminal justice, which the Fifth Amendment outlaws. It is a penalty imposed by courts for exercising a constitutional privilege. It cuts down on the privilege by making its assertion costly."

There are situations, however, in which prosecutorial comments and judicial instructions about the defendant's silence are permitted. The first occurs when the defense "opens the door" to comment by making false or misleading statements. The prosecution typically is permitted to respond to these in order to avoid unfairness to the state and because any additional prejudice to the defendant would be slight. For example, in *Lockett v. Ohio*, 438 U.S. 586 (1978), the Court permitted the prosecution in closing argument to repeatedly characterize the state's evidence as "unrefuted" and "uncontradicted," after the defense failed to fulfill a promise to the jury that it would contravene the state's evidence with witnesses of its own, including the testimony of defendant Lockett. The Court explained that the prosecutor's remarks "added nothing to the impression that had already been created by Lockett's refusal to testify after the jury had been promised a defense by her lawyer and told that Lockett would take the stand."

The second situation involves cautionary judicial comment via jury instructions. Instructions designed to alleviate prejudice — by warning the jury not to draw adverse inferences from the defendant's silence — are permitted and indeed required if the defense requests them. *Carter v. Kentucky*, 450 U.S. 288 (1981). The defendant in *Carter* requested that the jury be instructed: "The defendant is not compelled to testify and the fact that he does not cannot be used as an inference of guilt and should not prejudice him in any way." The trial court refused to give the instruction. The Supreme Court reversed Carter's conviction, holding that a trial court must give a "no-adverse-inference" jury instruction if the defendant so requests.

A cautionary jury instruction may even be given over a defendant's objection, although an instruction is not required by the Constitution in this circumstance. *Lakeside v. Oregon*, 435 U.S. 333 (1978). In *Lakeside*, after holding that the giving of a cautionary instruction over the defendant's objection does not violate the constitution, the Court remarked that state law may constitutionally prohibit cautionary instructions if they are not sought by defendants. The Court also noted that it may be "wise" for a trial judge not to give a cautionary instruction over a defendant's objection.

The need to avoid burdening constitutional rights, which underlies the "no comment" rule, presumably applies to the defendant's right to testify as well. Testimonial situations are trickier, however, because the defendant's testimony may raise legitimate issues that the prosecution is entitled to comment on and the jury to consider. Thus the Constitution does not necessarily bar adverse comment about a defendant's decision to take the stand. In *Portuondo v. Agard*, 529 U.S. 61 (2000), the Court held that the Fifth Amendment was not violated when a prosecutor, in closing argument, "called the jury's attention to the fact that the defendant had the opportunity to hear all other witnesses testify and to tailor his testimony accordingly." The comment merely asked the jury to do what it was entitled to do: evaluate the defendant's testimonial credibility in light of his ability to hear other witnesses before he took the stand.

IV. Handing the Case to the Jury: Instructions, Deliberations, and Verdicts

A. Jury Instructions in General

Both in advance of evidence taking and again after the close of evidence, the trial court gives the jury a raft of instructions. These range from instructions on appropriate jury conduct during trial, choosing a foreperson, guidance about evaluating certain types of evidence, and ultimately detailed recitations of the law governing the charges. The judge reads the instructions to the jury and sometimes, especially in complex cases, also provides a physical copy to be used during deliberations.

Often parties disagree on the appropriateness or the wording of instructions, and if the trial court decides to give an instruction with which they disagree, they must make an objection on the record if they wish to preserve the possibility of appealing on that ground. Note that appeals by the government on flaws in the instructions must be consistent with double jeopardy principles (see Chapter 15).

B. Instructions Implicating Due Process

Jury instructions sometimes implicate the defendant's constitutional rights. Instructions must, for example, comport with due process by conveying adequately the defendant's presumption of innocence and the prosecution's burden of proof. Although the words "presumption of innocence" need not be used in the instructions, the jury must be sufficiently instructed to ensure a fair trial, given all of the circumstances. *Kentucky v. Whorton*, 441 U.S. 786 (1979). In particular factual situations, such as when the instructions are "skeletal," the state's evidence weak, and the prosecution's closing argument replete with improper references to the defendant's status as an accused, the trial court's refusal to instruct the jury on the presumption of innocence may violate due process. *Taylor v. Kentucky*, 436 U.S. 478 (1978). The Court explained in *Taylor* that "one accused of a crime is entitled to have his guilt or innocence determined solely on the basis of the evidence introduced at trial, and not on grounds of official suspicion, indictment, continued custody, or other circumstances not adduced as proof at trial," and that an instruction on the presumption of innocence is one way of ensuring this right.

The constitution also requires appropriate instructions about the prosecution's burden of proof. The prosecution bears the burden of proof "beyond a reasonable doubt" on all of the elements of the offense, *In re Winship*, 397 U.S. 358 (1970), and jury instructions must adequately convey this information. Instructions that equate reasonable doubt with a "grave uncertainty" and an "actual substantial doubt," can be constitutionally problematic because they may suggest to the jury a higher standard of doubt than reasonable doubt actually requires—in other words, they allow for conviction on a showing less than "beyond reasonable doubt." *Cage v. Louisiana*, 498 U.S. 39 (1990). The test for reviewing courts is whether, given the totality of circumstances, there is a "reasonable likelihood that the jury understood the instructions to allow conviction based on proof insufficient to meet the *Winship* standard." *Estelle v. McGuire*, 502 U.S. 62 (1991). The failure to properly instruct on reasonable doubt constitutes a "structural error" that is not subject to harmless error review. *Sullivan v. Louisiana*, 508 U.S. 275 (1993). (See Chapter 16.)

C. Instructions about the Jury's Power to Nullify

The American criminal jury has the power to "nullify" the law by deciding not to convict even in the face of compelling evidence against the defendant. The power stems from the Double Jeopardy Clause, which forbids reprosecution after an acquittal (see Chapter 15). As a result of double jeopardy, the jury's decision to acquit is unreviewable and uncorrectable by the court through a judgment notwithstanding the verdict, even if the jury obviously acquitted for impermissible reasons. The power to nullify in the face of evidence beyond a reasonable doubt is a potent one because it overrules the legislature's definition of culpable conduct. It also ignores the trial court's legal instructions.

Powerful though their power is, juries typically are not informed about nullification. Instead, they are instructed to follow the law as given them by the trial judge. A few jurisdictions do permit instructions to inform jurors that they can "vote their conscience." An interest group called the "Fully Informed Jury Association" has attempted to increase the number of states permitting this type of instruction. It also works to inform the public about the jury's nullification power—even going so far as to reach out to jurors by calling them, leaving leaflets on their cars, and so on.

D. "Dynamite" Instructions during Deliberations

Once the jury has been instructed, it retires to deliberate. Its deliberations sometimes produce agreement, in which case it will issue a verdict. At other times, members of the jury will be unable to agree with one other, and they will inform the court that they are deadlocked. The trial court is permitted to attempt to break the deadlock by instructing the jury to listen to one another and consider each other's positions. This instruction is sometimes referred to as a "dynamite charge" or an "*Allen* charge," after a case in which the Supreme Court approved its use in federal trials. *Allen v. United States*, 164 U.S. 492 (1896). The trial court in that case delivered an instruction paraphrased in the Supreme Court record as follows:

> [The instruction was], in substance, that in a large proportion of cases absolute certainty could not be expected; that, although the verdict must be the verdict of each individual juror, and not a mere acquiescence in the conclusion of his fellows, yet they should examine the question submitted with candor, and with a proper regard and deference to the opinions of each other; that it was their duty to decide the case if they could conscientiously do so; that they should listen, with a disposition to be convinced, to each other's arguments; that, if much the larger number were for conviction, a dissenting juror should consider whether his doubt was a reasonable one which made no impression upon the minds of so many men, equally honest, equally intelligent with himself. If, upon the other hand, the majority were for acquittal, the minority ought to ask themselves whether they might not reasonably doubt the correctness of a judgment which was not concurred in by the majority.

Modern-day *Allen* charges employ very similar language.

Some criminal justice scholars have called for courts to disavow *Allen* charges, pointing to evidence that they decrease the quality of deliberations and increase the pressure on dissenting jurors to give in to the majority. See Samantha P. Bateman, *Blast It All: Allen Charges and the Danger of Playing with Dynamite*, 32 U. Hawaii L. Rev. 323 (2010). Defendants have made repeated Sixth Amendment challenges to verdicts obtained from "dynamited" juries. While these have been unsuccessful for the most part, some jurisdictions have restricted the circumstances in which *Allen* charges may be given — for example, permitting courts to deliver them only once to a particular jury. The Supreme Court has not taken an active role in evaluating these restrictions, letting the matter stand with the observation that "[t]he continuing validity of this Court's observations in *Allen* are beyond dispute." *Lowenfield v. Phelps*, 484 U.S. 231 (1988). Trial judges need to be careful not to learn about the reason for the jury's deadlock, or their vote on a particular charge, to avoid tailoring an *Allen* charge in a way that will be coercive toward returning a particular verdict.

Juries that are ultimately unable to reach a verdict are called "hung juries," and typically the trial judge will declare a mistrial. The double jeopardy implications of mistrials are discussed in Chapter 15.

E. Verdicts

The jury's issuance of a verdict does not necessarily end the possibility of constitutional problems related to its work. After a brief explanation of the prevalence in criminal cases of the "general verdict," this section will discuss several potential constitutional issues that may arise in connection with verdicts.

1. General and Special Verdicts

Juries in criminal cases are typically instructed to return what is known as a "general verdict": one that simply responds to each count in the indictment with "guilty" or "not guilty." The alternative would be a "special verdict," in which a jury might be asked to find certain facts or answer certain questions. In civil cases, special verdicts are common. In the criminal system, the disfavor cast on special verdicts has Sixth Amendment underpinnings: it is feared that directing the jury's attention to certain facts or questions will undermine its independence and focus it too heavily on particular issues.

2. Verdicts in Death Penalty Cases

Verdicts in capital cases are an exception to the "no special verdicts" rule in criminal cases. Supreme Court jurisprudence in capital cases requires the jury to consider potential aggravating and mitigating circumstances during the sentencing phase in a trial. Before a death sentence can be imposed, a jury must specifically find the presence of at least one aggravating circumstance or factor that, under the state's law, authorizes the imposition of a death sentence. *Ring v. Arizona*, 536 U.S. 584 (2002). As a result, verdicts in these cases typically identify aggravating circumstances that the jury agrees were proven beyond a reasonable doubt.

3. Verdicts That Are Seemingly Inconsistent

Sometimes juries issue verdicts that are seemingly inconsistent because they acquit the defendant of some charges while convicting him of others in a way that does not make logical sense. In most circumstances, this kind of inconsistency does not raise constitutional problems. *Dunn v. United States*, 284 U.S. 390 (1932). In *United States v. Powell*, 469 U.S. 57 (1984), the court upheld inconsistent verdicts of guilty on a compound offense and acquittal of the underlying felony. The Court noted that the verdicts might reflect the jury's decision to treat the defendant with lenity, and that jury lenity is a key component of the 6th Amendment's guarantees. Even if a jury treats co-defendants in a seemingly inconsistent manner after a joint trial, the Constitution is not violated. *United States v. Dotterweich*, 320 U.S. 277 (1943). The Court similarly has let stand judicial verdicts that are seemingly inconsistent. *Harris v. Rivera*, 454 U.S. 339 (1981).

Checkpoints

- The Sixth Amendment and the Due Process Clause provide criminal defendants with a right to be present during all critical stages of trial.

- The defendant may be tried *in absentia* if he waives the right to be present by voluntarily absenting himself after trial begins or by engaging in disruptive conduct.

- Some jurisdictions limit the proceedings that may take place *in absentia*, specifically prohibiting sentencing to take place without the defendant's presence.

- The defendant cannot be made to appear in shackles unless the trial court finds a special need in the particular circumstances of the case. Nor may the defendant be made to wear jail clothing in front of the jury.

- The forced medication of defendant, which may render her competent to stand trial, can be ordered only after the trial court engages in a four-factor analysis.

- The Constitution forbids adverse comment by the prosecution on the defendant's decision not to testify.

- Trial courts cannot instruct the jury that it may infer guilt from the defendant's silence, and the constitution requires, upon defendant's request, an instruction explaining the "no adverse inference" rule.

- Jury instructions can implicate the defendant's due process right, and in some circumstances an instruction about the presumption of innocence is required.

- The jury must be instructed properly about the prosecution's burden of proof beyond a reasonable doubt.

- The Constitution does not require the trial court to instruct the jury on its power to nullify, but a few jurisdictions permit such an instruction.

- If the jury deadlocks during deliberations, the Constitution permits a "dynamite" or *Allen* charge that encourages the jury to continue deliberating.

- Special verdicts are disfavored in criminal cases, but they are used in death penalty cases, in which the defendant has a right to a jury determination of aggravating factors that authorize the imposition of a capital sentence.

- The constitutional rights of the defendant are not implicated by verdicts that are seemingly inconsistent.

Chapter 14

Sentencing

I. Punishment Theory

Punishment theory often plays a role in determining the sentencing structure, as well as the individual sentence that is to be given to a defendant. Some of these theories are designated utilitarian (e.g., deterrence, rehabilitation), while others are considered retributive. Although each theory is often not exclusive to a particular system, a combination of the following punishment theories can play a role in the legislature's decision of how the sentencing scheme will work within the jurisdiction.

- *Deterrence*: A sentence arguably sends a message to potential future offenders that they will suffer if they commit a crime. Fear of suffering deters them from committing the crime. "Specific deterrence" focuses on deterring the convicted offender, "general deterrence" focuses on deterring other would-be offenders.
- *Education*: Criminal law is generally meant to address violations of a society's deepest moral principles. Punishment educates all of society's members on what those principles are and how seriously they are taken.

- *Rehabilitation*: Improving the offender's character, making him a better citizen, is the goal of rehabilitation. Punishment's focus thus shifts to re-forming the offender, such as by giving him job skills or treating his drug problem.
- *Restoration*: Restorative justice views criminal acts as a form of disease, in-juring the health not only of the offender and victim, but of the entire community. One central goal of punishment must be to heal both the in-dividuals and the community as a whole. The ultimate goal of punishment is for the community to re-embrace the ex-offender as an equal member.
- *Incapacitation*: An offender who is imprisoned cannot prey on those be-yond the prison's walls. The focus of this punishment theory is that so-ciety's safety should be paramount.
- *Retribution*: Retributive punishment is often said to be backward rather than forward-looking. Punishment is required because the offender com-mitted a wrong. Whether such punishment deters future crimes is irrel-evant. There are two common justifications for retribution: repaying a "debt to society" and "nullifying insult." A new theory, "empirical desert," bases sentencing on what level of retribution informed members of so-ciety think should be imposed under a specific sets of facts.

These goals are fuzzy and can conflict. Many sentencing statutes therefore specify a list of factors, sometimes a long list, for courts to consider. These factors may also be conflicting and ambiguous, and the statutes do not gener-ally specify how to weigh factors relative to one another. Nevertheless, legisla-tors have acted in the belief that greater detail will give judges more guidance.

A sentencing hearing would usually, at a minimum, involve the sentencing judge having before her a presentence report (PSR—often alternatively called a "probation officer's report"), a mental health report, and a statement of the offender's prior record.

II. Types of Sentence

A. Indeterminate versus Determinate Systems

The sentencing system designed by a legislature is typically thought of as either an indeterminate or determinate sentencing system. Indeterminate sys-tems generally mean those in which a judge has substantial discretion to im-pose a sentence within a broad range; "determinate" systems are those where the range is significantly narrowed, usually by sentencing guidelines specify-ing a range in months rather than years.

Thus, an armed robbery statute mandating a sentence of ten to twenty years typically would be an indeterminate system. The statute concerning the relevant offense of conviction imposes a minimum (ten years) and maximum (twenty years) sentence. The same robbery conviction in a determinate jurisdiction, by contrast, would be where the judge enters a specific sentence such as one hundred twenty (120) months.

Sentencing authority is not limited to the sentencing judge, but rather is shared among criminal justice institutions. In an indeterminate system, that includes not only the legislature and the trial judge, but also often a parole board. Many state legislatures at one time provided that a defendant must serve at least one-half the sentence before becoming eligible for parole. For example, an offender sentenced to twenty years might be released on parole after ten, but could be on parole no longer than the ten years remaining on the twenty-year sentence.

Additionally, there can be reductions for "good behavior" while in prison. Prison authorities generally made judgments whether an offender deserved good behavior credits. Some states mandated *immediate* reduction of a sentence for good behavior, though not yet earned, while sometimes still further reducing them for *earned* good behavior. Thus, the robber sentenced to twenty years in some jurisdictions could have the sentence reduced from twenty years to eighteen if statutes provided for an automatic two-year good behavior reduction. Following the one-half rule or day-for-day procedure, this individual might be eligible for parole after nine years (half of eighteen). However, this defendant could perhaps be able to further reduce the now-maximum eighteen year sentence by another two years, falling to sixteen years, if he or she earned two years' worth of good behavior credit.

Other states permitted parole eligibility to kick-in at the bottom of a sentence *range* imposed by the sentencing court. Thus, if sentenced to two to four years, the offender's parole eligibility began after two years in prison.

The misleading nature of sentences and lack of consistency in sentences received by defendants has led to a radical retrenchment of parole board authority by so-called "truth in sentencing" and similar legislation. Several states have abolished parole entirely (as has the federal system), with many more restricting it to nonviolent offenders.

B. Presumptive Sentencing

Some states, though specifying a wide sentencing range, identify a "presumptive" sentence, at least for certain offenses. In New Jersey, under N.J.S.A § 2C:44-1, for example, first degree felonies were long subject to a range of ten to twenty years imprisonment but with a presumed sentence of fifteen years. A wide range of statutorily-specified factors could be considered in determining whether to depart from the presumed sentence.

Other states, such as Colorado, C.R.S.A. 18-1.3-401, follow a similar approach but with a presumptive sentencing *range* rather than a specific presumptive sentencing point. As an illustration, anyone convicted in Colorado of a class 2 felony faces a presumptive sentencing range of from eight to twenty-four years imprisonment. To vary from this or any other presumptive sentence, the judge must make specific findings of extraordinary mitigating (to vary downward) or aggravating (to vary upward) circumstances. But in no event can the court impose a sentence less than one-half the minimum presumptive term or more than twice the maximum presumptive term. The statute also specifies certain extraordinary circumstances that require a sentence at least in the midpoint of the presumptive range (for example, committing a felony while on parole for another felony).

Courts have disagreed on the constitutionality of judges making such aggravating and mitigating findings in presumptive systems rather than the jury's doing so. For example, in *State v. Natale,* 878 A.2d 724 (N.J. 2005), the court invalidated New Jersey's presumptive system. But in *Lopez v. State,* 113 P.3d 713 (Colo. 2005), the court found Colorado's presumptive system consistent with jury trial right guarantees. This "*Apprendi/Booker*" jury-trial-right issue is discussed below.

C. Mandatory Minimum Sentences

In some jurisdictions the judiciary is not permitted to sentence a defendant below a certain sentence for a particular crime designated by the legislature. For example, some drug crimes will not allow the judge to sentence a defendant below a set number of years as designated by the legislature. Mandatory minimum sentencing statutes may also require a higher minimum than that specified in the statutory offense range if certain facts beyond merely committing the offense are found. Typically these facts concern the details of the crime (e.g., whether it involved use of a weapon to commit the burglary). If a burglary statute required a sentence of one to ten years, but the offender used a gun in committing a burglary, the mandatory minimum statute might instead require a sentence for this offender of at least five years. These statutes enhance prosecutorial discretion because a prosecutor remains free to ignore the facts triggering the mandatory minimum sentence, heightening prosecutorial power in plea-bargaining. Almost every state and the Federal government have some mandatory minimum statutes, with more than sixty federal offenses containing mandatory minimum provisions.

D. Recidivist or Habitual Offender Statutes

Recidivist or habitual offender statutes require higher minimum sentences within the statutory range for certain repeat offenders. The most infamous of such statutes are the "three-strikes" laws. These laws vary widely in details, some require that the two prior felonies, but not the current one, be violent, others require violence only in the current offense, while still other combinations abound. These statutes have a practical effect akin to mandatory minimum statutes but turn on prior crimes of the offender rather than details of the current crime.

E. Probation

Probation, if successfully completed, is a sentence of non-confinement. Probation is an option only where a statute permits a minimum sentence of zero years' incarceration. Probation is itself imposed, however, for a specific term of years. Thus, a judge might choose to impose five years' probation even though the statute permits up to a total period of ten years' punishment. Mandatory minimum statutes, where applicable, prohibit probation.

Probation usually involves conditions, minimally, that the defendant commit no new offenses. Other common conditions are that the defendant periodically report to a probation officer, successfully complete drug treatment, obtain a graduate equivalency diploma, pay fines and court costs, make restitution to the victim, obtain employment training, perform community service, or seek psychological therapy.

Probation violations, if reported by the probation officer to the sentencing judge, will result in a hearing and may lead to the violator's arrest to ensure an appearance at the hearing. If the court finds a violation, it can modify the conditions of continued probation or revoke it. If probation is revoked, the court may impose a longer term of probation or instead choose incarceration.

Probation violations are generally of two kinds: "technical" and "substantive." The meaning of these terms vary. Nevertheless, technical violations are usually relatively minor failures to comply with conditions meant to achieve rehabilitation, such as missing an appointment with a probation officer or failing to attend one scheduled drug treatment session. Such minor failures rarely initially result in probation revocation followed by imprisonment. On the other hand, a classic "substantive" violation is committing a new crime while on probation. That may result in probation revocation followed by imprisonment for that crime and a separate, perhaps consecutive, prison sentence for the new crime. Whatever they are called, there are a range of violations in between these extremes, such as a total failure to cooperate in drug-treatment that may make it more likely that probation will be revoked and replaced by harsher probationary terms of some term of imprisonment.

In many states, revoked probation exposes a violator to up to the maximum number of years to which the offender could have been imprisoned had he or she never been granted probation. That is true even if the violation occurred when probation was nearly completed. For example, a defendant initially facing a zero to ten-year sentence for purse-snatching, a minor form of robbery, might receive five years' probation. If this defendant violates probation after four years, however, he or she could be sentenced up to ten years in prison — the maximum time to which the defendant originally could have been imprisoned. The four years of successful probation will not be deducted from the ten-year maximum as "time served."

This consequence contrasts with that involved in a parole violation. A parole violator will have the total time on parole *and* in prison deducted from the remaining maximum time to which he or she originally could have been sentenced. Thus someone serving five years in prison, followed by four on parole, who violates parole after three years, has "served" eight years of a maximum ten-year penalty. If parole is revoked, the judge can choose to sentence the offender to imprisonment. But that term of imprisonment cannot exceed two more years because eight years (the total time imprisoned and on parole before violating it) served plus two years remaining equals the ten-year maximum sentence.

F. Intermediate Sanctions

"Intermediate" sanctions are those between straight (ordinary) probation and incarceration. For example, probation may be given with intensive supervision, or **Intensive Supervision Probation** (ISP). ISP, like many alternative sanctions, arose because of high recidivism rates among probationers. Typically, serious or modestly dangerous offenders, but not so serious or dangerous as to merit incarceration, or those with some small history of recidivism for non-violent offenses, are eligible for ISP. A repeat car thief might therefore qualify. The serial rapist, on the other hand, would more likely face incarceration, while the first-time possessor of a small quantity of marijuana might at most receive ordinary probation.

ISP probationers must meet with their probation officers often, sometimes five times per week. They must be subjected to curfew checks or frequent phone calls from their probation officer. They might be subjected to random drug testing or even home searches. Their days might be busy ones spent complying with just some of the conditions of probation that may potentially be imposed.

Another such "intermediate" sanction is **Diversion**, sometimes called "accelerated rehabilitative disposition," a form of pre-trial probation. With ordinary probation, a *convicted* offender is released subject to conditions. With pre-trial probation, the prosecutor agrees to hold off on proceeding with charges if the defendant waives speedy trial protections and successfully completes probation. If the defendant has no charges during the diversionary period, the prosecutor agrees to drop the charges entirely. Diversion programs are usually limited to non-violent first offenders. Recently, this procedure has been used extensively with corporate criminality. Corporations enter into Deferred Prosecution Agreements (DPA) and Non-Prosecution Agreements (NPA) that may involve no continued violations of the law, implementing corporate compliance procedures, and inserting a monitor into the corporation to assure compliance with the law.

Another example of an "intermediate" sanction would be **House Arrest.** Arrestees are allowed to leave their home only at specified times for specified purposes, such as working, schooling, or meeting their probation officers. House arrest is frequently enforced by electronic ankle bracelets notifying authorities if the offender leaves home at an impermissible time or travels an impermissible distance. House arrest may be imposed in lieu of incarceration or after a period of incarceration, depending on the laws of the individual jurisdiction.

A **Community Service Order** ("CSO") may also be used in some jurisdictions. This requires an offender to contribute a specified number of hours to community service. What service must be done is largely limited only by the judge's imagination. The offender might work in parks, schools, or hospitals. An offending drug addict may need to lecture high school students on the evils of cocaine, a convicted nurse required to heal the poor, or a repeat traffic offender to pick up highway trash.

Finally, it is common to see **Fines, Fees or Restitution** imposed as part of a sentence. When restitution is imposed, the victims may be compensated for the harm caused by the defendant. The maximum size of a fine is usually specified by statute.

III. Sentencing Procedure and Constitutional Rights

A. Sentencing Procedure

In the federal system, Federal Rule of Criminal Procedure 32 mandates that a probation officer conduct a presentence investigation and submit a report

(PSR) on that investigation to the court. For example, the probation officer's investigation will include information to enable the court to order restitution to any victim and will usually include an interview with the defendant. In the federal system, the PSR will also compute the guidelines range applicable for the defendant. Exceptions are made only where another statute specifically exempts a particular category of case from this requirement or where the court finds the information on the record sufficient to enable meaningful exercise of its sentencing authority without the required report, stating with specificity on the record why this is so. Most states have similar requirements.

Typical items contained in a PSR include any prior criminal record of the defendant, details of the crime, interviews with the defendant and his or her family, and information helpful to the judge who will be sentencing the defendant. In the federal system and many state systems, the parties each receive a copy of the report prior to sentencing and object to misstatements in the report as well as supplement the PSR with their own sentencing memorandum. When a defendant is entering a plea at the sentencing, the court will make certain that the plea is voluntary and that the accused understands all of his or her rights. (See Chapter 9).

B. Constitutional Rights

The Court has held, or at least suggested in *dicta*, that several trial rights do not apply at sentencing. In *Williams v. New York*, 337 U.S. 241 (1949), the Court suggested that prohibitions on hearsay evidence, presumably including Confrontation Clause prohibitions on admitting "testimonial" hearsay absent an opportunity to cross-examine the declarant, do not apply at sentencing. Although *Williams* was decided long before the Court held that the Confrontation Clause was incorporated against the states, the federal courts do not apply the restriction on hearsay evidence at sentencing hearings.

Outside the death penalty context, the Court has also held that the Double Jeopardy Clause generally has no application at sentencing. *Monge v. California*, 524 U.S. 721 (1998). That leaves the state free to seek higher sentences on appeal and to offer new evidence at re-sentencing to support a factual finding found on appeal to have been based on insufficient evidence. *United States v. DiFrancesco*, 449 U .S. 117 (1980). Correspondingly, a court may impose a more severe sentence after a second trial occasioned by appellate reversal of the first conviction so long as the higher sentence did not result from judicial vindictiveness. *North Carolina v. Pearce*, 395 U.S. 711 (1969); *United States v. Goodwin*, 457 U.S. 368 (1982); *Texas v. McCullough*, 475 U.S. 134 (1986); *Alabama v. Smith*, 490 U.S. 794 (1989). Indeed, the Court also permits a judge sentencing a defendant for one crime to take into account evidence that he or she committed another one, even if the defendant was *acquitted* of that other one at a trial, *United States v. Watts*, 519 U.S. 148 (1997), though state courts sometimes take a contrary position on state law grounds. *See, e.g.,* State v. Cote, 530 A.2d 775 (N.H. 1987); *State v. Patteson,* 673 N.E. 2d 1001 (Ohio Ct. App. 1996). The Court has reserved the question whether the collateral estoppel doctrine implicit in the Double Jeopardy Clause survives at sentencing. *Schiro v. Farley,* 510 U.S. 222 (1994).

The Court, however, has suggested in *dictum* that the prosecution's due process duty to disclose material exculpatory evidence applies at sentencing, at least in the capital context. *Brady v. Maryland,* 373 U.S. 83 (1963) (declaring the duty to apply to "guilt or to punishment"). Lower courts have extended this duty to noncapital sentencing proceedings too. *United States v. Severson,* 3 F.3d 1005 (7th Cir. 1993); *United States v. Weintraub,* 871 F.2d 1257 (5th Cir. 1989).

The right to counsel, including appointment of counsel for the indigent, likewise applies at sentencing. *Mempa v. Rhay,* 389 U.S. 128 (1967). Moreover, such counsel must provide *effective* sentencing assistance. *Glover v. United States,* 531 U.S. 198 (2001) (reversing a sentence on grounds of ineffective assistance of counsel). Although the Court has not decided whether convicted defendants have the right to proceed pro se or with counsel of their choice at sentencing, some lower courts have so decided.

Substantial aspects of the privilege against self-incrimination, as to facts relevant to the offense of conviction, or to other offenses for which he might potentially be prosecuted, apply at sentencing. *Mitchell v. United States,* 526 U.S. 314 (1999). A defendant may therefore refuse to testify about such facts at his sentencing hearing, and the judge may not hold that against the defendant. Yet the Court did not decide whether as to sentencing facts unrelated to proving a substantive offense, such as the degree of remorse or of commitment to successfully completing a drug treatment program, the defendant still may claim the privilege's shelter. The Court has also suggested in *dicta* that the privilege's bar on using compelled pre-trial statements against a defendant extends to sentencing, without actually so holding.

C. Who Decides: Judge or Jury?

"Sentencing courts have traditionally heard evidence and found facts without any prescribed burden of proof at all." *McMillan v. Pennsylvania,* 477 U.S. 79 (1986). Certainly, systems requiring sentencing judges to prove sentencing facts merely by a preponderance of the evidence generally satisfy due process. The Court has stated in *United States v. Watts,* 519 U.S. 148 (1997), in *dicta,* that "exceptional circumstances" might require the higher clear and convincing burden. Yet the Court has never found such circumstances.

The judge, however, is not always the proper sentencing body. Sometimes, as we will shortly discuss, the Constitution's Sixth Amendment demands that the jury find facts relevant to sentencing. In particular, the jury must find most such facts where they would increase the maximum guidelines sentence in a mandatory guidelines jurisdiction. The jury need not decide the ultimate sentence, though some jurisdictions at least sometimes permit that. But the jury *must find the facts relevant to* the guidelines sentence. Where that is so, the state must prove to the jury's satisfaction beyond a reasonable doubt all facts that may raise the otherwise-applicable mandatory guidelines maximum sentence. A small minority of states have chosen, as a matter of policy, to give juries a substantial role in noncapital sentencing. In states that have capital punishment, juries generally play a major role in capital sentencing proceedings. Outside capital cases, however, the vast majority of states have long left sentencing fact finding to the sentencing judge, regardless of the type of regime adopted — indeterminate or determinate, guidelines or not. Indeed, permitting sentencing fact finding by judges initially seemed to be a policy choice not subject to constitutional constraint, even with the rise of sentencing guidelines, whether advisory, presumptive, or mandatory. That freedom from constitutional constraint ended with a line of cases begun by *Apprendi v. New Jersey*, 530 U.S. 466 (2000).

The sentencing judge in *Apprendi* found by a preponderance of the evidence that the defendant had committed a firearms offense with "a purpose to intimidate ... because of race," a fact not proven at trial. The sentencing judge's finding raised the applicable sentencing range from five to ten years' up to ten-to-twenty years' imprisonment. The judge ultimately sentenced the defendant to twelve years in prison. The Court found that the fact finding process resulting in the enhanced sentence violated the defendant's Sixth Amendment right to a jury trial. The Court adopted this rule: "Other than the fact of prior conviction, any fact that increases the penalty for a crime, beyond the prescribed statutory maximum must be submitted to a jury and proved beyond a reasonable doubt."

The Court found no historical basis for distinguishing between "elements" to be proven beyond a reasonable doubt by the state at trial and "sentencing factors," an approach that would allow the state to circumvent the jury trial right simply by renaming what it must prove. Any time that proving a fact raises the statutory maximum sentence facing a defendant, the structural and other functions of the jury trial right are implicated. With that right comes the accompanying state burden to prove that fact beyond a reasonable doubt, the Court insisted.

Initially the Court had a limited scope of the *Apprendi* principle, finding that where the facts found merely raised the *minimum* but not the maximum prescribed statutory sentence it did not implicate the jury trial right. *Harris v. United States*, 536 U.S. 545 (2002). In *Alleyne v. United States*, 133 S. Ct. 2151 (2013), the Court overruled *Harris*, finding that "any fact that, by law, increases the penalty for a crime is an 'element' that must be submitted to the jury and found beyond a reasonable doubt." So too, in *Burrage v. United States*, 134 S. Ct. 881 (2014), the Court held that a "death results" enhancement that exposed the defendant to an increased minimum and maximum sentence provided an "element that must be submitted to the jury and found beyond a reasonable doubt." The Court also extended *Apprendi* in *Southern Union Company v. United States*, 132 S. Ct. 22344 (2012), holding that *Apprendi* applied to the imposition of fines.

Apprendi's principle was capacious enough to affect capital and not merely noncapital sentencing. Notably, in *Ring v. Arizona*, 536 U.S. 584 (2002), the Court invalidated an Arizona statute that permitted a judge to determine the presence of aggravating factors that could be used to impose a death sentence, relying specifically on the *Apprendi* principle. Ring had been convicted of felony murder. He could face a death sentence, however, only if he had been the killer and if aggravating factors existed that outweighed any mitigating ones. The trial judge relied upon an accomplice's testimony at the sentencing hearing to find that Ring was the killer. The trial judge also found two aggravating factors: first, that Ring did the crime for pecuniary gain; second, that the offense was committed in an especially heinous, cruel, or depraved manner. The trial judge found support for the latter finding in a witness's testimony that Ring had boasted about his marksmanship. The trial judge found that the one mitigating factor, Ring's having only a minimal prior criminal record, was of little weight and accordingly imposed the death penalty.

Although the Court engaged in an extensive analysis of precedent, it ultimately found the case to be a simple one. The trial judge had found facts that raised the maximum penalty to death. Such facts must be found, under *Apprendi*, by the jury, not the judge. The Court rejected arguments that aggravating factors in death penalty cases must be treated differently than other sorts of fact findings because trial judges are better able than jurors to prevent arbitrary impositions of the death penalty. Consequently, Ring's sentence violated the Sixth Amendment's protection of the right to a jury trial.

In other ways, *Apprendi*'s scope proved even wider outside the capital sentencing context. *Apprendi* left open the question whether the "prescribed statutory maximum" meant the maximum sentence authorized absent guidelines or instead included the maximum permitted by any applicable state sentencing guidelines. The Court chose the latter definition in *Blakely v. Washington*, 542 U.S. 296 (2004).

Blakely involved a defendant pleading guilty to a crime punishable by up to ten years' imprisonment. But the state's sentencing guidelines required, solely on the basis of the jury's verdict, a standard range punishment of 49 to 53 months in prison. The guidelines, however, authorized a higher range for "substantial and compelling reasons justifying an exceptional sentence." The judge found such reasons by concluding that the defendant committed his crime with "deliberate cruelty," thus sentencing the defendant to 90 months' imprisonment.

The Court reversed the sentence, defining *Apprendi's* statutory maximum to mean, "the maximum sentence a judge may impose *solely on the basis of the facts reflected in the jury verdict or admitted by the defendant....* In other words, the maximum [the judge may impose] *without* any additional findings." That definition "ensure[s] that the judge's authority to sentence derives wholly from the jury's verdict," allowing the jury to "exercise the control that the Framers intended." Because the state's sentencing reform act dictated application of a standard guidelines range with a specified maximum, additional factfinding increasing that statutory maximum, such as that the defendant acted with deliberate cruelty, went beyond the facts inherently found by the jury in its verdict. Such mandatory enhancement of the maximum guidelines penalty by additional fact finding therefore demanded that a jury, not a judge, find those facts.

Blakely, though addressing a state guidelines system, seemed to spell the death knell for the mandatory Federal Sentencing Guidelines, unless the Court found a way to distinguish the *Blakely* state from federal systems. Rather than permanently killing the Federal Guidelines, however, the Court temporarily killed them in *United States v. Booker*, 543 U.S. 220 (2005), then immediately resurrected them, zombie-like, in an altered form in which they became advisory rather than mandatory.

The government in *Booker* sought to distinguish the federal system from the state system at issue in *Blakely*. The *Blakely* guidelines were contained in statutes, while the federal ones were written by a Sentencing Commission, albeit one authorized by federal statute. The government argued that only legislative, not Commission, action defines the "statutory maximum." But the Court disagreed because in both cases "the relevant sentencing rules are mandatory and impose binding requirements on all sentencing judges." Consequently, as "the dissenting opinions in *Blakely* recognized, there is no distinction of constitutional significance between the Federal Sentencing Guidelines and the [government] procedures at issue in that case." That conclusion required that the Federal Guidelines be held unconstitutional, at least to the extent that they permitted judicial fact finding that could raise the maximum end of the Guidelines sentencing range. Obvious remedies would be either to strike down the Guidelines in their entirety or to preserve them but with jury fact finding replacing judicial fact finding. But the Court chose neither course.

Instead, the Court invalidated only those provisions of the Sentencing Reform Act that made the Guidelines mandatory. The effect, concluded the Court, was to render the Guidelines advisory. Because advisory guidelines do not automatically *mandate* a higher sentencing range, they do not, in the Court's view, implicate the right to a jury trial. The Court filled in seeming gaps created by this jury-rigged system. Sentencing judges must thus still "consider" the Guidelines after properly computing the Guidelines range. Judges are free, however, to deviate from the Guidelines. Appellate courts will override such deviations only if they are "unreasonable" in light of the Guidelines' purposes and those set forth in the federal Sentencing Reform Act.

Indeed, whether sentencing judges deviate from the Guidelines or not, they must always consider both the Guidelines and the Sentencing Reform Act and must explain the reasoning supporting their sentencing. Subsequent case law elaborates on the new system. It is important to stress that much fact finding occurs under the new advisory regime, but these facts may be found by the sentencing judge rather than by a jury. Moreover, once the relevant facts are found, the sentencing judge has substantial authority to weigh those facts, consider the policy goals of sentencing, and craft an appropriate sentence subject only to a fairly deferential standard of appellate review. The advisory guidelines approach aims to retain some measure of uniformity by drawing on the Commission's expertise as it is embodied in the Guidelines but leaves the sentencing judge more free than in the pre-*Booker* world to individualize the sentence to a particular offender's needs and circumstances. It is to the details of this advisory federal system to which this chapter next turns.

IV. Federal Sentencing

A. Preliminary Matters

The structure of federal sentencing comes from the Sentencing Reform Act of 1984. There was dissatisfaction with the existing indeterminate sentencing model that resulted in judicial disparity in sentences and uncertainty in the time that would be served by a sentence. The Act created a Sentencing Commission for the purpose of creating federal guidelines that would correct these two sentence disparities. The Act also abolished the parole system for future offenses. In *Mistretta v. United States*, 488 U.S. 361 (1989), the Court upheld the guidelines as promulgated by the United States Sentencing Commission as constitutional.

The Federal Sentencing Guidelines are complex. They cannot truly be understood without using them. The Guidelines are frequently amended, so details may change. The Guidelines were originally mandatory, providing only narrow grounds for departure. Because the Guidelines originally increased sentences based upon *judicial* factfinding, the Supreme Court in *Booker* held that such mandatory sentencing increases violate a defendant's Sixth Amendment right to a jury trial. Juries, not judges, must decide whether facts exist that could raise an offender's sentence over what it might otherwise be. The two exceptions to this rule, both of which are recited in the *Booker* case itself, are that judges may determine what prior offenses a defendant was convicted of committing and defendants may waive their right to jury factfinding. This jury-decision rule applies, however, only to mandatory guidelines. The federal Guidelines were indeed originally mandatory. Nevertheless, rather than invalidating them or mandating jury fact-finding, the Court simply declared the Guidelines advisory, invalidating only the statutory provision that made them mandatory. The Advisory Guidelines, concluded the Court, did not violate the Sixth Amendment.

Despite their advisory role, the Guidelines remain central to federal sentencing practice. Each sentencing judge must consider the Guidelines carefully and explain how the sentence was computed. Moreover, many judges continue to follow the Guidelines. Where judges depart from the recommended sentence, they must have reasonable grounds for doing so and must further explain those grounds. Additionally, despite the supposedly advisory nature of the Guidelines, judges effectively continue in engaging in "factfinding" when applying the Guidelines.

Guideline computations no longer end the matter. The sentencing court must next turn to the federal sentencing statute, 18 U.S.C. § 3553, to determine what sentence is consistent with that statute. Among the factors the judge must consider under that section are "the nature and circumstances of the offense and the history and characteristics of the defendant." Other circumstances to be considered include the seriousness of the offense, the needs to promote respect for the law, afford adequate deterrence, protect the public from further crimes by the defendant, provide him with needed educational or vocational training, avoid unwarranted sentencing disparities, and provide just punishment. The judge may choose a sentence outside the Guidelines based upon those statutory concerns so long as the judge considered the Guidelines and adequately explains the reasons for offering a different sentence.

B. The Guidelines

The core of the Guidelines is, of course, the sentencing grid or table. The *vertical* axis consists of offense severity scores increasing from offense level one to a maximum offense level of forty-three. The horizontal axis lists increasing criminal history categories numbered I up to a maximum of VI. In parentheses after each category number are "criminal history points." These points determine the criminal history category. For example, zero to one point is category I, seven to nine points is category IV, and 13 or more points is category VI. Users must thus compute criminal history points to determine the relevant criminal history category. Where each offense level intersects with each criminal history category, the Guidelines display a grid cell reciting the Guidelines sentencing range in months. Thus, someone convicted of a crime in Offense Level I and in criminal history category I receives a Guidelines sentence of "0–6" months of imprisonment.

The Guidelines Manual consists of eight chapters and three appendices for computing the defendant's guideline range. Chapter One recites definitions and general application principles.

Chapter Two discusses the offense levels for specific crimes and offense-specific adjustments that might apply to many crimes rather than only to a simple specific offense. The vast majority of federal crimes involve four offense categories: drug, economic, firearms, and immigration offenses.

Offense-specific conduct includes "relevant conduct." Relevant conduct, defined in § 1B1.3, extends to "all acts or omissions committed, aided, abetted, counseled, commanded, induced, procured, or willfully caused by the defendant ... that occurred during the commission of the offense of conviction, in preparation for that offense, or in the course of attempting to avoid detection or responsibility for that offense." For drug crimes and many other, though not all, offenses, relevant conduct extends to acts *and omissions* that were part of the "same course of conduct or common scheme or plan as the offense of conviction," even if not required to be proven as part of the offense of conviction's elements and even if no such proof was offered or received at trial.

Relevant conduct can likewise extend to the conduct of persons other than the defendant yet who were involved in the offense *even if conspiracy was never charged.* Such conduct applies to the defendant, however, only if it was reasonably foreseeable *and* done in furtherance of the jointly undertaken criminal activity. However, if these criteria are met, such conduct need not necessarily coincide with the scope of the entire conspiracy. Conspirators' conduct pre-dating defendant's joining the conspiracy, however, does not count against him even if he knew about that conduct.

On the other hand, relevant conduct can include conduct underlying dismissed, acquitted, and uncharged counts. The government generally has the burden of proving such conduct by a preponderance of the evidence at the sentencing hearing. *United States v. Watts*, 519 U.S. 148 (1997).

Chapter Two of the Guidelines also addresses adjustments to be made to the offense severity score that vary with the *specific offense of conviction*. For example, the offense level score will be adjusted based upon the defendant's "role in the offense." For example, there may be a downward adjustment in the offense level when the defendant is a "minimal participant," described as one "who plays a minimal role in concerted activity."

Chapter Three explains offense level adjustments that may apply to most offenses or to specialized categories of offense. For example, if a defendant abused a position of public or private trust or used a special skill in a way that significantly facilitates committing or concealing the offense, the offense level increases by two levels under section § 3B1.3. But this adjustment can be applied *only* if the abuse of trustee skill was not already included in the base offense level or a specific offense characteristic.

Chapter Three also provides for increasing a sentence where the defendant used or attempted to use someone less than eighteen years old to commit, or assist in avoiding commission or apprehension of, the offense, when a defendant intentionally selected any victim or property as the offense of conviction's object because of the actual or perceived race, color, religion, national origin, ethnicity, gender, disability, or sexual orientation of any person, or when the defendant knows or should have known that the victim was a vulnerable one. When the victim is an official, such as a current or former government officer or employee or a member of that officer or employee's immediate family and the offense of conviction was "motivated by" that victim's status, there can be an upward adjustment. Likewise, the Guidelines can increase if a victim was physically restrained during the course of the offense. A commonly used upward adjustment in a sentence is when the defendant "obstruct[s] or imped[es] the administration of justice."

Although Chapter Three generally addresses general adjustments that may apply to many types of offenses, several Chapter Three adjustments apply to specific categories of offenses. These categories include terrorism, use of body armor in drug trafficking crimes or crimes of violence, recklessly endangering another person during flight from a law enforcement officer, committing the current offense while on release for another federal offense, and false registration of a domain name.

Chapter Three also provides for adjustments that can lower the defendant's sentence. For example, a defendant who "clearly demonstrates" his "acceptance of responsibility for his offense" merits a two-level decrease in offense level. § 3E1.1(a). Pleading guilty is "significant evidence of acceptance of responsibility," so long as the offender truthfully admits to the conduct comprising the offense of conviction *and* truthfully admits to (or at least does not falsely deny) any associated relevant conduct. § 3E1.1, Application Note 3. On the other hand, pleading guilty does not guarantee an acceptance of responsibility adjustment "as a matter of right." Indeed, at times a guilty plea may be outweighed by other conduct inconsistent with accepting responsibility.

Chapter Four addresses the computation of criminal history points and categories. The Guidelines provide for computing a *single* offense level for a defendant convicted of multiple counts, whether they are charged in a single charging instrument (that is, a single indictment or information), or in separate ones consolidated for sentencing. Counts involving "substantially the same harm" constitute a single group. § 3D1.2. There can also be upward and downward departures premised on criminal history.

One also computes the criminal history under Chapter Four, with most prior sentences for crimes or juvenile adjudications being assigned a certain number of points based primarily on the sentence's length. Criminal history points, once finally computed, match to criminal history categories. For example, zero to one criminal history points equates to category I, while thirteen or more criminal history points equates to category VI. Typically, a white collar offender has no prior criminal activity and thus falls into category I.

Chapter Five looks at the use of the sentencing table or grid and the grounds for departures. One critical means for a defendant's obtaining a downward departure is when the government files a motion declaring that the defendant has "provided substantial assistance in the investigation or prosecution of another person who has committed an offense...." § 5K1.1. Only the prosecutor has the ability to file a § 5K1.1 motion, which made this section particularly important when the guidelines were mandatory. This section retains importance as cooperation can lower a sentence and it also may allow a court to go below a statutory mandatory minimum sentence. Another example of a downward departure is when diminished mental capacity substantially contributed to an offense's commission. § 5K2.13.

Chapter Six explains sentence and plea agreement procedures. The *Introductory Commentary* to Part B of this chapter declares that Commission policy on plea negotiation practices has the dual goal of promoting the purposes of sentencing outlined in 18 U.S.C. § 3553(a) and not perpetuating unwarranted sentencing disparities. The *Commentary* recognizes that sentencing pursuant to a guilty plea is nevertheless a judicial function and that the purpose of the policy statements is to ensure that any departure from the Guidelines is explained on the record.

Chapters Seven looks at guidelines for revocation of probation and supervised release procedures. The final chapter, Chapter Eight provides the sentencing guidelines for organizations. This chapter provides the methodology for computing a fine that a corporation will pay upon conviction. The Guidelines may be referenced in computing fines for deferred and non-prosecution agreements entered into between the government and an entity, even when the agreement is done outside the judicial system.

C. Post-*Booker* Sentencing

In a series of recent cases, the Court has offered details concerning fact finding and the exercise of judicial discretion under its new advisory Guidelines regime. This regime requires sentencing judges to consider the purposes of sentencing, to individualize sentences to some degree, and to consider Guidelines calculations as well.

In *Gall v. United States*, 552 U.S. 38 (2007), the Court articulated a multi-step process for sentencing judges to follow under *Booker*'s advisory Guidelines range. The Guidelines "should be the starting point and the initial benchmark" "to secure nationwide consistency." However, the sentencing judge should not presume that the Guidelines range is reasonable in any individual case. Accordingly, the judge must hear both parties' arguments as to what sentence they each deem appropriate, even if they argue for outside-the-Guidelines sentences.

The sentencing judge must next consider all the Sentencing Reform Act factors in 18 U.S.C. § 3553(a) to determine whether they support one party or the other's requested sentence or, presumably, a sentence that neither has requested. The judge "must make an individualized assessment based on the facts presented." This includes considering "the nature and circumstances of the offense and the history and characteristics of the defendant." It also necessitates considering the need for the sentence imposed, "the kinds of sentences available," the Sentencing Guidelines, any relevant policy statement issued by the Sentencing Commission, "the need to avoid unwarranted sentence disparities," and "the need to provide restitution to any victim." The sentence should be "sufficient, but not greater than necessary." The *Gall* Court noted "that § 3553(a) explicitly directs sentencing courts" to "begin their analysis with the Guidelines and remain cognizant of them throughout the sentencing process."

If, after going through the above process, the sentencing court decides to deviate from the Guidelines, the Court stated that it "must consider the extent of the deviation and ensure that the justification is sufficiently compelling to support the degree of the variance." *Gall* also requires an "adequate explanation" of the ultimate sentence chosen to enable informed appellate review. But this does not require, as the Court explained in *Rita v. United States*, 551 U.S. 338 (2007), a "full opinion in every case." The explanation needs merely to be sufficient to demonstrate to an appellate court that the sentencing judge has "considered the parties' arguments and has a reasoned basis for exercising his own legal decisionmaking authority." The explanation requirement is a statutory one recited in 18 U.S.C. § 3553(c), which means the judge "at the time of sentencing" must "state in open court the reasons for its imposition of the particular sentence."

Rita itself involved a defendant convicted by a jury of perjury and related charges. The parties and the sentencing judge had before them a presentence report explaining a recommended Guidelines range and included information relevant to a sentencing departure. That latter information outlined Rita's health, personal and family data, education, employment record, and meritorious military service. Each side presented their arguments at the sentencing hearing, with Rita arguing for a downward departure or deviation. Rita's counsel agreed on the record that his arguments on both scores rested on three points: first, Rita's poor physical condition; second, his being vulnerable to retaliation in prison because he had been involved in criminal justice work for the immigration service, resulting in a number of people going to prison; and third, his outstanding military service. The trial judge thereafter announced that it was appropriate to enter a sentence of imprisonment at the bottom of the Guidelines range. He added only that he was unable to conclude that the presentence report's recommendations were inappropriate and that "under [section] 3553 ... the public needs to be protected if it is true, and I must accept as true the jury verdict."

The Court found this statement of reasons adequate. The record made clear that the sentencing judge attentively listened to each argument and considered the supporting evidence. The judge was fully aware of, and carefully considered, the three reasons the defense offered for leniency. The context made clear that he found these reasons insufficient to justify departing or deviating from the Guidelines. More need not have been said. Although the law did not require more, the Court stated that a better practice in some cases will be to have the judge provide additional information:

We acknowledge that the judge might have said more. He might have added explicitly that he had heard and considered the evidence and argument; that (as no one before him denied) he thought the Commission in the Guidelines had determined a sentence that was proper in the mine rune of roughly similar perjury cases; and that he found that Rita's personal circumstances here were simply not different enough to warrant a different sentence. But context and the record made clear that this, or similar, reasoning, underlies the judge's conclusion. Where a matter is as conceptually simple as in the case at hand and the record makes clear that the sentencing judge considered the evidence and arguments, we do not believe the law requires the judge to write more extensively.

D. Appellate Review of Sentences

Both the government and the defense can appeal a sentence in the federal system. Appellate review of sentences, *Gall* declared, must be for "abuse-of-discretion." Review proceeds in two steps: first, determining whether the sentencing judge committed significant procedural error; second, considering the substantive reasonableness of the sentence under the deferential abuse-of-discretion standard.

The appellate court will consider the totality of the circumstances in conducting substantive reasonableness review. If the sentence is within the Guidelines range, the appellate court is free to, but is not required to, apply a presumption of reasonableness. But if the sentence is outside the Guidelines range, the appellate court may never, as noted earlier, apply a presumption of unreasonableness. The appellate court "may consider the extent of the deviation, but must give due deference to the district court's decision that the § 3553(a) factors, on a whole, justify the extent of the variance." However, simply because "the appellate court might reasonably have concluded that a different sentence was appropriate is insufficient to justify reversal of the district court."

The *Gall* Court rejected any requirements that Guidelines deviations be justified by extraordinary circumstances or proceed pursuant to a mathematical formula. Accordingly, the Court concluded, the Court of Appeals:

> clearly disagreed with the District Judge's conclusion that consideration of the § 3553(a) factors justified a sentence of probation; it believed that the circumstances presented here were insufficient to sustain such a marked deviation from the Guidelines range. But it is not for the Court of Appeals to decide *de novo* whether the justification for a variance is sufficient or the sentence reasonable. On abuse-of-discretion review, the Court of Appeals should have given due deference to the District Court's reasoned and reasonable decision that the § 3553(a) factors, on the whole, justified the sentence.

Starting with *Kimbrough v. United States*, 552 U. S. 85 (2007), the Court recognized that parties can challenge the validity of individual Guidelines simply because they have a reasoned basis for disagreeing with them. In *Kimbrough*, the then-controlling Guidelines contained a provision imposing a 100:1 ratio for sentencing for possessing or distributing crack, rather than powder, cocaine. Restated, possessing one gram of crack led to the same sentence as 100 grams of powder. The District Court instead imposed a substantially lower sentence, specifically, the fifteen-year statutory mandatory minimum. The District Court's reasons for doing so included the "disproportionate and unjust effect that crack cocaine guidelines have in sentencing." The United States Court of Appeals for the Fourth Circuit vacated the sentence, finding it per se unreasonable for the District Court judge to deviate from the crack Guidelines simply because of a disagreement with the policy judgment and impact they embody.

The United States Supreme Court rejected the Fourth Circuit's position, finding the District Court's sentence reasonable for the following reasons. First, crack and powder cocaine are chemically identical, with the same physiological and psychotropic effects. Yet the 100:1 ratio may result in a major powder cocaine supplier getting a shorter sentence than a low-level crack dealer.

Second, the crack Guidelines were not developed using the Commission's usual empirical approach of examining past sentencing practices. Instead, the ratio rested on assumptions of crack's greater harmfulness. But in a later report, the Commission concluded that crack was associated with less violence than previously assumed, had the same prenatal effects as powder, and did not result in the feared epidemic of crack use by youth. Moreover, the report concluded, the crack/powder cocaine disparity fostered "disrespect for and lack of confidence in the criminal justice system" given the "widely-held perception" that it promoted "unwarranted disparity based on race." Indeed, the severe federal court crack penalties were imposed "primarily upon black offenders."

For these and other reasons, the Commission later adopted newer Guidelines, albeit not governing Kimbrough's case, which ameliorated without eliminating the crack/powder disparity. Under these circumstances, concluded the Court, the sentencing judge had ample basis to reject the policy wisdom of the original 100:1 crack/powder ratio disparity contained in the Guidelines as they were applied to Kimbrough. Furthermore, noted the Court, the "Government acknowledges that the Guidelines 'are now advisory' and that, as a general matter, 'courts may vary [from Guidelines ranges] based solely on policy considerations, including disagreements with the Guidelines.'"

Technically, *Kimbrough* did not "invalidate" the original crack Guidelines. Instead, the case merely indicated that under certain conditions a sentencing judge is free to refuse to apply at least certain Guidelines on the grounds that they constitute bad policy or have an inadequate evidentiary basis, thus meriting little, if any weight. Although courts disagree, lower courts have shown a willingness to apply the *Kimbrough* analysis to a wide array of other individual Guidelines.

In *Pepper v. United States*, 131 S. Ct. 1229 (2011), the Court found it proper for a sentencing judge on remand for plenary re-sentencing to take into account evidence of the defendant's post-original-sentencing rehabilitation. A statutory provision, 18 U.S.C. § 3742(g)(2), prohibited imposing a non-Guidelines sentence at resentencing on a ground not relied upon at the prior sentencing. That provision thus treats post-sentencing rehabilitation as irrelevant. *Pepper* struck down that provision as inconsistent with *Booker*. Accordingly, the Court upheld the downward variance granted at resentencing. *Pepper* acknowledged the importance of considering rehabilitation as a ground for imposing a sentence *other than incarceration*—even considering post-sentencing rehabilitation upon resentencing. *Tapia v. United States*, 131 S. Ct. 2382 (2011), however, prohibits considering rehabilitation as a justification *for imposing incarceration* rather than rejecting it. *Tapia* similarly bars considering rehabilitation as a ground for determining incarceration's length.

V. Cruel and Unusual Punishment

A. Background

The Eighth Amendment declares that "Excessive bail shall not be required, nor excessive fines imposed, nor cruel and unusual punishments inflicted." The Fourteenth Amendment incorporates this provision to the States. Throughout the years, Courts have struggled with what constitutes "cruel and unusual punishment." Many of the cases exploring this issue involve capital punishment. Some punishments have been found to be categorically unconstitutional. Other punishments are examined under a proportionality review that looks at a totality of the circumstances inquiry to determine whether a sentence in a specific individual case is excessive. The Court described the proportionality principle as a "narrow" one that "'does not require strict proportionality between crime and sentence' but rather 'forbids only extreme sentences that are "grossly disproportionate" to the crime.'" *Graham v. Florida*, 560 U.S. 48 (2010).

In examining "cruel and unusual punishment," the Court has repeatedly noted that "[t]he Eighth Amendment 'is not fastened to the obsolete but may acquire meaning as public opinion becomes enlightened by a humane justice.'" *Hall v. Florida*, 134 S. Ct. 1986 (2014)(citing Weems v. United States, 217 U.S.

349 (1910)). One looks at the "evolving standards of decency that mark the progress of a maturing society."

B. Categorically Unconstitutional

The Court has found certain punishments as categorically unconstitutional. Such cases sometimes fall into two subsets, those concerning the nature of the offense and those considering the characteristics of the offender. Concerning the first subset, the Court has simply barred capital sentencing for crimes other than homicide. *Kennedy v. Louisiana*, 554 U.S. 407 (2008); *Enmund v. Florida*, 458 U.S. 782 (1982); *Coker v. Georgia*, 433 U.S. 584 (1977). Concerning the second subset, the Court has prohibited imposing the death penalty on those committing a murder when under age eighteen and those with low intellectual functioning. *Roper v. Simmons*, 543 U.S. 551 (2005) (juveniles); *Atkins v. Virginia*, 536 U.S. 304 (2002) (low intellectual functioning). Likewise, in *Graham v. Florida*, the Court went further in holding that it was unconstitutional to give a sixteen year old a life sentence without any opportunity for parole for a non-homicide offense.

Bother *Roper* and *Graham* focused on juveniles being different, finding first that they could not receive a death sentence for a homicide conviction and then a life sentence in a non-homicide case. In *Miller v. Alabama*, 132 S. Ct. 2455 (2012), the Court held that "the Eighth Amendment forbids a sentencing scheme that mandates life in prison without possibility of parole for juvenile offenders." The Court stated that

> [b]y requiring that all children convicted of homicide receive lifetime incarceration without possibility of parole, regardless of their age and age-related characteristics and the nature of their crimes, the mandatory sentencing schemes before us violate this principle of proportionality, and so the Eighth Amendment's ban on cruel and unusual punishment.

The approach in determining whether to create a categorical rule differs from the individual circumstances approach. In categorical rules cases, the Court first considers " 'objective indicia of society's standards, as expressed in legislative enactments and state practice' to determine whether there is a national consensus against the sentencing practice at issue." *Graham v. Florida*. If there is, the Court next determines "in the exercise of its own independent judgment whether the punishment in question violates the Constitution," guided by precedent and the Court's understanding of the Cruel and Unusual Punishment Clause's meaning. *Graham* was the first time that the Court considered whether to apply a categorical ban to a term of years sentence instead of to the death penalty. It imposed just such a ban.

Even when a categorical approach is used, there may be interpretation necessary to determine who fits within that category. In *Hall v. Florida*, the Court rejected a Florida statute that mandated an IQ score of 70 or below for a finding of intellectual disability that would forbid imposition of a death sentence. Execution of a man who scored a 71 instead of a 70 on the IQ test was rejected as "the law requires that he have the opportunity to present evidence of his intellectual disability, including deficits in adaptive functioning over his lifetime."

C. Proportionality Review

The Court first applied a proportionality analysis in *Weems v. United States*, 217 U.S. 349 (1910), where it struck down a sentence of fifteen years at hard labor in chains for falsifying a public document. Fifty years later, in *California v. Robinson*, 370 U.S. 660 (1962), the Court again used a proportionality approach to invalidate a ninety day prison sentence for being addicted to narcotics. There, the Court emphasized that proportionality turned not on anything inherent about the crime, the person, or the sentence but rather about their relationship to one another: "Even one day in prison would be a cruel and unusual punishment for the 'crime' of having a common cold." *Robinson* kicked off a decades long dispute among the Justices about the wisdom, scope, and meaning of proportionality analysis in noncapital cases. The one thing the Justices seemed to have a fair degree of agreement on, however, was the idea that "death is different," that is, that the Eighth Amendment analysis of the death penalty may proceed in a different way in capital than noncapital cases, though the Court was often unclear about just what were those differences. Justice Stewart, concurring in *Furman v. Georgia*, 408 U.S. 238 (1972), identified the logic of the distinction:

> The penalty of death differs from all other forms of criminal punishment not in degree, but in kind. It is unique in its total irrevocability. It is unique in its rejection of rehabilitation of the convict as a basic purpose of criminal justice. And it is unique, finally, in its absolute renunciation of all that is embodied in our concept of humanity.

The uniqueness of capital punishment led the Court first to prohibit it in adult rape cases, then juvenile homicides, then all nonhomicide offenses. *See Coker v. Georgia*, 433 U.S. 584 (1977) (rape); *Roper v. Simmons*, 543 U.S. 551 (2005) (juvenile homicides); *Kennedy v. Louisiana*, 554 U.S. 407 (2008) (all nonhomicides). The Court also prohibited executing the mentally retarded. *Atkins v. Virginia,* 536 U.S. 304 (2002).

In *Rummel v. Estelle,* 445 U.S. 263 (1980), the Court hinted that the difference between capital and noncapital cases for Eighth Amendment purposes was that in the latter cases sentences would rarely, if ever, be invalidated. "Outside the context of capital punishment," wrote Justice Rehnquist for the Court, "successful challenges to the proportionality of particular sentences have been exceedingly rare." Yet only three years later, in *Solem v. Helm,* 463 U.S. 277 (1983), the Court found that a life sentence imposed on a recidivist for a minor nonviolent felony was disproportionate to the crime committed. The proportionality principle, said the Court, was, even as applied to nonhomicide cases, "deeply rooted and frequently repeated in common-law jurisprudence." Nevertheless, rather than reversing *Rummel,* the Court distinguished it as a case in which, unlike in *Solem,* the defendant retained the possibility of release on parole.

But eight years after *Solem,* the Court in *Harmelin v. Michigan,* 501 U.S. 957 (1991), again seemed to limit proportionality to the death penalty arena. The Court thus rejected a first-offender's challenge to a life without parole sentence for possessing (an admittedly large amount of) cocaine. The Court explained that "[p]roportionality review is one of several respects in which we have held that 'death is different,' and have imposed protections that the Constitution nowhere else provides." Justice Kennedy authored a separate concurring opinion, however, that would later prove influential, Kennedy insisting that a gross disproportionality principle did still govern noncapital sentences.

In *Ewing v. California,* 538 U.S. 11 (2003), the Court embraced, at least in word if not in deed, Justice Kennedy's gross disproportionality principle in his *Harmelin* dissent. But the Court also repeated that successful application of that principle to noncapital cases would be "exceedingly rare," the case before it not being an exception to that rule. The Court thus upheld a recidivists' twenty-five to life sentence for stealing three golf clubs. Justice Scalia, in his concurring opinion, however, vigorously critiqued the Court's theoretical embrace of a disproportionality principle. For Scalia, the Eighth Amendment was more about the manner of punishment (for example, physical torture) than about its length.

In *Graham,* however, a majority of Justices embraced Justice Kennedy's gross disproportionality, case-specific principle and went even further, accepting at least some categorical bans on certain punishments in nonhomicide cases. The categorical ban analysis borrowed heavily from capital Eighth Amendment jurisprudence. This may diminish the argument that "death is different" when analyzing capital and noncapital cases. This position was strengthened in *Miller* by the Court's rejection of a mandatory life sentence for juveniles.

Checkpoints

- Punishment theory plays a role in determining the sentencing structure and sentences provided.

- Typically, a sentencing system is either an indeterminate or determinate sentencing system.

- Some states and the federal system have mandatory minimum sentences for certain offenses.

- Some states have habitual offender statutes that permit increased sentences for recidivists.

- Sentences can include imprisonment, probation, intermediate sanctions, and fines.

- Certain constitutional rights apply to sentencing, such as the right to counsel.

- In *Apprendi*, the Court held that the Sixth Amendment required that any fact that increases the penalty for a crime beyond the prescribed statutory maximum must be submitted to a jury and proved beyond a reasonable doubt.

- The *Apprendi* principle has been used by the Court to invalidate statutory provisions making the Federal Sentencing Guidelines mandatory, thus leaving them in place but having only advisory status.

- In federal court, a sentencing judge must thus still compute the Guidelines sentence but must next consider all statutory sentencing factors at 18 U.S.C. § 3553.

- A sentencing judge must state on the record the reasons for any sentence imposed and must provide an adequate justification for sentences outside the Guidelines.

- On appellate review, a reviewing court may, but need not, apply a presumption of reasonableness to within-Guidelines sentences, but the reviewing court may not apply a presumption of unreasonableness to outside-Guidelines sentences.

- The Eighth Amendment prohibits cruel and unusual punishments. Two lines of case law control: a case-specific inquiry and a categorical inquiry.

- The categorical prohibition has been used to invalidate death sentences for juveniles, those with low intellectual functioning, and life without parole for a nonhomicide juvenile offender.

- Courts may need to interpret a categorical rule such as when is an individual considered to be of low intellectual functioning.

- The case-specific inquiry generally governs and invalidates only sentences that are grossly disproportionate to the crime. There are two steps in this analysis: first, a facial examination of the sentence for gross disproportion (including an individualized examination of the offender's culpability, the severity of the crime, and the punishment imposed), then a comparative examination to other sentences within the same jurisdiction and within other jurisdictions for similar crimes.

Chapter 15

Double Jeopardy

Roadmap

- Three types of double jeopardy protection
- Four thresholds before double jeopardy will apply:
  - Criminal cases required
  - Same offense required — the *Blockburger* test
  - Same sovereign required
  - Jeopardy must have attached in first proceeding
- Dismissals, mistrials, and hung juries
- Appeals
- Reduced protection against multiple punishments
- Collateral estoppel as a double jeopardy guarantee

I. Introduction

The Fifth Amendment to the United States Constitution contains a number of provisions, including the guarantee that no person "be subject for the same offense to be twice put in jeopardy of life or limb." This is known as the prohibition against double jeopardy. According to the Supreme Court in *North Carolina v. Pearce*, 395 U.S. 711 (1969), the Double Jeopardy Clause contains distinct guarantees against:

- subsequent prosecution after an acquittal for the same offense;
- subsequent prosecution after a conviction for the same offense; and
- multiple punishments for the same offense.

The Double Jeopardy Clause serves several related purposes. During trial, it guarantees to the defendant the right to proceed to judgment before the original jury or judge, thus preventing the government from terminating a trial that does not seem to be going in its favor. Once a verdict has been handed down, the Clause preserves the finality of the criminal judgment and prevents the government from repeatedly attempting to convict or punish the defendant. Without a prohibition against double jeopardy, the government would have multiple chances to convict a defendant after refining its case, obtaining additional evidence, gaining a more sympathetic judge or jury, and/or simply exhausting the defendant. Even after sentencing, the government might be motivated to seek extra punishments after learning of additional evidence. Thus the Double Jeopardy Clause prevents government manipulation and oppression, allowing only one chance to convict and punish a defendant.

The importance of the Double Jeopardy Clause was highlighted by the Supreme Court in *Benton v. Maryland*, 395 U.S. 784 (1969), which held the protection applicable to individual states as well as the federal government because double jeopardy "represents a fundamental ideal in our constitutional heritage." For this reason the clause also has been applied to organizational defendants as well as individuals, although the Supreme Court has not addressed this question directly.

Double jeopardy typically is raised when the government seeks to reprosecute or repunish a defendant, and as a result it usually requires inquiry into a prior proceeding in order to determine whether the guarantee has been violated.

II. Four Double Jeopardy Thresholds

The Double Jeopardy Clause does not arise in every situation in which the government seeks to reprosecute or repunish a defendant. Instead, there are four thresholds that a defendant must meet in order to gain dismissal of a subsequent proceeding on double jeopardy grounds: the Double Jeopardy Clause applies only (1) in criminal cases, and (2) when the government is attempting to try or punish a defendant multiple times for the "same offense." Even then, the clause is implicated only (3) when the prosecuting government—or sovereign—is the same as the one that brought the previous criminal case. Finally, even if the first three thresholds are met, the Double Jeopardy Clause applies only (4) when jeopardy is "attached" in the first case. In other words, the clause only applies to the defendant actually was brought to trial or judgment on the facts, and the proceeding was not halted in a manner that permits a second proceeding.

Each of these four threshold matters will be discussed below. Keep in mind that the defendant must establish *each one* in order to convince the court to dismiss the subsequent proceeding.

A. Criminal Case

Because the framers of the Constitution explicitly limited double jeopardy protection to situations in which a defendant's "life or limb" is threatened, double jeopardy applies only to criminal prosecutions. *Both* the previous action *and* the subsequent one must be criminal in nature. Civil actions and administrative proceedings do not implicate the Clause, even if they result in punitive damages or asset forfeiture.

Usually the distinction between civil and criminal actions is fairly straightforward, but sometimes legislatures create fines and other penalties without clearly labeling them "criminal" or "civil." Can the government pursue these fines and penalties as "civil" ones and later bring criminal charges for the same conduct—or, reversing the order, pursue criminal charges first and then civil sanctions? Courts must use a two-part test to answer this question. First, the court must turn to the statute authorizing the fines or penalties involved in the "civil" proceeding and ask whether the legislature expressed a preference for labeling them "civil" or "criminal." If the legislature expressed a preference that the fines or penalties be imposed as criminal sanctions, then the double jeopardy guarantee is implicated.

If the legislative preference is for a "civil" punishment mechanism, then the court must engage in a second analysis, deciding whether there is "clear proof" that the penalties are sufficiently punitive in purpose or effect as to transform the civil proceeding into a criminal one. This "purpose or effect" test requires the court to consider and weigh the following factors:

(1) whether the sanction involves an affirmative disability or restraint; (2) whether it has historically been regarded as a punishment; (3) whether it comes into play only on a finding of *scienter* [in other words, culpable intent]; (4) whether its operation will promote the traditional aims of punishment—retribution and deterrence; (5) whether the behavior to which it applies is already a crime; (6) whether an alternative purpose to which it may rationally be connected is assignable for it; and (7) whether it appears excessive in relation to the alternative purpose assigned.

Hudson v. United States, 522 U.S. 93 (1997).

Hudson itself provides a good example of how this two-part analysis works in practice. Bank executives had been assessed large civil fines and were "debarred" (prohibited) from future participation in federal banking programs, after a federal agency concluded they had violated banking statutes. Later, they were indicted under federal criminal statutes for the same violations, and they moved to dismiss the indictment on double jeopardy grounds. The question was whether the fines and debarment in the first proceeding constituted criminal punishments. After articulating the two-part test described above, the Supreme Court examined the legislative intent underlying the fines and debarment, asking whether Congress, "in establishing the penalizing mechanism, indicated either expressly or impliedly a preference for one label or the other." The Court concluded that Congress intended for the penalties to be civil in nature. It then turned to the second step in the analysis, inquiring whether there was nonetheless "clear proof" that the statute "was so punitive either in purpose or effect, as to transform what was clearly intended as a civil remedy into a criminal penalty." Applying the factors set out above, the Court found a lack of "clear proof" that the fines or debarment were criminal in nature, and it permitted the subsequent criminal indictment to proceed.

There are a few cases in which courts have found "clear proof" that a civil penalty was so punitive as to serve as a criminal one. For example, in *Dye v. Frank*, 355 F.3d 1102 (7th Cir. 2004), a federal appellate court held that the state of Wisconsin could not assess a "drug tax" against a defendant already convicted in Wisconsin state court of drug violations, because the tax constituted a second punishment. The Seventh Circuit said the following as it engaged in the *Hudson* multi-factor analysis:

> [T]he Wisconsin legislature enacted the tax in order to promote the traditional aims of punishment such as retribution and deterrence.... [T]he tax is only applied to behavior that is already a crime. And although the [state] insists that this tax served an alternative revenue-raising purpose, ... the legislature never expected this tax law to raise revenue[;] rather, the legislature's purpose for drafting the original drug stamp tax bill was to learn the identity of drug dealers. A "tax" that is created in order to deter criminal conduct, which applies only to those violating criminal laws, and which serves no revenue-generating purpose is divorced from typical tax assessments and strikes this Court as punitive in nature.
>
> Furthermore, the high tax rate is indicative of criminal punishment rather than revenue-raising goals.... [C]ocaine is "taxed" at $200 per gram. The penalty for not paying the tax as soon as one obtains possession of the drugs is another $200 per gram. Our research indicates that cocaine has a market value of approximately $80 per gram. The tax assessment and penalty therefore total approximately five times the market value of the drugs. A "tax" that is five times the value of the item taxed is remarkably high and is more consistent with punishing ownership of the item than with raising revenue from ownership of

the good. Considering all of these factors, we therefore hold that the Wisconsin drug tax is fairly characterized as a criminal punishment for the purpose of double jeopardy analysis.

There are a few special situations in which proceedings that are technically "non-criminal" have been recognized as being categorically "criminal" in nature for double jeopardy purposes. In these situations, the reviewing court need not engage in the fact-specific *Hudson* analysis. The classic example is juvenile delinquency proceedings. Despite the fact that some states consider these proceedings to be "civil," the Supreme Court has held that they are categorically criminal in nature, at least where they can result in a deprivation of liberty. In *Breed v. Jones*, 421 U.S. 519 (1975), the Court explained that there is "no persuasive distinction ... between [juvenile delinquency proceedings] ... and a criminal prosecution, each of which is designed to vindicate the very vital interest in enforcement of criminal laws."

B. Same Offense: The *Blockburger* Test

Even where the prior and subsequent proceedings satisfy the "criminal case" threshold, double jeopardy is not implicated unless both proceedings involve the "same offense." To determine whether the offenses are the same, courts apply a test articulated in *Blockburger v. United States*, 284 U.S. 299 (1932). The *Blockburger* test compares the offense elements and asks whether each offense contains an element not found in the other. If so, then under the *Blockburger* test the offenses are not the same, leaving the government free to prosecute each one separately. But if all the elements of one offense are found in the other, then the offenses are the same, triggering double jeopardy protection. Because this test often confuses people, it can be described as follows:

§ If only *one* of the offenses contains an element not found in the other, they constitute the "same offense." In that situation, the offense containing the additional element generally is considered the "greater" offense and the other is a "lesser included" offense.

§ If *each* of the offenses contains an element not found in the other, then they do *not* constitute the "same offense."

The following scenario illustrates an application of the *Blockburger* test. Say a defendant is charged with, and convicted of, robbery, which is defined in the jurisdiction as "the taking of money or goods in the possession of another, from his or her person, by force or intimidation." Later, the prosecution discovers that the defendant was carrying a gun during the robbery, and it charges him with armed robbery, which is defined in the jurisdiction as "robbery while armed." Under the *Blockburger* test, robbery and armed robbery are the "same offense" for double jeopardy purposes, because all of the elements of robbery are included within the elements of armed robbery:

Robbery elements	Armed robbery elements
taking	taking
money or goods	money or goods
in the possession of another	in the possession of another
from his or her possession	from his or her possession
by force or intimidation	by force or intimidation
	while armed

As you can see, only the armed robbery offense contains an additional element, and so the *Blockburger* test is satisfied. The armed robbery prosecution would not be able to proceed, because the defendant already was prosecuted for the "lesser included" offense of robbery. On the other hand, if the first prosecution had been for highway robbery, defined as robbery in a public place, then the second prosecution (for armed robbery) could be brought because each offense would contain an element not found in the other ("public place" in the first case and "while armed" in the second). This is true even if both prosecutions involved the same conduct.

The *Blockburger* test has been criticized because it does not protect defendants against multiple prosecutions involving the same conduct, as illustrated in the last example above. At one point, the Supreme Court disavowed it, recognizing in *Grady v. Corbin*, 495 U.S. 508 (1990), a broader analysis, called the "same conduct" test, that would have prohibited the second prosecution in the highway robbery/armed robbery scenario. Within a few years, however, the Court overturned *Grady* and returned to the *Blockburger* test. See *United States v. Dixon*, 509 U.S. 688 (1993). Some states have retained their own double jeopardy protections that duplicate *Dixon* or otherwise reach further than *Blockburger* to prevent multiple prosecutions based on the same conduct.

The Supreme Court has created two exceptions to the *Blockburger* test. The first applies where events taking place after the original conviction change the scope of the defendant's criminal liability. Imagine an incident of reckless driving that results in a severely injured victim who dies years later. Even though the *Blockburger* test would suggest that reckless driving (driving a vehicle recklessly) and vehicular homicide (causing death by driving a vehicle recklessly) are the same offense, an earlier prosecution for reckless driving would not preclude the prosecution from pursuing the homicide charge after the victim dies, because of an exception articulated in *Brown v. Ohio*, 432 U.S. 161 (1977), that applies when the prosecution "is unable to proceed on the more serious charge at the outset because the additional facts necessary to sustain that charge have not occurred or have not been discovered despite the exercise of due diligence."

The Court created a second exception in the felony murder context. In *Harris v. Oklahoma*, 433 U.S. 682 (1977), it held that robbery and felony murder based on robbery were the same offense, despite the fact that each offense, as defined by Oklahoma law, contained an element not found in the other. Felony murder, of course, required a killing—an element not present in the offense of robbery. Robbery required proof of a forcible taking of property—an element not necessarily required by felony murder, which penalizes the causing of a death during the commission of a felony. After the state prosecuted Harris for felony murder, the Court held that double jeopardy barred it from a subsequent prosecution for robbery. The Court explained that, although the felony murder charge did not require proof of forcible taking of property, the actual felony murder case against Harris had been based on a forcible taking.

The Court in *Harris* based its double jeopardy analysis in part on an examination of the prosecution's proof in the first proceeding, as opposed to simply analyzing how the legislature defined the two offenses. It remains to be seen whether, and if so how, the Court will choose between these two different approaches—one focusing purely on elements and the other on the circumstances of the successive prosecutions.

C. Same Sovereign

Defendants will get no relief from multiple prosecutions for the same offense if the sovereigns pursuing those offenses are different. This "dual sovereignty" doctrine, articulated in *United States v. Lanza*, 260 U.S. 377 (1922), permits the federal government, state governments, tribal governments, territorial governments, and foreign governments to prosecute offenses regardless of whether another sovereign has already done so. The doctrine acknowledges that different sovereigns, which derive power from different sources, are entitled to vindicate their separate interests. It also recognizes that "[e]very citizen of the United States is also a citizen of a State or territory. He may be said to owe allegiance to two sovereigns and may be liable to punishment for an infraction of the laws of either." *Abbate v. United States*, 359 U.S. 187 (1959).

An example of the dual sovereignty doctrine at work can be found in *Heath v. Alabama*, 474 U.S. 82 (1985). Larry Heath and his wife lived in Alabama, just a few miles from that state's border with Georgia. Heath contracted in Georgia with two men to kill his pregnant wife, and they apparently carried out the arrangement by kidnapping her in Alabama and transporting her over the state line into Georgia before killing her. After Georgia authorities arrested Heath, he confessed and pleaded guilty to murder in exchange for a sentence of life in prison with the possibility of parole. Three months later, an Alabama grand jury indicted Heath with the capital offense of murder during a kidnapping. Heath's double jeopardy claim was rejected by Alabama state courts, and he was convicted and sentenced to death. The Supreme Court upheld the Alabama judgment, affirming that "successive prosecutions by two States for the same conduct are not barred by the Double Jeopardy Clause" and rejecting Heath's contention that Alabama's interest in prosecuting him had been satisfied by the Georgia prosecution. The Court explained,

> [a] State's interest in vindicating its sovereign authority through enforcement of its laws by definition can never be satisfied by another State's enforcement of its own laws. Just as the Federal Government has the right to decide that a state prosecution has not vindicated a violation of the "peace and dignity" of the Federal Government, a State must be entitled to decide that a prosecution by another State has not satisfied its legitimate sovereign interest. In recognition of this fact, the Court consistently has endorsed the principle that a single act constitutes an "offence" against each sovereign whose laws are violated by that act. The Court has always understood the words of the Double Jeopardy Clause to reflect this fundamental principle.

Alabama executed Larry Heath in 1992.

A key limitation of the dual sovereignty doctrine is found in the fact that local governments, such as counties and municipalities, are not independent sovereigns. Instead, they are political subdivisions of their states. As a result, once a state or one of its subdivisions has prosecuted a defendant, a subsequent prosecution against the defendant for the same offense cannot be brought by that state or any subdivision within it.

The dual sovereignty doctrine is best known for enabling the federal government to use its greater power and resources to pursue defendants who have avoided conviction in state courts. In the Rodney King beating case, for instance, federal prosecutors gained convictions of police officers who, in a previous state court trial, had been acquitted of the beatings. For a detailed explanation of the case, see *Koon v. United States*, 518 U.S. 81 (1996). Although many Americans lauded the doctrine's use in that case, it has been heavily criticized in other situations for enabling government oppression of defendants.

Recognizing the potential for oppression that arises from successive prosecutions by multiple sovereigns, the federal government has adopted a policy that "several offenses arising out of a single transaction should be alleged and tried together and should not be made the basis of multiple prosecutions." *Petite v. United States*, 361 U.S. 529 (1960). Under this policy (known as "the *Petite* policy"), the federal government voluntarily foregoes such prosecutions except in extraordinary cases. But where the federal government decides to exercise its prerogative to bring a successive prosecution, the *Petite* policy does not confer on the defendant the right to seek dismissal of the indictment.

The dual sovereignty doctrine also has been criticized for creating the potential for "sham" prosecutions. In *Bartkus v. Illinois*, 359 U.S. 121 (1959), for instance, a defendant acquitted of bank robbery in federal court claimed that his subsequent prosecution in state court was a pretext that enabled the federal government to gain a second chance to convict him. To bolster his contention, the defendant demonstrated that the Federal Bureau of Investigation had shared all of its evidence with state prosecuting authorities. He was even able to prove that the FBI had continued to investigate him — and to turn evidence over to state prosecutors — *after* the federal acquittal. The Supreme Court was not impressed with this showing, pointing out that it is "conventional practice" for federal and state authorities to cooperate with one another. According to the Court, the record did not "support the claim that the State of Illinois in bringing its prosecution was merely a tool of the federal authorities, who thereby avoided the prohibition of the Fifth Amendment."

D. Defendant Put to Trial or Judgment

The Double Jeopardy Clause is not implicated until, in the first criminal prosecution, the defendant actually is put in jeopardy of conviction. This happens when his or her guilt or innocence is put before a trier of fact. In a case involving a jury trial, jeopardy "attaches" when the jury is empanelled and sworn. This is a bright-line test from which the Court has never varied. See *Martinez v. Illinois*, 134 S. Ct. 2070 (2014). In a non-jury case, jeopardy attaches when the judge begins to hear evidence or accepts a guilty plea. Before that time — before jeopardy attaches — an indictment may be dismissed and refiled without implicating the Double Jeopardy Clause.

Because the typical double jeopardy claim is brought in a motion to dismiss a subsequent case, the question becomes whether jeopardy attached *in the first case*. If jeopardy attached in the first case, and if the other thresholds are met, then the subsequent case usually must be dismissed because it cannot be brought to trial or judgment without violating the defendant's double jeopardy rights.

III. Special Situations

Generally, when a defendant can establish the four thresholds, double jeopardy will prevent a subsequent prosecution. There are a few situations, however, in which this general rule does not apply. Each of these is discussed below.

A. Government Denied One Complete Chance to Convict

The government must be given one complete chance to bring the defendant to judgment. Double jeopardy will not bar subsequent prosecution when the government was prevented from bringing the defendant to judgment in the previous case through no fault of its own. There are several ways in which the government might be denied the chance of conviction.

1. Dismissals and Mistrials at Defendant's Request

Sometimes a case is dismissed or a mistrial is declared before judgment but after jeopardy attaches. If the action (a) comes at the defendant's request, (b) was not required because of government bad faith, or (c) was ordered for reasons other than the sufficiency of the evidence, the government typically will be permitted to prosecute again. Dismissals or mistrials in this context often involve pretrial problems, such as defects in the indictment or pretrial delay, that are raised and decided after jeopardy attached. Examples of these will be given below.

a. Pretrial Issues

In *Lee v. United States*, 432 U.S. 23 (1977), the Court found no double jeopardy violation when the government embarked on a subsequent prosecution of Lee. A trial court had dismissed the first case against him, at the close of evidence at trial, on the ground that the indictment was defective. The Court reasoned that the dismissal was at the defendant's request and did not involve a determination on the merits.

In *United States v. Scott*, 437 U.S. 82 (1978), the dismissal was a result of pretrial delay. The defendant was charged with three counts of illegal drug distribution, and he moved to dismiss the first and second counts on the ground of the delay. The trial court did not rule on the dismissal motion until after the close of the evidence at trial. At that time, it dismissed the first two counts, because it determined that the pretrial delay on those counts had prejudiced the defendant's opportunity to adequately defend himself at trial. The third count was given to the jury, which acquitted. When the government appealed the dismissal of the first two counts, the defendant claimed the appeal violated his double jeopardy rights because it put him in danger of a retrial. The Supreme Court permitted the appeal to go forward, saying that "in a case such as this the defendant, by deliberately choosing to seek termination of the proceedings against him on a basis unrelated to factual guilt or innocence of the offense of which he is accused, suffers no injury cognizable under the Double Jeopardy Clause if the Government is permitted to appeal from such a ruling ... [T]he Double Jeopardy Clause, which guards against Government oppression, does not relieve a defendant from the consequences of his voluntary choice."

b. Trial Issues

When events take place at trial that cause the defendant to move for a mistrial—in other words, a dismissal because of trial error that could prejudice the factfinder—double jeopardy does not prevent a retrial unless the prosecution "goaded" the defendant into the motion by engaging in conduct intended to provoke a mistrial request. Without evidence of goading, a defendant's mistrial motion will be considered "a deliberate election on his part to forgo his valued right to have his guilt or innocence determined before the first trier of fact," and double jeopardy will not bar the prosecution from bringing the defendant to trial again. *Oregon v. Kennedy*, 456 U.S. 667 (1982).

In *Kennedy*, the defendant's mistrial motion was motivated by the prosecution's suggestion, in a question directed at its witness, that the defendant was a "crook." The defendant, charged with theft of an oriental rug, had attempted during cross-examination to establish that the witness, an oriental rug expert, was biased against him, by eliciting that the witness once had filed a criminal complaint against him. During its redirect questioning, the government attempted to explain the reasons for the witness's decision to file the complaint, but it was prevented from doing so by the defendant's objections. Finally, this exchange took place:

> Prosecutor: Have you ever done business with the Kennedys?
> Witness: No, I have not.
> Prosecutor: Is that because he is a crook?

At this, the defendant moved for a mistrial, apparently reasoning that the jury would be prejudiced by the suggestion. The trial court granted the motion. When the state attempted to retry him, the defendant claimed a double jeopardy violation, but the trial court found that "it was not the intention of the prosecution in this case to cause a mistrial." That finding, said the Supreme

Court, insulated the mistrial from double jeopardy implications and rendered the prosecution free to bring the defendant to trial again.

c. Distinguishing Dismissals from Rulings on Sufficiency

In either of these dismissal contexts, it can be difficult to distinguish between judicial determinations on the sufficiency of the evidence (which constitute acquittals, thereby implicating double jeopardy) from dismissals on other grounds (which do not). The form of the judge's action is not controlling. Where the record is unclear, the key is to look for indications that the trial court's decision "represents a resolution of some or all of the factual elements of the offense charged." See *United States v. Martin Linen*, 430 U.S. 564 (1977). As the Court explained in *Martinez v. Illinois*, an acquittal encompasses "any ruling that the prosecution's proof is insufficient to establish criminal liability for an offense." Even if the trial court erred in granting an acquittal, double jeopardy bars retrial. See *Evans v. Michigan*, 133 S. Ct. 1069 (2013). In *Evans*, the trial court granted an arson defendant's motion for judgment of acquittal because the prosecution had failed to establish that the building he had allegedly burned was not a dwelling house (arson of a dwelling would have been charged under a different statute). On appeal, it became clear that under state law, the prosecution was not required to establish the nature of the building. Nevertheless, the Court reversed *Evans*'s conviction, reiterating a statement it had made in several previous cases: "a mistaken acquittal is an acquittal nonetheless." In response to the state's argument that such a rule creates windfalls for defendants, the Court observed that states are free to deny to trial courts the power to grant midtrial acquittals. States can require trials to continue through to verdict, and if a jury verdict of guilty is returned, it can be reinstated if the judge's acquittal is found to be erroneous. Reinstating a jury verdict does not implicate double jeopardy, as is discussed in Part B. on p. 336.

2. Dismissals and Mistrials Not at Defendant's Request: Manifest Necessity

In some cases, events at trial may cause either the prosecution to move for dismissal or mistrial, or the trial court to dismiss or declare a mistrial even though the defendant did not move for such relief. These cases require a different double jeopardy analysis, because they do not involve the defendant's "deliberate election ... to forgo his valued right to have his guilt or innocence determined before the first trier of fact." Instead, they invoke the interest of the public in fair trials and just judgments, and they require courts to inquire whether "there is a manifest necessity for the mistrial, or the ends of public justice would otherwise be defeated." *United States v. Dinitz*, 424 U.S. 600

(1976). This test accords discretion to the trial court to evaluate all of the cir-cumstances and balance the defendant's right to a determination by the first trier of fact against the public's interest in justice. Where justice cannot be attained without discontinuing the trial, the trial court may declare dismissal or mis-trial, and the defendant may be retried without violating the Double Jeopardy Clause.

In *Illinois v. Somerville*, 410 U.S. 458 (1973), the Supreme Court permitted a second prosecution of Donald Somerville when a trial court declared a mis-trial, at the prosecution's request, after the first day of trial. The prosecution moved for the mistrial after the jury was sworn (recall that this event marks the attachment of jeopardy), because it realized only at that time that the indict-ment was fatally deficient. Under Illinois law, the prosecution could not amend the indictment. Instead, it was required to go back to the grand jury for a new indictment—a procedure that required dismissal of the original charges. After the trial court granted the prosecution's motion for a mistrial, a new indictment was obtained and Somerville was brought to trial again and convicted. He raised his double jeopardy claim in a habeas corpus action. The Supreme Court found no double jeopardy violation, emphasizing that the trial court was in the best po-sition to determine whether "manifest necessity" existed. While it eschewed cat-egorical rules, it suggested a "general approach" to the manifest necessity question:

> While virtually all of the cases turn on the particular facts and thus es-cape meaningful categorization, it is possible to distill from them a gen-eral approach, premised on the public justice policy ... to situations such as that presented by this case. A trial judge properly exercises his discretion to declare a mistrial if an impartial verdict cannot be reached, or if a verdict of conviction could be reached but would have to be re-versed on appeal due to an obvious procedural error in the trial. If an error would make reversal on appeal a certainty, it would not serve the ends of public justice to require that the Government proceed with its proof when, if it succeeded before the jury, it would automatically be stripped of that success by an appellate court. While the declaration of a mistrial on the basis of a rule or a defective procedure that would lend itself to prosecutorial manipulation would involve an entirely different question, such was not the situation ... in the instant case.

If the prosecution appears to be manipulating the situation to its advan-tage, then a trial court's "manifest necessity" finding may be overturned. For example, in *Downum v. United States*, 372 U.S. 734 (1963), the Court held a second prosecution barred when a trial court granted a mistrial at the prose-cution's request because its primary witness was missing. The motion occurred after the jury was sworn, and the record established that "[t]he prosecution knew, prior to the selection and swearing of the jury, that this witness could not be found and had not been served with a subpoena." Similarly, in *Martinez v. Illinois*, the Court observed that the absence of witnesses "generally does not constitute the kind of extraordinary and striking circumstance in which a trial court may exercise discretion to discharge the jury before it has reached a verdict."

3. Hung Juries

"Hung juries" and "deadlocked juries" involve a special mistrial rule. These terms refer to juries that cannot agree on verdicts of acquittal or conviction. Typically in this situation, a judge will not declare a mistrial unless he or she has asked the jury at least once to try to reach agreement in good faith. If the jury is unable to do so, a mistrial may be declared and the defendant tried anew without violating the Double Jeopardy Clause. The hung jury rule is a categorical one—there is no need for the court to question whether "manifest necessity" exists. As the Supreme Court has stated, "we have constantly adhered to the rule that a retrial following a 'hung jury' does not violate the Double Jeopardy Clause.... This rule accords recognition to society's interest in giving the prosecution one complete opportunity to convict those who have violated its laws." *Richardson v. United States*, 468 U.S. 317 (1984).

B. Appeals

When, at a defendant's request, a reviewing court reverses a conviction because of procedural errors during trial, double jeopardy does not prevent the government from retrying the defendant on all counts of conviction from which he appealed. This is because the appeal constitutes the defendant's waiver of his double jeopardy right as to those counts.

There are two important limitations to this rule, however. The first applies to the situation in which a defendant is charged with a greater offense (murder, for example) but convicted only of a lesser included offense (say, manslaughter). If the defendant successfully appeals the lesser offense conviction because of trial errors, the government must limit its reprosecution to that lesser offense if the jury expressly or implicitly acquitted on the greater offense. Express acquittal on the greater offense takes place where a jury reports "not guilty" on the verdict form as to the greater offense and "guilty" on the verdict form as to the lesser. Sometimes juries simply indicate "guilty" as to the lesser offense and are silent as to the greater. These situations create an implied acquittal on the greater offense. See *Green v. United States*, 355 U.S. 184 (1957); *Price v. Geor-*

gia, 398 U.S. 323 (1970). But if the jury is hung and returns no formal verdict, the "implied acquittal" doctrine is not available to prevent retrial on all counts, even if the jury reported in court that it did not believe the defendant to be guilty of the greater offense. This is because the jury's report is not a verdict and does not enjoy the "finality necessary to constitute an acquittal." *Blueford v. Arkansas*, 132 S. Ct. 2044 (2012).

The second limitation to the rule that permits retrials after successful defense appeals is this: The government cannot reprosecute the defendant if the appellate court reverses a conviction on the ground that the government's evidence was insufficient to constitute proof beyond a reasonable doubt. This is because the appellate court's finding constitutes an acquittal—a judgment on the evidence—that must be given the same finality as a judgment emanating from a trial jury or judge. *Burks v. United States*, 437 U.S. 1 (1978).

So far we have been talking about appeals brought by defendants. What about appeals by the government? Ordinarily, the Double Jeopardy Clause does not permit government appeals, because these would threaten to put the defendant in jeopardy again. There are a few exceptions. The government may appeal pre-trial decisions, because jeopardy has not yet attached. And, as discussed above, there are situations in which the government may appeal from decisions during trial that have the effect of denying it the opportunity to have one complete chance to convict. Finally, the government may appeal if doing so does not threaten the defendant with another round of jeopardy. This situation can arise in a jury trial if the jury votes to convict but the trial judge issues a judgment of acquittal. In this situation, the government is permitted to appeal the judgment of acquittal, because if it is overturned, the jury's conviction can be reinstated without putting the defendant through a second trial. Note, however, that if a judge orders an acquittal and there is no jury verdict of conviction to fall back on, the government cannot appeal even if the judge's order is "egregiously erroneous." *Fong Foo v. United States*, 369 U.S. 141 (1969).

Appeals by the government are limited by statute as well as by the Constitution. Many such federal and state statutes specify that the government may not appeal once the defendant has been put in jeopardy. For example, the federal Criminal Appeals Act, 18 U.S.C. section 3731, provides,

> [i]n a criminal case an appeal by the United States shall lie to a court of appeals from a decision, judgment, or order of a district court dismissing an indictment or information or granting a new trial after verdict or judgment, as to any one or more counts, or any part thereof, except that no appeal shall lie where the Double Jeopardy Clause of the United States Constitution prohibits further prosecution.

IV. Multiple Punishments for the Same Offense in the Same Proceeding

When the government seeks multiple punishments for the same offense in the same proceeding, the Double Jeopardy Clause affords reduced protection. In this situation, courts must defer to legislative intent. If the court determines that the legislature intended to create multiple punishments for the same offense, then the Double Jeopardy Clause is not violated.

The Supreme Court announced this approach in *Missouri v. Hunter*, 459 U.S. 359 (1983), and the facts of that case are helpful to understanding the rule. Hunter was arrested for robbing a grocery store at gunpoint. He was charged, convicted, and sentenced under Missouri statutes that criminalize both "armed robbery" and "armed criminal action." He appealed on double jeopardy grounds. By the time the case reached the Supreme Court, Missouri state courts already had determined that the two offenses constituted the "same offense" for double jeopardy purposes. They also had determined that the Missouri legislature had intended to create two separate punishments for the offenses. The Supreme Court upheld the punishments, explaining that,

> [t]he Double Jeopardy Clause is cast explicitly in terms of being "twice put in jeopardy." We have consistently interpreted it to protect an individual from being subjected to the hazards of trial and possible conviction more than once for an alleged offense. Because respondent has been subjected to only one trial, it is not contended that his right to be free from multiple trials for the same offense has been violated. Rather, the Missouri court vacated respondent's conviction for armed criminal action because of the statements of this Court that the Double Jeopardy Clause also protects against multiple punishments for the same offense ... [I]t is clear that the Missouri Supreme Court has misperceived the nature of the Double Jeopardy Clause's protection against multiple punishments. With respect to cumulative sentences imposed in a single trial, the Double Jeopardy Clause does no more than prevent the sentencing court from prescribing greater punishment than the legislature intended.

In other words, so long as a legislature intends to punish defendants separately—even cumulatively—for the same offense, it may do so. The courts' only role is to ensure that it is following legislative intent.

There has been much discussion about the *Hunter* rule. Some have criticized it, questioning the meaning of a constitutional guarantee whose limits do not apply to legislatures. Others have supported the rule, pointing out that the legislative branch has virtually free rein to create criminal punishments, subject only to the 8th Amendment's cruel and unusual punishments clause.

V. Collateral Estoppel

From courses in civil procedure, you may recall learning about the doctrine of collateral estoppel, also known as "issue preclusion." The doctrine prevents the re-litigation of any issue of ultimate fact that has already been determined with finality in a previous lawsuit involving the same parties. Collateral estoppel rarely crops up in criminal cases, but when it does, it implicates the Double Jeopardy Clause. According to the Supreme Court in *Ashe v. Swenson*, 397 U.S. 436 (1970), the Double Jeopardy Clause prevents the government from retrying a defendant on an issue that a previous trier of fact has already decided in the defendant's favor.

The rule is best understood by studying the facts of *Ashe* itself. There, Bob Ashe was alleged to have been one of "three or four" masked men who robbed six poker players at gunpoint. He was charged with a separate robbery offense for each of the six victims, and the prosecution first brought him to trial on a count involving victim Knight. The only issue at trial was whether Ashe had been one of the robbers, and the prosecution's identification evidence was weak. After the jury acquitted Ashe, the prosecution brought him to trial six weeks later, this time on a count involving another victim. The state had re-fined and strengthened its identification evidence, and Ashe was convicted. Ashe's appeal on collateral estoppel grounds required him to establish that the first jury had acquitted him after determining an issue of ultimate fact — whether he was one of the robbers. The jury's acquittal, he argued, indicated that the prosecution had failed to prove that fact. The argument was challenging because the verdict of acquittal, like most criminal verdicts, was a "general" one — it did not identify particular issues that the jury considered or findings that it made. Given the circumstances of the case, however, the Supreme Court was able to conclude that the jury indeed had found the prosecution's identification evidence lacking. There simply was no other issue on which the jury could have based its acquittal, and because the issue had already been decided in Ashe's favor, the Double Jeopardy Clause prohibited re-litigation before another trier of fact.

Claims of collateral estoppel involve reviewing courts with a highly fact-specific task. In the words of the *Ashe* decision, they must "examine the record of a prior proceeding, taking into account the pleadings, evidence, charge, and other relevant matter, and conclude whether a rational jury could have grounded

its verdict upon an issue other than that which the defendant seeks to foreclose from consideration."

A recent illustration of the complexity of these inquiries can be found in
Yeager v. United States, 557 U.S. 110 (2009). Yeager was a senior Enron executive when the company inflated the value of its stock by falsely touting the success of one of its fiber-optic ventures. During this time, Yeager sold massive
amounts of his own Enron shares. He claimed that he did not know that the
fiber-optics venture was riddled with problems. Nevertheless he was prosecuted
for securities fraud ("knowingly and willfully participat[ing] ... in a scheme to
defraud in connection with ... false statements or material omissions") and insider trading (selling shares "while in the possession of material non-public information"). After a 13-week trial and lengthy jury deliberations, a jury acquitted
him on the fraud counts, but was unable to reach a verdict on the insider trading counts. The court declared a mistrial with respect to the latter counts. The
government reinitiated proceedings against Yeager on the "mistried" insider
trading counts. Claiming collateral estoppel, Yeager moved to dismiss, arguing that the jury's acquittals on the fraud counts meant it had necessarily found
that he did not possess "material non-public [insider] information" (in other
words, that he did not know about the fiber-optic problems)—an ultimate fact
that the government would have to prove in order to convict him on the insider trading counts. Evaluating Yeager's dismissal motion, the district court
and court of appeals disagreed on what the jury necessarily found:

> • The district court rebuffed Yeager's claim, holding the jury had nec-
> essarily found only that Yeager did not knowingly participate in a scheme
> to defraud. Because the jury had not necessarily resolved the issue of his
> possession of insider information, the district court determined that
> the second prosecution did not implicate Double Jeopardy protections.
> • The court of appeals felt the jury's acquittals meant that it had nec-
> essarily found that Yeager lacked insider information. But the fact that
> the jury could not agreed to acquit on the insider trading counts was
> problematic to the court because a rational jury, having concluded
> the Yeager did not possess insider information, would have acquitted
> him on the insider trading counts as well as the securities fraud counts.
> The inconsistency in the jury's actions left the court of appeals un-
> able "to decide with any certainty what the jury necessarily deter-
> mined." As a result, it affirmed the district court despite the
> disagreement between the two courts about the jury's findings.

The Supreme Court granted review on the question of "whether an apparent
inconsistency between a jury's verdict of acquittal on some counts and its fail-

ure to return a verdict on other counts affects the preclusive force of the acquittals under the Double Jeopardy Clause of the Fifth Amendment." The Court answered the question in the negative, holding that the hung counts should not have been considered in the collateral estoppel analysis:

A hung count is not a "relevant" part of the record of the prior proceeding. Because a jury speaks only through its verdict, its failure to reach a verdict cannot—by negative implication—yield a piece of information that helps put together the trial puzzle. A mistried count is therefore nothing like the other forms of record material that *Ashe* suggested should be part of the preclusion inquiry. Unlike the pleadings, the jury charge, or the evidence introduced by the parties, there is no way to decipher what a hung count represents. Even in the usual sense of "relevance," a hung count hardly makes the existence of any fact more probable or less probable. A host of reasons—sharp disagreement, confusion about the issues, exhaustion after a long trial, to name but a few—could work alone or in tandem to cause a jury to hang. To ascribe meaning to a hung count would presume an ability to identify which factor was at play in the jury room. But that is not reasoned analysis; it is guesswork. Such conjecture about possible reasons for a jury's failure to reach a decision should play no part in assessing the legal consequences of a unanimous verdict that the jurors did return.

Despite the clarification in *Yeager* about the irrelevance of hung juries, in many situations, it will still be impossible for a reviewing court to discern whether a jury's verdict necessarily meant that it determined a particular fact. In those situations the Double Jeopardy Clause will not bar the subsequent prosecution.

Collateral estoppel is rarely raised in criminal cases, and is even more rarely raised successfully. Nevertheless, it plays an important role in prosecutorial charging and trial decisions. These decisions involve the concept of joinder, discussed in Chapter 4.

Checkpoints

- The Double Jeopardy Clause has applicability to multiple prosecutions after acquittal or conviction and to multiple punishments.

- The goal of the clause is to prevent government manipulation and oppression, and it restricts the government to one complete chance to convict and punish a defendant.

- The Double Jeopardy Clause creates fundamental liberties and is incorporated through the Fourteenth Amendment to the states.

- Double jeopardy typically is raised when a second proceeding is initiated, and it requires an inquiry into the first proceeding.

- Double jeopardy does not apply unless the defendant establishes four thresholds:

  - The pertinent proceedings are criminal ones;

  - The offenses involved are determined to be the "same offense," using the *Blockburger* test;

  - The proceedings have been brought by the same sovereign; and

  - Jeopardy attached in the first proceeding.

- The government has "one complete chance to convict," which means that dismissals and mistrials sometimes do not prevent it from re-prosecuting the defendant.

- If the defendant moves for dismissal or mistrial, re-prosecution is permitted unless either the government "goaded" the defendant into making the request or the dismissal or mistrial was based on sufficiency of the evidence.

- If the government moves for dismissal or mistrial, or if the court dismisses or declares a mistrial of its own accord, the "manifest necessity" standard applies.

- Hung juries do not prevent reprosecution.

- A successful appeal by a defendant does not prevent re-prosecution unless the appellate court made a determination on the sufficiency of evidence.

- Typically double jeopardy bars the government from appealing, but it may do so if success on appeal would not require another trial.

- The multiple punishments prong of the Double Jeopardy Clause prevents multiple punishments in the same proceeding only if the legislature did not intend to create multiple punishments.

- The Double Jeopardy Clause has collateral estoppel implications that prohibit the government from retrying a defendant on an issue of fact that already has been determined in defendant's favor by a trier of fact.

Challenging a Conviction

I. Introduction

A defendant convicted of a crime, whether by a verdict or guilty plea, can question how the court resolved a number of issues that arose in the case, such as police actions during the investigation, improprieties in a search warrant or execution of an arrest, and the conduct of the trial or plea proceeding, including sentencing. There are numerous grounds for challenging a conviction and sentence, and the customary remedy granted for a violation of the defendant's rights is a new trial or other proceeding in which the harmful effects of the violation will not be felt. Even if there is a violation of a defendant's rights, however, a court may conclude that the error was "harmless" and provide no relief.

For a few specified types of violations, such as the speedy trial right, a court will reverse a conviction and prohibit a retrial on the charges or bar a prosecution from proceeding further. Similarly, if the government did not introduce sufficient evidence to establish every element of the offense beyond a reasonable doubt, then an appellate court must reverse the conviction and direct that no further proceedings occur under the Double Jeopardy Clause.

Appealing a decision of the trial court must await a conviction and entry of a final judgment, which usually occurs after sentencing. If the defendant is acquitted, there can be no appeal by the prosecution because that would threaten a defendant's double jeopardy right (see Chapter 15). Pursuant to the *collat-*

eral order doctrine, there are only a few orders of the trial court that can be appealed immediately because they are "too important to be denied review and too independent of the cause itself to require that appellate consideration be deferred until the whole case is adjudicated." *Cohen v. Beneficial Industrial Loan Corp.,* 337 U.S. 541 (1949).

Under the common law, there was no guaranteed right to appeal a criminal conviction, and the Constitution does not furnish such a protection to a defendant. In *McKane v. Durston,* 153 U.S. 684 (1894), the Supreme Court stated:

> A review by an appellate court of the final judgment in a criminal case, however grave the offense of which the accused is convicted, was not at common law, and is not now, a necessary element of due process of law. It is wholly within the discretion of the state to allow or not to allow such a review.

That said, every state and the federal government provides a defendant with at least one appeal *as of right,* which means the defendant may exercise the right to appeal without having to request the appellate court to review the case. Thus, the Supreme Court has not had to confront its holding in *McKane v. Durston,* which was decided long before the extension of many protections for criminal defendants under the Due Process Clause.

II. Trial Court Review

A defendant may request that a court grant a new trial if required due to an error in the proceeding. This is based on the traditional principle that a trial court has broad authority to grant a new trial if it concludes that there was a miscarriage of justice that led to the guilty verdict. A new trial cannot be ordered if a defendant is acquitted of a charge. In almost every state, and the federal system, the burden is on the defendant to establish grounds for a new trial, at least if it is based on a non-constitutional error, such as the erroneous admission of evidence.

A motion for a new trial is usually filed with the judge who presided over the initial proceeding that led to the conviction — because that person has the best understanding of the case and can evaluate the claims of error and their effect, if any, on the verdict. Under Federal Rule of Criminal Procedure 29, a defendant can move for a judgment of acquittal or, in the alternative, a new trial after a conviction. The judge usually rules on the acquittal motion first, and then decides the new trial motion. If the acquittal motion is denied but the new trial motion granted, then the case proceeds to the subsequent trial.

A federal statute, 18 U.S.C. § 3731, authorizes the federal government to appeal a decision dismissing charges or granting a new trial, so long as the appeal does not violate a defendant's double jeopardy rights. A successful appeal merely reinstates the original verdict and does not subject a person to an impermissible second proceeding under the Double Jeopardy Clause. The statute provides:

> In a criminal case an appeal by the United States shall lie to a court of appeals from a decision, judgment, or order of a district court dismissing an indictment or information or granting a new trial after verdict or judgment, as to any one or more counts, or any part thereof, except that no appeal shall lie where the double jeopardy clause of the United States Constitution prohibits further prosecution.

A. Newly-Discovered Evidence

A common justification for seeking a new trial is on the basis of newly-discovered evidence. A number of high profile exonerations based on DNA evidence are examples of claims raised years after the original conviction that seek to reverse a verdict and have a second chance to gain an acquittal. As a general matter, however, courts are hostile to claims of newly-discovered evidence. The general skepticism about such claims is particularly evident in cases involving non-scientific evidence, such as the discovery of a new witness or the recantation of testimony by an important witness for the prosecution.

A motion based on newly-discovered evidence generally must meet the following requirements, known as the *Berry* test (*Berry v. Georgia*, 10 Ga. 511 (Ga. 1851)):

- That the evidence is newly discovered and was unknown to the defendant at the time of trial;
- That the evidence is material and not just impeachment evidence of a witness;
- That the evidence is likely to produce an acquittal; and
- That failure to learn of the evidence was not because of a lack of diligence by the defendant and his counsel.

Motions for a new trial are subject to severe time restrictions and deferential standards of appellate review. Federal Rule of Criminal Procedure 33(b)(1) requires the motion to be filed within three years of the guilty verdict, otherwise the defendant can only avail himself of collateral procedures to challenge a conviction (see Chapter 17). While a few states do not have time limits to move for a new trial, most require the motion be filed within one to three years of the conviction, and a few mandate the claim be filed within as little as 60 days from the conclusion of the prosecution. In *Herrera v. Collins*, 506 U.S. 390 (1993), the Supreme Court stated "we cannot say that Texas' refusal to entertain petitioner's newly discovered evidence eight years after his conviction transgresses a principle of fundamental fairness rooted in the traditions and conscience of our people."

The justifications for these restrictive rules for allowing a new trial motion on the basis of recently obtained evidence are (1) the need for verdict finality and (2) the efficiency of the judicial system that cannot allow for verdicts to be regularly challenged months (or years) after the end of the trial. It is often the case that memories will have faded and evidence may no longer be available if a new proceeding were ordered. In *Herrera*, the Court rejected a claim that denial of any right to seek a new trial based on a claim of actual innocence in a death penalty case was unconstitutional, stating:

> [B]ecause of the very disruptive effect that entertaining claims of actual innocence would have on the need for finality in capital cases, and the enormous burden that having to retry cases based on often stale evidence would place on the States, the threshold showing for such an assumed right would necessarily be extraordinarily high.

B. DNA Testing

A majority of the states allow prisoners access to DNA evidence so that independent tests can be performed to determine whether they are innocent of the crime for which they were convicted. The statutes have two basic components: (1) requirements regarding what the prisoner must prove about the state of the evidence and establishing the proper chain of custody; and (2) requirements that the prisoner show that a favorable result will follow from access to the DNA. If the prisoner meets these two criteria, then there is a right to access the DNA evidence for use in scientific testing. Many states limit access to DNA evidence to cases in which identity was an issue in the trial, so the scientific testing can reasonably be expected to exonerate the defendant. If the testing shows the defendant is not tied to the DNA, then there is provided a procedure for having the conviction overturned.

III. Appeals

While there is no constitutional right to appeal, at least one level of appellate review is available in every state and at the federal level. Most states have a two-tier appellate system. The first appeal is *as of right*, sometimes called a first-tier appeal, which means the defendant need not seek the permission of a court to have the case reviewed. Three states do not furnish an automatic right to appellate review in criminal cases, but do provide significant procedural safeguards that virtually guarantee an appeal, at least after a trial. A *discretionary appeal* is one in which the appellate court chooses whether to consider the case on the merits, and it can limit the appeal to certain specified issues. The Supreme Court and the highest court in the states generally exercise discretionary review of cases, except in limited circumstances, such as death penalty cases in which an automatic appeal is available.

A defendant normally must wait until the judgment of conviction is final, which usually takes place after sentencing and the trial court's rulings on any post-verdict motions, such as requests for a new trial or a judgment of acquittal. Some states limit the right to appeal after a guilty *plea* by providing only discretionary review rather than an appeal as of right. In addition, courts have upheld provisions in plea agreements waiving the right to appeal the conviction or sentence, although a claim that the waiver was not knowing, intelligent, and voluntary may invalidate such a provision.

In death penalty cases, most states provide an automatic appeal to the highest appellate court in the state, while some provide it to an intermediate appellate court. Federal death penalty cases are first appealed to the appropriate federal circuit court of appeals. For some minor offenses, the appeal is to a higher-level trial court, which may conduct a *de novo* trial.

A. Grounds for an Appeal

1. Identifying Objections

Appellate courts, by rule or judicial precedent, require that a defendant identify for the trial court any ruling or action that is a violation of the rules or a defendant's rights, and provide the basis for the objection, in order to have the issue considered on appeal. Federal Rule of Criminal Procedure 51(b) provides:

> A party may preserve a claim of error by informing the court—when the court ruling or order is made or sought—of the action the party wishes the court to take, or the party's objection to the court's action and the grounds for that objection. If a party does not have an opportunity to object to a ruling or order, the absence of an objection does not later prejudice that party.

The objection can be raised in different ways, such as by submitting a motion to the court, lodging an oral objection on the record, or seeking reconsideration of a decision. Under the older common law rules, a party had to note an "exception" for the record to preserve the issue for appeal, but that requirement has been dropped in most jurisdictions.

The Supreme Court explained in *Puckett v. United States*, 556 U.S. 129 (2009), that the rationale for requiring an objection is to prevent "a litigant from 'sandbagging' the court—remaining silent about his objection and belatedly raising the error only if the case does not conclude in his favor." Failure to bring an objection to the trial court's attention ordinarily bars appellate review of the issue on a subsequent motion or on appeal, unless the problem amounts to *plain error*. The issue of preserving a claim of error for subsequent review arises most frequently in connection with objections to a ruling under the evidence rules and claims of improper argument or questioning of a witness.

2. Interlocutory Appeals

In federal cases, the Supreme Court ruled that appellate review was only available upon the entry of a final judgment unless the issue comes within the *collateral order doctrine*. In *Cohen v. Beneficial Industrial Loan Corp.*, 337 U.S. 541 (1949), the Court held that an appeal of a non-final judgment was permissible only for those issues which "finally determine claims of right separable from, and collateral to, rights asserted in the action, too important to be denied review and too independent of the cause itself to require that appellate consideration be deferred until the whole case is adjudicated." This is called an *interlocutory appeal*, and in criminal prosecutions the Court has allowed appeals before a final judgment of conviction for the following constitutional issues:

- A motion to dismiss for a violation of the Double Jeopardy Clause (*Abney v. United States*, 431 U.S. 651 (1977));
- A claim of a violation of the Excessive Bail Clause (*Stack v. Boyle*, 342 U.S. 1 (1951)); and
- A motion to dismiss for a violation of the Speech or Debate Clause (*Helstoski v. Meanor*, 442 U.S. 500 (1979)).

A number of states allow interlocutory appeals for specified issues, such as jury instructions or a decision whether the judge should recuse himself or herself from the proceeding. In addition, the government can appeal an order suppressing evidence if it would seriously hamper the successful prosecution of the defendant because that decision could not be appealed under the Double Jeopardy Clause if the defendant were acquitted of the charge. 18 U.S.C. §3731.

3. The Appellate Process

Once the trial court enters a final judgment of conviction, then the defendant can file a notice of appeal and pursue review of any claimed errors in the proceeding. Even if a defendant pleads guilty, there is a right to seek review of any errors in the plea or sentencing proceedings, although prosecutors frequently include a waiver of the right to appeal in the plea agreement. In some cases, a defendant enters a *conditional plea*, reserving the right to challenge a pre-trial ruling in the case, such as the denial of a motion to suppress evidence.

For certain minor offenses tried in a low-level court, sometimes referred to as a district or magistrate court, the state may allow for a trial *de novo* before a higher court, such as a circuit court, as the means of appealing an adverse decision. In that circumstance, the higher court conducts a completely new trial, and the outcome of the prior proceeding will not affect the outcome of the second prosecution. In rejecting a claim that the second trial violated a defendant's double jeopardy rights, the Supreme Court held in *Justices of Boston Municipal Court v. Lydon*, 466 U.S. 294 (1984):

> Although admittedly the Commonwealth at the de novo trial will have the benefit of having seen the defense, the defendant likewise will have had the opportunity to assess the prosecution's case. Because in most cases the judge presiding at the bench trial can be expected to acquit a defendant when legally insufficient evidence has been presented, it is clear that the system provides substantial benefits to defendants, as well as to the Commonwealth.

B. Right to Counsel

The Supreme Court's holding in *McKane v. Durston* that the states are not obligated to provide appellate review of a conviction means the Sixth Amendment right to counsel does not apply at that stage of the case. If a state does grant a first appeal as of right, then, under the Due Process and Equal Protection Clauses, it must provide counsel for an indigent defendant.

The Court first confronted the issue of what rights an indigent defendant has on appeal in *Griffin v. Illinois*, 351 U.S. 12 (1956). It held that when a state conditions the opportunity to pursue an appeal on a party submitting a trial transcript, then it must provide an indigent defendant with a free transcript. The Court stated, "There can be no equal justice where the kind of trial a man gets depends on the amount of money he has. Destitute defendants must be afforded as adequate appellate review as defendants who have money enough to buy transcripts."

In *Douglas v. California*, 372 U.S. 353 (1963), the Court extended *Griffin* in holding that for an appeal as of right the state must appoint counsel for an indigent defendant seeking review of a conviction. It stated that "where the merits of the one and only appeal an indigent has as of right are decided without benefit of counsel, we think an unconstitutional line has been drawn between rich and poor."

For discretionary appeals, the Court took a different approach and held in *Ross v. Moffitt*, 417 U.S. 600 (1974), that appointed counsel was not required. The defendant was represented on his first appeal as of right by appointed counsel, and the Court explained

> [t]he duty of the State under our cases is not to duplicate the legal arsenal that may be privately retained by a criminal defendant in a continuing effort to reverse his conviction, but only to assure the indigent defendant an adequate opportunity to present his claims fairly in the context of the State's appellate process.

Appeals to the Supreme Court, and the highest courts of most states, are discretionary, and these courts only review a small fraction of the cases it receives. Similarly, a collateral attack on a conviction, such as a habeas corpus petition (see Chapter 17), is discretionary. Therefore, counsel need not be provided to an indigent defendant—although a person is free to retain private counsel and in some instances the court will appoint counsel.

In *Halbert v. Michigan*, 545 U.S. 605 (2005), the Court applied *Douglas* rather than *Ross* to invalidate a state's procedure that denied indigent defendants who entered guilty pleas the right to appointed counsel to challenge the plea in the court of appeals. The Court found that because the appellate court considered the merits of the underlying claim and indigent defendants "are generally ill-equipped to represent themselves," the appeal was the type of "first-tier" proceeding that required the appointment of counsel.

C. Death Penalty Appeals

When a death sentence is given, most states provide for a direct appeal as of right to the highest court to review any claims of error. For example, the California state constitution provides, "The Supreme Court has appellate jurisdiction when judgment of death has been pronounced." CAL. CONST. art. 6, § 11(a). Under the federal death penalty statute, the circuit court of appeals reviews the sentence, similar to the process for appeals in other cases. For defendants sentenced to death in state court prosecutions, federal law provides for the appointment of counsel in a clemency proceeding and collateral attack on the sentence in federal court. 18 U.S.C. § 3599(a)(2).

Most direct death penalty appeals are *automatic*, although the federal statute does not require appellate review of the sentence. When an appeal is required, the appropriate court will review the case without the defendant having to seek consideration. Although there are cases in which a defendant waived the right to direct appeal of a death sentence, the courts usually review the record of the case even when the defendant does not want the appeal to go forward to ensure there was no serious error that affected the proceeding.

IV. Harmless and Plain Error

In *United States v. Hasting*, 461 U.S. 499 (1983), the Supreme Court noted that "given the myriad safeguards provided to assure a fair trial, and taking into account the reality of the human fallibility of the participants, there can be no such thing as an error-free, perfect trial, and that the Constitution does not guarantee such a trial." Courts recognize that not every error in a trial, or in the preliminary proceedings leading up to a conviction, necessitates the reversal of the conviction. Courts have developed the doctrines of *harmless error* and *plain error* to determine whether problems in the judicial process are significant enough to warrant reversing a conviction and ordering a second trial, or perhaps even dismissing the charge altogether.

Federal Rule of Criminal Procedure 52 is similar to the approach taken in most states in the treatment of different types of error. If the initial decision of the trial court was correct, then Federal Rule 52 has no application. An error that did not *prejudice* the defendant is harmless error under Federal Rule 52(a) and disregarded by the reviewing court, even though a defendant properly objected to the decision. If the objected error prejudiced the defendant, then it is a *reversible error* rather than a harmless one and the court will usually overturn the conviction and remand the case for a new trial.

Federal Rule 52(b) deals with plain error, which is an error so fundamental that a new trial or other relief should be granted, even though the defendant *failed to object* to the action at the time of the challenged decision. In order to rise to the level of plain error, the problem must be clear, prejudicial to the defendant, and the error "seriously affect[ed] the fairness, integrity, or public reputation of judicial proceedings."

A. Harmless Error

1. Non-Constitutional Error

The determination of whether an error is harmless involves a balancing process by the reviewing court which considers the type of error involved, its impact on the proceeding below, and the strength of the government's case after factoring out the error. Of course, this process is speculative, because the error did occur and it may be impossible to assess its probable impact long after the conclusion of the trial. Nevertheless, in *Kotteakos v. United States*, 328 U.S. 750 (1946), the Supreme Court set forth the basic structure for harmless error review:

> If, when all is said and done, the conviction is sure that the error did not influence the jury, or had but very slight effect, the verdict and the judgment should stand, except perhaps where the departure is from a constitution norm or a specific command of Congress. * * * But if one cannot say, with fair assurance, after pondering all that happened without stripping the erroneous action from the whole, that the judgment was not substantially swayed by the error, it is impossible to conclude that substantial rights were not affected. The inquiry cannot be merely whether there was enough to support the result, apart from the phase affected by the error. It is rather, even so, whether the error itself had substantial influence. If so, or if one is left in *grave doubt*, the conviction cannot stand. (Italics added).

In applying the *Kotteakos* harmless error test, a court considers the circumstances of the particular case, so the importance of particular holdings in other cases is minimal because of the unique facts in every prosecution. This standard applies to *non-constitutional error*, and the grave doubt requirement is a difficult one to establish.

Appellate courts frequently begin the harmless error analysis by making clear that it must review the entire record to ascertain the probable effect of the error on the outcome, taking into account all the evidence. The burden of proof is on the prosecution to establish that the error was harmless. In a close case, it is more likely that an error affected the outcome and will lead to a reversal, while even an obvious error that could impact a case will be viewed as harmless if there is significant evidence of the defendant's guilt apart from the tainted material or questioning.

In assessing whether an error was harmless, errors related to the admission of evidence will not lead to a reversal if the facts shown by that evidence were before the jury through other properly admitted evidence. Similarly, the erroneous exclusion of evidence is harmless if other evidence is admitted show-ing the same facts. If an error occurs and the court later gives a curative instruction to the jury or takes other corrective action, then the error is much more likely to be viewed as harmless. For example, if the court allows testimony over the defendant's objection, and the next day reverses itself and decides it should not have admitted the testimony, an instruction to the jury to disregard the witness's statements is usually viewed by an appellate court as *sufficient* to ren-der the error harmless because of the presumption that jurors obey the court's instructions.

2. Constitutional Error

At one time, any constitutional error was viewed as necessarily harmful, and, therefore, a conviction would be reversed. The Supreme Court's decision in *Chapman v. California*, 386 U.S. 18 (1967), however, extended the harmless error analysis to violations involving the Constitution. In *Chapman*, the defendant objected to the prosecutor's disparaging comments at trial regarding defen-dant's failure to testify—comments which violated the Fifth Amendment. In the course of finding that the error required reversal of the conviction, the Court stated that "there may be some Constitutional errors which in the set-ting of a particular case are so unimportant and insignificant that they may, con-sistent with the Federal Constitution, be deemed harmless, not requiring the automatic reversal of the conviction."

This is called *trial error*, and since *Chapman*, the Court has applied harm-less error analysis to, *inter alia*, the admission of illegally-obtained evidence, Confrontation Clause violations, prosecutions prohibited by *ex post facto*, in-terrogations in violation of the Sixth Amendment right to counsel, denial of the right of cross-examination, breach of a plea agreement, and improper jury instructions that did not include all the elements of the offense.

The Court identified certain types of error as falling outside the harmless error analysis and, instead, constitute *structural error*, which require *automatic re-versal* of a conviction without regard to any prejudice to the defendant because of the error's presumed impact on the proceeding. *Chapman*'s initial list of such significant errors involved the admission of a coerced confession, denial of the right to counsel at a critical stage, and the right to an impartial judge. In *Arizona v. Fulminante*, 499 U.S. 279 (1991), however, the Court reversed its position on coerced confessions and instead applied the harmless error analysis to this claimed violation.

The Court has identified additional types of structural error requiring automatic reversal, including a double jeopardy violation, an improper reasonable doubt instruction that shifted the burden of proof to the defendant, denial of the right to counsel of choice, failure to allow a defendant to represent himself, and *Batson* error. If the analysis of a constitutional violation already incorporates an assessment of prejudice, such as for ineffective assistance of counsel or a *Brady* violation, then harmless error does not apply because the assessment of whether there was a violation already involves a prejudice determination.

In assessing the impact of the error, the burden is on the prosecution to establish *beyond a reasonable doubt* that the error was harmless. This is a much more exacting standard than under *Kotteakos*, which applies to non-constitutional errors, such as a violation of the rules of criminal procedure or evidence, or a right granted by statute. Thus, identifying the standard is critical, and defendants usually seek to characterize an error as one coming within the category of *structural error*, and if not that then *Chapman* error, rather than being subject to the more permissive *Kotteakos* analysis. Even with the higher standard, in practice most constitutional errors fall under *Chapman* and do not trigger a reversal of the conviction, because courts still look to the strength of the government's evidence in assessing the impact on the conviction.

B. Plain Error

While the usual rule is that a defendant must object to a trial court's ruling or that claim of error is waived, appellate courts are authorized to correct a violation that rises to the level of *plain error*. Federal Rule 52(b) provides that a "plain error that affects substantial rights may be considered even though it was not brought to the court's attention." All states recognize some form of the plain error review to allow an appellate court to remedy glaring or egregious violations of a defendant's rights.

1. Plain

Exactly what constitutes plain error is not entirely clear. Courts have used language to describe errors to which defendant did not object that can be recognized as "obvious and substantial," "serious and manifest," and "seriously prejudicial." None of these phrases are particularly helpful, and the application of the plain error rule is highly fact specific. A key rationale for the plain error rule is to protect defendants from a serious injustice, so the strength or weakness of the evidence against him will be a relevant consideration. Courts also look at whether allowing the error to remain uncorrected will "seriously affect the fairness, integrity, or public reputation of judicial proceedings." In *Henderson v. United States*, 133 S. Ct. 1121 (2013), the Supreme Court clarified that the error must be plain *at the time of the decision of the trial judge*, or at least by the time of appellate consideration of the issue due to a subsequent change in the law. If the law was unsettled, then the error would not be plain and so it would fall outside Federal Rule 52(b).

2. Olano *Test*

In *United States v. Olano*, 507 U.S. 725 (1993), the Supreme Court considered whether the presence of alternate jurors during the jury's deliberations in violation of a federal rule that restricted those who can be present constituted plain error. It set forth three requirements for correcting a forfeited error:

- The ruling must be an *actual error*, and the Court distinguished between waiver and forfeiture. If a right has been waived, then the failure to uphold that right at trial is not an error but instead a decision by the defendant to forego the protection afforded. On the other hand, if the right was forfeited by defense counsel's failure to object to the violation, then is has not been waived and "there has been an 'error' within the meaning of Rule 52(b) despite the absence of a timely objection."
- The error must be plain, which the Court described as "obvious"—a rather unhelpful synonym.
- The plain error must have affected *substantial rights*, which means that the error was prejudicial and there was a reasonable probability that the error affected the outcome of the trial or other proceeding. Note that this is the same standard for the harmless error analysis under Rule 52(a), but the crucial difference is that for a claim of plain error "[i]t is the defendant rather than the Government who bears the burden of persuasion with respect to prejudice."

Failure to object to an alleged violation or error means that it will be much more difficult to obtain a reversal of a conviction because the plain error standard is higher than for other forms of error. Unlike *Kotteakos* and *Chapman,* the burden is on the defendant to establish the prejudice rather than on the government to show the absence of any significant harm.

3. Permissive

Even if these three requirements are met, *Olano* held that "Rule 52(b) is permissive, not mandatory. If the forfeited error is 'plain' and 'affect[s] substantial rights,' the Court of Appeals has authority to order correction, but is not required to do so." While a defendant need not establish his actual innocence to receive a remedy under the plain error rule, the appellate court's power is limited to correcting only those errors that "seriously affect the fairness, integrity or public reputation of judicial proceedings." In deciding *Olano*, the Supreme Court found that permitting the alternates to remain during the deliberations was both erroneous and plain, but it did not affect the defendant's substantial rights because he could not demonstrate any prejudice from the presence of the alternate jurors in the jury room during deliberations.

The Court reiterated the *Olano* test a few years later in *Johnson v. United States*, 520 U.S. 461 (1997), a perjury prosecution in which the trial court did not submit the materiality element of the offense to the jury to decide. The Court stated:

> Under that test, before an appellate court can correct an error not raised at trial, there must be (1) "error," (2) that is "plain," and (3) that "affects substantial rights." * * * If all three conditions are met, an appellate court may then exercise its discretion to notice a forfeited error, but only if (4) the error "seriously affect[s] the fairness, integrity, or public reputation of judicial proceedings."

The *Johnson* Court rejected the claim that the failure to submit an element of the crime to the jury was structural error, requiring automatic reversal of the conviction. Instead, it found that even if the error met the first three requirements, the evidence of materiality was overwhelming and largely uncontroverted, so "there is no basis for concluding that the error 'seriously affect[ed] the fairness, integrity, or public reputation of judicial proceedings.' Indeed, it would be the reversal of a conviction such as this which would have that effect."

4. Prejudice

While some plain error claims fail on the first two prongs of rising to the level of "error" and being "obvious," most cases are decided on whether or not prejudice can be demonstrated; then the consideration is whether the court should exercise its discretion to overturn the guilty verdict to remedy the violation. The plain error rule can be applied to violations in the process of accepting a defendant's guilty plea, *United States v. Dominguez Benitez*, 542 U.S. 74 (2004), even though the defendant admitted guilt, and, therefore, it would appear to be difficult to establish any prejudice from the error. The plain error test does not apply, however, to errors in a state court proceeding that were not raised until a federal *habeas corpus* challenge to the conviction (see Chapter 17).

Checkpoints

- While there is no constitutional right to appeal, the states and the federal government grant at least one appeal of a criminal conviction.

- A defendant can request that the trial court order a new trial or other proceeding to remedy errors.

- The most common remedy for a violation of a defendant's rights is a new trial.

- The states impose time limits on a defendant's right to request a new trial based on newly-discovered evidence, with significant hurdles to establishing a claim.

- A defendant seeking to appeal a ruling of the trial court must lodge a contemporaneous objection, unless it would be futile.

- If defendant did not object to an error, an appellate court will only review the claim under the restrictive plain error standard.

- In the federal system and many states, a defendant cannot challenge a trial court ruling or decision until after conviction and entry of a final judgment in the case.

- Interlocutory appeals in federal cases are permitted for alleged violations of double jeopardy, excessive bail, and the speech or debate protection afforded to members of Congress.

- If a state provides an appeal as of right, then due process requires that an indigent defendant be furnished counsel.

- A state need not provide counsel for a discretionary appeal, or for a collateral attack on a conviction.

- For most errors in a trial, including constitutional errors, the court must determine whether the violation was harmless.

- The government bears the burden of showing an error that violates a defendant's constitutional rights was harmless beyond a reasonable doubt.

- A non-constitutional error only requires a court to find that the error did not have a substantial influence on the outcome of the case.

- Certain types of violations entail structural error rather than trial error, and reversal of the conviction is automatic.

- The defendant bears the burden of showing that an un-objected error affected substantial rights and that it calls into question the fairness, integrity, or public reputation of the judicial proceedings.

- Even if an error is plain, either at the time of trial or during a subsequent appeal, the rule is permissive and the appellate court has discretion in deciding whether to grant relief.

Chapter 17

Collateral Review of Convictions

I. Introduction

After the appellate review process is complete (see Chapter 16), a defendant may continue to seek review of his or her conviction or sentence through post-conviction proceedings, also called collateral review. Post-conviction remedies exist for both state and federal prisoners.

Some states have statutes that provide defendants with state court post-conviction procedures, so that these prisoners can challenge their criminal convictions beyond their states' appellate processes. After state processes are exhausted, those in state custody may turn to the federal courts for relief. Congress' Act of February 5, 1867 and later court decisions authorize federal courts to hear state prisoners pleas for relief from state court convictions. *See McCleskey v. Zant*, 499 U.S. 467 (1991).

Federal prisoners also may seek relief after completion of their appellate review. For example, a prisoner may ask a court to re-examine his or her conviction when the law has changed, when the defendant believes trial or appellate counsel was ineffective, or perhaps when new evidence is discovered that calls into question the guilt of the defendant. The federal system provides a process for post-conviction criminal matters for those convicted in federal court.

In the federal system there are writs of coram nobis and habeas corpus. Coram nobis is a petition filed by an individual who is no longer in custody, but continues to suffer the collateral effects of a conviction. In contrast to coram nobis, federal habeas petitions are filed by individuals who remain in custody, though a loose definition of custody has been used by courts. The habeas process is prescribed by statute and includes cases coming from both state and federal courts. Additionally, the U.S. Constitution provides that "[t]he privilege of the Writ of Habeas Corpus shall not be suspended, unless when in Cases of Rebellion or Invasion the public Safety may require it."

State court petitioners seeking federal habeas corpus relief are governed by 28 U.S.C. § 2254. Post-appellate federal petitions are governed by 28 U.S.C. § 2255. The ability of federal judges to issue writs of habeas corpus and the procedures to be used in handling these writs are controlled by 28 U.S.C. § 2241 et. seq.

Whether the petitioner's case arose in federal or state court, he or she will face many obstacles in pursuing claims for habeas relief. There are limited areas subject to review, and new rules established by Supreme Court decisions often do not operate retroactively. There is also a strict timing restriction on the filing of these petitions. Additionally, there is a requirement that the defendant have exhausted all state remedies before pursuing the matter in federal court. Courts preclude many habeas claims because petitioners failed to raise them in earlier proceedings. Successive petitions also are frowned upon and require explicit court approval.

The Antiterrorism and Effective Death Penalty Act of 1996 (AEDPA) places added obstacles in front of federal and state prisoners seeking writs of habeas corpus, such as limits on second petitions. Although AEDPA imposed "new conditions" for habeas, it did "not deprive" the Court "of jurisdiction to entertain original habeas petitions." *Felker v. Turpin*, 518 U.S. 651 (1996). Following enactment of the AEDPA, "habeas corpus with respect to a claim adjudicated on the merits in state court" is prohibited "unless that adjudication 'resulted in a decision that was contrary to, or involved an unreasonable application of, clearly established Federal law, as determined by the Supreme Court of the United States.'" *Penry v. Johnson*, 532 U.S. 782 (2001).

As one might suspect, there are many who file habeas actions, but few actually succeed. Despite the complexity of these matters, defendants are not automatically afforded the right to counsel with their habeas petitions, except in capital matters. The Supreme Court has stated, however, in *Haines v. Kerner*, 404 U.S. 519 (1972), that the petitions of pro se defendants are held to "less stringent standards than formal pleadings drafted by lawyers."

II. Habeas and Post-Conviction Statutes

Prior to focusing on common issues that arise in habeas matters, this next section provides an overview of the key statutes for habeas and post-conviction review in the federal system. Later parts delve into specific issues that arise when prisoners bring habeas petitions.

A. Federal Habeas for Prisoners in State Custody

State cases can make their way into federal court for habeas review under 28 U.S.C. § 2254. These petitions are often referred to simply as 2254 motions. The basis is that the defendant is "in custody pursuant to the judgment of a State court," and that the custody is "in violation of the Constitution or laws or treaties of the United States." 28 U.S.C. § 2254(a). Federal habeas corpus is not available "for errors of state law," such as challenges to a state parole board determination. *Swarthout v. Cooke*, 131 S. Ct. 859 (2011).

To obtain relief, the applicant has to have exhausted all state remedies, which means he or she must have pursued and completed the appellate and post-conviction processes of the state system and any other procedures available in the state. Additionally, there either has to be no state means for correcting the constitutional violation complained of, or the circumstances make it an ineffective process for this applicant. 28 U.S.C. § 2254(b)(1). Even when there has been an exhaustion of state remedies, federal courts can deny the habeas petition without a hearing. 28 U.S.C. § 2254(b)(2).

The scope of reviewable claims is limited. If the matter was reviewed in state court, then the claim must have resulted in "a decision that was contrary to, or involved an unreasonable application of, clearly established Federal law, as determined by the Supreme Court" or "a decision that was based on an unreasonable determination of the facts in light of the evidence presented in the

State court proceeding." 28 U.S.C. § 2254(d). The state court is not bound to accompany its decision with an explanation. *Harrington v. Richter*, 131 S. Ct. 770 (2011). In *Harrington*, and its companion case issued the same day, *Premo v. Moore*, 131 S. Ct. 733 (2011), the Court stressed the importance of giving deference to state court decisions, even when the subject matter pertains to ineffective assistance of counsel. In *Premo*, the Court stated that if "the state post conviction court's decision involved no unreasonable application of Supreme Court precedent," it should stand.

It is difficult to establish an unreasonable application of Supreme Court precedent unless the petitioner's facts are identical, or nearly so, to those in the applicable precedent. In *White v. Woodall*, 134 S. Ct. 1697 (2014), the petitioner could not establish that the trial court unreasonably applied Supreme Court precedent when it refused to give his requested "no adverse inference" instruction during the penalty phase of his capital trial. The petitioner had not testified during that part of the trial, and because he had a Fifth Amendment right not to do so, he wished the jury to be instructed that it should not draw any adverse inferences from his silence. Prior Supreme Court decisions had established that (1) a trial court must give such a requested "no adverse inference" instruction during the guilt/innocence phase of a capital trial; (2) the Fifth Amendment privilege against self incrimination applies during the penalty phase; and (3) during judicial sentencing, an adverse inference cannot be based on a defendant's silence. But because the Court had never directly held that a no adverse inference instruction must be given at the penalty phase, it declined to find that the trial court's refusal constituted an unreasonable application of precedent.

On the other hand, if the state court fails to apply the proper constitutional test, then its decision involves an unreasonable application of clearly established law. In *Lafler v. Cooper*, 132 S. Ct. 1376 (2012), the petitioner raised ineffectiveness of counsel after his trial counsel urged him to reject a favorable plea offer. On direct appeal, the state appellate court failed to apply *Strickland* to assess his claim and instead simply evaluated his rejection of the plea for its "knowing and voluntary" character. The Court granted relief, explaining that "[a]n inquiry into whether the rejection of a plea is knowing and voluntary … is not the correct means by which to address a claim of ineffective assistance of counsel.… By failing to apply *Strickland* to assess the ineffective-assistance-of-counsel claim respondent raised, the state court's adjudication was contrary to clearly established federal law. And in that circumstance the federal courts in this habeas action can determine the principles necessary to grant relief."

When reviewing habeas claims, courts must presume factual determinations of state courts to be correct. In *Cullen v. Pinholster*, 131 S. Ct. 1388 (2011), the Supreme Court held that review under § 2254(d)(1) is "limited to the record in existence at that same time." An applicant disputing factual determinations bears a heavy burden of "rebutting the presumption of correctness by clear and convincing evidence." 28 U.S.C. § 2254(e)(1). Put another way, the rules of habeas relief "do not permit federal judges to so casually second-guess the decisions of their state-court colleagues." *Burt v. Titlow*, 134 S. Ct. 10 (2013).

Federal courts do not hold evidentiary hearings to establish facts unless the claim relies on a new constitutional rule that the Supreme Court has allowed to operate retroactively. This is rare since most rulings of the Supreme Court are meant to operate prospectively. An evidentiary hearing also can be held when there is "a factual predicate that could not have been previously discovered through the exercise of due diligence." Irrespective of whether it is a situation of a new rule operating retroactively or something that could not have been previously discovered, it is necessary that the error be one that is "substantial" or have an "injurious effect." If the defendant would still be found guilty, even with the new rule or new evidence, there is no basis for habeas relief. 28 U.S.C. § 2254(e)(2). Further ineffectiveness of counsel in federal or state post-conviction matters is not a basis for habeas relief. 28 U.S.C. § 2254(i).

B. Relief for Prisoners in Federal Custody

Federal prisoners who wish to challenge their convictions and sentences must do so under 28 U.S.C. § 2255. Like the remedy for state prisoners, § 2255 applies to those in custody. Here again, lower courts often use a loose definition of custody that includes those who on probation or some form of supervised release. Section 2255 allows a petition for unconstitutional or illegal sentences, those "in excess of the maximum authorized by law," or "otherwise subject to collateral attack." 28 U.S.C. § 2255(a). The defendant must exhaust his or her remedies in the courts prior to taking a habeas route. 28 U.S.C. § 2255(e). The statute has a time limit of one year for a motion under this section, with explicit statements in the statute of how the time is computed. 28 U.S.C. § 2255(f). The statute also limits "second or successive" motions, requiring that they be certified by the court as containing either harmful newly discovered evidence or a new rule that has retroactive application.

C. Rules of Procedure

Habeas procedure is controlled by 28 U.S.C. § 2241 et. seq. Habeas actions are civil matters, despite the fact that they review criminal convictions or sentences. The statutes govern how venue is attained (§ 2241), what the application should look like (§ 2242), the power of the court to direct a response (§ 2243), the need for finality and preclusion of successive petitions (§ 2244), presentation of facts from lower courts (§ 2245), and use of evidence (§§ 2246–47). State or federal prisoners seeking habeas relief can use forms provided by the federal court system.

III. Scope of Available Relief

A. Limitations

Often referred to as "gatekeepers" to habeas relief, there are limitations that narrow the availability of using this vehicle for review. While habeas review permits federal consideration of claims from state courts, there are several obstacles such as timing requirements, limitations on new rules, and requirements on the nature of the error that serves as barriers to success on habeas review. For example, AEDPA imposed "a 1-year period of limitation" to "apply to an application for a writ of habeas corpus by a person in custody pursuant to the judgment of a State court." Under 28 U.S.C. § 2244(d)(1), the starting point for this time limit (for federal as well as state prisoners) is "the date on which the factual predicate of the claim or claims presented could have been discovered through the exercise of due diligence," but in *Holland v. Florida*, 560 U.S. 631 (2010), the Supreme Court noted that the one-year statute of limitations for habeas petitions is subject to equitable tolling if the petitioner exercised due diligence but was prevented by "extraordinary circumstances" from bringing his claim within the year. In *Holland*, the Court remanded the case to the Court of Appeals to determine if there were extraordinary circumstances warranting equitable tolling. There also is a "miscarriage of justice" exception for AEDPA's statute of limitations in cases raising convincing claims of actual innocence, as discussed below.

In addition to being subject to a very short statute of limitations, habeas claims are limited by subject matter. One type of claim that is precluded from habeas review is a Fourth Amendment search and seizure error that was previously considered by a state court. In *Stone v. Powell*, 428 U.S. 465 (1976) the Court stated that "where the State has provided an opportunity for full and fair litigation of a Fourth Amendment claim, the Constitution does not require that a state prisoner be granted federal habeas corpus relief on the ground that evidence obtained in an unconstitutional search or seizure was introduced at his trial." The rationale for this exception is the unique role played by the exclusionary rule—"deterrence of police conduct that violates Fourth Amendment rights." The Court was concerned that if the Fourth Amendment exclusionary rule were "applied indiscriminately it may well have the opposite effect of generating disrespect for the law and administration of justice." Thus, the Court saw a value in applying the Fourth Amendment's exclusionary rule in state trials and on direct appeal from these trials. But to extend it to habeas review would add a small value in relation to the costs — the release of an otherwise guilty individual. The Court stated, "[t]here is no reason to believe, however, that the overall educative effect of the exclusionary rule would be appreciably diminished if search-and-seizure claims could not be raised in federal habeas corpus review of state convictions."

The habeas bar articulated in *Stone v. Powell* has not been extended to other constitutional violations. Thus, it does not preclude a habeas petition premised on a Fifth Amendment *Miranda* violation. *See Withrow v. Williams*, 507 U.S. 680 (1993). Likewise, Sixth Amendment claims of ineffective assistance of counsel may also be brought under a habeas petition. *See Kimmelman v. Morrison*, 477 U.S. 365 (1986).

B. New Rules

Many petitions for habeas relief have been predicated on a Supreme Court decision that changed the law upon which the prisoner was previously indicted, tried, or sentenced. In these cases, the appellate review process has passed, and the only avenue available for the prisoner is the habeas route. The convicted prisoner, observing that the law had changed, attempts to obtain relief because of the new rule established by the Supreme Court. Prior to the Supreme Court's decision in *Teague v. Lane*, 489 U.S. 288 (1989), prisoners could successfully claim that a new rule should be applied to them. This landmark decision, however, limits the retroactive application of new rules in habeas matters. The Antiterrorism and Effective Death Penalty Act "codifies *Teague* to the extent that *Teague* requires federal habeas courts to deny relief that is contingent upon a rule of law not clearly established at the time the state conviction became final." *Williams v. Taylor*, 529 U.S. 362 (2000).

In *Teague v. Lane*, the Court examined whether a prisoner could obtain habeas review in order to apply the Court's holding in *Batson v. Kentucky*, 476 U.S. 79 (1986) to his case. *Batson* prohibited racial discrimination in the exercise of peremptory challenges. See Chapter 10. The defendant in *Teague* sought the benefit of this decision, but the Court held that habeas is not available for "new constitutional rules of criminal procedure" in cases "which have become final before the new rules [were] announced." Thus, the defendant could not receive the benefit of the *Batson* decision because it was decided after he had proceeded through the non-habeas portion of the judicial process. Similarly, the Court held in *Chaidez v. United States*, 133 S. Ct. 1103 (2013), that it had announced a new rule of procedure, which would not apply retroactively to cases on collateral review, when it held in *Padilla v. Kentucky*, 559 U.S. 356 (2010), that the Sixth Amendment requires defense counsel to provide advice about the risk of deportation that accompanies a guilty plea.

According to Justice Harlan in *Teague v. Lane*, there are two situations in which new rules may apply to habeas petitioners: (1) when a new rule "places certain kinds of primary, private individual conduct beyond the power of the criminal law-making authority to proscribe"; and (2) when a new rule "requires the observance of those procedures that are 'implicit in the concept of ordered liberty.' " This second exception is considered reserved for "watershed rules of criminal procedure."

What constitutes a "watershed rule" has been the subject of Court decisions. In *Whorton v. Bockting*, 549 U.S. 406 (2007), the Supreme Court examined this question in deciding whether a leading confrontation clause case, *Crawford v. Washington*, 541 U.S. 36 (2004) (see Chapter 12), should be applied retroactively. The defendant's conviction and appeal occurred prior to the Court's holding in *Crawford*. Finding that *Crawford's* holding was not retroactive, the Court in *Whorton v. Bockting* found that the new rule in this case was of a procedural nature as opposed to substantive. Thus, the only basis for consideration was whether this new rule was a "watershed rule of criminal procedure." To be a watershed rule it must meet one of two tests: (1) "the rule must be necessary to prevent an impermissibly large risk of an inaccurate conviction" or (2) "the rule must alter our understanding of the bedrock procedural elements essential to the fairness of a proceeding." The rule in this case was not comparable to a rule like *Gideon*, which provided indigents the right to counsel in felony cases. It did not "effect a profound and sweeping change." Thus, *Crawford's* new rule would not meet *Teague v. Lane's* "watershed rule" exception and would not have retroactive application.

C. Substantial or Injurious Effect

Habeas relief premised on a trial error requires that there be a showing that the error "had a substantial and injurious effect or influence in determining the jury's verdict." *Brecht v. Abrahamson*, 507 U.S. 619 (1993). This standard is not the same as the demanding (to the state) "harmless error" standard used by state courts in appellate cases under *Chapman v. California*, 386 U.S. 18 (1967), which requires reversal if the error contributed in the slightest to the verdict. Rather, courts are instructed to use the "more forgiving" (to the state) federal standard from *Kotteakos v. United States*, 328 U.S. 750 (1946) which permits courts to affirm convictions in the face of errors that had some influence on the verdict, so long as that influence was not substantial.

D. Adequate and Independent State Grounds

Habeas is also limited in that federal courts will not take up state court questions that "rest on a state law ground that is independent of the federal question and adequate to support the judgment." *Coleman v. Thompson*, 501 U.S. 722 (1991). In *Lee v. Kemma*, 534 U.S. 362 (2002), petitioner was deprived of a requested continuance to find subpoenaed witnesses that were suddenly missing. The Missouri court denied the continuance as "defective under the State's rules." The issue on habeas was whether the state ground was adequate to preclude habeas. The Court held "that the Missouri Rules, as injected into this case by the state appellate court, did not constitute a state ground adequate to bar federal habeas review."

In contrast, in *Walker v. Martin*, 131 S. Ct. 1120 (2011), the Supreme Court examined whether California's time limitation on habeas applications qualified as an independent state ground that should bar review. As opposed to employing a specific deadline on habeas claims, California instructed "petitioners to file known claims 'as promptly as the circumstances allow.' " Reaffirming its decision in *Beard v. Kindler*, 558 U.S. 53 (2009), the Court in *Walker v. Martin* found that state procedural bars could serve as adequate and independent grounds for denying federal habeas petitions. "California's time rule, although discretionary, meets the 'firmly established' criterion, as *Kindler* comprehended that requirement."

E. Enemy Combatants

Several cases considered whether enemy combatants held at Guantanamo Bay, Cuba have the right to use the habeas corpus process. In *Rasul v. Bush*, 542 U.S. 466 (2004) the Court held "that § 2241 confers on the District Court jurisdiction to hear petitioners' habeas corpus challenges to the legality of their detention at the Guantanamo Bay Naval Base." Congress then passed the Detainee Treatment Act of 2005 that amended section 2241 to provide that "no court, justice, or judge shall have jurisdiction to hear or consider an application for a writ of habeas corpus filed by or on behalf of an alien detained by the" Department of Defense at Guantanamo Bay, Cuba. In *Hamdan v. Rumsfeld*, 548 U.S. 557 (2006), the Court held that this provision did not apply to the case brought by petitioners. Congress again responded, this time passing the Military Commissions Act, which authorized the trial of enemy combatants by military commission, rather than Article III federal courts, and in Section 7 expressly denied access to courts (by habeas corpus or otherwise) to those categorized as enemy combatants. In *Boumediene v. Bush*, 553 U.S. 723 (2008), the Supreme Court held that the procedures under the Detainee Treatment Act "are not an adequate and effective substitute for habeas corpus" and that section 7 of the Military Commissions Act "operates as an unconstitutional suspension of the writ." Although the Supreme Court allowed petitioners to use the habeas corpus process, the Court did not resolve whether the petitioners were entitled to have the writ granted.

IV. Exhaustion of Remedies

It has long been a requirement that those seeking habeas relief from state court judgments must first exhaust all state remedies. Since it is considered important that there not be unnecessary conflict caused by federal courts ruling on issues within the jurisdiction of state courts, as a matter of comity (respect for other courts) federal courts would not act until the state court first had the opportunity to consider and act on the matter. *Ex Part Royall*, 117 U.S. 241 (1886). Today, exhaustion requirements are incorporated into federal statutes, but the comity rationale continues to be expressed in court decisions.

Section 2254 specifically requires that state prisoners seeking habeas relief in federal court need to have exhausted all state remedies prior to seeking federal relief. Exhaustion of state remedies requires that all available state court procedures to address the question first be used. 28 U.S.C. § 2254 (c). If there is no process in state court to address the issue or "circumstances exist that render such process ineffective to protect the rights of the applicant" then the habeas motion is not precluded by a failure to exhaust state remedies. 28 U.S.C. § 2254 (b)(1). A state can waive the exhaustion requirement, but this requires an express waiver by the state's counsel. 28 U.S.C. § 2254 (b)(3).

Questions can arise in determining when an issue is fully exhausted. Exhaustion does not require a petitioner to relitigate an issue in a collateral proceeding that has been addressed on direct appeal. Likewise, if the State passes on the claim or ignores it, it can be assumed "that further state proceedings would be useless." *Castille v. Peoples*, 489 U.S. 346 (1989). In *Castille*, Justice Scalia differentiated these scenarios from claims that are "presented for the first and only time in a procedural context in which its merits will not be considered unless 'there are special and important reasons therefor.'" This would not be considered a "fair presentation" and exhaustion may be necessary unless the state procedurally precluded the issue from being presented in state court. Likewise, failing to present a claim to a state supreme court when there is discretionary review in that court, will mean that the petitioner has not exhausted his or her remedies. See *O'Sullivan v. Boerckel*, 526 U.S. 838 (1999).

In some instances the petitioner may have a mixed question, meaning that it is partly exhausted and partly still eligible for state court review. In *Rose v. Lundy*, 455 U.S. 509 (1982), decided before the passage of AEDPA and its one-year statute of limitations, the Supreme Court endorsed a "total exhaustion rule" by which petitions with mixed questions would either get dismissed for failure to exhaust remedies or limited in consideration only to the exhausted claims. The rationale was to promote comity, while "not unreasonably impair[ing] the prisoner's right to relief." Petitioners at the time *Lundy* was decided could, if their petitions were dismissed, return to state court in order to exhaust all claims, and then refile their petitions. AEDPA's statute of limitations changed this landscape, because it is not tolled by the filing of a petition for habeas corpus. Thus, a petitioner would most likely not have time to return to state court for exhaustion. Some federal circuits have called for a reevaluation of *Lundy*. See *Zarvela v. Artuz*, 254 F.3d 374, 379 (2d Cir. 2001).

The Supreme Court has not done so, but it has held that in AEDPA's aftermath a district court has discretion to grant a "stay and abeyance" when a mixed question is involved. *Rhines v. Weber*, 544 U.S. 269 (2005). The Court explained that this procedure essentially tolls the statute of limitations while the petitioner returns to state court to exhaust his remedies: "[u]nder this procedure, rather than dismiss the mixed petition pursuant to *Lundy*, a district court might stay the petition and hold it in abeyance while the petitioner returns to state court to exhaust his previously unexhausted claims. Once the petitioner exhausts his state remedies, the district court will lift the stay and allow the petitioner to proceed in federal court." The district court's discretion to grant a stay and abeyance is circumscribed by AEDPA's underlying purposes of reducing time delays and streamlining procedures. For this reason, it would be an abuse of discretion for a district court to grant a stay and abeyance unless there were a good reason for the petitioner's failure to exhaust, or if the unexhausted claims were plainly meritless, or without placing "reasonable time limits on a petitioner's trip to state court and back."

Pro se defendants may not be aware of the consequences of having mixed questions and the need to meet the time limits that apply to habeas proceedings. Nevertheless courts are not under an obligation to instruct these prisoners. As the Supreme Court stated in *Pliler v. Ford*, 542 U.S. 225 (2004), "[r]equiring district courts to advise a *pro se* litigant in such a manner would undermine district judges' role as impartial decisionmakers."

Exhaustion is also required for federal prisoners filing under § 2255. In this instance it is necessary that the defendant have first addressed the issues in the court that initially sentenced him or her. Here again, an exception exists when "the remedy by motion is inadequate or ineffective to test the legality of his detention." 28 U.S.C. § 2255 (e).

V. Procedural Default

A habeas petition is not the appropriate vehicle for raising new matters. Typically the prisoner's issues presented in the petition have been considered by an earlier court. Just as there is a requirement to exhaust remedies in state or federal court prior to bringing a habeas petition, issues should not be raised for the first time in a habeas petition. It is considered a procedural default, and a bar to proceeding on the habeas petition, when matters were not previously considered by prior courts handling the case.

A rationale for requiring that matters be raised prior to the habeas petition is to afford respect for the state or federal court that initially heard the matter. If that court did not have an opportunity to hear the issue, then it was deprived of the opportunity to review and correct any possible problems.

Although procedural defaults can preclude habeas review, several exceptions exist. Reviewing courts look at whether there is a "cause" for the procedural default and whether there would be "prejudice" resulting from not allowing the matter to now be heard despite a failure to have it previously considered. Courts also look at claims of "actual innocence." These exceptions to the procedural default rule are aimed at avoiding a "fundamental miscarriage of justice."

A. Cause and Prejudice Test

In *Fay v. Noia*, 372 U.S. 391 (1963), the Supreme Court held that habeas corpus rights should not be denied to a prisoner despite his failure to "comply with a state procedural requirement." Two co-defendants were released following an appeal because it was determined that their confessions had been coerced. A third defendant, Noia, did not raise this issue despite his confession also being coerced. The Court held that habeas corpus was a proper remedy for the defendant in this situation.

Later cases, however, make it more difficult for a defendant to pursue habeas corpus when there is a procedural default. In *Wainwright v. Sykes*, 433 U.S. 72 (1977), certiorari was granted "to consider the availability of federal habeas corpus to review a state convict's claim that testimony was admitted at his trial in violation of his rights under *Miranda v. Arizona.*" The defendant, however, failed to make a contemporaneous objection, and only raised the issue in a "motion to vacate the conviction, and, in the State District Court of Appeals and Supreme Court, petitions for habeas corpus." Taking a different approach than was taken in *Fay v. Noia*, the Supreme Court in *Wainwright v. Sykes* expressed a concern that allowing such habeas petitions would allow for "'sandbagging' on the part of defense lawyers, who may take their chances on a verdict of not guilty in a state trial court with the intent to raise their constitutional claims in a federal habeas court if their initial gamble does not pay off."

Although *Wainwright v. Sykes* provided a more restrictive approach to allowing habeas review following a procedural default, it offered as a relief the "cause" and "prejudice" test of a prior case. This exception to procedural default was offered so that the rule would "not prevent a federal habeas court from adjudicating for the first time the federal constitutional claim of a defendant who in the absence of such an adjudication [would] be the victim of a miscarriage of justice." The contours, however, of the "cause and prejudice" test were left for later decisions as this defendant had offered "no explanation whatever for his failure to object at trial," and the other substantial evidence presented "negate[d] any possibility of actual prejudice resulting to the respondent from the admission of his inculpatory statement."

Cases since *Wainwright v. Sykes* have developed what is permissible under the "cause and prejudice" test. For example, "[a]ttorney ignorance or inadvertence" has been held not to be a sufficient basis for "cause" for overcoming a procedural default, because under agency principles, a client bears the risk of negligent conduct on the part of his attorney. *Coleman v. Thompson*, 501 U.S. 722 (1991). But if a petitioner has been "abandoned" by his pro bono state post-conviction attorney, he may establish cause for his failure to follow state procedural rules governing the timing of appeals. See *Maples v. Thomas*, 132 S. Ct. 912 (2012). In *Maples*, a death row prisoner in Alabama was represented by two attorneys from Sullivan & Cromwell in New York, as well as local counsel whose role was limited to managing logistics for the New Yorkers. When the New York attorneys left Sullivan & Cromwell for new employment, they failed to notify Maples or local counsel. Thereafter, the state court denied Maples' post-conviction petition and mailed a copy of its order to Sullivan & Cromwell and to local counsel. The Sullivan & Cromwell copy was returned unopened to the Alabama court, and local counsel, assuming that the New York attorneys would undertake an appeal, did nothing. The time for appeal ran out before Maples could find assistance. The Supreme Court, while acknowledging that negligence on the part of post-conviction counsel ordinarily does not qualify as cause, held that a "markedly different situation" was presented in Maples situation, because he had been abandoned without notice and the abandonment severed the principal-agent relationship.

The *Coleman* rule also does not apply "[w]here, under state law, claims of ineffective assistance of trial counsel must be raised [for the first time] in an initial-review collateral proceeding." If the petitioner had no counsel for that proceeding, or if counsel was ineffective, the petitioner may establish cause for his procedural default of a claim of ineffective assistance at trial. *Martinez v. Ryan*, 132 S. Ct. 1309 (U.S. 2012). Similarly, if state court procedures make it virtually impossible for petitioners to raise ineffective assistance of counsel claims on direct appeal, it would be unfair to bar them from raising these claims in habeas proceedings, and the procedural default may be excused. *Trevino v. Thaler*, 133 S. Ct. 1911 (2013).

Federal prisoners are not barred by the "cause and prejudice" rule from bringing claims of ineffective assistance of counsel for the first time in post-conviction proceedings, rather than on direct appeal to the federal circuit courts. In *Massaro v. United States*, 538 U.S. 500 (2003), the Supreme Court held that "the procedural-default rule is neither a statutory nor a constitutional requirement, but it is a doctrine adhered to by the courts to conserve judicial resources and to respect the law's important interest in the finality of judgments." Requiring criminal defendants to bring ineffective assistance of counsel claims on direct appeal would not advance those objectives, because the factual predicates for those claims would not have been developed. According to the Court, "[t]he better-reasoned approach is to permit ineffective-assistance claims to be brought in the first instance in a timely motion in the district court under § 2255 whether or not the petitioner could have raised the claim on direct appeal."

Cause for failure to raise a claim may be found if "a constitutional claim is so novel that its legal basis is not reasonably available to counsel." *Reed v. Ross*, 468 U.S. 1 (1984). However, *Reed* was decided prior to *Teague v. Lane* and may no longer be good law, according to some of the federal circuits. *See United States v. Moss*, 252 F.3d 993, 1002 (8th Cir. Neb. 2001); *Daniels v. United States*, 254 F.3d 1180, 1194 (10th Cir. 2001). According to the Tenth Circuit in *Daniels*, "If one has cause for not raising a constitutional claim in earlier petitions because it is sufficiently 'novel,' that same novelty ensures the claim is barred from application on collateral review as a new rule under *Teague* (unless one of two exceptions applies)."

Even when the petitioner is able to show that he or she has a "cause" for the procedural default, this is insufficient for relief absent a showing that prejudice occurred. In *Strickler v. Green*, 527 U.S. 263 (1999), the Supreme Court examined "cause" noting that the petitioner had "established cause for failing to raise a *Brady* (See Chapter 8) claim prior to federal habeas because (a) the prosecution withheld exculpatory evidence; (b) petitioner reasonably relied on the prosecution's open file policy as fulfilling the prosecution's duty to disclose such evidence; and (c) the Commonwealth confirmed petitioner's reliance on the open file policy by asserting during state habeas proceedings that petitioner had already received 'everything known to the government.'" But the petitioner was unsuccessful because there was no showing of prejudice since he was not able to show that his conviction or sentence would have been different if he had been given the discovery material.

B. Actual Innocence

In addition to allowing a habeas matter to proceed when there is "cause" for the procedural default and when "prejudice" would exist if the petition was barred, claims of "actual innocence" also provide an exception to the procedural default rule. It is difficult, however, to succeed with these claims. In *Murray v. Carrier*, 477 U.S. 478 (1986), the Supreme Court stated that "in an extraordinary case, where a constitutional violation has probably resulted in the conviction of one who is actually innocent, a federal habeas court may grant the writ even in the absence of a showing of cause for the procedural default." The Court later clarified that in order "to show 'actual innocence' the petitioner must demonstrate by clear and convincing evidence that, but for a constitutional error, no reasonable juror would have found the petitioner eligible for the death penalty under the applicable state law." *Sawyer v. Whitley*, 505 U.S. 333, 336 (U.S. 1992). Explaining the critical nexus between "actual innocence" and "constitutional error," the Court in *Herrera v. Collins*, 506 U.S. 390 (1993), dismissed a petitioner's claim of actual innocence based on newly discovered evidence, because the claim was not tied to a constitutional error. The Court noted that "the existence merely of newly discovered evidence relevant to the guilt of a state prisoner is not a ground for relief on federal habeas corpus," as the remedy is to "ensure that individuals are not imprisoned in violation of the Constitution — not to correct errors of fact." A claim of actual innocence, the Court stated, "is not itself a constitutional claim, but instead a gateway through which a habeas petitioner must pass to have his otherwise barred constitutional claim considered on the merits." Although some innocence claims might be considered, in this case the Court noted that petitioner still had the remedy of executive clemency. A strong dissent started with the statement that "[n]othing could be more contrary to contemporary standards of decency, ... or more shocking to the conscience, ... than to execute a person who is actually innocent."

Claims of newly discovered evidence do get a boost of sorts from AEDPA: as was noted above, its one-year statute of limitations does not begin running until "the date on which the factual predicate of the claim or claims presented could have been discovered through the exercise of due diligence." See § 2244(d)(1)(D). The Court has held that "a convincing showing of actual innocence" may extend the time further. See *McQuiggin v. Perkins*, 133 S. Ct. 1924 (2013). Years after his conviction became final, Perkins obtained three affidavits consistent with his theory of innocence, but it was not until five years after obtaining them that he filed his petition for habeas corpus alleging ineffective assistance of counsel. Perkins did not qualify for "equitable tolling" of the statute of limitations because he could not demonstrate "(1) that he ha[d] been pursuing his rights diligently, and (2) that some extraordinary circumstance stood in his way and prevented timely filing." Nevertheless, the Court held, a petition in these circumstances could be heard under a "miscarriage of justice exception" that "applies to a severely confined category: cases in which new evidence shows it is more likely than not that no reasonable juror would have convicted the petitioner." Although the petitioner's lack of due diligence does not bar him from gaining the advantage of the exception, "unexplained delay in presenting new evidence bears on the determination whether the petitioner has made the requisite showing [of innocence]." Perkins himself was unlikely to be successful because the federal district court already had found that his newly discovered evidence did not meet the standard.

Some petitioners have been successful with actual innocence arguments. For example, a remand was granted to allow the prisoner to show that his defaulted claim of an unintelligent plea should be considered on the merits. *See Bousley v. United States*, 523 U.S. 614 (1998). In *House v. Bell*, 547 U.S. 518 (2006), the Court found that the prisoner had "made the stringent showing required by this exception" and the Court allowed the habeas petition to proceed.

VI. Successive Petitions

For many years, defendants could file multiple petitions seeking habeas relief in federal court. As each was denied, a new petition could be filed. A limit on successive petitions was available through abuse-of-the-writ principles.

Specific limits on the number of times that one can file a habeas petition are of recent vintage, with AEDPA providing limited accessibility to habeas after the denial of a first petition. Federal and state habeas now require that the defendant receive a certificate of appealability (COA) from a federal appellate court in order to file a second or successive habeas petition. The requirements governing a COA and second and successive habeas petitions are statutory and found in 28 U.S.C. § 2244 (b); 28 U.S.C. § 2253(c), Rule 9, and 28 U.S.C. § 2255(h). Rule 11 also provides the process with a COA and the discretion a court has in directing arguments on whether to issue the Order.

Rule 9, a rule governing cases that proceed under section 2254 (cases coming from state courts), provides that "[b]efore presenting a second or successive petition, the petitioner must obtain an order from the appropriate court of appeals authorizing the district court to consider the petition as required by 28 U.S.C. § 2244(b)(3)." A similar reference is made to section 2244 in section 2255 cases (cases coming from federal courts). 28 U.S.C. § 2255(h) provides that second and successive motions have to be certified as provided by 28 U.S.C. § 2244.

28 U.S.C. § 2244 is titled "finality of determination," as it provides definitive rules that limit successive habeas petitions from going forward. 28 U.S.C. § 2244 (b)(1) provides that claims previously presented get dismissed. If the claim was not previously presented, but it is included in a second or successive habeas petition, it gets dismissed unless the defendant can show one of two situations. The defendant has to show either that his or her claim relies on a new rule of constitutional law that was made retroactive, or that "the factual predicate for the claim could not have been discovered previously through the exercise of due diligence" and these new facts present a harmful error. 28 U.S.C. § 2244 (b)(2). Even when one of these conditions exist, the defendant filing a "second or successive habeas corpus application has to secure a COA to proceed." 28 U.S.C. § 2244(b)(3). This requires the approval of a three judge appellate court finding that "the application makes a prima facie showing that the application satisfies the requirements of this subsection." 28 U.S.C. § 2244(b)(3)(C). There is no appellate review of this decision (28 U.S.C. § 2244(b)), but the defendant can use federal rules of appellate procedure to have the denial reconsidered.

An initial question can arise as to what constitutes a second or successive petition. In *Slack v. McDaniel*, 529 U.S. 473 (2000), the Supreme Court addressed this question in a case in which the defendant filed a second habeas petition after his first was dismissed on procedural grounds — a failure to exhaust state remedies. The Court held that this was not to be considered a second habeas petition for purposes of rules limiting second and successive petitions. The dismissal of an initial petition for failure to exhaust state remedies, followed by the exhaustion of those remedies, allows the petitioner to then proceed with a habeas petition as if it were a first petition. The Court also noted that this also extends to mixed petitions that get dismissed before the district court gets to adjudicate the claim. These, too, are not considered second or successive petitions.

The Supreme Court also provided guidance for when a pro se litigant filed a motion seeking relief, but may not have characterized that motion as a petition for habeas under section 2255. In *Castro v. United States*, 540 U.S. 375 (2003), the Court held that a "court cannot so recharacterize a pro se litigant's motion as the litigant's first § 2255 motion *unless* the court informs the litigant of its intent to recharacterize, warns the litigant that the recharacterization will subject subsequent § 2255 motions to the law's 'second or successive' restrictions, and provides the litigant with an opportunity to withdraw, or to amend, the filing." (emphasis in original). A failure to do this will mean that the petitioner's motion "will not count as a § 2255 motion for purposes of applying § 2255's 'second or successive' provision."

A new rule made retroactive is one basis upon which a successive petition can be filed. In *Tyler v. Cain*, 533 U.S. 656 (2001), the Supreme Court examined when a new rule issued by the Court would be considered retroactive for purposes of filing a second or successive habeas petition. The Court held that there are three prerequisites required for success in filing a second or successive petition premised on a retroactive new rule. "First, the rule on which the claim relies must be a 'new rule' of constitutional law; second, the rule must have been 'made retroactive to cases on collateral review by the Supreme Court'; and third, the claim must have been 'previously unavailable.'"

VII. Coram Nobis

Writs of coram nobis are not as common as those for habeas corpus. Once an individual is no longer subject to prison or probationary status following prison, but continues to suffer the collateral effects of a conviction, he or she may seek relief by filing a petition for coram nobis. The collateral consequences of his or her conviction may include circumstances such as a loss of a license (e.g. law license), inability to secure a gun permit, or the deprivation of voting rights.

At common law, the writ of coram nobis corrected factual errors. It was used for federal courts and also had a limited use in states. In *United States v. Morgan*, 346 U.S. 502 (1954), the Court looked at the confusion as to whether one could file a writ of coram nobis after the passage of the federal habeas statute. A 19-year-old defendant had plead guilty to a federal offense and served a four-year sentence. He was then convicted in state court and sentenced to a longer sentence because of the prior federal conviction. He filed a writ of corum nobis claiming that his waiver in the initial case was not competent because of his youthful status and his failure to be afforded counsel. The federal district court treated this as a habeas matter and refused it because he "was no longer in custody" for this first offense. Finding the error to be "of fundamental character" the court of appeals reversed. The Supreme Court affirmed the court of appeals, allowing the use of the writ of coram nobis to present the defendant's post-conviction issue. It held that this remedy continued even after the passage of the federal habeas statute, 28 U.S.C. §2255. Justice Reed, writing for the majority, stated that the defendant was "entitled to an opportunity to attempt to show that this conviction was invalid." There was a four-person dissent to this position.

Checkpoints

- Post-conviction remedies exist for both state and federal prisoners.

- States often have post-appellate procedures to review convictions in extenuating circumstances.

- State cases can make their way into federal court for habeas review under 28 U.S.C. § 2254, and these are often termed 2254 motions.

- Federal post-appellate matters proceed under 18 U.S.C. § 2255, and are often called 2255 matters.

- The Antiterrorism and Effective Death Penalty Act (AEDPA) placed added obstacles to a defendant succeeding on a habeas petition.

- Except in capital cases, there is no automatic right to counsel in habeas cases.

- Habeas matters are civil actions.

- Fourth Amendment claims that were provided an opportunity for a full and fair hearing at trial, even when the claim is premised on an unconstitutional search or seizure, are excluded from receiving habeas review.

- New rules do not get applied retroactively for habeas unless the rule is substantive or it is a watershed rule of criminal procedure.

- To be applied retroactively as a watershed rule, it must be a rule either necessary to prevent an impermissibly large risk of an inaccurate conviction or the rule must be on the level of *Gideon*, one that alters our understanding of the bedrock procedural elements essential to the fairness of a proceeding.

- The AEDPA requires federal habeas courts to deny relief that is contingent upon a rule or law not clearly established at the time the state conviction became final.

- If habeas is premised on a trial error, it requires that there be a showing that the error "had a substantial and injurious effect or influence in determining the jury's verdict."

- Congress cannot suspend the right to habeas corpus for individuals held as enemy combatants.

- State prisoners cannot proceed with a habeas petition in federal court until they have exhausted all state remedies that are available.

- Comity is a rationale for requiring that prisoners have exhausted remedies in the state system prior to proceeding to federal court.

- A federal habeas petition is not precluded when there is no process in state court or when the process would be ineffective.

- A state prisoner's remedies can be considered exhausted for purposes of a habeas petition when the issue was litigated on direct appeal or when a state proceeding would be useless.

- If a question is mixed, with part exhausted and part still having a remedy, a total exhaustion rule applies.
- Courts have some discretion in staying proceedings involving mixed questions.
- Federal prisoners also must exhaust all remedies in the initial federal courts prior to proceeding with a petition for habeas relief.
- Habeas will be barred as a procedural default if an issue has not been previously litigated.
- Procedural defaults will not preclude a habeas petition when there is a "cause" for the procedural default and resulting "prejudice."
- Attorney ignorance or inadvertence is not sufficient "cause" to overcome a procedural default, but ineffective assistance of counsel can be.
- "Cause" may be found when there is a novel constitutional claim with a legal basis not reasonably available to counsel.
- Procedural defaults will not preclude a habeas petition when there is a showing of "actual innocence."
- The Antiterrorism and Effective Death Penalty Act (AEDPA) restricts successive petitions.
- To overcome the successive petition rule, it is necessary that the defendant show that he or she has a claim that relies on a new rule that was made retroactive or that there is a factual error that rises to the level of harmfulness, that even with due diligence could not have been discovered.
- Defendants filing second or successive habeas petitions need to secure a certificate of appealability (COA) from a federal appellate court.
- Successive habeas petitions premised on a new rule of constitutional law require that there be a new rule that the Supreme Court made retroactive to cases on collateral review, and the claim must have been previously unavailable.
- Petitions filed after the dismissal of an initial petition on procedural grounds, are not considered to be successive petitions.
- Writs of coram nobis are filed by those who are no longer in custody, but continue to suffer the collateral effects of a conviction.

Mastering Criminal Procedure, Volume 2: The Adjudicatory Stage Master Checklist

Preliminary Proceedings in a Prosecution

❏ After an arrest or charges are filed, a defendant will have an initial appearance before a judge.

❏ A court will inform the defendant of the charges, determine whether counsel must be appointed, and make an initial decision regarding release of the defendant.

❏ The Eighth Amendment does not grant a right to bail, only requiring that it not be excessive.

❏ A defendant can be detained if the person presents a risk of flight or a threat to the community.

❏ In many jurisdictions, a defendant can have charges reviewed at a preliminary hearing at which the government must establish probable cause.

❏ A grand jury indictment involves a determination of probable cause that can eliminate the requirement to hold a preliminary hearing in many jurisdictions.

❏ The grand jury both investigates cases and determines whether there is sufficient evidence to charge a defendant.

❏ Grand jury subpoenas are generally enforceable because the power to investigate is broad.

❏ A witness called to testify before a grand jury can invoke privileges, including the Fifth Amendment privilege to refuse to answer questions unless granted immunity from prosecution.

❏ Dismissal of charges before trial does not prevent the government from refiling the charges at a later time.

❏ The government can file charges involving different crimes in a single proceeding against a defendant, and two or more defendants can be joined together for a single trial on related charges.

❑ Venue for a prosecution is based on where the crime was committed, and can be in multiple locations.

❑ In most jurisdictions, venue must be proven by a preponderance of the evidence.

❑ The determination of a violation of the Sixth Amendment speedy trial right is based on a balancing of the time from when a charge was filed, the reason for the delay, defendant's assertion of the right, and prejudice from the delay.

❑ Delay in filing charges violates due process if the defendant can show actual prejudice.

❑ A defendant has a right to counsel for all "critical stages" of a criminal prosecution, from the filing of charges through the first appeal as of right.

❑ The right to counsel includes the right to have counsel appointed if the person cannot afford to retain an attorney,

❑ A defendant has the right to effective assistance of counsel in all proceedings in which there is a right to counsel, and the right to effective assistance of counsel applies both to appointed and retained counsel.

❑ The test for ineffective assistance of counsel is (a) whether the lawyer committed serious error(s) that a reasonable attorney would not commit and (b) whether the defendant was prejudiced.

❑ A competent defendant has the right to self-representation so long as the right to assistance of counsel is knowingly and voluntarily waived.

❑ Discovery in criminal cases is largely controlled by statutes, procedural rules and ethics mandates that require the government to turn over specified evidence.

❑ Due process requires the prosecution to turn over evidence that is exculpatory and material in terms of a defendant's guilt or punishment.

❑ Exculpatory evidence includes impeachment material that can undermine the credibility of a government witness.

Plea Bargaining

❑ A plea bargain is treated as a contract between the prosecutor and defendant, with a court interpreting its terms under contract principles.

❑ A defendant must waive constitutional rights in order to enter a guilty plea, and a court must ensure the waiver of those rights is knowing and voluntary.

❑ If a plea bargain is breached, a court can allow a party to withdraw from the agreement, or require specific performance of the agreement, such as ordering a new sentencing hearing for the defendant.

The Criminal Trial

❏ A defendant has a federal constitutional right to a jury trial in any case in which the potential punishment is more than six months imprisonment.

❏ The pool of potential jurors must represent a "fair cross-section" of the community.

❏ Jurors are questioned during *voir dire* to determine whether they can fairly judge the case, and a party can challenge a juror for cause based on potential bias.

❏ The parties are provided, by statute or rule, with a number of peremptory challenges that permit the removal of a potential juror from the pool for any reason not prohibited by statute, rule, Supreme Court decision or ethics mandates.

❏ Unique rules pertain to striking jurors in death penalty cases based on their views on capital punishment.

❏ The Supreme Court has restricted the use of peremptory challenges based on the race or gender of the juror, and either the defendant or the prosecutor can challenge the exercise of a peremptory challenge.

❏ A defendant has the right to a public trial, which includes all aspects of the trial, unless the judge determines there are strong reasons for closing a portion of the trial.

❏ A defendant can seek a change of venue based on prejudicial pretrial publicity, and a judge can try to mitigate the impact of publicity by engaging in detailed *voir dire* of the potential jurors.

❏ The lawyers involved in a case can be restricted in what they say publicly to avoid prejudicing potential jurors, but the First Amendment makes it very difficult to impose a gag order on the press from reporting on a case.

❏ The Confrontation Clause requires that a defendant have an opportunity to cross-examine a witness.

❏ Under *Crawford*, testimonial evidence cannot be admitted without having the person present at trial and subject to cross-examination.

❏ A statement by one defendant that implicates a co-defendant is not admissible at a joint trial of the defendants unless there is a complete redaction of any reference to the co-defendant, or the defendant who made the statement testifies and is subject to cross-examination.

❏ The Compulsory Process Clause requires the government to assist the defendant in obtaining evidence and witnesses for trial.

❏ A defendant cannot be compelled to testify at trial, nor may the prosecutor comment on a defendant's decision not to testify.

❏ A witness can be compelled to testify by furnishing immunity that protects the person from having the testimony used in a subsequent prosecution or to develop investigative leads.

❑ A defendant has the right to be present for all critical stages of a prosecution.

❑ A jury of twelve is the usual rule, and required in federal prosecutions, but a criminal conviction is permissible by a jury with as few as six members in some states.

❑ A court may not instruct a jury that it must or should infer an element of the offense from certain evidence, although the court can instruct the jury that it is permitted to draw inferences from circumstantial evidence.

❑ Although a jury has the right to nullification by ignoring the instructions and returning a "not guilty" verdict, in most jurisdictions there is no right to instruct the jury on this authority.

❑ If a jury is deadlocked, the court can give an instruction asking them to reconsider the evidence and try to reach a unanimous verdict.

❑ Although most jurisdictions require jury unanimity in finding a defendant guilty or not guilty, states can authorize a verdict by a vote as low as 9-3, but in states that permit 6-person juries, verdicts must be unanimous.

❑ A jury can return inconsistent verdicts, and there is no constitutional right to have an inconsistent verdict overturned.

❑ In death penalty cases, the jury must specify the aggravating and mitigating factors it found in finding in favor of capital punishment.

Sentencing

❑ Punishment theory plays a role in the sentencing structure and sentences provided, but punishments cannot violate the Eight Amendment's prohibition against "Cruel and Unusual Punishments."

❑ Sentencing systems are typically indeterminate or determinate, with some states also having mandatory minimum sentences and habitual offender statutes.

❑ The Federal Sentencing Guidelines provide a complex mechanism for ascertaining the recommended sentencing range that includes an analysis of the offense conduct, criminal history, circumstances of the offender and victim, and the impact of mandatory minimum sentences.

❑ The Federal Sentencing Guidelines have moved from being mandatory to now being advisory.

Post-Trial Proceedings

❑ A jury must determine any facts that increase the defendant's sentence beyond the statutory maximum or the applicable guidelines range.

❑ A defendant has a right to speak to the judge before sentence is imposed.

❏ There is a rebuttable presumption of judicial vindictiveness when a defendant successfully appeals a conviction and is then convicted again and the court imposes a higher sentence, although the presumption can be rebutted.

❏ The Cruel and Unusual Punishment Clause invalidates only grossly disproportional sentences.

❏ There is no constitutional right to an appeal, but every jurisdiction grants a defendant at least one appeal as of right after a convictions.

❏ An indigent defendant has the right under equal protection to the appointment of counsel on a first appeal as of right, but not for a discretionary appeal.

❏ If a defendant did not object to an error, then an appellate court will usually only review the claim for "plain error."

❏ Most errors, including constitutional errors, during the pretrial and trial phase of a case are subject to "harmless error" analysis.

❏ If the error involved a constitutional right, then the government bears the burden of showing that it was harmless beyond a reasonable doubt.

❏ An error that affects the structural fairness of the proceeding requires automatic reversal of a conviction.

❏ After a direct appeal of a conviction has been completed, a defendant can challenge a conviction in a federal civil proceeding claiming that the restraint on the defendant is unconstitutional or violates a federal statutory right.

❏ There are substantial procedural barriers to federal court habeas corpus review of state and federal convictions.

❏ Congress cannot suspend the right of habeas corpus for enemy combatants.

❏ Before filing a federal habeas corpus action, a state defendant must exhaust all available remedies in the state courts for review of the conviction and sentence.

❏ Habeas corpus is not available for an issue that has not been previously litigated, unless a defendant can show legitimate "cause" for the failure to raise the issue, as well as prejudice.

❏ The Double Jeopardy Clause protects against multiple punishments and a second prosecution for the same offense.

❏ The *Blockburger* test determines whether two crimes are the "same offense" by comparing the elements of the offenses to determine whether each contains an element the other does not.

❏ A mistrial does not prohibit a subsequent reprosecution, if it is supported by manifest necessity; nor does a pretrial dismissal of charges prohibit a subsequent prosecution.

❏ Jeopardy attaches when the jury is sworn in, or in a bench trial when the first witness testifies.

❏ A successful appeal by a defendant overturning a conviction does not prevent a retrial unless the grounds for reversal are insufficient evidence of the crime.

❏ If a court denies a defendant's motion to dismiss charges because of a double jeopardy violation, the defendant may appeal immediately to prevent against a second proceeding.

Index